投资肯尼亚法律必读

（中英文对照）

Required Readings of Laws on Investment in Kenya

(In Chinese & English)

李 智 何烈辉 朱晓琛 等编译

上海大学出版社
·上海·

图书在版编目(CIP)数据

投资肯尼亚法律必读:英汉对照/李智等编译. —
上海:上海大学出版社,2023.10
ISBN 978-7-5671-4831-4

I.①投… Ⅱ.①李… Ⅲ.①法律—基本知识—肯尼亚—汉、英 Ⅳ.①D942.4

中国国家版本馆 CIP 数据核字(2023)第 186151 号

责任编辑 严 妙
封面设计 缪炎栩
技术编辑 金 鑫 钱宇坤

投资肯尼亚法律必读(中英文对照)
李 智 何烈辉 朱骁琛 等编译
上海大学出版社出版发行
(上海市上大路 99 号 邮政编码 200444)
(https://www.shupress.cn 发行热线 021-66135112)
出版人 戴骏豪

*

南京展望文化发展有限公司排版
上海普顺印刷包装有限公司印刷 各地新华书店经销
开本 787mm×1092mm 1/16 印张 27.25 字数 697 千字
2023 年 11 月第 1 版 2023 年 11 月第 1 次印刷
ISBN 978-7-5671-4831-4/D·254 定价 88.00 元

版权所有 侵权必究
如发现本书有印装质量问题请与印刷厂质量科联系
联系电话: 021-36522998

本书是上大法学文库"非洲法律系列"之二,受上海大学法学院和北京中凯(上海)律师事务所资助,特此表示感谢!

前　　言

后疫情时代,全球经济仍然笼罩在疫情的阴霾之下,"一带一路"沿线国家的经济潜力为中国投资者带来了破局的希望。非洲国家是"一带一路"倡议的重要合作伙伴,据世界银行最新发布的报告预计,到2035年非洲地区总出口量将增加近29%,其中区域内出口将增长逾81%,对区域外国家出口将增长19%[①]。基于非洲国家的经济增长趋势,译者继登上"非洲之巅"——出版《投资埃塞俄比亚法律必读》一书之后,又推开"非洲东大门"——出版《投资肯尼亚法律必读》,助力中国投资者成为非洲这片投资蓝海的弄潮儿。

肯尼亚是撒哈拉以南非洲第三大经济体,也是这一地区最多元、最发达的经济体之一。肯尼亚东邻索马里,南接坦桑尼亚,西连乌干达,北与埃塞俄比亚、南苏丹交界,东南濒临印度洋,赤道横穿东西,东非大裂谷纵贯南北,海岸线长536千米。它以优越的地理位置、相对完善的经济基础,发挥着向东非、中非辐射的重要作用。农业、服务业和工业是肯尼亚国民经济的三大支柱,旅游业是仅次于农业的第二大外汇收入来源。

相关国际组织预测,肯尼亚将是后疫情时代非洲经济复苏和增长最快的国家。以2020年为例,肯尼亚全年经济实现正增长,增长率约为0.6%。肯尼亚注重基础设施投入,具有较为发达的交通环境,截至2021年6月,肯尼亚航空提供45条国际航线,通达37个国家和地区。

世界银行发布了《2020年营商环境报告》,对全球190个经济体的营商环境进行了分析和排名,其中肯尼亚排名第56名。得益于良好的营商环境建设,中国投资者对于在肯尼亚投资抱有较大的热情。2021年,我国与肯尼亚双边贸易额达69.62亿美元,同比增长25.2%。其中,中方出口67.35亿美元,同比增长24.5%;进口2.27亿美元,同比增长50.5%。2021年,我国企业对肯尼亚直接投资达3.5亿美元[②]。中国企业对肯尼亚投资多集中在建筑、房地产、制造业等领域。其中典型的投资项目有:中国武夷投资9 600万美元的内罗毕建筑产业化基地,中国路桥投资约6.7亿美元的内罗毕机场收费快速路项目等。

值得一提的是,肯尼亚数字经济发展在非洲处于领先地位,在数字经济蓬勃发展的今天,肯尼亚欢迎中国投资者参与未来数字经济合作和数字化建设。

历史与未来相拥、人类与自然共生的肯尼亚在中国投资者的智慧之火上浇上利益之油。肯尼亚的投资机遇就如马赛马拉大草原上的动物大迁徙一样,只有有耐心又猎奇的投资者才能捕捉其中的机遇。中国投资者如何在肯尼亚迸发智慧之火?如何捕捉机会?本书或可从法

---

① 商务部对外投资和经济合作司:对外投资合作国别(地区)指南-肯尼亚(2021版),第27页,https://www.investgo.cn/upfiles/swbgbzn/2021/kenniya.pdf,最后访问日期:2023年4月13日。

② 商务部:中国-肯尼亚经贸合作简况(2021年),http://www.mofcom.gov.cn/article/tongjiziliao/sjtj/xyfztjsj/202302/20230203385083.shtml,最后访问日期:2023年4月13日。

律层面给出答案。

第一编介绍投资法规。《外国投资保护法》旨在保护经批准的外国投资及相关事项,明确了外国投资者许可证的申请条件,规定了引进外国资产的批准期限,对促进和保护外国投资作出了特别安排。《投资促进法》协助投资者获得投资所需的许可证等激励措施,确定了申请投资证明的审核程序,赋予外籍人士入境许可证,对外国投资者不当行为予以处罚。《竞争法》通过规定竞争管理局和竞争法庭的设立、权力和职能,列举了限制性贸易行为,认定了经营者不当集中和合并的行为,并为消费者提供了诸种福利,从而实现国民经济的公平竞争等目标。《公私合营法》专门设计了私人当事方的选择程序,以规范私营团体参与基础设施或开发项目的融资等商业行为;通过系列措施简化公私合营关系的监管框架,包括设立公私合营委员会以及要求披露项目协议。

第二编呈现劳动法规。《就业法》确立了三大原则,即"禁止强迫劳动""就业歧视"和"性骚扰";从就业、雇佣关系及其解除两个角度宣布并定义员工的基本权利;为雇主雇用雇员设置了以工资保障为核心的基本条件,包括雇主应提供足够的卫生用水、适当的食物以及充足适当的药物供雇员使用;就儿童雇员以及外国服务合同这两个特殊问题作出特别规定;就事后救济而言,该法规定的争议解决程序涉及劳资纠纷案件申诉和管辖等事项。

第三编勾画税收法规。为促进数字经济的发展,肯尼亚国家财政和规划内阁秘书特别制定了《数字服务税收条例》。该条例提纲挈领地明晰了"数字市场""数字市场提供商"等重要概念的内涵,限定了数字服务税的适用范围,简化了数字服务税登记流程,并与《税收程序法》(2015)的规定进行了衔接。

第四编涉猎经济特区法规。《经济特区法》指定了经济特区划定标准,对经济特区的开发管理模式和特区内主体的权利义务作出了规定,包括有权取得、处置或转让特区内土地或资产;就成立经济特区管理局和一站式服务中心两个专门性机构,免除管理局工作人员善意行为的个人责任作出了规定;要求管理局特设基金会管理财务事项;规定以颁发经营许可证的方式监管经济特区的业务开展;确立了印花税豁免等经济特区内企业享有的优惠政策。

第五编描述反商业贿赂法规。为预防、调查和惩罚腐败、经济犯罪和相关犯罪,肯尼亚政府制定了《反腐败和经济犯罪法》,设立了肯尼亚反腐败委员会和反腐败咨询理事会。该法不仅包括已支付的贿赂,还涵盖了主动提出或承诺将给予贿赂的行为;不论贿赂收受地点是否在肯尼亚,只要参与方为肯尼亚公民或公司,均在该法管辖范围内。依据该法,公私部门将需要根据自身规模及运营范围来建立相应程序以防止贿赂及腐败的发生,否则管理层可能因缺少必要的防范程序被追究责任。

在曾任国务院原特区办公室综合司司长的柳孝华先生和曾任中国开发区协会副秘书长的周振邦先生的引荐下,译者得以与肯尼亚的中资公司取得联系,从而得到中国武夷肯尼亚分公司副总经理罗自成先生和综合管理部副经理徐田女士的大力支持。同时,本书的出版得益于上海大学法学院院长李凤章教授和上海大学ADR与仲裁研究院院长文学国教授的鼎力支持。

作为"上大法学文库-非洲法律系列之二",本书与系列之一的《投资埃塞俄比亚法律必读》具有类似的功效:一为已在肯尼亚发展的企业与个人更好地投资提供法律参考;二为打算去肯尼亚投资的企业与个人提供法律指南;三为政府的决策者提供法律索引;四为相关研究的学者提供法律铺陈。

本书的编译过程充满着曲折,在疫情严峻的形势下,译者们凭着对肯尼亚法律的热情,在不懈的坚持下,本书才得以与读者见面。虽然经过几轮校对,但翻译不当或错误在所难免,恳请各位专家与读者不吝赐教。在肯尼亚的投资尝试,如同本书的出版一般,只要勤于坚持、勇于探索,就一定可以捕捉到弥足珍贵的机遇。走,到肯尼亚投资去!

本书的翻译分工如下:
1. 《外国投资保护法》——姚甜甜、何烈辉
2. 《投资促进法》——姚甜甜、朱骁琛
3. 《竞争法》——万欣怡、张津瑶、魏林强
4. 《公私合营法》——李　智、应文娇、朱骁琛
5. 《就业法》——李　智、陈克豪
6. 《数字服务税收条例》——肖　静
7. 《经济特区法》——肖　静、文怡筱
8. 《反腐败和经济犯罪法》——曾凡勇、魏林强

全书译校统稿:李　智
译校统稿助理:魏林强

翻译团队介绍:
李　智,女,民商法博士,上海大学法学院教授、博士生导师。
何烈辉,男,历史学博士,达之路控股集团董事长。
朱骁琛,女,上海师范大学非洲研究中心博士研究生。
姚甜甜,女,上海大学法学院 2021 级民商法硕士研究生。
肖　静,女,上海大学法学院 2021 级民商法硕士研究生。
应文娇,女,上海大学法学院 2021 级民商法硕士研究生。
陈克豪,男,上海大学法学院 2021 级法律硕士研究生。
曾凡勇,男,上海大学法学院 2021 级刑法硕士研究生。
魏林强,男,上海大学法学院 2021 级知识产权法硕士研究生。
万欣怡,女,上海大学法学院 2022 级民商法硕士研究生。
张津瑶,女,上海大学法学院 2022 级民商法硕士研究生。
文怡筱,女,上海大学法学院 2023 级诉讼法硕士研究生。

本书首次定稿于 2023 年 4 月 15 日。书稿三审期间,本书涉及的部分法律被修订,笔者立即组织部分译者重新对书稿进行了修改与补充编译,特此说明!

本书最终定稿于 2023 年 10 月 25 日
上海大学东区法学院 609 室

李　智

目　　录

第一编　投　资　法　规

第一部　外国投资保护法（第518章）（2017年修订版）

1. 简称 …………………………………………………………………… 2
2. 释义 …………………………………………………………………… 2
3. 外国投资者可申请并获得证书 ……………………………………… 2
4. 证书的修改 …………………………………………………………… 3
5. 批准期限内引进的外国资产 ………………………………………… 3
6. 废除 …………………………………………………………………… 3
7. 利润转移等 …………………………………………………………… 3
8. 强制征收 ……………………………………………………………… 4
8A. 废除 ………………………………………………………………… 4
8B. 促进和保护投资的特别协议 ……………………………………… 4
9. 法规和指令 …………………………………………………………… 4
附录　肯尼亚宪法 …………………………………………………… 4

第二部　投资促进法（2004年第6号法令）（2014年修订版）

第一部分　总则 ………………………………………………………… 7
  1. 简称 ………………………………………………………………… 7
  2. 定义 ………………………………………………………………… 7
第二部分　投资证书——申请和颁发等 ……………………………… 8
  3. 申请 ………………………………………………………………… 8
  4. 获得证书的权利 …………………………………………………… 8
  5. 申请的审核程序 …………………………………………………… 8
  6. 颁发证书 …………………………………………………………… 8
  7. 取得证书的条件 …………………………………………………… 9
  8. 转让 ………………………………………………………………… 9
  9. 修改 ………………………………………………………………… 9
  10. 撤销 ……………………………………………………………… 9

11. 审查管理局的决定 ··· 9
第三部分　投资证书——福利 ·· 9
12. 获得特定许可证的权利 ·· 9
13. 外籍人士入境许可的权利 ·· 10
第四部分　肯尼亚投资管理局 ·· 11
14. 管理局以法人团体身份存续 ·· 11
15. 职能 ··· 11
16. 管理局理事会 ··· 11
17. 理事长、委任成员的任期 ·· 12
18. 理事长、委任成员的辞职 ·· 12
19. 理事长、委任成员的罢免 ·· 12
20. 理事会成员津贴 ··· 12
21. 理事会程序 ··· 12
22. 理事会秘书 ··· 12
23. 管理局常务理事 ··· 12
24. 其他人员 ··· 12
25. 豁免 ··· 12
第五部分　国家投资委员会 ·· 13
26. 委员会成立 ··· 13
27. 职能 ··· 13
第六部分　其他 ··· 13
28. 误导管理局等罪行 ··· 13
29. 不当泄露依法获取信息的罪行 ·· 13
30. 规章 ··· 14
31. 第 485 章的废除 ··· 14
32. 已废除法令保留的一般权限等 ·· 14
附录 ··· 14
附录一　申请投资证书的审议程序 ··· 14
附录二　投资证书持有人有权获得的许可证 ······································· 15
附录三　管理局理事会关于业务和事务行为规则 ······························· 18

第三部　竞争法（2010 年第 12 号法令）（2019 年修订版）

第一部分　总则 ··· 21
1. 简称 ··· 21
2. 释义 ··· 21
3. 本法目的 ··· 23
4. 表达的解释 ··· 23
5. 适用 ··· 24
6. 域外行为 ··· 24

第二部分　管理局的设立、权力和职能 ……………………………………… 25
　　7. 管理局的设立 …………………………………………………………… 25
　　8. 管理局业务与事务的管理 ……………………………………………… 25
　　9. 管理局的职能 …………………………………………………………… 25
　　10. 管理局成员 ……………………………………………………………… 26
　　11. 管理局成员的薪酬 ……………………………………………………… 26
　　12. 总干事 …………………………………………………………………… 26
　　13. 工作人员 ………………………………………………………………… 26
　　14. 公章 ……………………………………………………………………… 27
　　15. 管理局的授权 …………………………………………………………… 27
　　16. 个人责任保护 …………………………………………………………… 27
　　17. 管理局的损害赔偿责任 ………………………………………………… 27
　　18. 进行调查的权力 ………………………………………………………… 27
　　19. 管理局部门的设置 ……………………………………………………… 28
　　20. 保密 ……………………………………………………………………… 28

第三部分　限制性贸易行为 …………………………………………………… 29
　　A－限制性协议、行为和决定
　　21. 限制性贸易行为 ………………………………………………………… 29
　　B－适用于贸易协会的限制性贸易行为
　　22. 适用于行业协会的行为 ………………………………………………… 30
　　C－滥用支配地位
　　23. 支配地位的认定标准 …………………………………………………… 31
　　24. 滥用支配地位 …………………………………………………………… 31
　　24A. 滥用买方权力 ………………………………………………………… 32
　　D－特定限制性行为的豁免
　　25. 给予特定限制性行为豁免 ……………………………………………… 33
　　26. 豁免申请的决定 ………………………………………………………… 33
　　27. 豁免的撤销或修改 ……………………………………………………… 33
　　28. 知识产权豁免 …………………………………………………………… 34
　　29. 专业规则的豁免 ………………………………………………………… 34
　　30. 授予、撤销或修改豁免的通知 ………………………………………… 35
　　E－对禁止行为的调查
　　31. 管理局的调查 …………………………………………………………… 35
　　32. 进入和搜查 ……………………………………………………………… 35
　　33. 管理局取证的权力 ……………………………………………………… 36
　　34. 管理局的拟议决定 ……………………………………………………… 36
　　35. 召开听证会进行口头陈述 ……………………………………………… 36
　　36. 调查后的行动 …………………………………………………………… 37
　　37. 临时救济 ………………………………………………………………… 37

38. 和解 ·· 37
39. 管理局决定的公布 ·· 37
40. 向法庭提出上诉 ··· 37

第四部分 合并 ·· 38

41. 合并的定义 ··· 38
42. 对合并的控制 ··· 38
43. 向管理局发出拟议合并的通知 ······································ 39
44. 拟议合并的确定期限 ·· 39
45. 关于拟议合并的听证会 ·· 39
46. 拟议合并的决定 ·· 39
47. 撤销对拟议合并的批准 ·· 40
48. 法庭复核管理局的决定 ·· 41
49. 遵守其他法律和上诉 ·· 41

第五部分 经营者不正当集中的控制 ································· 41

50. 经营者不正当集中的认定 ·· 41
51. 听证会 ·· 42
52. 处置权益的命令 ·· 42
53. 对管理局命令提出上诉 ·· 43
54. 犯罪及处罚 ·· 43

第六部分 消费者福利 ··· 43

55. 虚假或误导性陈述 ·· 43
56. 不正当行为 ·· 43
57. 商业交易中的不正当行为 ·· 44
58. 对公众的警告通知 ·· 45
59. 产品安全标准和不安全商品 ·· 45
60. 产品信息标准 ·· 45
61. 消费者须知 ·· 46
62. 管理局宣布产品安全或信息标准 ································ 47
63. 不合适商品的责任 ·· 47
64. 瑕疵商品责任 ·· 47
65. 制造商不明 ·· 47
66. 抗辩 ·· 48
67. 与肯尼亚标准局的协商 ·· 48
68. 向政府机构转交投诉 ·· 48
69. 消费者团体的通知 ·· 48
70. 犯罪及处罚 ·· 48
70A. 管理局对投诉开展调查 ··· 48

第七部分 竞争法庭的设立和权力 ···································· 48

71. 竞争法庭的设立 ·· 48

72. 向法庭上诉的程序 ··· 49
73. 有权向法庭上诉的人 ··· 49
74. 上诉的审理和裁决 ·· 49
75. 法庭将上诉发回重审 ··· 50
76. 待决上诉的规定 ··· 50
77. 管理局的上诉权 ··· 50

第八部分 财政规定 ·· 50
78. 管理局的资金 ·· 50
79. 财政年度 ·· 50
80. 年度预算 ·· 51
81. 账目及审计 ··· 51
82. 资金投资 ·· 51

第九部分 其他 ··· 51
83. 年度报告 ·· 51
84. 禁止披露的信息 ··· 52
85. 工作人员披露私人利益 ·· 52
86. 可展开调查的时间 ·· 52
87. 妨碍法令的施行 ··· 52
88. 不遵守传票的规定 ·· 52
89. 不遵从命令 ··· 53
89A. 宽大处理程序 ·· 53
90. 其他罪行 ·· 53
91. 一般处罚 ·· 53
92. 地方法院的管辖权 ·· 53
93. 规则 ·· 53

第十部分 废除、保留和过渡性条款 ·· 53
94. 定义 ·· 53
95. 资产及其他财产 ··· 53
96. 权利、权力和法律责任等 ··· 54
97. 法律诉讼 ·· 54
98. 借调至管理局 ·· 54
99. 废除第504章 ·· 54
100. 储蓄 ·· 54

附录 关于管理局的规定 ·· 54

第四部 公私合营法（2021年第14号法令）

第一部分 总则 ··· 58
1. 简称 ··· 58
2. 释义 ··· 58

3. 法案的目的 …… 59
4. 法案的适用 …… 60
5. 法案优先适用 …… 60

第二部分 公私合营委员会

6. 公私合营委员会 …… 60
7. 成员资格和任期 …… 60
8. 委员会的职权 …… 60
9. 离职 …… 61
10. 小组委员会 …… 61
11. 委员会的授权 …… 61
12. 委员会事务的处理 …… 61
13. 行为准则 …… 61
14. 报酬 …… 62
15. 理事会 …… 62
16. 总干事 …… 62
17. 理事会工作人员 …… 62
18. 借调工作人员到理事会 …… 62
19. 理事会的职能 …… 62

第三部分 公私合营

20. 项目协议 …… 63
21. 公私合营协议 …… 63
22. 缔约方的职责 …… 63
23. 公私合营协议期限的确定 …… 64
24. 项目协议的执行 …… 64
25. 项目清单的提交 …… 64
26. 国家清单和优先项目清单 …… 64
27. 资格预审程序 …… 65
28. 政府支持措施 …… 65
29. 成交费用及可回收的项目开发成本 …… 65

第四部分 项目鉴定和私人当事方的选择

30. 项目鉴定、选择和优先排序 …… 65
31. 项目准备和实施 …… 66
32. 可行性研究 …… 66
33. 可行性报告的审批 …… 66
34. 缔约方的技术专长 …… 66
35. 标准和程序 …… 67
36. 或有负债的限额 …… 67

第五部分 公私合营采购方式

37. 采购方式 …… 67

目　录

38. 直接采购 ··· 68
39. 直接采购程序 ·· 68
40. 私人发起的提案 ·· 68
41. 对私人发起的提案的尽职调查 ·· 69
42. 对私人发起的提案的评估 ··· 69
43. 私人发起的提案的项目开发 ··· 70
44. 采购设计 ··· 72
45. 限制性招标 ··· 72
46. 资格申请 ··· 73
47. 私人当事方的资格 ·· 73
48. 资格预审委员会 ·· 73
49. 私人当事方的资格取消 ··· 73
50. 招标书 ··· 74
51. 提交标书 ··· 74
52. 竞争性对话 ··· 74
53. 联合体投标 ··· 74
54. 提案评审小组 ··· 75
55. 评标和评标报告 ·· 75
56. 投标人违约 ··· 75
57. 谈判 ··· 76
58. 项目和风险评估报告 ··· 76
59. 委员会审批项目和财务风险评估报告 ·· 77
60. 项目审批 ··· 77
61. 项目协议的执行 ·· 77
62. 投标的取消 ··· 77
63. 待议会审批的协议 ·· 77

第六部分　郡政府的公私合营 ·· 78

64. 郡政府项目协议 ·· 78
65. 郡议会批准 ··· 78
66. 郡项目清单 ··· 78
67. 第五部分的适用 ·· 78

第七部分　项目公司,披露和项目协议 ··· 78

68. 项目公司 ··· 78
69. 公布项目协议执行信息 ··· 79
70. 项目协议各方的最低义务 ··· 79
71. 适用法律 ··· 79
72. 项目协议的修改和变更 ··· 80
73. 项目管理 ··· 80
74. 借调缔约方雇员 ·· 81

  75. 申诉委员会 ……………………………………………………………………… 81
  76. 秘书 ……………………………………………………………………………… 81
  77. 报酬 ……………………………………………………………………………… 81
  78. 利益冲突 ………………………………………………………………………… 81
  79. 罪行 ……………………………………………………………………………… 81
  80. 法令 ……………………………………………………………………………… 82
第八部分 财务规定 …………………………………………………………………… 82
  81. 公私合营项目促进基金 ………………………………………………………… 82
  82. 财务报告、审计和项目执行报告 ……………………………………………… 82
第九部分 其他规定 …………………………………………………………………… 82
  83. 本土化 …………………………………………………………………………… 82
  84. 罪行及处罚 ……………………………………………………………………… 83
  85. 国家官员或公职人员根据本法参与投标 ……………………………………… 84
  86. 检查公私合营处所等 …………………………………………………………… 84
  87. 2003 年第 3 号第五、六部分的适用 …………………………………………… 84
  88. 年度报告 ………………………………………………………………………… 84
  89. 条例 ……………………………………………………………………………… 84
第十部分 救济和过渡性规定 ………………………………………………………… 85
  90. 释义 ……………………………………………………………………………… 85
  91. 成员及工作人员 ………………………………………………………………… 85
  92. 救济 ……………………………………………………………………………… 85
  93. 废除 ……………………………………………………………………………… 85
附录 ………………………………………………………………………………………… 85
  附录一 关于委员会的业务和事务的管理规定 ……………………………… 85
  附录二 公私合营安排 ………………………………………………………… 86
  附录三 项目协议中规定的最低合同义务 …………………………………… 88

第二编 劳 动 法 规

第五部 就业法(2007 年第 11 号法令)(2023 年修订版)

第一部分 总则 ………………………………………………………………………… 90
  1. 简称 ………………………………………………………………………………… 90
  2. 释义 ………………………………………………………………………………… 90
  3. 适用 ………………………………………………………………………………… 92
第二部分 一般原则 …………………………………………………………………… 93
  4. 禁止强迫劳动 …………………………………………………………………… 93
  5. 就业歧视 ………………………………………………………………………… 93
  6. 性骚扰 …………………………………………………………………………… 94

第三部分　雇佣关系 ·· 95
　7. 服务合同 ·· 95
　8. 口头和书面合同 ·· 95
　9. 服务合同的一般条款 ··· 95
　10. 雇用细则 ··· 95
　11. 初步详情说明 ·· 97
　12. 纪律处分声明 ·· 97
　13. 变更声明 ··· 97
　14. 可合理查阅的文件或集体协议 ·· 98
　15. 告知员工其权利 ··· 98
　16. 执行 ·· 98

第四部分　工资保障 ·· 99
　17. 工资、津贴等的支付、处理和收回 ··· 99
　18. 工资或薪金到期时 ·· 100
　19. 工资扣除 ··· 100
　20. 工资明细表 ·· 101
　21. 法定扣除声明 ·· 102
　22. 修改工资条文和扣款声明的权力 ·· 102
　23. 工资保证金 ·· 102
　24. 雇员死亡 ··· 103
　25. 被错误扣留或扣除报酬的返还 ··· 103

第五部分　就业权利和义务 ·· 103
　26. 基本最低的就业条件 ·· 103
　27. 工作时间 ··· 103
　28. 年假 ·· 103
　29. 产假 ·· 104
　29A. 收养前休假 ·· 104
　30. 病假 ·· 105
　31. 住房 ·· 105
　31A. 已删除 ··· 105
　31B. 经济适用房征税 ··· 105
　31C. 雇主的义务 ·· 105
　32. 水 ··· 106
　33. 食物 ·· 106
　34. 医疗护理 ··· 106

第六部分　终止和解雇 ·· 106
　35. 终止通知 ··· 106
　36. 代通知金 ··· 107
　37. 临时雇佣转换为定期合同 ·· 107

38. 雇主豁免通知 ·· 107
39. 旅途中到期的合同可以延期 ·· 108
40. 因裁员而终止 ·· 108
41. 因不当行为被解雇前的通知和听证 ·· 108
42. 试用合同的终止 ·· 108
43. 终止的理由证明 ·· 109
44. 即时解雇 ·· 109
45. 不公平终止 ·· 109
46. 终止或纪律处分的原因 ··· 110
47. 即时解雇和不公平解雇的申诉 ·· 110
48. 代表 ··· 111
49. 不当解雇和不公平解雇的补救措施 ·· 111
50. 须予指导的法院 ·· 111
51. 服务证明 ·· 111

第七部分 保护儿童 ··· 112

52. 释义 ··· 112
53. 禁止最恶劣的童工形式 ··· 112
54. 向劳工官员或警察申诉 ··· 112
55. 劳工官员取消和禁止合同的权力 ··· 113
56. 禁止雇用13岁至16岁的儿童 ·· 113
57. 禁止与13至16岁儿童签订书面合同 ··· 113
58. 限制雇用13至16岁的儿童从事机械作业 ·· 113
59. 雇用儿童的时间限制 ·· 113
60. 紧急情况 ·· 114
61. 儿童就业登记册 ·· 114
62. 童工的体检 ·· 114
63. 年龄的确定 ·· 114
64. 非法雇用儿童的处罚 ·· 114
65. 儿童死亡或受伤的处罚 ··· 114

第八部分 雇主破产 ··· 115

66. 雇主破产 ·· 115
67. 破产的定义 ·· 115
68. 本部适用的债务 ·· 115
69. 根据第68条支付的金额限额 ·· 115
70. 相关官员的角色 ·· 116
71. 向劳资法庭申诉 ·· 116
72. 权利的转让和救济 ··· 116
73. 知情权 ··· 117

| 第九部分 | 就业记录 | 117 |

74. 雇主保存的记录 · 117
75. 虚假条目等 · 118

| 第十部分 | 就业管理 | 118 |

76. 空缺通知 · 118
77. 职位填补或撤销的通知 · 119
78. 终止雇佣的通知 · 119
79. 雇员登记处 · 119
80. 豁免 · 119
81. 本部分罪行 · 119

| 第十一部分 | 外国服务合同 | 119 |

83. 格式和认证 · 119
84. 认证前的要求 · 119
85. 外国服务合同的担保 · 119
86. 诱使他人根据非正式合约出国的犯罪 · 120

| 第十二部分 | 争议解决程序 | 120 |

87. 劳资纠纷案件的申诉和管辖 · 120
88. 其他法律规定的一般处罚和犯罪 · 120
89. 外国签订服务合同的救济 · 120
90. 诉讼时效 · 121

| 第十三部分 | 其他规定 | 121 |

91. 规则 · 121
92. 废除第226章和救济条款 · 122
93. 过渡性条文 · 122

第三编 税 收 法 规

第六部 所得税法(第470章)
所得税(数字服务税)条例(2020)

1. 引用与生效 · 124
2. 释义 · 124
3. 数字服务 · 124
4. 数字服务税的适用 · 125
5. 用户位置 · 125
6. 总交易额 · 125
7. 登记 · 125
8. 任命税务代表 · 125
9. 简易税务登记 · 125

10. 会计和付款 ··· 126
11. 申报表修改 ··· 126
12. 记录 ··· 126
13. 处罚 ··· 126

第四编　经济特区法规

第七部　经济特区法(2015年第16号法令)(2023年修订版)

第一部分　总则 ··· 128
  1. 简称及生效 ··· 128
  2. 释义 ··· 128
  3. 本法的目的 ··· 129

第二部分　经济特区 ·· 130
  4. 经济特区的宣布 ·· 130
  5. 经济特区划定标准 ·· 130
  6. 被视为出口和进口到肯尼亚的货物 ·· 131
  7. 经济特区内的商品和服务 ·· 131
  8. 经济特区货物的运出 ··· 132
  9. 经济特区企业收支情况 ··· 132

第三部分　经济特区管理局 ··· 132
  10. 管理局的设立 ·· 132
  11. 管理局的职能 ·· 132
  12. 理事会 ··· 133
  13. 理事会的业务和事务处理 ·· 133
  14. 理事会的权力 ·· 133
  15. 理事酬金 ··· 134
  16. 首席执行官 ·· 134
  17. 管理局工作人员 ·· 134
  18. 管理局授权 ·· 134
  19. 个人责任免除 ·· 134
  20. 公章 ·· 134

第四部分　财务规定 ·· 135
  21. 基金会的设立 ·· 135
  22. 财政年度 ··· 135
  23. 年度预算 ··· 135
  24. 账目和审计 ·· 135
  25. 资金投入 ··· 136

第五部分　监管规定 ………………………………………………………………… 136
　　26. 经济特区经营许可证 ………………………………………………………… 136
　　27. 申请及颁发许可证 …………………………………………………………… 136
　　28. 经济特区开发商和经营者资质 ……………………………………………… 137
　　29. 经济特区企业 ………………………………………………………………… 137
　　30. 许可证登记册 ………………………………………………………………… 137

第六部分　经济特区企业的权利和义务 ……………………………………………… 137
　　31. 经济特区内允许的活动 ……………………………………………………… 137
　　32. 经济特区内的设施 …………………………………………………………… 138
　　33. 经济区开发商或经营者的权利和义务 ……………………………………… 138
　　34. 经济特区企业的权利 ………………………………………………………… 139
　　35. 经济特区企业、开发商和经营者的权益 …………………………………… 139

第七部分　其他规定 …………………………………………………………………… 140
　　36. 内阁秘书的权力 ……………………………………………………………… 140
　　37. 争议解决 ……………………………………………………………………… 140
　　38. 印花税的豁免 ………………………………………………………………… 140
　　39. 条例 …………………………………………………………………………… 140
　　40. 过渡 …………………………………………………………………………… 141

附录 ……………………………………………………………………………………… 141
　　附录一　经济特区的类型 ………………………………………………………… 141
　　附录二　关于理事会业务和事务处理的规定 …………………………………… 141

第五编　反商业贿赂法规

第八部　反腐败和经济犯罪法(2003年第3号法令)(2023年修订版)

第一部分　总则 ………………………………………………………………………… 144
　　1. 简称 ……………………………………………………………………………… 144
　　2. 释义 ……………………………………………………………………………… 144

第二部分　特别法官的委任 …………………………………………………………… 145
　　3. 任命特别法官的权力 …………………………………………………………… 145
　　4. 由特别法官审理的案件 ………………………………………………………… 145
　　5. 特别法官的程序和权力 ………………………………………………………… 146

第三部分　肯尼亚反腐败委员会和咨询理事会 ……………………………………… 146
　　A—肯尼亚反腐败委员会 …………………………………………………………… 146
　　6. 废除 ……………………………………………………………………………… 146
　　7. 废除 ……………………………………………………………………………… 146
　　8. 废除 ……………………………………………………………………………… 146

9. 废除 ·· 146
　　10. 废除 ·· 146
　　11. 废除 ·· 146
　　12. 废除 ·· 146
　　13. 废除 ·· 146
　　14. 废除 ·· 146
　　15. 废除 ·· 146
　　B—肯尼亚反腐败咨询理事会 ··· 146
　　16. 咨询理事会的成立 ·· 146
　　17. 咨询理事会的职能 ·· 147
　　18. 咨询理事会的独立性 ··· 147
　　19. 删除 ·· 147
　　20. 主席、副主席 ·· 147
　　21. 咨询理事会秘书 ··· 147
　　22. 咨询理事会的程序 ·· 147
第四部分　调查 ··· 148
　　23. 调查员 ··· 148
　　24. 调查员的身份证明 ·· 148
　　25. 未调查的投诉 ·· 148
　　25A. 停止调查 ·· 148
　　26. 嫌疑人财产陈述 ··· 149
　　27. 提供信息的要求等 ·· 149
　　28. 提供记录和财产 ··· 149
　　29. 搜查住所 ·· 150
　　30. 提供或发现物品的可接受性 ·· 150
　　31. 旅行证件的交还 ··· 150
　　32. 逮捕人 ··· 151
　　33. 可能影响调查的披露 ··· 151
　　34. 冒充调查员 ··· 151
　　35. 调查报告 ·· 151
　　36. 季度报告 ·· 151
　　37. 检控年度报告 ·· 152
第五部分　罪行 ··· 152
　　38. "代理人"和"委托人"的含义 ·· 152
　　39. 删除 ·· 152
　　40. 建议的秘密引诱 ··· 152
　　41. 欺骗委托人 ··· 153
　　42. 利益冲突 ·· 153

43. 受托人委任的不当利益 ……………………………………………… 153
44. 投标操纵等 …………………………………………………………… 153
45. 公共财产和税收保护等 ……………………………………………… 154
46. 滥用职权 ……………………………………………………………… 154
47. 可疑财产的处理 ……………………………………………………… 154
47A. 企图、阴谋等 ………………………………………………………… 154
48. 对本部分所订罪行的处罚 …………………………………………… 155
49. 惯例不作为抗辩理由 ………………………………………………… 155
50. 不可能,无意图等不作为辩护理由 ………………………………… 155

第六部分 不当利益的赔偿和追回

51. 赔偿责任 ……………………………………………………………… 155
52. 不正当利益的责任 …………………………………………………… 155
53. 责任——其他规定 …………………………………………………… 155
54. 定罪赔偿令 …………………………………………………………… 156
55. 没收来源不明资产 …………………………………………………… 156
56. 保留可疑财产的命令等 ……………………………………………… 157
56A. 任命接管人 …………………………………………………………… 157
56B. 庭外和解 ……………………………………………………………… 158
56C. 资金和其他资产的追回 ……………………………………………… 158

第七部分 证据

57. 作为证据的来源不明资产等 ………………………………………… 158
58. 有行为证明的腐败推定 ……………………………………………… 159
59. 证明财产价值的证书等 ……………………………………………… 159
60. 与共犯有关的规则等 ………………………………………………… 159
61. 职位证明及补偿 ……………………………………………………… 159

第七 A 部分 执行

61A. 针对委员会的执行 …………………………………………………… 159

第八部分 其他

62. 因被指控犯有腐败或经济犯罪被停职 ……………………………… 159
63. 因被判腐败或经济犯罪而停职等 …………………………………… 160
64. 因被判腐败或经济犯罪而被取消资格 ……………………………… 160
65. 对举报人的保护 ……………………………………………………… 160
66. 妨碍根据本法行事的人等 …………………………………………… 161
67. 在肯尼亚境外的行为——犯罪 ……………………………………… 161
68. 法规 …………………………………………………………………… 161

第九部分 废除、过渡和修订

69. 释义 …………………………………………………………………… 161
70. 废除第 65 章 ………………………………………………………… 161

71. 废除法下的罪行 ··· 161
72. 临时理事等 ··· 161
73. 移交自肯尼亚警察部队反腐败部门 ··· 162
74. 对第 22 章第 42 条的修订 ·· 162

附录 ·· 162
  附录一　关于委员会工作人员的规定 ··· 162
  附录二　关于咨询理事会成员的规定 ··· 164
  附录三　关于商业行为及咨询理事会事务的规定 ····································· 166

Contents

GROUP ONE   INVESTMENT LAWS AND REGULATIONS

TITLE ONE   FOREIGN INVESTMENTS PROTECTION ACT
(CHAPTER 518) (Revised Edition 2017)

1. Short title ········· 168
2. Interpretation ········· 168
3. Foreign investors may apply for and be granted certificates ········· 168
4. Amendment of certificate ········· 169
5. Foreign assets to be brought in during approved period ········· 170
6. *Repealed by Act No. 6 of 1994, s. 74.* ········· 170
7. Transfer of profits, etc. ········· 170
8. Compulsory acquisition ········· 170
8A. *Repealed by Act No. 6 of 1994, s. 74.* ········· 171
8B. Special arrangement for investment promotion and protection ········· 171
9. Regulations and directions ········· 171
SCHEDULE   THE CONSTITUTION OF KENYA ········· 171

TITLE TWO   THE INVESTMENT PROMOTION ACT
(NO. 6 OF 2004) (Revised Edition 2014)

PART I   PRELIMINARY ········· 175

1. Short title ········· 175
2. Definitions ········· 175

PART II   INVESTMENT CERTIFICATES – APPLICATION AND ISSUE, ETC. ········· 176

3. Applications ········· 176
4. Entitlement to certificate ········· 176
5. Procedures for consideration of application ········· 177
6. Issue of certificate ········· 177

7. Conditions of certificate 177
8. Transfer 177
9. Amendment 177
10. Revocation 177
11. Review of Authority decision 177

PART III INVESTMENT CERTIFICATES – BENEFITS 178
12. Entitlement to certain licences 178
13. Entitlement to entry permits for expatriates 179

PART IV KENYA INVESTMENT AUTHORITY 180
14. Authority continued as body corporate 180
15. Functions 180
16. Board of Authority 181
17. Term of office of Chairman, appointed members 181
18. Resignation of Chairman, appointed members 181
19. Removal of Chairman, appointed members 181
20. Allowances of board members 182
21. Procedures of the board 182
22. Secretary of board 182
23. Managing director of Authority 182
24. Other staff 182
25. Immunity 182

PART V NATIONAL INVESTMENT COUNCIL 182
26. Council established 182
27. Functions 183

PART VI MISCELLANEOUS 183
28. Offence, misleading Authority, etc. 183
29. Offence, improperly divulging information acquired under Act 183
30. Regulations 184
31. Repeal of Cap. 485 184
32. General authority, etc. under repealed Act continued 184

SCHEDULES 184
  FIRST SCHEDULE   PROCEDURES FOR CONSIDERATION OF APPLICATION FOR INVESTMENT CERTIFICATE 184
  SECOND SCHEDULE   LICENCES TO WHICH THE HOLDER OF AN INVESTMENT CERTIFICATE MAY BE ENTITLED 185
  THIRD SCHEDULE   PROVISIONS AS TO THE CONDUCT OF BUSINESS AND AFFAIRS OF THE BOARD OF THE AUTHORITY 189

TITLE THREE COMPETITION ACT (NO. 12 OF 2010) (Revised Edition 2019)

PART I PRELIMINARY 192
   1. Short title 192
   2. Interpretation 192
   3. Objects of the Act 194
   4. Interpretation of expressions 195
   5. Application 196
   6. Extra-territorial operation 196

PART II ESTABLISHMENT, POWERS AND FUNCTIONS OF THE AUTHORITY 197
   7. Establishment of the Authority 197
   8. Conduct of business and affairs of the Authority 197
   9. Functions of the Authority 197
   10. Members of the Authority 198
   11. Remuneration of members of the Authority 199
   12. Director-General 199
   13. Staff 199
   14. Common seal 200
   15. Delegation by the Authority 200
   16. Protection from personal liability 200
   17. Liability of the Authority for damages 201
   18. Power to hold inquiries 201
   19. Establishment of divisions of the Authority 202
   20. Confidentiality 202

PART III RESTRICTIVE TRADE PRACTICES 203
   A – Restrictive Agreements, Practices and Decisions 203
   21. Restrictive trade practices 203
   B – Restrictive Trade Practices Applicable to Trade Associations 205
   22. Application to practices of trade associations 205
   C – Abuse of Dominant Position 206
   23. Criteria for determining dominant position 206
   24. Abuse of dominant position 206
   24A. Abuse of buyer power 207
   D – Exemption of Certain Restrictive Practices 208
   25. Grant of exemption for certain restrictive practices 208

26. Determination of application for exemption ……… 209

27. Revocation or amendment of exemption ……… 209

28. Exemption in respect of intellectual property rights ……… 210

29. Exemption in respect of professional rules ……… 210

30. Notification of grant, revocation or amendment of exemption ……… 211

E – Investigation into Prohibited Practices ……… 211

31. Investigation by Authority ……… 211

32. Entry and search ……… 212

33. Power of Authority to take evidence ……… 213

34. Proposed decision of Authority ……… 213

35. Hearing conference to be convened for oral representation ……… 214

36. Action following investigation ……… 214

37. Interim relief ……… 214

38. Settlement ……… 215

39. Publication of decision of Authority ……… 215

40. Appeals to the Tribunal ……… 215

PART IV MERGERS ……… 215

41. Merger defined ……… 215

42. Control of mergers ……… 216

43. Notice to be given to Authority of proposed merger ……… 217

44. Period for making determination in relation to proposed merger ……… 217

45. Hearing conference in relation to proposed merger ……… 217

46. Determination of proposed merger ……… 218

47. Revocation of approval of proposed merger ……… 219

48. Review of decisions of Authority by Tribunal ……… 219

49. Compliance with other laws and appeals ……… 220

PART V CONTROL OF UNWARRANTED CONCENTRATION OF ECONOMIC POWER ……… 220

50. Identifying unwarranted concentration of economic power ……… 220

51. Hearing conference ……… 221

52. Orders to dispose of interests ……… 222

53. Appeals from the Authority's order ……… 222

54. Offences and penalties ……… 222

PART VI CONSUMER WELFARE ……… 223

55. False or misleading representations ……… 223

56. Unconscionable conduct ……… 223

57. Unconscionable conduct in business transactions ……… 224

58. Warning notice to public ... 225
59. Product safety standards and unsafe goods ... 226
60. Product information standards ... 226
61. Notice to consumers ... 227
62. Authority to declare product safety or information standards ... 228
63. Liability in respect of unsuitable goods ... 229
64. Liability for defective goods ... 229
65. Unidentified manufacturer ... 230
66. Defence ... 230
67. Consultations with the Kenya Bureau of Standards ... 230
68. Referral of complaints to Government agencies ... 230
69. Notification by Consumer bodies ... 230
70. Offences and penalty ... 231
70A. Authority to initiate investigation into complaint ... 231

PART VII ESTABLISHMENT AND POWERS OF THE COMPETITION TRIBUNAL ... 231

71. Establishment of the Competition Tribunal ... 231
72. Procedure on appeals to the Tribunal ... 232
73. Persons entitled to appeal to the Tribunal ... 232
74. Hearing and determination of appeal ... 232
75. Tribunal to refer appeals back for reconsideration ... 233
76. Provisions pending determination of appeal ... 233
77. Authority's right of appeal ... 233

PART VIII FINANCIAL PROVISIONS ... 233

78. Funds of the Authority ... 233
79. Financial year ... 234
80. Annual estimates ... 234
81. Accounts and audit ... 234
82. Investment of funds ... 235

PART IX MISCELLANEOUS ... 235

83. Annual reports ... 235
84. Prohibition on disclosure of information ... 235
85. Disclosure of private interest by staff ... 236
86. Time within which investigation may be initiated ... 236
87. Hindering administration of Act ... 236
88. Failure to comply with summons ... 236
89. Failure to comply with order ... 236
89A. Leniency programme ... 237

90. Other offences ·················· 237
91. General penalty ·················· 237
92. Jurisdiction of magistrate's courts ·················· 237
93. Rules ·················· 237
PART X REPEAL, SAVINGS AND TRANSITIONAL PROVISIONS ·················· 237
94. Definition ·················· 237
95. Assets and other property ·················· 238
96. Rights, powers, liabilities, etc ·················· 238
97. Legal proceedings ·················· 238
98. Secondment to Authority ·················· 238
99. Repeal of Cap. 504 ·················· 239
100. Savings ·················· 239
SCHEDULE PROVISIONS AS TO THE AUTHORITY ·················· 239

TITLE FOUR THE PUBLIC PRIVATE PARTNERSHIPS ACT (NO. 14 OF 2021)

PART I PRELIMINARY ·················· 243
1. Short title ·················· 243
2. Interpretation ·················· 243
3. Object of the Act ·················· 245
4. Application of Act ·················· 245
5. Act to prevail ·················· 246
PART II PUBLIC PRIVATE PARTNERSHIP COMMITTEE ·················· 246
6. Public Private Partnership Committee ·················· 246
7. Qualification and terms of members ·················· 246
8. Functions and powers of the Committee ·················· 247
9. Vacation of office ·················· 247
10. Subcommittees ·················· 248
11. Delegation by the Committee ·················· 248
12. Conduct of the business of the Committee ·················· 248
13. Code of conduct ·················· 248
14. Remuneration ·················· 248
15. Directorate ·················· 248
16. Director-General ·················· 248
17. Staff of the Directorate ·················· 249
18. Secondment of staff to the Directorate ·················· 249
19. Functions of the Directorate ·················· 249
PART III PUBLIC PRIVATE PARTNERSHIPS ·················· 250
20. Project agreements ·················· 250

21. Public private partnership arrangements 250
22. Duties of contracting authorities 251
23. Determination of the duration of public private partnership agreements 251
24. Execution of project agreements 252
25. Submission of project lists 252
26. National list and priority list of projects 252
27. Prequalification procedures 253
28. Government support measures 253
29. Success fees and recoverable project development costs 253

PART IV PROJECT IDENTIFICATION AND SELECTION OF PRIVATE PARTIES 254

30. Project identification, selection and prioritisation 254
31. Project preparation and implementation 254
32. Feasibility studies 254
33. Approval of feasibility reports 255
34. Technical expertise of contracting authorities 255
35. Standards and procedures 255
36. Limitation of contingent liabilities 256

PART V PUBLIC PRIVATE PARTNERSHIPS PROCUREMENT METHODS 256

37. Procurement methods 256
38. Direct procurement 257
39. Procedure for direct procurement 257
40. Privately-initiated proposals 258
41. Due diligence on privately-initiated proposals 259
42. Evaluation of privately-initiated proposals 259
43. Project development of privately-initiated proposals 260
44. Procurement design 262
45. Restricted bidding 263
46. Requests for qualification 264
47. Qualification of private parties 264
48. Prequalification committees 264
49. Disqualification of private parties 265
50. Invitations to bid 265
51. Submission of bids 266
52. Competitive dialogue 266
53. Bids by consortiums 266
54. Proposal evaluation teams 267
55. Evaluation of bids and evaluation reports 267

56. Non-compliance by bidders ·· 268

57. Negotiations ·· 268

58. Project and risk assessment reports ·· 269

59. Approval of project and financial risk assessment reports by the Committee ······ 269

60. Approval of projects ·· 270

61. Execution of project agreements ·· 270

62. Cancellation of tenders ··· 270

63. Agreements to be ratified by Parliament ··································· 271

PART VI PUBLIC PRIVATE PARTNERSHIPS BY COUNTY GOVERNMENTS ······ 271

64. Project agreements by county governments ······························ 271

65. Approved by county assemblies ··· 271

66. County project lists ·· 272

67. Part V to apply ·· 272

PART VII PROJECT COMPANIES, DISCLOSURES AND PROJECT AGREEMENTS
·· 272

68. Project companies ·· 272

69. Publishing information on execution of project agreements ············ 273

70. Minimum obligations of parties to a project agreement ················· 273

71. Applicable law ·· 274

72. Amendment and variation of project agreements ························· 274

73. Project management ··· 274

74. Secondment of employees of contracting authority ······················· 275

75. Petition Committee ··· 275

76. Secretary ··· 276

77. Remuneration ··· 276

78. Conflict of interest ·· 276

79. Offences ·· 276

80. Decree ·· 277

PART VIII FINANCIAL PROVISIONS ··· 277

81. Public Private Partnership Project Facilitation Fund ····················· 277

82. Financial reporting, audit and project performance reports ············· 277

PART IX MISCELLANEOUS PROVISIONS ······································ 278

83. Local content ·· 278

84. Offences and penalties ·· 278

85. Participation of State officers or public officers in tenders under this Act ······ 279

86. Inspection of public private partnership premises, etc. ·················· 280

87. Application of Part V and Part VI of No. 3 of 2003 ······················ 280

88. Annual report ·· 280

89. Regulations 280
PART X SAVINGS AND TRANSITIONAL PROVISIONS 281
90. Interpretation 281
91. Members and staff 281
92. Savings 282
93. Repeal 282
SCHEDULES 282
FIRST SCHEDULE   PROVISIONS AS TO THE CONDUCT OF BUSINESS AND AFFAIRS OF THE COMMITTEE 282
SECOND SCHEDULE   PUBLIC PRIVATE PARTNERSHIP ARRANGEMENTS 283
THIRD SCHEDULE   MINIMUM CONTRACTUAL OBLIGATIONS REQUIRED TO BE SPECIFIED IN A PROJECT AGREEMENT 285

GROUP TWO   LABOR LAWS AND REGULATIONS

TITLE FIVE   THE EMPLOYMENT ACT (NO. 11 OF 2007) (Revised Edition 2023)

PART 1 PRELIMINARY 289
1. Short title 289
2. Interpretation 289
3. Application 292
PART II GENERAL PRINCIPLES 293
4. Prohibition against forced labour 293
5. Discrimination in employment 293
6. Sexual harassment 294
PART III EMPLOYMENT RELATIONSHIP 295
7. Contract of service 295
8. Oral and written contracts 296
9. General provision of contract of service 296
10. Employment particulars 297
11. Statement of initial particulars 298
12. Statement on disciplinary rules 299
13. Statement of changes 299
14. Reasonably accessible document or collective agreement 300
15. Informing employees of their rights 300
16. Enforcement 301

PART IV   PROTECTION OF WAGES ……… 301
17. Payment, disposal and recovery of wages, allowances, etc. ……… 301
18. When wages or salaries due ……… 303
19. Deduction of wages ……… 304
20. Itemised pay statement ……… 305
21. Statement of statutory deductions ……… 305
22. Power to amend provisions on pay and statements of deductions ……… 306
23. Security bond for wages ……… 306
24. Death of an employee ……… 306
25. Repayment of remuneration wrongfully withheld or deducted ……… 307

PART V   RIGHTS AND DUTIES IN EMPLOYMENT ……… 307
26. Basic minimum conditions of employment ……… 307
27. Hours of work ……… 308
28. Annual leave ……… 308
29. Maternity leave ……… 308
29A. Pre-adoptive leave ……… 309
30. Sick leave ……… 309
31. Housing ……… 310
31A. *Deleted* ……… 310
31B. Affordable Housing Levy ……… 310
31C. Obligations of the employer ……… 311
32. Water ……… 311
33. Food ……… 311
34. Medical attention ……… 311

PART VI   TERMINATION AND DISMISSAL ……… 312
35. Termination notice ……… 312
36. Payment in lieu of notice ……… 313
37. Conversion of casual employment to term contract ……… 313
38. Waiver of notice by employer ……… 314
39. Contract expiring on a journey may be extended ……… 314
40. Termination on account of redundancy ……… 314
41. Notification and hearing before termination on grounds of misconduct ……… 315
42. Termination of probationary contracts ……… 315
43. Proof of reason for termination ……… 315
44. Summary dismissal ……… 315
45. Unfair termination ……… 316
46. Reasons for termination or discipline ……… 317
47. Complaint of summary dismissal and unfair termination ……… 317

48.	Representation	318
49.	Remedies for wrongful dismissal and unfair termination	318
50.	Courts to be guided	319
51.	Certificate of service	319

PART VII PROTECTION OF CHILDREN — 320

52.	Interpretation	320
53.	Prohibition of worst forms of child labour	320
54.	Complaint to the labour officer or police officer	320
55.	Powers of labour officer to cancel and prohibit contracts	321
56.	Prohibition of employment of children between thirteen years and sixteen years of age	322
57.	Prohibition of written contracts for child between thirteen and sixteen years of age	322
58.	Restriction in employing child of between thirteen and sixteen years of age to attend machinery	322
59.	Time restriction in employing a child	322
60.	Emergencies	323
61.	Registers of child in employment	323
62.	Medical examination of a child employee	323
63.	Determination of age	323
64.	Penalty for unlawful employment of child	323
65.	Penalty in case of death or injury of a child	324

PART VIII INSOLVENCY OF EMPLOYER — 324

66.	Insolvency of employer	324
67.	Definition of insolvency	324
68.	Debts to which Part applies	325
69.	Limitation on amount payable under section 68	325
70.	Role of relevant officer	325
71.	Complaint to Industrial Court	326
72.	Transfer of rights and remedies	326
73.	Power to obtain information	327

PART IX EMPLOYMENT RECORDS — 328

74.	Records to be kept by employer	328
75.	False entries etc.	329

PART X EMPLOYMENT MANAGEMENT — 329

76.	Notification of vacancies	329
77.	Notification of filling or abolition of post	329
78.	Notification of termination of employment	329

79. Regiser of employees ··· 329
80. Exemptions ··· 330
81. Offence under Part ··· 330

PART XI FOREIGN CONTRACTS OF SERVICE ··· 330
83. Form and attestation ··· 330
84. Requirement before attestation ··· 330
85. Security in foreign contract of service ··· 330
86. Offence to induce person to proceed abroad under informal contract ··· 331

PART XII DISPUTES SETTLEMENT PROCEDURE ··· 331
87. Complaint and jurisdiction in cases of dispute between employers and employees ··· 331
88. General penalty and offences under other laws ··· 331
89. Saving of contracts of service made abroad ··· 332
90. Limitations ··· 332

PART XIII MISCELLANEOUS PROVISIONS ··· 332
91. Rules ··· 332
92. Repeal of Cap. 226 and savings ··· 333
93. Transitional provisions ··· 334

GROUP THREE   TAX LAWS AND REGULATIONS

TITLE SIX   THE INCOME TAX ACT (*Cap. 470*)
THE INCOME TAX (DIGITAL SERVICE TAX) REGULATIONS, 2020

1. Citation and commencement ··· 336
2. Interpretation ··· 336
3. Digital services ··· 336
4. Application of digital service tax ··· 337
5. User location ··· 337
6. Gross transaction value ··· 337
7. Registration ··· 338
8. Appointment of a tax representative ··· 338
9. Simplified tax registration ··· 338
10. Accounting and payment ··· 338
11. Amendment of returns ··· 339
12. Records ··· 339
13. Penalties ··· 339

GROUP FOUR   SPECIAL ECONOMIC ZONES LAWS AND REGULATIONS

TITLE SEVEN   THE SPECIAL ECONOMIC ZONES ACT (NO. 16 OF 2015) (Revised Edition 2023)

PART I   PRELIMINARY 341
   1. Short title and commencement 341
   2. Interpretation 341
   3. Object and purpose of Act 343

PART II   THE SPECIAL ECONOMIC ZONES 344
   4. Declaration of special economic zones 344
   5. Criteria for designating special economic zones 345
   6. Goods to be considered as exported and imported into Kenya 345
   7. Goods and services within a special economic zone ... 346
   8. Removal of goods from a special economic zone 346
   9. Receipts and payments of special economic zone enterprises ... 347

PART III   THE SPECIAL ECONOMIC ZONES AUTHORITY ... 347
   10. Establishment of the Authority 347
   11. Functions of the Authority 347
   12. Board of Directors 348
   13. Conduct of business and affairs of the Board 349
   14. Powers of the Board 349
   15. Remuneration of directors 349
   16. Chief Executive Officer 349
   17. Staff of the Authority 350
   18. Delegation by the Authority 350
   19. Protection from personal liability 350
   20. Common seal 350

PART IV   FINANCIAL PROVISIONS 351
   21. Establishment of the Fund 351
   22. Financial year 351
   23. Annual estimates 351
   24. Accounts and audit 352
   25. Investment of funds 352

PART V   REGULATORY PROVISIONS 352
   26. Licence to operate in special economic zone 352

27. Application and issue of licence ·· 353
28. Qualifications of a special economic zone developer and operator ············ 353
29. Special economic zone enterprises ·· 354
30. Register of licences ·· 354

PART VI RIGHTS AND OBLIGATIONS OF SPECIAL ECONOMIC ZONE ENTITIES ·· 354

31. Activities permitted within a special economic zone ·· 354
32. Facilities within a special economic zone ·· 355
33. Rights and obligations of an economic zone developer or operator ············ 355
34. Rights of special economic zone enterprises ·· 356
35. Benefits accruing to special economic zone enterprises, developers and operators
 ·· 357

PART VII MISCELLANEOUS PROVISIONS ·· 358

36. Powers of the Cabinet Secretary ·· 358
37. Dispute resolution ·· 358
38. Exemption from Stamp duty ·· 358
39. Regulations ·· 358
40. Transition ·· 359

SCHEDULES ·· 359

FIRST SCHEDULE TYPES OF SPECIAL ECONOMIC ZONES ·· 359
SECOND SCHEDULE PROVISIONS AS TO THE CONDUCT OF BUSINESS
 AND AFFAIRS OF THE BOARD ·· 359

GROUP FIVE ANTI-CORRUPTION AND ECONOMIC CRIMES LAWS AND REGULATIONS

TITLE EIGHT ANTI-CORRUPTION AND ECONOMIC CRIMES ACT (NO. 3 OF 2003) (Revised Edition 2023)

PART I PRELIMINARY ·· 363

1. Short title ·· 363
2. Interpretation ·· 363

PART II APPOINTMENT OF SPECIAL MAGISTRATES ·· 365

3. Power to appoint special magistrates ·· 365
4. Cases triable by special Magistrates ·· 365
5. Procedure and powers of special Magistrates ·· 365

PART III KENYA ANTI-CORRUPTION COMMISSION AND ADVISORY BOARD
 ·· 366

A—Kenya Anti-Corruption Commission ·· 366

6. *Repealed by Act No. 22 of 2011, s. 37.* 366
7. *Repealed by Act No. 22 of 2011, s. 37.* 366
8. *Repealed by Act No. 22 of 2011, s. 37.* 366
9. *Repealed by Act No. 22 of 2011, s. 37.* 366
10. *Repealed by Act No. 22 of 2011, s. 37.* 366
11. *Repealed by Act No. 22 of 2011, s. 37.* 366
12. *Repealed by Act No. 22 of 2011, s. 37.* 366
13. *Repealed by Act No. 22 of 2011, s. 37.* 366
14. *Repealed by Act No. 22 of 2011, s. 37.* 366
15. *Repealed by Act No. 22 of 2011, s. 37.* 366
B—Kenya Anti-Corruption Advisory Board 366
16. Establishment of Advisory Board 366
17. Functions of Advisory Board 367
18. Independence of Advisory Board 367
19. *Deleted by Act No. 18 of 2014, Sch.* 367
20. Chairman and Vice-chairman 367
21. Secretary to Advisory Board 367
22. Procedures of the Advisory Board 367

PART IV   INVESTIGATIONS 368
23. Investigators 368
24. Identification for investigators 368
25. Complaint not investigated 368
25A. Cessation of investigations 368
26. Statement of suspect's property 369
27. Requirement to provide information, etc. 370
28. Production of records and property 370
29. Search of premises 371
30. Admissibility of things produced or found 371
31. Surrender of travel documents 371
32. Arrest of persons 372
33. Disclosure that may affect investigation 372
34. Impersonating investigator 372
35. Investigation report 373
36. Quarterly reports 373
37. Annual report on prosecutions 373

PART V   OFFENCES 374
38. Meaning of "agent" and "principal" 374
39. *Deleted by Act No. 47 of 2016, s. 23.* 374
40. Secret inducements for advice 374

41. Deceiving principal ... 374
42. Conflicts of interest ... 375
43. Improper benefits to trustees for appointments ... 375
44. Bid rigging, etc. ... 375
45. Protection of public property and revenue, etc. ... 376
46. Abuse of office ... 376
47. Dealing with suspect property ... 376
47A. Attempts, conspiracies, etc. ... 377
48. Penalty for offence under this Part ... 377
49. Custom not a defence ... 377
50. Impossibility, no intention, etc., not a defence ... 377

PART VI COMPENSATION AND RECOVERY OF IMPROPER BENEFITS ... 378
51. Liability for compensation ... 378
52. Liability for improper benefits ... 378
53. Liability—miscellaneous provisions ... 378
54. Compensation orders on conviction ... 378
55. Forfeiture of unexplained assets ... 379
56. Order preserving suspect property, etc. ... 380
56A. Appointment of receiver ... 380
56B. Out of court settlement ... 381
56C. Recovery of funds and other assets ... 382

PART VII EVIDENCE ... 382
57. Unexplained assets, etc., as corroboration ... 382
58. Presumption of corruption if act shown ... 382
59. Certificates to show value of property, etc. ... 382
60. Rule, etc., relating to accomplices ... 383
61. Certificates to show office and compensation ... 383

PART VIIA EXECUTION ... 383
61A. Execution against the Commission ... 383

PART VIII MISCELLANEOUS ... 383
62. Suspension, if charged with corruption or economic crime ... 383
63. Suspension, etc., if convicted of corruption or economic crime ... 384
64. Disqualification if convicted of corruption or economic crime ... 384
65. Protection of informers ... 385
66. Obstructing persons under this Act, etc. ... 385
67. Conduct outside Kenya—offences ... 385
68. Regulations ... 386

PART IX REPEAL, TRANSITION AND AMENDMENTS ... 386
69. Interpretation ... 386

70. Repeal of Cap. 65 386
71. Offences under repealed Act 386
72. Temporary Director, etc. 386
73. Transfer from anti-corruption unit of the Kenya Police Force 386
74. Amendment of section 42 of Cap. 22 387

SCHEDULES 387

    FIRST SCHEDULE PROVISIONS RELATING TO THE STAFF OF THE COMMISSION 387

    SECOND SCHEDULE PROVISIONS RELATING TO MEMBERS OF THE ADVISORY BOARD 390

    THIRD SCHEDULE PROVISIONS AS TO THE CONDUCT OF BUSINESS AND AFFAIRS OF THE ADVISORY BOARD 392

第一编
投 资 法 规

第一部
外国投资保护法（第 518 章）

2017 修订版 [1990]

由全国法律报告委员会经总检察长授权公布

www.kenyalaw.org

第518章
外国投资保护法

[批准日期：1964年12月11日]

[施行日期：1964年12月15日]

旨在保护经批准的外国投资及相关事项的议会法案

[1964年第35号法令,1976年第6号法令,1988年第7号法令,
1994年第6号法令,2009年第8号法令]

1. 简称

本法可称为《外国投资保护法》。

2. 释义

（1）在本法中,除非上下文另有规定,否则——

"**所批准的**"任何企业、外币、期间、金额或数额是指第3条签发的相关证书中规定的任何企业、货币、期间、金额或数额；

"**外国资产**"包括外币、信贷、权利、利益或财产,通过支出外币、提供外债、使用或利用外国权利、利益或财产而获得的货币、信贷、权利、利益或财产,以及第3条签发的与获批企业相关的证书持有人对该企业的投资所获得的任何利润；

"**外国人**"是指非肯尼亚公民,包括非在肯尼亚注册成立的法人团体；

"**部长**"是指当时负责财政事务的部长。

（2）为免生疑问,特此声明,就货币而言,只要相关款项来自肯尼亚以外,不得因其在英联邦其他地区而不作为外国资产,且该货币不得因其在肯尼亚及境外而不作为外币。

[1976年第6号法令,附录]

3. 外国投资者可申请并获得证书

（1）拟在肯尼亚投资的外国人可向部长申请证明拟投资的企业为本法所批准的企业。

（2）部长应考虑根据第（1）款提出的每一项申请,如果他确信在任何情况下该企业将促进肯尼亚的经济发展或对肯尼亚有利,可酌情颁发证书给申请人。

（3）*根据1988年第7号法令第3条予以删除。*

（4）每份证书均须载明——

（a）持有人的姓名；

（b）企业的名称和类型；

（c）证书持有人投资或将投资于该企业的外国资产的数额分为以下几部分：

（i）资本,就本法而言,被视为证书持有人在企业中权益的固定数额,应以肯尼亚货币或相关外币在证书中予以记载；和

（ii）任何贷款,就本法而言,应当以肯尼亚货币或相关外币表示；

（d）已投资或拟投资的外币；

（e）根据1976年第7号法令第3条予以删除；

（f）就本法而言，必要或适当的其他事项。

（5）如果外国资产尚未投入，除第（3）款规定的细节外，应出具附条件证明，说明其投资期限。

[1976年第6号法令，附录；1988年第7号法令，第3条]

4. 证书的修改

部长可修改根据第3条颁发的证书——

（a）在任何情况下，如果部长确信其他外国国民已经继承了证书持有人的企业权益，则用继承人姓名代替原持有人的姓名。

但部长不得因持有人直接或间接支出非外国资产，而用已获得持有人利益的人的姓名替代原持有人的姓名；

（b）持有人死亡的，企业的利益应转移给其他人；

（c）企业名称变更的，用变更后的名称替代原名称；

（d）在任何情况下，持有人投资或将投资新的外国资产到企业，或持有人已根据本法撤回或支付其投资的任何部分，所批准金额的变动应以肯尼亚货币或相关外币表示；

（e）在任何情况下，如果投资包括收购法人团体的股份或股票，并且新股或股票不是通过投资非外国资产的方式取得的，则修改其数量或金额以及其类型；

（f）经证书持有人书面同意，更改批准的外币；

（g）延长外国资产的投资期限；和

（h）符合上述规定并经持有人书面同意，以必要或适当的其他方式。

[1976年第6号法令，附录；1988年第7号法令，第4条]

5. 批准期限内引进的外国资产

如果在根据本法颁发证书时，证书所涉及的任何外国资产或其中的一部分尚未投资于批准的企业，则应在批准的期限内投入该笔资产，如果没有在该期限内完成投资的，该证书应视为已被撤销。

6. 根据1994年第6号法令第74条予以废除。

7. 利润转移等

尽管有现行有效的其他法律的规定，对于该证书所涉及的获批准企业，证书持有人可以按现行汇率将获批准的外币转出肯尼亚——

（a）对外国资产投资所产生的利润，包括税后未资本化的留存利润：

根据本法，因出售企业全部或部分资产或对资产重估而引起投资的资本价值增加，不得视为该投资产生的利润。

（b）根据本法，证书中载明的资本代表并被视为证书持有人在企业中的股权的固定数额：

但是——

（i）根据第4条的规定，对上述资本数额进行修改或变更的，应以修改或变更后的数额代替原数额；和

　　　　　（ii）自证书签发或自最后一次修订或变更以来,不得在证书(经修订或变更后规定的资本)中增加额外的金额或数额,以表示投资资本价值的任何增加;和

　　（c）贷款的本金和利息应在证书中予以载明。

　　　　　　[1976年第6号法令,附录;1988年第7号法令,第5条;1994年第6号法令,第74条]

8. 强制征收

　　不得强制占有经批准的任何企业或其财产,也不得强制取得对该企业或财产的权益或权利,但依据《宪法》第75条及本法附录中转载的关于强制占有和征收以及全额和及时补偿的规定实行的除外。

8A. *根据1994年第6号法令第74条予以废除。*

8B. 促进和保护投资的特别协议

　　（1）财政部长可不时通过公报发布公告,宣布该公告中规定的协议在其期限内有效,该协议是与任何国家政府达成的旨在促进和保护该国在肯尼亚投资的协议。

　　（2）本节下的通知可以通过后续通知进行修改或撤销,通知的修改或撤销可以包含部长认为必要或适当的过渡条款或终止日期。

　　　　　　　　　　　　[2009年第8号法令,第66条]

9. 法规和指令

　　为了更好地实施本法,部长可以制定法规或作出指令,并规定本法证书申请的方式,以及这些申请应附带的信息。

附录
[第8节]
肯尼亚宪法

75. 保护财产免受剥夺

　　（1）不得强制占有任何种类的财产,也不得强制取得任何种类财产的利益或权利,满足下列条件的情形除外,即——

　　　　（a）出于国防、公共安全、公共秩序、公共道德、公共卫生、城乡规划的目的,或以促进公共利益的方式开发或利用任何财产,需要占有或取得财产的;和

　　　　（b）对享有该财产利益或权利的人造成困扰的,应当作出合理的说明;和

　　　　（c）对于占有和取得,全额补偿的及时赔付应由相关法律做出规定。

　　（2）凡对被强制占有或取得的财产享有权益或权利的人,均有权就以下事项直接诉诸高等法院以——

　　　　（a）确定其利益或权利,占有或取得财产、利益或权利的合法性,及其有权获得补偿的数额;和

　　　　（b）获得及时的补偿:

　　如果议会规定,就(a)项所述事项应通过上诉的方式进行(对该财产享有权利或利益的人可行使该权利),则应向高等法院以外的依法有管辖权的法庭或当局提出,以确定该事项。

　　（3）首席大法官可根据高等法院或由高等法院依第(2)款赋予管辖权的其他法庭或机构

的惯例和程序制定规则,或在第(2)款条件下,根据其他法庭或当局之运行制定规则(包括关于向高等法院提出申请或上诉或向其他法庭或机构提出申请的期限规则)。

(4) *根据1977年第13号法令第3条予以删除。*

(5) *根据1977年第13号法令第3条予以删除。*

(6) 根据法律的授权,下列事项不视为违反第(1)款或第(2)款——
 (a) 在有关法律对占有或取得任何财产作出规定的范围内——
  (i) 符合税收、关税、税率、税费或其他税款的规定的;
  (ii) 根据肯尼亚法律,无论是在民事诉讼中还是在刑事诉讼中被定罪后,对违法行为进行处罚的;
  (iii) 涉及出租、租赁、抵押、销售单据、质押或合同的;
  (iv) 在确定民事权利或义务的诉讼中,执行法院的判决或命令的;
  (v) 当财产处于危险状态或对人类、动物或植物的健康有害,有合理必要这样做的;
  (vi) 由于涉及诉讼时效的任何法律;或者
  (vii) 就土地而言,在为进行审查、调查、审判或询问的必要期间内,或为进行土壤保护、其他自然资源保护,或从事与农业发展、改良有关的工作(即土地所有者或占用人已被要求实施,而无合理理由拒绝实施或未能实施的发展或改良的相关工作)的必要期间内;

该条文(或视属何情况而定),在其授权下所做的事情须被证明在民主社会是合理的;或者
 (b) 在有关法律对占有或取得以下财产作出规定的范围内——
  (i) 敌方财产;
  (ii) 当管理财产是为了有权享有其实益权益的人的利益时,死者、精神不健全者或未满18岁者的财产;
  (iii) 当管理破产个人或法人团体的债权人的利益时,或管理该财产受益人的利益时,被判定破产的个人或清算中的法人团体的财产;或者
  (iv) 为使信托生效,当根据法院的指令,将受信托约束的财产给予信托文件或法院指定的受托人时,受信托约束的财产。

(7) 如果国会法案规定强制占有或强制征收任何为公共目的而设立的法人团体(除议会提供的资金外,其他资金不允许投入)的财产、利益或权利,则依据该法案所做的任何行为不应被视为违反本节的规定或与本节不一致。

第二部
投资促进法（2004年第6号法令）

2014 修订版 [2004]
由全国法律报告委员会经总检察长授权公布

www.kenyalaw.org

2004 年第 6 号法令
投资促进法

［批准日期：2004 年 12 月 31 日］

［施行日期：2005 年 10 月 3 日］

旨在协助投资者获得投资所需的许可证、提供其他援助和激励措施以促进投资及相关目的的议会法案

［2004 年第 6 号法令，2005 年第 123 号法律公告，
2005 年第 6 号法令，2014 年第 19 号法令］

第一部分
总　　则

1. 简称

本法可称为《投资促进法(2004)》。

2. 定义

在本法中，除非上下文另有规定，否则——

"**管理局**"是指根据第 14 条存续的肯尼亚投资管理局；

"**外国投资者**"是指——

(a) 非肯尼亚公民的自然人；

(b) 由非肯尼亚公民的一人或数人控股的合伙企业；或者

(c) 根据肯尼亚以外的国家的法律注册成立的公司或其他法人团体。

"**投资**"是指投资者对本国或外国资本的出资，包括由企业或为企业创设或收购商业资产，以及企业的扩大、重组、改进或恢复；

"**投资证书**"是指根据本法签发的投资证明；

"**许可证**"包括法律以任何形式要求的注册、准许、批准或授权；

"**本国投资者**"是指——

(a) 作为肯尼亚公民的自然人；

(b) 由肯尼亚公民控股的合伙企业；

(c) 根据肯尼亚法律注册成立，且多数股份由肯尼亚公民持有的公司；或者

(d) 根据肯尼亚法律设立的信托或信托公司，其中多数受托人和受益人为肯尼亚公民。

"**部长**"是指负责投资相关事务的部长。

第二部分
投资证书——申请和颁发等

3. 申请

（1）本国投资者可向管理局申请投资证书。

（2）拟在肯尼亚投资的外国投资者可向管理局申请投资证书。

（3）申请投资证书应符合规定格式。

（4）管理局可要求澄清和补充信息。

［2005年第6号法令，第55条］

4. 获得证书的权利

（1）在以下情况下，申请人有权获得投资证书——

（a）申请完整，并符合本法规定的适用条件；

（b）外国投资者的投资金额至少为10万美元或其他等值货币；

（c）本国投资者的投资金额至少为100万先令或其他等值货币；和

（d）投资及其相关活动合法且有利于肯尼亚。

（2）就第（1）款（d）项而言，在确定一项投资及其相关活动是否对肯尼亚有利时，管理局应考虑投资及活动将在多大程度上符合（a）、（b）和（c）项规定的条件，以及是否符合下列（d）、（e）、（f）、（g）和（h）项规定的任何或全部条件——

（a）为肯尼亚人创造就业机会；

（b）为肯尼亚人带来新的技能或技术；

（c）为税收或其他政府收入作出贡献；

（d）向肯尼亚转让技术；

（e）通过出口或进口代替的方式增加外汇；

（f）使用国内的原材料、供应品和服务；

（g）用增值的方式加工本国资源、自然资源和农业资源；

（h）利用、推广、开发和实施信息和通信技术；

（i）管理局认为的其他对肯尼亚有利的因素。

［2005年第6号法令，第56条］

5. 申请的审核程序

附录一中规定的程序应适用于对申请投资证书的审核。

6. 颁发证书

（1）如果管理局决定颁发投资证书，则应在申请人要求之日颁发。

（2）管理局可以申请人因投资而设立的公司或为实现投资目的所组建的其他商业组织为名义颁发投资证书。

（3）*根据2005年第6号法令第57条予以删除。*

（4）不持有投资证书的本国投资者，应向管理局登记该投资。

［2005年第6号法令，第57条］

7. 取得证书的条件

投资证书应符合——

(a) 本法规定的条件;和

(b) 管理局在颁发证书时明确规定的条件。

8. 转让

(1) 投资证书只有经管理局书面批准才能转让。

(2) 投资证书的转让,受本法规定的限制。

9. 修改

应证书持有人的要求,管理局可根据本法的限制规定,修订该投资证书。

10. 撤销

(1) 管理局可以下列理由撤销投资证书——

(a) 该证书是基于申请人提供的错误信息而颁发的;

(b) 该投资证书是通过欺诈的手段取得的;或者

(c) 违反获得投资证书的条件。

(2) 若管理局拟撤销投资证书,则须至少提前 30 天书面通知持有人撤销投资证书的理由,并须让持有人有机会陈述证书不应被撤销的理由。

11. 审查管理局的决定

(1) 申请投资证书的人或者持有或曾经持有投资证书的人可以请求部长任命专家组来审查管理局有关该申请或证书的决定。

(2) 在收到根据第(1)款提出的请求后,部长应任命下列人员组成专家组——

(a) 任职至少 10 年的主席;和

(b) 另外两名在法律、经济或商业方面经验丰富的成员。

(3) 在进行审查后,专家组可作出下列一项或多项决定——

(a) 确认、更改或撤销上诉的决定;

(b) 指示管理局根据专门小家组作出的指示,重新考虑有关事项;

(c) 下令支付费用。

(4) 部长可根据本条制定管理专家组程序的规则。

(5) 根据部长制定的规则,专家组可规范其程序。

(6) 专家组具有与法院相同的权力,可下令以确保人员出席、出示文件或调查以及惩处藐视法规的行为。

(7) 部长可任命专家组秘书和为适当履行专家组职能所需的其他工作人员。

(8) 专家组成员应获得由部长确定的津贴和费用。

(9) 专家组的费用,包括专家组成员的津贴和费用,应由政府支付。

第三部分
投资证书——福利

12. 获得特定许可证的权利

(1) 投资证书应列明附录二中所列的拟投资所必需,以及投资证书持有人在申请时依法有权获得的许可证。
(2) 在颁发投资证书后,以下规定适用于根据第(1)款在证书中列明的许可证——
  (a) 投资证书的持有人有权获得颁发的许可证,但须符合附录二或投资证书中规定的条件,并在投资证书颁发后12个月内提出申请并支付适当费用(如有);
  (b) 在许可证颁发之前或投资证书颁发后12个月内,无论何者发生在前,如果符合附录二或投资证书中规定的条件,以及第(3)款规定的缴费要求,则该许可证被视为已颁发。
(3) 投资证书持有人应在证书颁发后6个月内,根据相关法律规定,支付在投资证书中列明的许可证的费用。
(4) 为更明确起见,第(2)款(a)项规定的许可证权利仅适用于许可证的首次颁发,并且在首次颁发后,颁发许可证所依据的法律适用于其他所有许可证,包括许可证的撤销或续期。
(5) 对于根据本条有权获得许可证的投资证书持有人,管理局应对其许可证颁发提供便利。

13. 外籍人士入境许可的权利
(1) 根据《移民法》(第172章),投资证书持有人有权获得以下入境许可证——
  (a) 管理人员或技术人员的3张A类入境许可证;和
  (b) 所有人、股东或合伙人的3张H、I或J类入境许可证。
(2) 根据本条,首次颁发的许可证的有效期为2年。
(3) 根据本条,若许可证到期时被重新颁发或被颁发给不同的雇员、所有人、股东或合伙人,则投资证书持有人有权获得该许可证。
(4) 投资证书持有人如果属于《移民法》(第172章)所禁止移民的人,则无权获得该许可证。
(5) 根据本条,获得许可证的持证人须遵守肯尼亚的法律。
(6) 对于第(1)款下的每份许可证,投资证书持有人有权获得——
  (a) 许可证持证人的每个受抚养人的亲属通行证;和
  (b) 许可证或根据(a)项发出的通行证所要求的再入境许可证。
(7) 第(4)款和第(5)款经必要修改后适用于第(6)款规定的通行证或再入境许可证。
(8) 根据本条获得许可证或通行证的条件是——
  (a) 已申请许可证或通行证;
  (b) 已支付适当费用(如有);和
  (c) 已支付或提供《移民法》(第172章)要求的存款或保证金。
(9) 尽管有第(8)款(b)项的规定,第(1)款(b)项规定的许可证首次颁发不收取任何费用。
(10) 如果在投资证书颁发时,第(1)款(a)项规定的入境许可证已经颁发给投资证书持有人的雇员,则该许可证应被视为证书持有人有权根据第(1)款(a)项获得的许可证之一。
(11) 如果在投资证书颁发时,第(1)款(b)项规定的进入许可证已颁发给投资证书持有人或持有人的所有人、股东或合伙人,则该许可证应被视为证书持有人有权根据第(1)款(b)项获得的许可证之一。
(12) 投资证书持有人根据本条有权获得的许可证和通行证,管理局应对其颁发提供便利。

（13）为更加明确起见，除投资证书持有人有权根据本条获得的许可证或通行证之外，本节不限制根据《移民法》（第172章）规定的其他许可证或通行证的颁发。

第四部分
肯尼亚投资管理局

14. 管理局以法人团体身份存续

根据《投资促进中心法》（第485章）设立的投资促进中心在此继续作为本法的法人团体，称为肯尼亚投资管理局。

15. 职能

（1）管理局应促进和便利在肯尼亚的投资。

（2）为促进和便利投资，管理局应——

 （a）通过下列方式协助外国和本国投资者以及潜在投资者——

  （i）颁发投资证书；

  （ii）协助获得任何必要的许可证和通行证；

  （iii）根据《所得税法》（第470章）、《海关和消费税法》（第472章）、《增值税法》（第476章）或其他法律，协助获得激励或豁免；和

  （iv）提供信息，包括投资机会信息或资金来源信息。

 （b）在国内和国际上提升在肯尼亚投资的机会；

 （c）审查投资环境并就促进和便利投资的变革，包括许可证条件变革向政府和其他当局提出建议；

 （d）完善管理投资场地、地产或土地及其相关设施；

 （e）在其认为必要的情况下，在本国和其他国家任命代理人代表管理局执行某些职能；

 （f）实施管理局认为将促进和便利投资的其他举措。

16. 管理局理事会

（1）管理局应设理事会，负责管理局的总体指导和管理。

（2）管理局理事会由下列人员组成——

 （a）由总统任命的1名理事长；

 （b）管理局常务理事；

 （c）内阁秘书；

 （d）各部委中负责下列事项的常任秘书——

  （i）财政；

  （ii）贸易和工业；

  （iii）农业；

  （iv）土地；

  （v）地方当局；和

（vi）规划。

(e)《出口加工区法》(第517章)规定的出口加工区管理局的行政长官；

(f) 出口促进委员会的行政长官；和

(g) 部长任命的6名成员。

(3) 任何人除非在法律、经济、商业、工业或管理领域有杰出成就,否则不得获委任为理事长或根据第(2)款(g)项获委任为成员。

17. 理事长、委任成员的任期

理事长或根据第16条第(2)款(g)项委任的成员,任期为3年,可连任。

18. 理事长、委任成员的辞职

(1) 理事长可向总统递交书面辞呈。

(2) 根据第16条第(2)款(g)项委任的成员可向部长递交书面辞呈。

19. 理事长、委任成员的罢免

(1) 根据第(2)款所述理由,总统可以罢免理事长,部长可以罢免根据第16条第(2)款(g)项委任的成员。

(2) 第(1)款所述的理由如下——

(a) 理事长或成员无合理理由连续三次缺席已获通知的管理局理事会会议；

(b) 理事长或成员破产；

(c) 理事长或成员被判犯有涉及不诚实、欺诈或道德败坏的罪行；

(d) 理事长或成员因长期患有身体或精神疾病而无法履行其职责；或者

(e) 理事长或成员因其他原因不能或不适合履行其职务。

20. 理事会成员津贴

管理局应向管理局理事会成员支付由部长确定的津贴和费用。

21. 理事会程序

(1) 管理局理事会的业务和事务应根据附录三的要求进行。

(2) 除附录三另有规定外,管理局理事会可规范自己的程序。

22. 理事会秘书

管理局常务理事为管理局理事会秘书。

23. 管理局常务理事

(1) 管理局理事会须委任一名常务理事,作为管理局的行政长官,并在理事会的指示下,负责管理局的日常运作。

(2) 常务理事的聘用条款及条件,须由管理局理事会决定。

(3) 常务理事的任期不得超过8年。

24. 其他人员

(1) 除常务理事外,管理局可委任其认为适当的其他人员。

(2) 除常务理事外的工作人员的聘用条款及条件,由管理局决定。

25. 豁免

管理局工作人员、理事会成员或理事委员会对根据本法善意的作为或不作为不承担个人责任。

第五部分
国家投资委员会

26. 委员会成立

作为非法人机构的国家投资委员会特此成立,由以下成员组成——

(a) 由总统或由总统指定的部长担任理事长;

(b) 部长负责的有关事项——

(i) 财政;

(ii) 贸易和工业;

(iii) 农业;

(iv) 土地;

(v) 地方当局;

(vi) 规划;

(vii) 旅游和信息;和

(viii) 环境、自然资源和野生动物。

(c) 肯尼亚中央银行行长;

(d) 管理局理事会理事长;

(e) 由总统任命的代表私营部门的12人,其在法律、经济、商业、工业或管理领域具有突出表现。

27. 职能

(1) 国家投资委员会的职能是——

(a) 向政府和政府机构提供在肯尼亚增加投资和促进经济增长的建议;和

(b) 制定和执行政府有关经济和投资的政策,以促进公共和私营部门之间的合作。

(2) 在根据第(1)款执行其职能时,委员会应——

(a) 监测经济环境,以确定投资和经济增长的障碍,并提出促进投资和经济增长的激励措施;

(b) 监测肯尼亚的经济发展,以确定可能无法从经济发展中受益的区域;和

(c) 就促进投资和经济发展咨询公共和私营部门的人士的意见和建议。

第六部分
其 他

28. 误导管理局等罪行

任何人故意向管理局提交虚假或误导性信息以获取投资证书或获得管理局的任何协助,即属犯罪,一经定罪,可处以100万先令以下罚款或2年以下监禁,或两者并罚。

29. 不当泄露依法获取信息的罪行

任何人无正当理由泄露依本法行事过程中获得的信息,即属犯罪,一经定罪,可处以100

万先令以下罚款或 2 年以下监禁,或两者并罚。

30. 规章

(1) 部长可以制定规章以更好地执行本法的规定。

(2) 在不违反第(1)款的情况下,内阁秘书可就以下事项制定规章——

　　(a) 修订附录二;

　　(b) 明确须颁发工作许可证的雇员类别;

　　(c) 规定审查投资者的程序。

[2014 年第 19 号法令,第 41 条]

31. 第 485 章的废除

《投资促进中心法》(第 485 章)被废除。

32. 已废除法令保留的一般权限等

(1) 在《投资促进中心法》被第 31 条废除之前,根据该法取得的一般授权应被视为本法规定的投资证书而存续。

(2) 在《投资促进中心法》被第 31 条废除之前,根据该法(第 485 章)对一般授权的申请,应被视为本法规定的对投资证书的申请而存续。

附录一
申请投资证书的审议程序
[第 5 节]

1. 定义

在本附录中——

"**工作日**"是指星期六、星期日或公众假期以外的日期。

2. 申请报告

(1) 在收到完整的申请后 10 个工作日内,管理局应就申请准备书面报告。

(2) 当收到第 3 条第(3)款要求的任何澄清或补充信息时,视为已收到申请。

3. 决定

在申请报告完成后 5 个工作日内,管理局应就申请作出决定。

4. 决定通知书

在管理局作出决定后 5 个工作日内,管理局应当将决定书面通知送达申请人。

5. 如果决定拒绝颁发投资证书,管理局应——

　　(a) 准备书面理由;

　　(b) 根据第 4 条向申请人发出通知,附上一份理由副本和根据第 2 条准备的报告副本;和

　　(c) 在管理局作出决定后的 5 个工作日内,向部长提交申请书副本、理由副本和根据第 2 条准备的报告副本。

6. 如果决定迟延,申请人可向部长投诉——

(1) 如果申请人向管理局提交完整申请后的 25 个工作日内没有收到管理局根据第 4 条作出的决定通知,该申请人可以向部长提出书面投诉。

(2) 部长应对根据第(1)款提出的投诉进行调查,并在收到投诉后的 15 个工作日内将调查结果通知申请人。

7. 环境、健康或安全问题的特殊规定

(1) 如果申请提出下列问题,则适用本条——

(a) 管理局认为应提交给其他人或机构关于环境、健康或安全问题;或者

(b) 需获其他人或机构批准或同意的问题。

(2) 如果申请提出第(1)款所述的问题,管理局应将该问题转送给适当的人或机构,并通知该申请人。

(3) 就本附录中规定的任何期间的适用而言,根据第(2)款的规定,从转送相关个人或机构之日起到收到相关回复的期间不计算在内。

8. 管理局应与有关当局联络,以确定投资证书的申请人是否有权合法获得附录二所列的投资所需的许可证。

附录二
投资证书持有人有权获得的许可证

[第 12 条,第 30 第(2)款,附录 1 第 8 条]

总　　则

1. 根据《工业注册法》(第 118 章)进行注册。

   条件:在投资证书颁发后 6 个月内提交注册详情。

2. 《贸易许可法》(第 497 章)规定的许可证,包括附条件的许可证。

3. 《进出口和基本供给法》(第 502 章)规定的进口许可证或出口许可证。

4. 根据《工厂法》(第 514 章)将场所注册为工厂。

5. 根据《工厂法》(第 514 章)第 69G 条批准的计划。

6. 《地方政府法》(第 265 章)规定的许可证,包括根据该法制定的规章。

7. 根据《地方政府法》(第 265 章),包括根据该法或《公共卫生法》(第 242 章)制定的规章,授权或同意进行工厂或场所的建设。

   条件:工厂或场所符合所有设计要求,并且在法律要求的任何检查或证书执行或颁发之前,工厂或场所不得使用。

8. 1996 年《实体规划法》(1996 年第 6 号)第 33 条规定的开发许可以及该法第 30 条第(7)款中所述的合规证书。

9. 根据《工业培训法》(第 237 章)规定的命令进行注册。

   条件:在投资证书颁发后 6 个月内提交注册详情。

10. 《运输许可法》(第 404 章)规定的私人承运许可证。

11. 根据《标准法》(第 496 章)使用标准化标记的许可证。

12. 《水法》(2002 年第 8 号)第 25 条规定要求的许可证。

13. 《湖泊和河流法》(第 409 章)规定的蒸汽船许可证。

14. 《环境管理与协调法》(1999 年第 8 号)规定的环境影响许可证。

酒　　店

15.《酒店和餐馆法》(第494章)规定的酒店许可证。

　　条件：提供该法令第5条第(4)款要求的由卫生官员出具的健康证明。

16. 根据《酒店和餐馆法》(第494章)为投资证书中指定的人颁发的酒店经理许可证。

17.《酒店和餐馆法》(第494章)规定的餐馆许可证。

　　条件：提供该法令第5条第(4)款要求的由卫生官员出具的健康证明。

18. 根据《酒店和餐馆法》(第494章)为投资证书中指定的人颁发的餐馆经理许可证。

19.《售酒许可法》(第121章)规定的一般零售售酒许可证和酒店售酒许可证。

餐　　馆

20.《酒店和餐馆法》(第494章)规定的餐馆许可证。

　　条件：提供该法令第5条第(4)款要求的由卫生官员出具的健康证明。

21. 根据《酒店和餐馆法》(第494章)为投资证书中指定的人颁发的餐馆经理许可证。

22.《售酒许可法》(第121章)规定的餐馆售酒许可证。

销售、制备食物等

23.《食品、药品和化学品法》(第254章)规定的许可证，允许使用场所销售、制备、储存或展示食物以供出售。

农业——总则

24. 根据《农业法》(第318章)第22条第(6)款进行注册。

除虫菊种植

25.《除虫菊法》(第340章)规定的种植除虫菊的许可证。

剑麻产业

26. 根据《剑麻法》(第341章)注册为种植者。

　　条件：剑麻产业要求的细则。

　　(登记)规则应在投资证书颁发后6个月内提交。

27.《剑麻法》(第341章)规定的工厂许可证。

玉米、小麦等的碾磨

28.《国家谷物和农产品委员会法》(第338章)规定的磨坊主许可证。

茶　　厂

29.《茶叶法》(第343章)规定的制造许可证。

糖　　厂

30.《糖法》第200号(2001年第10号)规定的经营糖厂或粗糖厂的许可证。

咖啡交易

31. 2001年《咖啡法》(2001年第9号)规定的购买、销售、研磨、仓储、出口或以其他方式经营咖啡业务或进行咖啡交易的许可证。

32. 2001年《咖啡法》(2001年第9号)规定的许可转移。

乳制品行业

33. 根据《乳业法》(第336章)第五部分进行注册。

　　条件：在投资证书颁发后6个月内提交该法第32条要求的详细信息。

34. 根据《乳业法》(第 336 章)为投资证书中指定的人颁发的乳品经理许可证。

35. 《乳业法》(第 336 章)规定的零售许可证。

36. 根据《公共卫生法》(第 242 章)下的《公共卫生(牛奶和乳制品)规则》将营业场所注册为牛奶场。

　　条件:提供本条要求的卫生官员所出具的健康报告。

37. 《公共卫生法》(第 242 章)下的《公共卫生(牛奶和乳制品)规则》规定的牛奶供应商许可证。

原皮和皮革贸易法

38. 《原皮和皮革贸易法》(第 359 章)规定的买方许可证。

39. 《原皮和皮革贸易法》(第 359 章)规定的出口商许可证或进口商许可证。

40. 《原皮和皮革贸易法》(第 359 章)规定的场所注册证书。

培 根 工 厂

41. 《养猪业法》(第 361 章)规定的培根工厂许可证。

42. 《养猪业法》(第 361 章)规定的生猪屠宰许可证。

43. 《动物疾病法》(第 364 章)下的《动物疾病(猪疾病防治)规则》规定的养猪许可证。

屠 宰 场

44. 《肉类控制法》(第 356 章)下的《肉类控制(本国屠宰场)条例》规定的屠宰场经营许可证。

45. 《肯尼亚肉类委员会法》(第 363 章)第 8 条第(1)款(a)项规定的许可证。

46. 《养猪业法》(第 361 章)规定的生猪屠宰许可证。

47. 《动物疾病法》(第 364 章)下的《动物疾病(猪疾病防治)规则》规定的养猪许可证。

消 毒 工 厂

48. 《肥料和动物饲料法》(第 345 章)规定的消毒工厂许可证。

在蒙巴萨的肉类出口和船只肉类供应

49. 《肯尼亚肉类委员会法》(第 363 章)第 8 条第(1)款(b)项规定的许可证。

股 票 交 易

50. 《股票交易员许可法》(第 498 章)规定的股票交易员许可证。

渔　　业

51. 《渔业法》(第 378 章)规定的船舶登记证书。

52. 《渔业法》(第 378 章)规定的捕鱼许可证。

53. 《渔业法》(第 378 章)规定的外国渔船许可证。

制 造 药 品

54. 《制药和毒物法》(第 244 章)规定的制造许可证。

药　　店

55. 根据《制药和毒物法》(第 244 章)对场所进行注册。

害虫防治产品

56. 《害虫防治产品法》(第 346 章)规定的场所许可证。

机动车零部件或配件交易

57. 《机动车部件和配件法》(第 520 章)规定的交易机动车部件或配件的许可证。

二手机动车交易

58.《二手机动车法》(第484章)规定的开展买卖二手机动车业务的许可证。

废旧金属交易

59.《废旧金属法》(第503章)规定的许可证。

公共交通

60.《运输许可证法》(第404章)规定的公共承运人许可证。

条件：许可证受该法第8条第(2)款规定的条件约束。

矿 业

61.《采矿法》(第306章)规定的探矿权。

62.《采矿法》(第306章)规定的在特定土地上的独家勘探许可证。

63.《采矿法》(第306章)规定的对特定土地的租赁。

64.《野生动物(保护和管理)法》(第376章)第10条规定的对国家公园内特定土地的使用许可。

贵金属交易

65.《未加工贵金属贸易法》(第309章)规定的买卖未加工贵金属的许可证。

钻石交易

66.《钻石工业保护法》(第310章)规定的钻石经销商许可证。

电 影

67.《电影和舞台剧法》(第222章)规定的电影许可证。

电影制作

68.《电影和舞台剧法》(第222章)规定的拍摄许可证。

69.《野生动物(保护和管理)法》(第376章)规定的在国家公园拍摄电影的授权。

租购业务

70.《租购法》(第507章)规定的开展租购业务的许可证。

拍 卖

71.《拍卖师法》(1996年第5号)规定的许可证。

附录三
管理局理事会关于业务和事务行为规则
[第21节]

1. 会议

（1）理事会在每个财政年度应至少召开4次会议，并且两次会议间隔时间不得超过4个月。

（2）会议应由理事会秘书根据理事长的指示或至少5名理事会成员的要求召集。

（3）除非全体成员另有约定，否则会议召开前应至少提前7天通知每位成员。

（4）会议应由理事长主持，在理事长缺席时，由理事会为此目的选出一名人员主持。

（5）第16条第(2)款(b)、(c)、(d)、(e)或(f)项规定的成员可以指定下列人员之一在其缺席时代表其出席理事会会议——

（a）该成员的代理人；或者

（b）受该成员授权且级别与其相同或更高的人。

2. 法定人数

9名理事会成员构成法定人数。

3. 表决

理事会的决定应由出席并参加表决的多数成员作出，在票数相等的情况下，主持会议的人应投第二票或决定票。

4. 委员会

（1）理事会可设立委员会并将其认为适当的职能委托给委员会。

（2）理事会可任命非理事会成员的人士为根据第（1）款设立的委员会的成员。

第三部
竞争法（2010 年第 12 号法令）

2019 修订版 [2010]

由全国法律报告委员会经总检察长授权公布

www.kenyalaw.org

2010 年第 12 号法令
竞争法

[批准日期:2010 年 12 月 30 日]
[施行日期:2011 年 8 月 1 日]

旨在促进和保障国民经济的公平竞争;保护消费者免受不公和误导性市场行为的侵害;对竞争管理局和竞争法庭的设立、权力和职能及相关目的作出规定的议会法案

[2010 年第 12 号法令,L. N. 73/2011,L. N. 23/2011,2014 年第 16 号法令,
2015 年第 25 号法令,2016 年第 49 号法令,2017 年第 11 号法令,
2018 年第 18 号法令,2019 年第 27 号法令]

第一部分
总　　则

1. 简称
本法可称为《竞争法》(2010)。

2. 释义
在本法中,除非上下文另有规定,否则——

"**协议**"在用于行业惯例时,包括合同、约定或协定,无论其法律上是否可执行。

"**资产**"包括任何有形或无形的不动产或动产、知识产权、商誉、权利财产、权利、许可证、诉讼或索赔的财产以及其他任何具有商业价值的资产。

"**管理局**"是指本法第 7 条规定的竞争管理局。

"**买方权力**"是指一个企业或企业集团以产品或服务购买者的身份施加的影响——

　　(a) 以从供应商处获得更优惠的条件;或者

　　(b) 以强加长期机会成本,包括损害或保留利益,如果实施该行为,该长期机会成本将与该行为导致的企业或企业集团的任何长期成本不相称。

"**竞争**"和"**竞争者**"的定义分别见本法第 4 条。

"**协同行为**"是指公司之间通过直接或间接接触实现的合作或协调行为,该行为取代了公司的独立行动,但不等同于协议。

"**消费者**"包括以非转售目的购买或要约购买商品或服务的人,但不包括为了生产或制造商品以供销售而购买商品或服务的人。

"**消费者团体**"包括以任何名称命名的居民协会和经注册的消费者群体。

"**郡政府**"是指根据《宪法》第 76 条①第(1)款设立的郡政府。

---

① 经核对,译者认为此处为《宪法》最新版本的第 176 条。

"**客户**"包括购买或要约购买商品或服务的人。

"**总干事**"指根据本法第 12 条任命的总干事。

"**市场支配地位**"的含义见本法第 4 条,其中"**支配地位**"应据此解释。

"**企业**"是指业务经营企业。

"**货物**"包括:

(a) 船舶、飞机和车辆;

(b) 动物,包括鱼类;

(c) 矿物、树木和作物,无论是地上物、地下物或者土地附着物;和

(d) 煤气、水和电。

"**中间产品**"是指在生产制造过程中用作投入的货物。

"**许可证**"是指允许被许可人提供或获取商品或服务,或进行任何其他活动的执照、许可证或授权。

"**地方当局**"*根据 2016 年第 49 号法令第 2 条予以删除。*

"**制造**"包括以转售为目的对商品进行改造以增加商品价值的任何人工过程,以及单个企业内与运输方式无关的任何包装或重新包装的操作。

"**市场**"的定义见本法第 4 条。

"**市场力量**"是指公司控制价格、排除竞争或在一定程度上独立于其竞争对手、客户或供应商的力量。

"**成员**"就管理局而言,指管理局的理事长和其他成员。

"**合并**"是指在肯尼亚境内或境外对股份、业务或其他资产的收购,从而导致肯尼亚的企业、部分企业或企业资产的控制权以任何方式发生变化,包括接管。

"**部长**"是指目前负责财政的部长。

"**人**"包括法人团体;

"**掠夺性行为**"是指试图将竞争对手赶出市场或阻止其进入市场的行为或策略。

"**公认的消费者团体**"是指为本法目的而得到管理局承认的消费者团体。

"**出售**"包括出售或要约出售的协议,"**要约出售**"应被视为包括公开所售商品、提供口头或书面报价单以及表示愿意进行任何交易的任何行为或通知。

"**服务**"包括任何权利(包括与不动产或动产有关的利益和有关的权利)、利益、特权或便利,不限于上述一般规定,包括根据任何合同为以下方面提供、授予的权利、利益、特权或便利——

(a) 工作的履行,包括专业性质的工作,无论是否供应货物;

(b) 休闲、娱乐、交通、广播、旅游、消遣、教育或教学设施的提供、使用或享用;

(c) 保险;

(d) 银行业务;

(e) 贷款;

(f) 咨询;

(g) 私人专业实践,

以及以特许权使用费、贡金、征税或类似费用的形式支付报酬的任何权利、利益或特权,但

不包括根据雇佣合同履行工作或供应货物。

"国营公司"的含义可以参照《国营公司法》(第446章)的规定。

"供应"——

  (a) 就货物而言,包括通过出售、交换、租赁、出租或租购的方式供应或再供应;和

  (b) 就服务而言,包括提供、授予或给予。

"供应商"也应作相应解释。

"肯尼亚的大部分地区"是指肯尼亚的一部分,包括区、镇议会、市议会。

"贸易"包括商业。

"行业协会"是指为促进其成员或由其成员所代表的个人的利益而成立的团体或个人(无论是否成立)。

"法庭"是指根据本法第71条设立的竞争法庭。

"业务经营"是指由个人、合伙企业或信托公司及行业协会在生产、供应、分销商品或提供服务方面为获取利益或报酬而开展的业务。

"经营者不正当集中"是指两个不同的企业或公司之间存在交叉董事关系,生产实质上相似的商品或提供相似的服务,其市场份额合计超过40%。

[2014年第16号法令,第31条;2016年第49号法令,第2条;2019年第29号法令,第2条]

3. 本法目的

本法的目的是通过在肯尼亚全国范围内促进和保护市场的有效竞争,防止不公平和误导性市场行为,增加肯尼亚人民的福利,以便——

  (a) 提高商品和服务的生产、分销和供应效率;

  (b) 促进创新;

  (c) 最大限度地提高资源的有效分配;

  (d) 保护消费者;

  (e) 创造有利于外国和本国的投资环境;

  (f) 履行国家在区域一体化倡议中有关竞争事务的义务;

  (g) 使国家竞争法、政策和做法符合最佳国际惯例;和

  (h) 提升国有企业在世界市场上的竞争力。

4. 表达的解释

(1) 本法中提及的以下表述应根据本条规定进行解释——

  (a) "竞争"是指肯尼亚市场上的竞争,是指两个或多个人——

    (i) 供应或试图供应给;或者

    (ii) 获取或试图获取自,

使用相同或替代的商品或服务的市场中的主体;

  (b) 如果双方彼此有竞争关系或将会有竞争关系,则双方互为"竞争者",除非双方作为协议的当事方,很可能相互竞争;

  (c) "市场"是指肯尼亚或肯尼亚大部分地区的市场,是指特定种类的商品或服务之间,以及这些商品或服务的供应者或需求者之间,或者潜在供求者或需求者之间,在供应或需求方面替代的合理可能范围。

(2) 在评估对竞争的影响或确定一个主体是否具有市场支配地位时,除其他相关事项外,还应考虑以下事项:
  (a) 由非肯尼亚居民或在肯尼亚经营业务的主体进口货物或提供服务;和
  (b) 相关市场的经济情况,包括在市场上提供或获取商品或服务的主体的市场份额、这些主体扩大其市场份额的能力以及新进入市场的潜力。
(3) 一个主体在市场上具有支配地位,如果该主体——
  (a) 生产、供应、分销或以其他方式控制的货物不少于在肯尼亚或其大部分地区生产、供应或分销的任何种类的货物总额的一半;
  (b) 提供或以其他方式控制的服务不少于在肯尼亚或其大部分地区提供的服务的一半。

[2014年第16号法令,第32条]

5. 适用

(1) 本法适用于所有从事贸易的主体,包括政府、国有公司和地方当局;
(2) 如果本法的规定与任何其他法律中有关竞争、消费者福利和管理局的权力或职能的规定有冲突的,以本法的规定为准;
(3) 如果负责公共监管的机构对本法规定由特定部门管理的行为具有管辖权,则管理局和该机构应——
  (a) 确定并建立共同管辖区域的管理程序;
  (b) 促进合作;
  (c) 提供信息交换和机密信息的保护;和
  (d) 确保本法规则的一致适用:

但是在与竞争和消费者福利有关的所有事项中,如果存在任何冲突、不协调或不一致,则应以管理局的决定、指令、法规、规则、命令和决议为准。

(4) 尽管有第(1)款的规定,但是政府不承担本法规定的任何罚款或处罚,也不应因违反本法规定而被起诉。
(5) 就本条而言,在不影响"**贸易**"在其他方面的含义的情况下——
  (a) 在政府、国有公司或郡政府开展的业务中出售或收购一项业务、部分业务或资产的行为,构成从事贸易的行为;
  (b) 以下行为不构成从事贸易——
    (i) 征收税款;
    (ii) 授予或撤销执照、许可证和授权;
    (iii) 收取执照、许可证和授权的费用;
    (iv) 政府、国有公司或郡政府内部的交易。

[2016年第49号法令,第3条]

6. 域外行为

本法适用于在肯尼亚境外通过以下主体实施的行为——
  (a) 肯尼亚公民或通常居住在肯尼亚的人;
  (b) 在肯尼亚注册成立或在肯尼亚境内经营业务的法人团体;

（c）向肯尼亚或在肯尼亚境内供应或获取商品或服务的相关人员；或者

（d）在肯尼亚境外收购股份或其他资产，导致对肯尼亚境内企业、企业的一部分或企业资产的控制发生变化的任何人。

第二部分
管理局的设立、权力和职能

7. 管理局的设立

（1）兹设立一个机构，称为竞争管理局。

（2）管理局应是独立的，且应独立、公正、不偏不倚地履行其职能，行使其权力。

（3）管理局为拥有公章的永续存在的法人团体，并能够以其法人名义——

（a）起诉和被诉；

（b）购买或以其他方式获取、持有、抵押和处置动产和不动产；

（c）借款；和

（d）为适当履行本法规定的职能而进行或执行其他所有必要的事项或行为，且这些事项和行为可以法人名义合法进行或执行。

8. 管理局业务与事务的管理

（1）管理局业务和事务的管理和规范须按照附录规定。

（2）除附录另有规定外，管理局可规范自己的程序。

9. 管理局的职能

（1）管理局的职能为——

（a）促进和加强对本法的遵守；

（b）接收和调查法人、自然人和消费者团体的投诉；

（c）促进公众对本法规定的义务、权利和救济措施以及管理局的职责、职能和活动的了解、认识和理解；

（d）促进消费者团体的建立，并制定其能遵守的良好和适当的标准和规则，以保护竞争和消费者福利；

（e）承认根据国家相关法律正式注册的消费者团体是在其业务领域内代表消费者向竞争管理局申诉的适当机构；

（f）向消费者提供与本法规定的个人义务、消费者权利和可获得的救济措施有关的信息及指南；

（g）调查和研究与竞争和消费者利益保护有关的事项；

（h）研究政府政策、程序和方案、立法和立法建议，以评估它们对竞争和消费者福利的影响，并公布研究结果；

（i）调查在整个经济运行过程中或在特定环节内的竞争阻碍，包括进入和退出市场，并公布调查结果；

（j）调查监管机构的政策、程序和方案，以评估其对竞争和消费者福利的影响，并公布调查结果；

（k）参与政府、政府委员会、监管机构和其他机构有关竞争和消费者福利的审议和程序；

（l）就与竞争和消费者福利有关的事项向政府、政府委员会、监管机构和其他机构进行交涉；

（m）在所有与竞争和消费者福利有关的事项上与监管机构和其他公共机构进行联络；

（n）就与竞争和消费者福利有关的事项向政府提供建议。

（2）根据 L.N. 23/2011 附录予以删除。

[L.N. 23/2011,附录]

10. 管理局成员

（1）管理局应由以下成员组成——

（a）由总统任命的 1 名理事长；

（b）现任负责财政的该国家部门常任秘书或其代表；

（c）现任负责贸易的该国家部门常任秘书或其代表；

（d）总检察长或其代表；

（e）根据本法第 12 条任命的总干事；和

（f）其他 5 名成员由部长从在竞争和消费者福利事务方面经验丰富的人员中任命，其中一名应在消费者福利事务方面经验丰富。

（2）根据第（1）款（f）项被提名管理局成员者，在被任命前，应由议会通过相关的议会委员会进行审查和批准。

[2018 年第 18 号法令,附录]

11. 管理局成员的薪酬

管理局成员应获得部长批准的报酬、费用、津贴和支出的费用。

12. 总干事

（1）管理局应设有一名总干事，经议会批准，由管理局从具有竞争事务方面知识和经验的人员中任命。

（2）总干事应按照管理局不时在委任文书中或以其他书面形式确定的聘用条款和条件任职，但总干事任期为 5 年，最多可连任两届。

（3）总干事应是管理局的当然成员，但无权在管理局的任何会议上投票。

（4）总干事应是管理局的首席执行官，并在管理局的指示下负责管理局的日常管理工作。

13. 工作人员

（1）管理局应聘用其认为适当的工作人员，以便能够履行其职责和行使权力；

（2）管理局可在其认为适当的情况下聘请顾问和专家，协助其履行职责和行使权力。

（3）管理局应制定竞争性选拔程序以任命工作人员、顾问和专家。

（4）管理局雇用工作人员和聘请顾问和专家的条款及条件应由管理局决定，但应包括以下事项——

（a）工作人员、顾问或专家一旦出现任何利益冲突，应立即以书面形式通知管理局，如果不遵守这一要求，无论是故意还是过失，都将被立即解雇；

（b）当管理局知悉利益冲突时，无论是根据（a）项发出通知还是通过任何其他方式，管理局可指示该人不参加与其有利益冲突的任何事项的审议，在这种情况下，该人须遵从该指示。

（5）在雇用或聘用任何人之前，管理局须向该人取得关于任何现有利益冲突的书面声明。

（6）管理局雇用的全职雇员不得从事任何其他有偿工作。

（7）管理局可与政府部门和其他政府机关和机构签订协议，在其认为适当的情况下共享特定雇员的服务。

（8）管理局应在其年度报告中列入其竞争性选拔程序及其雇佣规则的说明。

14. 公章

（1）管理局的公章应由总干事或管理局指示的其他人保管，除非有管理局的命令，否则不得使用。

（2）管理局的公章加盖在文件上并经过正式认证后，应由司法和官方正式通知，除非有相反的证明，否则管理局根据本条作出的任何必要命令或授权应被推定为已正式发出。

（3）加盖管理局的公章须经管理局理事长和总干事签字确认：

在理事长或总干事缺席的情况下，管理局应在任何特定事项上提名一名管理局成员代表理事长或总干事认证管理局的公章。

15. 管理局的授权

（1）管理局可通过一般授权或以授权书规定的其他方式将其权力授予其任何成员，但下列情况除外——

（a）本法规定的决策职责；

（b）授权本身；和

（c）撤销或更改授权的权力。

（2）授权应根据授权书行使。

（3）管理局可随时撤销或更改授权。

16. 个人责任保护

（1）管理局成员或管理局的任何职员、工作人员或代理人所做的事项，如果该事项或事情是为执行管理局的职能、权力或职责而善意地做出的，成员、官员、工作人员、代理人或任何按其指示行事的人应以个人名义对任何诉讼、索赔或要求承担法律责任。

（2）管理局或管理局根据本法授权的人出于善意做出或将要做出的任何直接或间接造成损失、损害或伤害的事情，均不向任何人支付赔偿。

（3）任何人根据管理局的指示所做或据称做出的行为在任何法庭被起诉或检控而产生的费用，如果法院认为该行为是善意的，则应由管理局的一般资金支付，否则由该行为人自行承担相关费用。

17. 管理局的损害赔偿责任

管理局因行使本法或其他法律赋予的权利，或者全部或部分未能履行其职责，对任何人本人、财产或利益造成的损失或损害，第16条的规定不得免除管理局的赔偿责任。

18. 进行调查的权力

（1）管理局可在以下情况下进行调查或部门调研——

（a）认为对履行其职能而言是必要或适宜的；

（b）部长以书面形式向管理局发出指示，要求其对指示中指定的事项进行调查或部门调研。

（2）部长根据第（1）款（b）项作出的指示应指明管理局向部长提交报告的期限。

（3）在适当的情况下，调查或部门调研结束后，管理局应在其提交给部长的报告中确定与经营者不正当集中有关的因素，并提出可能改善这种情况的措施和建议。

（4）应监管机构的要求，或出于自身要求，管理局可对任何影响竞争、滥用买方权力或消费者福利的事项进行调查，并在合理期限内提供报告。

（5）管理局应通过以下方式就拟进行的调查或部门调研发出通知——

（a）在公报以及至少一种全国发行的日报上发布通知，指明——

（i）拟进行调查的主题；

（ii）邀请公众在指定期限内就该主题提出意见；和

（iii）在部长的指示下进行调查时，由部长规定职权范围；

（b）将调查的书面通知，以及（a）项中的信息发送给——

（i）管理局认为利益可能受到调查结果影响的企业；

（ii）管理局认为在该事件中具有利益的行业和消费者组织；

（iii）部长。

（6）任何人、企业、行业协会或团体都应有义务提供给管理局为履行本部分规定的调查或部门调研的法定职责而要求的信息。

［2016年第49号法令，第4条；2019年第27号法令，第3条］

19. 管理局部门的设置

（1）管理局可设置其认为能够适当地履行本法规定的职能的一个或多个部门。

（2）管理局应任命一名或多名管理局员工为各部门的主管。

（3）总干事负责对管理局的日常活动进行管理以及对其员工的职责进行监督和分配。

20. 保密

（1）就本条而言，"材料"包括与本法适用的任何事项有关的任何信息、文件或证据。

（2）无论因法律强制规定还是其他情况，任何人向管理局提供或披露任何材料，都可以要求对该材料的全部或部分予以保密。

（3）提出保密要求之前向管理局以外的人披露材料的情形，则不视为违反了本条的规定。

（4）有口头证据时，可以在提出证据时以口头方式提出要求；在所有其他情况下，应采用书面形式，并由要求人在指定材料上签字，并陈述理由。

（5）如果管理局确信材料属于机密性质，并且——

（a）其披露可能会对任何人的竞争地位产生不利影响；或者

（b）因其他原因具有商业敏感性，

则管理局须为该材料保密。

（6）管理局应书面通知提出保密要求的人是否决定给予保密的决定，如未给予保密，则管理局应在发出该通知后的14天内，将该材料视为机密。

（7）若保密要求——

（a）是与自愿提供给管理局的材料有关的；和

（b）管理局决定不对该材料的全部或部分进行保密，

提供该材料的人可根据第（6）款的决定在14天内将该材料连同其他随附的材料一起从管理局撤回。

（8）尽管管理局已根据第（5）款批准了保密要求，但管理局可在以下情况下披露该材料——

（a）如有以下情况，可在不通知任何其他人的情况下随时披露——

（i）向另一履行本法规定的职能的人进行披露；

（ii）披露是在提供材料的人同意的情况下进行的；

（iii）披露是由其他法律授权或要求的；或者

（iv）披露是由法院或依法组成的法庭授权或要求的；

（b）管理局认为——

（i）披露该材料不会对提供材料的人或与材料有关的人造成损害；或者

（ii）尽管披露该材料会对提供该材料的人或与该材料相关的人造成损害，但披露该材料的公共利益大于其损害，并且管理局已提前14天书面通知相关人员其拟根据本条规定披露该材料。

（9）任何人对管理局根据本条作出的不同意保密材料或披露机密材料的决定不服的，在管理局根据本条有义务对材料保密期间，可随时就该决定向法庭提出上诉，管理局在法庭对上诉作出裁决之前，应继续将该材料视为机密。

（10）任何人在未经本条授权的情况下披露机密信息，即属犯罪。

第三部分
限制性贸易行为

A-限制性协议、行为和决定

21. 限制性贸易行为

（1）企业之间的协议、企业协会的决定、企业的决定或企业的协同行为，其目的或作用是阻止、干扰或减少在肯尼亚或其部分地区的商品或服务的贸易竞争的，则被禁止，除非根据本部分 D 节的规定予以豁免。

（2）第（1）款中所述的协议、决定和协同行为，包括以下各方达成的协议——

（a）横向关系的当事人，即在贸易竞争中交易的企业；或者

（b）纵向关系的当事人，即企业及其供应商或客户或两者兼有。

（3）在不影响第（1）款规定的一般情况下，该款特别适用于符合以下条件的任何协议、决定或协同行为——

（a）直接或间接确定购买价格或销售价格或任何其他贸易条件；

（b）通过分配客户、供应商、区域或特定类型的商品或服务来划分市场；

（c）涉及串通投标的行为；

（d）涉及维持最低转售价的行为；

(e) 限制或控制生产、市场渠道或准入、技术开发或投资；

(f) 对与其他交易方的同等交易实施不同的条件,从而使其处于竞争的不利地位；

(g) 在签订合同时,要求其他缔约方接受附加条件,而这些附加条件就其性质或商业惯例而言,与该合同的主要内容无关；

(h) 以非公平、合理和无歧视的方式使用知识产权的行为；

(i) 以其他方式阻止、干扰或限制竞争。

(4) 第(3)款(d)项不得阻止商品或服务的供应商或生产商向商品的转销商或服务的提供者推荐转售价格,但前提是——

(a) 供应商或生产商向转销商及提供者明确规定,建议的价格不具有约束力；和

(b) 如果产品上或任何与产品或服务有关的文件或物品上附有供应商或生产商推荐的价格,那么在该价格旁边应标注"建议价格"。

(5) 第(1)款中规定的具有禁止性质的协议或协同行为,在下列情况下应被视为存在于两个或多个企业之间：

(a) 一个企业拥有另一个企业的重大权益,或至少共有一名董事或一名大股东；和

(b) 企业联合体从事第(3)款所述的任何行为。

(6) 如果企业或有关董事或股东能够证明合理基础的存在,即企业所从事的行为都是对市场普遍情况的正常商业反应,第(5)款规定的推定可以被推翻。

(7) 就第(5)款而言,"董事"包括——

(a) 《公司法》(第486章)所定义的公司董事；

(b) 就社团企业而言,与他人共同负责管理的人；

(c) 信托的受托人；或者

(d) 就个人或合伙经营的企业而言,该企业的所有人或合伙人；

(e) 就任何其他企业而言,单独或与他人共同负责管理的人员。

(8) 第(1)款不适用于以下双方之间达成的协议或以下各方所从事的行为——

(a) 公司及其全资子公司或该子公司的全资子公司；或者

(b) 公司以外的企业,且每个企业均由同一人或相同的多人所有或控制。

(9) 任何人违反本条规定,即属犯罪,一经定罪,将被处以5年以下的监禁或1000万先令以下的罚款,或两者并罚。

[2014年第16号法令,第33条]

B-适用于贸易协会的限制性贸易行为

22. 适用于行业协会的行为

(1) 以下由行业协会实施或代表行业协会的行为被宣布为限制性贸易行为——

(a) 任何善意从事或打算从事与协会有关贸易的人被不合理地排除在该协会之外,在确定此种排除是否合理时,管理局除审查有关的其他事项外,还可审查该协会任何规则的适用情况以及这些规则的合理性；

(b) 行业协会直接或间接向其成员或其任何级别的成员提出与以下内容相关的建议：

(i) 此类成员或此种级别的成员收取或将要收取的价格,或价格中包含的利

润,或用于计算这些价格时使用的定价公式;或者

（ii）此类成员或此种级别的成员的销售条款(包括折扣、信用、交付以及产品和服务保证条款)及直接影响价格、包含在价格中的利润率或在计算价格时使用的定价公式。

（2）第(1)款(b)项所述的行业协会的建议应被视为限制性行业行为,不论该建议中的陈述是否会被建议针对的成员或同级别成员所遵守。

（3）任何人为了直接或间接地使行业协会能够违反或规避本法的规定而提出的建议,应被视为已由该行业协会提出。

（4）凡由行业协会或其代表向其成员或任何级别成员就影响其成员交易条件的任何事项是否采取行动提出明示或暗示的具体建议,在成员赞成协会并互相遵守协会的建议的前提下,如果彼此达成协议,尽管与协会章程或规则相违背,本法的规定仍适用。

（5）行业协会成员以书面形式明确通知协会,其完全不参与该协会达成的协议,或者视情况而定,其不会采取行动或不采取该协会明示或暗示的建议中提到的行动,在没有相反证据的情况下,该成员不得被视为该协议的缔约方,或视情况而定,不得被视为同意遵守该建议的协会成员。

（6）任何人违反本条规定,即属犯罪,一经定罪,可处以5年以下监禁或1 000万先令以下的罚款,或两者并罚。

C - 滥用支配地位

23. 支配地位的认定标准

（1）就本条而言,"**支配地位的企业**"是指下列企业——

（a）在肯尼亚或肯尼亚大部分地区生产、供应、分销或以其他方式控制不少于二分之一的任何种类的全部商品;或者

（b）在肯尼亚或肯尼亚大部分地区提供或以其他方式控制不少于二分之一的服务。

（2）尽管有第(1)款的规定,在以下情况下,企业也应被视为本法中具有支配地位的企业——

（a）尽管不具有支配地位,但至少控制40%至50%市场份额,除非其能证明其不具有市场支配力;或者

（b）控制40%以下的市场份额,但具有市场支配力。

［2014 年第 16 号法令,第 34 条］

24. 滥用支配地位

（1）禁止任何在肯尼亚或肯尼亚大部分地区的市场滥用支配地位的行为。

（2）在不影响第(1)款规定的一般性的情况下,滥用支配地位包括:

（a）直接或间接施加不公平的买卖价格或其他不公平的交易条件;

（b）通过掠夺性或其他方法限制生产、市场销路或市场准入、投资、分销、技术开发或技术进步;

（c）对与其他交易方的同等交易适用不同的条件;和

（d）在签订合同时,要求其他缔约方接受附加条件,而这些附加条件就其性质或商业惯例而言,与该合同的主要内容无关;和

(e) 滥用知识产权。

（2A）*根据2019年第27号法令第4条予以删除。*

（2B）*根据2019年第27号法令第4条予以删除。*

（2C）*根据2019年第27号法令第4条予以删除。*

（2D）*根据2019年第27号法令第4条予以删除。*

（3）任何人违反本条规定，即属犯罪，一经定罪，可处以5年以下的监禁或1 000万先令以下的罚款，或两者并罚。

［2016年第49号法令，第5条；2019年第27号法令，第4条］

24A. 滥用买方权力

（1）禁止在肯尼亚市场或肯尼亚大部分地区滥用买方权力。

（2）如果管理局确定某个部门或企业正在实施或可能实施滥用买方权力的行为，则可以监控该部门或企业的活动，并通过强制实行报告和审慎要求来确保合规。

（3）管理局可要求可能实施滥用买方权力行为的行业和部门制定一项具有约束力的行为准则。

（4）在裁定任何与滥用买方权力有关的投诉时，管理局应考虑所有相关情况，包括——

(a) 有关企业之间合同条款的性质和确定；

(b) 为使用基础设施所要求的付款；和

(c) 支付给供应商的价款。

（5）构成滥用买方权力的行为包括——

(a) 无正当理由违反约定付款条件延迟付款；

(b) 在没有通知或通知期过短的情况下，无正当理由单方面终止或威胁终止商业关系；

(c) 违反约定的合同条款，无正当理由拒绝接收或退回全部或部分货物；

(d) 强行要求供应商为商品或服务的推广提供资金，以此将成本或风险转移给商品或服务供应商；

(e) 将本应由买方承担的商业风险转移给供应商；

(f) 要求提供不利于供应商的优惠条件或限制对其他买方的供应；

(g) 在难以实质性替代买方的情况下，进行小幅而重要的降价，或将价格降低至行业竞争水平以下；或者

(h) 买方为将竞争对手排除在市场之外，承诺提高投入价格。

（6）在调查滥用买方权力的投诉时，管理局应以买方企业与供应商之间的现有协议为基础，无论协议是否为书面。

（7）买方企业与供应商之间的协议内容应包括：

(a) 支付条款；

(b) 付款日期；

(c) 逾期付款的利率；

(d) 经合理通知后终止和变更合同的条件；和

(e) 争端解决机制。

（8）管理局应公布与利益相关方、相关政府机构和总检察长协商制定的行为准则。

（9）任何人违反第（1）款的规定，即属犯罪，一经定罪，应处以5年以下的监禁或1 000万先令以下的罚款，或两者并罚。

[2019年第27号法令,第5条]

D—特定限制性行为的豁免

25. 给予特定限制性行为豁免

（1）任何企业或企业协会均可向管理局提出申请，就以下事项从本部分A节或B节的规定中予以豁免——

    （a）任何协议或协议类型；

    （b）任何决定或决定类型；

    （c）任何协同行为或协同行为类型。

（2）根据第（1）款提出的豁免申请应——

    （a）以规定的形式和方式作出；

    （b）附上规定的或管理局可能合理要求的信息。

（3）管理局须就根据第（1）款收到的申请，在公报中发出通知——

    （a）说明申请人所寻求豁免的性质；和

    （b）呼吁利害关系人在通知发出后30日内，向管理局提交其认为与此申请有关的书面陈述。

26. 豁免申请的决定

（1）在考虑豁免申请和利害关系人提交的陈述后，管理局应就该申请作出决定，并可以——

    （a）批准豁免；

    （b）拒绝给予豁免，并相应地通知申请人及说明拒绝的理由；或者

    （c）出具许可证书，表明其认为，根据其掌握的事实，该项或该类协议、决定或协同行为不构成对本部分A节或B节中所载禁止性行为的违反。

（2）如果管理局认为在公共政策方面有特殊的和令人信服的理由，说明该项或该类协议、决定、协同行为应被排除在本部分A节或B节所载的禁止性行为之外的理由，则管理局可以批准豁免。

（3）在根据第（2）款作出决定时，管理局应考虑该项或该类协议、决定或协同行为在多大程度上促进或导致，或者可能促进或导致以下情况——

    （a）维持或促进出口；

    （b）改善或者防止商品生产、销售的下降或服务提供的减少；

    （c）促进任何行业的技术或经济的进步或稳定；

    （d）为公众获得的利益超过或将超过因该项或该类协议、决定或协同行为导致或可能导致的竞争减少。

（4）管理局可在其认为合适的条件和期限内给予豁免。

27. 豁免的撤销或修改

（1）如果管理局在根据第26条授予豁免或颁发清关证书后，确信——

(a) 授予豁免或颁发清关证书是根据严重不正确或误导性的信息进行的；
(b) 自授予豁免或颁发证书以来,情况发生了重大变化；
(c) 给予豁免的条件未被遵守。

管理局可视情况撤销或修改该豁免,或撤销清关证书。

(2) 如果管理局根据第(1)款提议撤销或修改豁免或撤销清关证书,应当——
(a) 将拟采取的行动以书面通知获得该豁免或证书的人,以及管理局认为其他可能与该事项有利害关系的人；和
(b) 要求上述人员在收到通知后30天内向管理局提交其关于拟采取的行动的陈述。

(3) 在不遵守豁免条件的情况下,无论管理局是否因此而撤销或修改豁免,管理局均可向法庭申请就该不遵守的情况处以罚款,可附或不附任何其他命令。

(4) 任何人不遵守豁免条件,即属犯罪。

28. 知识产权豁免

(1) 管理局可根据申请,并在管理局确定的条件下,就行使根据任何法律获得或受保护的与版权、专利、设计、商标、植物品种或任何其他知识产权相关的任何权利或权益的协议或行为给予豁免。

(2) 第25、26和27条应参照适用于本条规定的豁免。

29. 专业规则的豁免

(1) 专业协会的规则如果含有阻止、歪曲或削弱市场竞争的效果,则应以书面或规定的方式向管理局申请第(2)款规定的豁免。

(2) 管理局可豁免专业协会的全部或部分规则,使其在特定时期内不受本部分A节的规定约束,但考虑到国际通行的规范,如果这些规则中所包含的任何限制具有防止或大幅减少市场竞争的效果,则有理由要求维持——
(a) 专业标准；或者
(b) 该专业的一般功能。

(3) 在收到根据第(1)款提出的申请后,管理局应——
(a) 在公报中刊登申请通知；
(b) 允许利害关系方自该通知发出之日起30日内就该申请作出陈述；和
(c) 咨询负责管理与申请相关专业的法律事项的政府机构或部门。

(4) 在收到并考虑申请及相关的呈件或信息后,管理局应——
(a) 向申请人发出书面通知,批准豁免或拒绝申请；
(b) 若拒绝申请,应书面说明理由；和
(c) 在公报上公布该决定。

(5) 如果管理局认为规则的全部或部分内容,不应再根据本条获得豁免,管理局可在下述情况发生后的任何时间撤销对此类规则或该等规则有关部分的豁免——
(a) 在公报上公布豁免的撤销；
(b) 允许利害关系方自该通知发出之日起30日内就豁免作出陈述；和
(c) 咨询第(3)款(c)项提及的负责的部长。

(6)规则的豁免与豁免的撤销自管理局指定之日起生效。

(7)就本条而言,"**专业协会**"是指根据法律设立或注册的行业公认的主导团体,但不包括行业协会和行业游说机构或团体。

(8)任何行业协会——
 (a) 其规则限制具有阻止、干扰或减少肯尼亚市场竞争的效果,并且未按照第(1)款和第(2)款的要求申请豁免;或者
 (b) 已根据第(1)款申请豁免,但未能遵守管理局拒绝其申请的决定,即构成犯罪,且任何官员或任何人违反该规定发布指导方针或规则,一经定罪,将被处以5年以下的监禁或1 000万先令以下的罚款,或两者并罚。

[2014年第16号法令,第35条;2019年第27号法令,第6条]

30. 授予、撤销或修改豁免的通知

(1)管理局须在切实可行的范围内,尽快安排在公报上公布根据本部分的任何条文授予的每项豁免,以及每项被撤销的豁免及其理由。

(2)经内阁秘书批准,管理局可通过公报公告,将任何类型的决定、行为或企业或企业之间的协议排除在本部分规定的适用范围之外。

[2014年第16号法令,第36条]

E-对禁止行为的调查

31. 管理局的调查

(1)管理局可主动或在收到任何人或政府机构或国家部门提供的资料或投诉后,对涉嫌构成或可能构成侵犯以下规定的任何行为或可能行为进行调查:
 (a) 与限制性贸易惯例有关的禁令;
 (b) 与滥用支配地位有关的禁令;或者
 (c) 与滥用买方权力有关的禁令。

(2)如果管理局在收到任何人就第(1)款规定的涉嫌侵权行为的投诉或调查申请后,决定不进行调查,则管理局应书面通知其理由。

(3)*根据L.N. 23/2011附录予以删除。*

(4)如果管理局决定进行调查,可以通过规定的方式向任何人送达书面通知,要求其——
 (a) 以签署的书面形式,由自然人或法人团体的董事或成员或其他主管人员、工作人员或代理人签名,依通知中指明的时间和方式,向管理局提供通知中指明的管理局认为与调查相关的任何信息;
 (b) 向管理局或通知中指明代表管理局的人,出示通知中指明的管理局认为与调查相关的文件或物品;
 (c) 按通知中指定的时间和地点到管理局作证或出示通知中指定的文件或物品;和
 (d) 如果他拥有与调查有关的记录,需将这些记录的副本提供给管理局,或者按照通知指定的时间和方式将记录提交给管理局以供备份。

[L.N. 23/2011,附录;2019年第27号法令,第7条]

32. 进入和搜查

(1)凡管理局认为有必要根据本部分进行调查时,其书面授权的人员可进入任何由贸易

商、制造商、生产商、佣金代理人、结算及转运代理、运输商或其他被认为掌管有关资料及文件的人占用或控制下的任何场所并检查该场所的任何货物、文件和记录。

(2) 根据第(1)款授予的权力进入场所时,获得书面授权的人应在对场所、货物、文件和记录进行检查之前,通知场所负责人或合理地表现为暂时负责该场所的人,其将根据本法行使权力;

(3) 被授权人可以使用场所内的任何计算机系统,或要求场所内任何人协助其使用该计算机系统,以便——

(a) 搜索该计算机系统中包含或可获得的任何数据;
(b) 从该数据中复制相关记录;
(c) 获取该计算机的输出以检查和备份;
(d) 扣押,或在必要时将任何与调查有关的物品带出场所进行检查和保管并出具收据。

(4) 管理局在执行本节授予的任务时,可寻求警察和其他执法机构的协助。

33. 管理局取证的权力

(1) 管理局可接收其认为可能有助于有效处理调查的任何陈述、文件、信息或事项,但声明、文件、信息或事项应当符合法院的可采性要求,否则不得作为证据接收。

(2) 在宣誓或确认后,管理局可向出席会议的人取证,因此管理局的任何成员均可主持宣誓或确认。

(3) 管理局可准许任何人作为证人出庭提供证据,并在管理局认为合适的情况下,以宣誓或确认的方式核实书面陈述。

(4) 出席管理局会议的人有权享有与在高等法院出庭的证人相同的豁免权和特权。

34. 管理局的拟议决定

(1) 如果在调查结束后,管理局提议作出的决定——

(a) 违反本部分 A 节规定的一项或多项禁令;
(b) 违反本部分 B 节规定的一项或多项禁令;或者
(c) 违反本部分 C 节规定的一项或多项禁令,

应将其拟议的决定以书面通知可能受该决定影响的每个企业。

(2) 第(1)款中所述的通知应——

(a) 说明管理局拟议决定的理由;
(b) 列明管理局可能考虑提供的救济细节;
(c) 通知每个企业,可以就管理局的拟议决定或(b)项中规定的任何事项,在通知规定的期限内——
(i) 向管理局提交书面陈述;和
(ii) 说明是否需要向管理局作出口头陈述的机会。

[2016 年第 49 号法令,第 6 条]

35. 召开听证会进行口头陈述

(1) 如果企业表示需要向管理局作出口头陈述的机会,管理局须——

(a) 召开会议,由管理局确定会议的日期、时间和地点;和

（b）将日期、时间和地点书面通知——
(i) 相关的一个或多个企业；
(ii) 就管理局调查的行为向管理局提出投诉的人；
(iii) 管理局认为适宜出席会议的任何其他人。

（2）根据第（1）款收到会议通知的任何人，可由他在会议上需要其协助的人陪同，包括律师。

（3）会议的程序可由主体所允许的非正式的方式进行。

（4）管理局应安排保存足以载列参会人员所提出的事项的会议记录。

（5）管理局如认为参会人员已获合理的机会表达意见，可终止会议。

36. 调查后的行动

在考虑所有书面陈述和会议上提出的事项后，管理局可采取以下措施——
（a）宣布作为管理局调查标的的行为违反本部分A、B或C节所载的禁令；
（b）限制该企业从事该行为；
（c）指示相关企业采取行动以补救或消除该侵权行为或其影响；
（d）对有关企业处以不超过该企业上一年度在肯尼亚年总营业额10%的罚款；或者
（e）给予任何其他适当的救济。

〔2016年第49号法令，第7条〕

37. 临时救济

（1）如果管理局有合理的理由相信，企业已经从事、正在从事或打算从事的行为涉嫌违反本部分A、B或C节所载的禁令，则管理局有必要采取紧急行动，以达到以下目的——
（a）防止对任何个人或此类人造成严重的、无法弥补的损害；或者
（b）保护公共利益，

管理局可通过书面命令指示该相关企业停止并放弃从事该类行为，直至正在进行的调查结束为止。

〔2016年第49号法令，第8条〕

38. 和解

（1）管理局可在对涉嫌违反本部分所载禁令的行为进行调查的期间或调查后，与有关企业订立和解协议。

（2）第（1）款提及的协议可包括——
（a）对申诉人的损害赔偿金；
（b）拟处罚款的金额。

39. 管理局决定的公布

（1）管理局应在公报上刊登根据第37条采取的行动和第38条提及的协议通知。

（2）第（1）款所述的通知应包括——
（a）所涉及的每家企业的名称；和
（b）作为诉讼或和解协议主体的行为性质。

40. 向法庭提出上诉

（1）任何人对管理局根据本部分作出的决定不服的，应在收到管理局决定后30日内以书

面形式向法庭提出上诉。

（2）根据第（1）款对法庭的裁决不服提出上诉的一方，可以在该裁决的通知送达其本人之日起 30 日内就该裁决向高等法院提出上诉，且高等法院的裁决为终局裁决。

[2014 年第 16 号法令，第 37 条]

第四部分
合　并

41. 合并的定义

（1）就本部分而言，一个或多个企业直接或间接收购或控制另一企业的全部或部分业务，即为合并。

（2）第（1）款中所述的合并可以任何方式实现，包括——

(a) 购买或租赁股份、收购权益或购买其他有关企业的资产；

(b) 收购能够独立经营企业的部分业务的控股权益，无论该业务是否由公司经营；

(c) 由位于肯尼亚境内或境外的另一企业收购处于接管中的企业；

(d) 以任何方式获得外国企业的控股权，而该外国企业已取得其在肯尼亚的子公司的控股权；

(e) 就联合企业而言，获得另一企业的控制权或能够独立经营的被收购企业的一部分的控制权；

(f) 纵向一体化；

(g) 企业之间通过采取的任何策略或手段进行股份交换，导致所有权结构发生重大变化；或者

(h) 与其他企业合并、收购或任何其他组合。

（3）个人控制企业，如果该人——

(a) 拥有企业已发行股本或业务及资产一半以上的收益；

(b) 有权在企业的股东大会上投出多数票，或有能力直接或通过该企业的受控实体控制多数票进行投票；

(c) 能够同意或否决该企业的大多数董事的任命；

(d) 控制一家控股公司，且是《公司法》（第 486 章）中规定公司的子公司；

(e) 如果该企业是信托企业，有能力控制受托人的大多数投票，或者任命大多数受托人，或者任命或更改信托的大多数受益人；

(f) 如果该企业是被提名企业，拥有大部分成员的利益，或者直接控制或有权控制被提名企业的大多数投票；或者

(g) 有能力以与一般商业实践中可行使(a)项至(f)项所述控制要素的人以相类似的方式对企业的政策产生实质性影响。

[2016 年第 49 号法令，第 9 条]

42. 对合并的控制

（1）管理局可与内阁秘书协商并通过公报通知，以确立被本部分规定排除在外的合并

标准。

（2）任何人,无论是单独或与任何其他人联合或合作,均不得实施本部分适用的拟议合并,除非该拟议合并——

　　（a）经管理局批准;和

　　（b）按照批准的附带条件执行。

（3）在没有管理局授权的情况下进行的第41条所述的合并,不具有任何法律效力,相关合并协议对参与方规定的义务也不得在法律程序中强制执行。

（4）收购企业支付的全部收购价款应视为本条所指的合并的实施,最高首付款未超过约定收购价20%的不构成合并的实施。

（5）任何人违反本条规定,即属犯罪,一经定罪,可处以5年以下的监禁或1 000万先令以下的罚款,或两者并罚。

（6）管理局可处以不超过该企业上一年度在肯尼亚的总营业额10%的罚款。

[2016年第49号法令,第10条]

43. 向管理局发出拟议合并的通知

（1）拟议合并的,各企业应以书面或规定的方式将该计划通知管理局。

（2）管理局在收到根据第(1)款发出的通知之日起30日内,可以书面形式要求相关企业提供进一步资料。

44. 拟议合并的确定期限

（1）在符合第(2)款规定的情况下,管理局须就收到的依照第43条的拟合并事项,考虑并作出决定——

　　（a）在管理局收到通知之日起的60日内确定合并期限;或者

　　（b）如果管理局根据第43条第(2)款的规定要求其提供进一步资料,则在管理局收到资料之日起的60日内确定合并期限;或者

　　（c）如果根据第45条召开听证会议,则在会议结束之日起的30天内确定合并期限。

（2）如果管理局认为第(1)款(a)、(b)或(c)项所确定的期限因复杂情况应当延长,则可在该期限届满前,将合并期限延长的事宜以书面通知有关企业,但不得超过该通知所指明的60日期限。

45. 关于拟议合并的听证会

（1）如果管理局认为适当,可决定召开与拟议合并有关的会议。

（2）如果管理局认为确定有必要召开会议的,应在第44条第(1)款(a)项或(b)项或该条第(2)款所述期限届满之前,视情况而定,以书面形式向所涉企业发出合理通知——

　　（a）召开会议;

　　（b）规定日期、时间和地点;和

　　（c）规定会议审议的事项。

46. 拟议合并的决定

（1）在就拟议合并作出决定时,管理局可以——

　　（a）批准实施合并;

　　（b）拒绝批准实施合并;或者

　　　　（c）附条件地批准实施合并。
　　（2）管理局可根据其认为与拟议合并所涉情况相关的任何标准,对拟议合并作出决定,包括——
　　　　（a）拟议合并在多大程度上可能阻止或减少竞争,限制贸易或任何服务的提供,或危及供应或服务的连续性;
　　　　（b）拟议合并在多大程度上可能导致任何企业,包括未作为一方当事人参与拟议合并的企业,获得或加强其市场支配地位;
　　　　（c）拟议合并在多大程度上可能给公众带来利益,而这种利益将超过任何企业,包括未作为一方当事人参与拟议合并的企业,获得或加强其市场支配地位可能带来的损害;
　　　　（d）拟议合并在多大程度上可能影响某一特定工业部门或地区;
　　　　（e）拟议合并在多大程度上可能影响就业;
　　　　（f）拟议合并在多大程度上可能影响小型企业进入市场或在市场中的竞争力;
　　　　（g）拟议合并在多大程度上可能会影响本国工业在国际市场上的竞争力;和
　　　　（h）可能从拟议合并中获得的与研发、技术效率、产量增加、货物或服务的有效分配以及市场准入有关的任何利益。
　　（3）为考虑拟议合并,管理局可将拟议合并的详情转介调查员,该调查员可包括管理局的工作人员或任何其他合适的人,其就第（2）款所述标准进行调查并撰写报告,并将该报告通知相关企业。
　　（4）根据第（3）款规定作出转介后,有关调查员应尽快——
　　　　（a）调查上述提议;和
　　　　（b）在管理局指明的日期前,向管理局提交调查报告。
　　（5）任何人,包括未作为一方当事人参与拟议合并的主体,可以自愿向调查员或管理局提交与拟议合并有关的任何文件、宣誓书、声明或其他相关信息。
　　（6）管理局须——
　　　　（a）就其对拟议合并作出的决定发出通知——
　　　　　　（i）以书面形式向拟议合并的各方发出通知;和
　　　　　　（ii）通过公报发出通知;和
　　　　（b）为决定出具书面理由——
　　　　　　（i）如果禁止或有条件地批准拟议合并;或者
　　　　　　（ii）如果应合并任意一方的要求。

47. 撤销对拟议合并的批准
　　（1）管理局在考虑根据第（2）款作出的陈述后,若出现以下情形可随时撤销批准实施拟议合并的决定——
　　　　（a）该决定是基于合并方负责的严重不正确或具有误导性的信息而做出的;或者
　　　　（b）未遵守批准合并所附带的对实施具有重大意义的条件。
　　（2）如果管理局根据第（1）款提出撤销其批准决定,应将拟议的行动书面通知参与合并的每一企业以及管理局认为的该事项的利益相关人,并要求其在收到通知后30日内向管理局作出关于拟议行动的任何陈述。
　　（3）尽管有第（1）款和第（2）款的规定，管理局可处不超过上一年度总营业额10%的罚款。
　　（4）作为合并各方的任何人——
　　　　（a）提供了严重不正确或误导性的信息；或者
　　　　（b）未遵守批准合并的任何附加条件，
　　导致该合并根据本条被撤销的，即属犯罪，一经定罪，则处以1 000万先令以下罚款或5年以下监禁，或两者并罚。

[2016年第49号法令，第11条]

48. 法庭复核管理局的决定

　　（1）在管理局根据第46条第（6）款的规定在公报上就其对某项拟议合并决定发出通知后的30日内，合并各方可按法庭确定的形式，向法庭提出复核管理局决定的申请。
　　（1A）一方在收到管理局根据第46条第（6）款的规定发出的书面决定后，可就该决定向法庭提出上诉。
　　（2）在收到根据第（1）款提出的申请后30日内，法庭应通过公报对复核申请进行通知，并邀请利害关系人依通知规定的时间和方式就待审事项向法庭提交意见书。
　　（3）自提出复核申请之日起4个月内，法庭须作出以下裁决——
　　　　（a）推翻管理局的决定；
　　　　（b）通过命令施加限制或列入条件以修改管理局的决定；
　　　　（c）确认管理局的决定；或者
　　　　（d）将该事项发回管理局按具体条件予以重审。
　　（4）法庭应——
　　　　（a）就复审所作的裁决发出通知：
　　　　　　（i）以书面形式通知管理局和参与拟议合并的各方；和
　　　　　　（ii）通过公报通知；和
　　　　（b）向管理局和有关各方出具作出该裁决的书面理由。
　　（5）法庭可以根据本条规定确定复核程序。

[2016年第49号法令，第12条]

49. 遵守其他法律和上诉

　　（1）管理局或法庭根据本部分复核后批准的拟议合并，并不免除企业遵守任何相关法律的义务。
　　（2）根据本部分对法庭的裁决不服提出上诉的一方，可以在该裁决的通知送达其本人之日起30日内就该裁决向高等法院提出上诉，且高等法院的裁决为终局裁决。

第五部分
经营者不正当集中的控制

50. 经营者不正当集中的认定

　　（1）管理局应审查对经济的不利影响超过了生产或分销一体化效率优势的经营者集中情

形,以保持肯尼亚商品和服务的生产分配结构。

(2)管理局应调查其有理由认为可能存在具有经营者不正当集中因素的任何经济部门,为此,管理局可以要求该部门的任何参与者允许管理局及其书面授权的人员查阅与所有权模式、市场结构和销售份额有关的记录。

(3)管理局可要求任何拥有第(2)款所述记录的人向其提供该记录的副本。

(4)就本部分而言,经营者不正当集中应被视为损害公共利益,考虑到本国当前的经济状况以及与特定情况相关的其他因素,其影响是或将是——

  (a)不合理地增加与商品的生产、供应、分销或提供任何服务有关的成本;

  (b)不合理地提高——

    (i)商品的销售价格;或者

    (ii)从商品的生产、供应、分销或从提供任何服务中获得的利润;或者

  (c)减少、干扰、阻止或限制任何商品的生产、供应、分销(包括销售或购买)或提供任何服务方面的竞争;

  (d)导致任何商品或服务质量的下降;或者

  (e)导致任何商品或服务的生产、供应或分销的不充分。

51. 听证会

(1)如果受调查的任何企业经济部门提出要求,或者管理局认为适当,可以决定就有关经营者不正当集中的拟议决定举行听证会。

(2)如果管理局决定举行听证会,则应向相关企业
发出合理的书面通知——

  (a)召开听证会;

  (b)指定举行会议的日期、时间和地点;和

  (c)规定会议审议的事项。

(3)在计划或举行听证会时,管理局对于是否存在经营者不正当集中的决定应在听证会结束之前中止。

(4)听证会不应仅因有关企业不合作而不做出结论。

52. 处置权益的命令

(1)完成调查后,管理局可以发布命令,指示其认为在相关部门出现经营者不正当集中情形的主体,由该主体处置其生产、分销或服务供应方面的权益,以消除不正当集中。

(2)除第(1)款外,管理局可单独或连同该款作出处置权益的命令,命令有关主体遵守其认为必要的其他条件,以消除不正当集中。

(3)根据第(1)款作出处置权益的命令,可能伴随出售个人在企业中的全部或部分受益权,或出售该人控制的制造商、分销商或服务供应商的集团或连锁企业中的一个或多个单位。

(4)当引入控制不同组成部分的独立管理单位导致效率降低、每单位的生产成本提升的实质集中情形出现时,不得根据本节发布命令,以细分生产设备。

(5)根据本条作出的命令,管理局应确定有足够的时间,以便有序处置利益或遵守管理局施加的任何条件,以免对相关人员造成不应有的价值损失。

53. 对管理局命令提出上诉

（1）若对管理局根据本部分作出的命令不服的,可按规定形式向法庭提出上诉。

（2）根据第（1）款对法庭的裁决不服提出上诉的一方,可以在该裁决通知送达本人之日起 30 日内就该裁决向高等法院提出上诉。高等法院的裁决为终局裁决。

54. 犯罪及处罚

（1）任何人,无论是委托人还是代理人,无论是本人还是代理人——

（a）未在指定的上诉期内对管理局根据本部分作出的命令提出上诉,违反或不遵守该命令;

（b）在法庭宣布对作出上诉的裁决后,违反或不遵守管理局根据本部分作出的经法庭确认或修改的命令,

即属犯罪。

（2）根据本部分对法庭的裁决不服提出上诉的一方,可在该裁决送达其本人之日起 30 日内就该裁决向高等法院提出上诉,高等法院的裁决为终局裁决。

（3）任何人被裁决犯有本部分规定的罪行的,应处以 5 年以下监禁或 1 000 万先令以下罚款,或两者并罚。

第六部分
消费者福利

55. 虚假或误导性陈述

任何人在与供应或可能供应货品或服务有关的贸易中,或在与以任何方式供应或使用货品或服务有关的宣传活动中,有下列情形,即属犯罪——

（a）其作出以下虚假陈述——

（i）商品具有特定的标准、质量、价值、等级、成分、款式或型号,或具有特定的历史或特定的先前用途;

（ii）服务具有特定的标准、质量、价值或等级;

（iii）商品是新的;

（iv）特定人已同意购买商品或服务;

（v）商品或服务具有其不具备的赞助、批准、性能特征、配件、用途或利益;

（vi）产品具有本不具备的赞助、批准或隶属关系;

（b）其就以下方面作出虚假或误导性陈述——

（i）商品或服务的价格;

（ii）商品维修或商品备件的可获得设施;

（iii）商品的原产地;

（iv）对任何商品或服务的需求;或者

（v）任何条件、保证、担保、权利或补救措施的存在、例外或影响。

56. 不正当行为

（1）任何人在与向他人供应或可能供应商品或服务有关的贸易中,从事在任何情况下都

不正当的行为,即属犯罪。

(2) 在不限制管理局为确定某人是否在向他人(在本款中称为"消费者")供应或可能供应货物或服务方面违反了第(1)款规定时,管理局可考虑——

  (a) 该人与消费者的谈判地位中的相对优势;

  (b) 消费者是否因为其行为而须遵守某些条件,但这些条件并非为保护个人合法利益的合理必要条件;

  (c) 消费者是否能够理解与商品或服务的供应或可能供应有关的任何文件;

  (d) 与有关商品或服务的供应或可能供应有关的主体代表,是否对消费者或代表消费者的人施加了任何不适当的影响或压力,或使用了任何不公平的手段;和

  (e) 消费者可以从其他供应商处获得相同或同等商品或服务的金额和情形。

(3) 任何人在提供银行、小额信贷和保险及其他服务时,如果相关收费和费用在征收之前或提供服务之前未提醒消费者注意,不得以任何名目单方面收取费用。

(4) 消费者有权从服务提供商处获悉为提供服务而征收的任何名目的费用。

(5) 任何人不得仅因为该人就该供应或可能的供应提起诉讼,或者将与该供应或可能的供应有关的争议或索赔提交仲裁,而被视为从事本条规定的不正当的行为。

(6) 为确定某人是否在向他人供应或可能供应商品或服务方面违反了第(1)款——

  (a) 管理局不应考虑在被指控的违法行为发生时无法合理预见的任何情况;和

  (b) 管理局可考虑在本法生效前从事的行为或存在的情况。

(7) 本条中提及的商品或服务是指通常为个人、家庭使用或消费而获得的商品或服务。

(8) 本条中提及的商品供应或可能供应不包括为再供应或在贸易中使用或改造而供应或可能供应的商品。

57. 商业交易中的不正当行为

(1) 从事贸易中的人出现以下行为,应构成犯罪——

  (a) 向他人供应或可能供应商品或服务;或者

  (b) 从他人处购买或可能购买商品或服务,

以从事在任何情况下都不正当的行为。

(2) 在不限制的情况下,管理局为确定供应商在向商业消费者供应或可能供应商品或服务方面是否违反了第(1)款时,管理局可考虑——

  (a) 供应商和商业消费者谈判地位的相对优势;

  (b) 商业消费者是否因为供应商的行为而须遵守某些条件,但这些条件并非为保护供应商合法利益的合理必要条件;

  (c) 商业消费者是否能够理解与任何商品或服务的供应或可能供应有关的文件;

  (d) 与商品或服务的供应或可能供应有关的供应商或代表该供应商的主体,是否对商业消费者或代表商业消费者的人施加了不当影响或压力,或任何不公平的手段;

  (e) 商业消费者可以从供应商以外的人处获得相同或同等商品或服务的金额和情形;

  (f) 供应商对商业消费者的行为和供应商对其他类似商业消费者之间交易行为一致的程度;

（g）任何适用行业规范的要求；
　　（h）商业消费者是否有理由相信供应商会遵守其他行业准则的要求；
　　（i）供应商不合理地未向商业消费者披露的程度——
　　　　（i）供应商可能影响商业消费者利益的任何预期行为；和
　　　　（ii）因供应商的预期行为给商业消费者带来的任何风险（即供应商应当预见的、商业消费者无法察觉的风险）；
　　（j）供应商愿意与商业消费者就任何商品或服务供应合同的条款和条件进行协商的程度；
　　（k）供应商和商业消费者行为的诚信程度。

58. 对公众的警告通知
　　（1）管理局应发布包含以下一项或两项内容的通知——
　　（a）通知中所指明的货物种类正在接受调查的声明，以确定该商品是否会对任何人造成伤害；
　　（b）通知中规定的使用某类商品可能涉及的风险警告。
　　（2）如果第（1）款所述的调查已经完成，管理局应尽快在至少一份全国性日报上发布书面通知，公布调查结果，说明是否根据本法对商品采取了行动，以及何种行动。
　　（3）管理局可将本条所规定的职能委托给政府的相关专门机构。

59. 产品安全标准和不安全商品
　　（1）任何人在贸易中提供拟供消费者使用或可能供消费者使用的商品，如果该商品属于以下类型，即属犯罪——
　　（a）有规定的产品安全标准但不符合该标准；
　　（b）根据本条规定，存在宣布该商品为不安全商品的有效通知；或者
　　（c）根据本条规定，存在永久禁止使用该商品的有效通知。
　　（2）凡——
　　（a）任何人供应不符合产品安全标准的商品，即违反本条规定；
　　（b）任何人由于商品的缺陷或危险特性，或由于缺少与商品有关的特定信息而遭受损失或损害；和
　　（c）如果商品符合该标准，该人将不会遭受损失或损害，
就本法而言，该人应被视为因提供商品而遭受损失或损害。
　　（3）凡——
　　（a）因本条发出的认定某类商品为不安全商品或应被永久禁用的通知正在实施，任何人供应该类商品的行为违反本条规定；和
　　（b）任何人由于商品的缺陷或危险特性，或由于缺少与商品特性有关的特定信息而遭受损失或损害，
就本法而言，该人应被视为因提供商品而遭受损失或损害。

60. 产品信息标准
　　（1）在贸易中，任何人提供拟供消费者使用或可能供消费者使用的商品，而该商品的产品信息标准属于已被规定的类型，除非该人已就该类商品遵循了该标准，否则即属犯罪。

(2) 管理局可以通过有关特定种类商品予以规定,制定产品信息标准,其中包括以下要求——
　　(a) 披露与商品的性能、成分、内容、制造或加工方法、设计、构造、抛光或包装有关的信息;和
　　(b) 在商品上或附于商品一起披露该信息的形式和方式,向使用商品的人提供有关商品数量、质量、性质或价值的信息是合理且必要的。
(3) 第(1)款不适用于拟在肯尼亚境外使用的商品。
(4) 如果有适用于商品的——
　　(a) 商品仅供出口的声明;或者
　　(b) 通过使用法规授权用于本条的词语,表明商品拟在肯尼亚境外使用的声明,就本条而言,除非有相反的证明,否则应推定商品将用于此用途。
(5) 就第(4)款而言,在以下情况下,声明应被视为适用于商品——
　　(a) 该声明被编织、印制、加工或附在商品上;或者
　　(b) 该声明适用于随商品提供的封面、标签、卷轴或物品。
(6) 第(5)款中提及的封面包括塞子、玻璃、瓶子、器皿、盒子、胶囊、箱子、框架或包装物的封面,而该款中提及的标签包括票证的封面。
(7) 就本法而言,在下列情况下,个人应被视为因提供商品而遭受了损失或损害——
　　(a) 任何人未遵守与商品有关的产品信息标准而供应商品,构成违反本条规定;
　　(b) 个人由于不了解与商品有关的特定信息而遭受损失或损害;和
　　(c) 如果该人遵守了与商品有关的标准,则该人不会遭受损失或损害。

61. 消费者须知
(1) 如果任何人(在本条中称为"供应商")在本法生效之日或之后,在贸易中供应拟供消费者使用或可能由消费者使用的商品,并且——
　　(a) 管理局认为该商品可能或将会对任何人造成伤害;
　　(b) 该商品有规定的商品安全标准,而不符合该标准;或者
　　(c) 该商品属于根据第58条规定的有效通知所涉及的商品种类;
　　(d) 管理局认为供应商没有采取令人满意的行动来防止该商品对任何人造成伤害,管理局应发出适当的通知,要求供应商按照第(2)款采取行动。
(2) 管理局应在第(1)款规定的情况下,要求供应商——
　　(a) 在通知规定的期限内召回商品;
　　(b) 在通知规定的期限内,以通知规定的方式向公众或通知中指定的人员披露以下一项或多项信息——
　　　　(i) 缺陷的性质,或通知中确定的商品的危险特性;
　　　　(ii) 通知中确定的商品使用的危险情况;或者
　　　　(iii) 通知中规定的商品处置程序;
　　(c) 在通知规定的期限内,以通知规定的方式向公众或通知中指定的人员告知供应商承诺在通知规定的期限内——
　　　　(i) 修理商品除非通知表明商品的危险特性;
　　　　(ii) 更换商品;或者

(iii) 将商品的价款退还给(无论是由供应商还是由其他人)供应商品的人。

（3）在管理局公布第(1)款(c)项所述的通知之前,管理局应通知受影响的一方,并让其有机会陈述该通知不应被公布的理由。

（4）管理局应考虑根据第(3)款作出的陈述,并在21日内传达其关于公布的决定。

（5）任何人对管理局根据第(4)款作出的决定不服的,可向法庭提出上诉。

62. 管理局宣布产品安全或信息标准

（1）对于通知中指定种类的产品,由规定的协会或机构制定或批准的特定标准或部分特定标准,或通知中增加或变更的标准或部分标准,管理局应通知公众这类标准为本法规定的产品安全标准。

（2）在已发出通知的情况下,通知中提及的标准或部分标准,以及通知中补充或变更的标准或部分标准,视情况而定,应被视为本法规定的产品安全标准。

63. 不合适商品的责任

（1）凡——
(a) 在贸易中,企业制造的商品供应给另一人,而该人购买并转卖的;
(b) 任何人(无论是否从该企业获得商品的人)以拍卖以外的方式向消费者提供该商品;
(c) 消费者为特定目的购买商品,该公司或直接,或通过给消费者供货的人或与消费者进行谈判的人明示或暗示地知悉该目的;
(d) 商品被不合理使用,无论其是否是此类商品的通常供应目的;和
(e) 消费者或从其处获得商品的人,或者通过消费者或以消费者的名义取得货物所有权的人因商品被不合理使用而遭受损失或损害;

该企业应对消费者或其他人的损失或损害承担赔偿责任,消费者或该人可以在有管辖权的法院对该企业提起诉讼,追索赔偿金额。

（2）第(1)款不适用于——
(a) 如果商品由于以下原因不能合理地适用于第(1)款所述的目的——
(i) 任何人(非企业或企业的雇员或代理人)的行为或过失;或者
(ii) 独立于人为控制的原因;发生在商品脱离企业控制之后;或者
(b) 情况表明,消费者不依赖或者不合理地依赖企业的技能或判断。

64. 瑕疵商品责任

（1）在贸易中供应其制造的商品,若该商品存在瑕疵,致使个人遭受损失或者伤害的,该供应商应当就个人遭受的损失或者伤害承担赔偿责任。

（2）遭受损失或损害的个人可以通过法院诉讼获得赔偿。

65. 制造商不明

（1）欲提起赔偿诉讼的人如果不确定商品的制造商,可以向其所知的该商品的供应商发出书面请求,要求其提供具体的信息,以确定——
(a) 制造该商品的人;或者
(b) 向被请求的供应商提供商品的供应商。

（2）如果在该人根据第(1)款提出一个或多个请求后30天内,仍不知道作为诉讼标的的

该商品的制造商,且该人或作为供应商的每一人——

  (a) 被提出请求;和

  (b) 没有遵守该请求,

则就该诉讼而言,应被视为涉诉产品的制造商。

66. 抗辩

(1) 在根据第 64 条提起的诉讼中,如果存在以下情况,可作为抗辩理由——

  (a) 涉诉商品导致损失的瑕疵在商品供应时不存在;

  (b) 仅由于遵守强制性标准导致商品存在此种瑕疵;

  (c) 在实际制造商提供这些商品时,科学或技术知识的水平不足以发现该瑕疵;或者

  (d) 如果该瑕疵包含在其他成品中,则只能归因于——

    (i) 成品的设计;

    (ii) 成品上或附带的标记;或者

    (iii) 成品制造商提供的说明或警告。

67. 与肯尼亚标准局的协商

就本法而言,管理局应就涉及商品定义和规格以及商品质量分级的所有事项与肯尼亚标准局协商。

68. 向政府机构转交投诉

在适当的情况下,管理局有权将消费者投诉转介给政府的专门机构,由这些机构作出适当的决定,并相应地通知管理局和投诉人。

69. 消费者团体的通知

(1) 公认的消费者团体有权将任何涉嫌违反本部分规定的侵权行为通知管理局。

(2) 收到消费者团体的通知后,管理局应进行必要的调查。

(3) 向管理局发出通知的消费者团体应与管理局合作,对涉嫌违反本部分规定的行为进行调查。

70. 犯罪及处罚

任何人违反本部分的规定,即属犯罪,一经定罪,处以 5 年以下监禁或 1 000 万先令以下罚款,或两者并罚。

70A. 管理局对投诉开展调查

(1) 根据本部分的规定,管理局可以主动或在收到任何人、政府机构、部委或消费者团体的信息或投诉后,对消费者投诉进行调查。

(2) 对消费者投诉的调查适用本法第 31、32、33、34、35、36、37、38、39 和 40 条的规定。

[2016 年第 49 号法令,第 13 条]

第七部分
竞争法庭的设立和权力

71. 竞争法庭的设立

(1) 兹设立一个法庭,称为竞争法庭,行使本法赋予的职能。

(2) 该法庭应由以下人员组成——
    (a) 1名主席,应为具有7年以上经验的律师;和
    (b) 2—4名其他成员,

由部长任命。

(3) 法庭成员的任期在其任命文书中指明不得超过5年,除非在该期限届满之前——
    (a) 该成员以书面形式向部长提出辞职;或者
    (b) 部长认为该成员因精神或身体虚弱而不适合履行其职责,或该成员至少连续3次未出席法庭会议,撤销其任命。

(4) 法庭会议的法定人数为1名主席和2名成员。

(5) 法庭成员有权获得部长确定的费用和津贴。

(6) 部长可与法庭协商制定规则——
    (a) 规定向法庭提出上诉的方式以及支付上诉的相关费用;
    (b) 规定法庭在审理上诉时应采用的程序和法庭应保存的记录;
    (c) 规定法庭的开庭方式以及开庭的地点和时间;
    (d) 以更好地执行本法关于法庭及其上诉的规定。

72. 向法庭上诉的程序

在根据本法提起的上诉中——
    (a) 上诉人应在确定的审理日期和时间内亲自出庭或由辩护律师出庭,但如果有证据使法庭确信,由于上诉人不在肯尼亚境内、生病或其他合理原因,无法在规定的日期和时间出席庭审,法庭可在认为必要的合理时间内推迟该审理;
    (b) 诉讼费用应由法庭酌情决定。

73. 有权向法庭上诉的人

以下人员可以行使本法所赋予的上诉权:
    (a) 根据管理局依据本法作出的决定,任何——
        (i) 被指示停止或不重复任何贸易行为的人;
        (ii) 被下达停止令或其他临时命令的人;
        (iii) 获准在该命令规定的条件下继续或重复贸易行为的人;
        (iv) 被指示采取某些措施,协助受禁止贸易行为不利影响的现有或潜在供应商或客户的人;
        (v) 被责令支付罚金或罚款的人;或者
        (vi) 不服管理局的停止令或其他临时命令的人;
    (b) 在(a)项所述的命令是针对某一类人的情况下,属于或代表该类人的任何人;或者
    (c) 根据第46条作出的命令,任何——
        (i) 被禁止继续进行拟议合并的人;或者
        (ii) 被授权在命令规定的条件下进行拟议合并的人。

74. 上诉的审理和裁决

(1) 在任何情况下,法庭认为符合当事各方或其中任何一方的利益,并且不违背相关人员

的利益或公共利益,可以命令以非公开方式召开听证会或部分听证会。

(2)法庭可发布命令,禁止在其受理的任何上诉(无论是公开审理还是不公开审理)中公布关于诉讼程序或诉讼程序任何部分的报告或说明,但不得作出该等命令,禁止公布上诉各方的姓名、名称,或法庭的任何决定。

(3)在裁决任何上诉时,法庭可以确认、修改或撤销上诉所针对的命令或该命令的任何部分。

75. 法庭将上诉发回重审

(1)尽管第73条有规定,但法庭可在任何情形下,指示管理局就上诉所涉及的全部或任何指定的、一般或特定的事宜进行重新审议,而不是根据该条对上诉作出裁决。

(2)在根据本条作出任何指示时,法庭应——

(a)告知管理局相关理由;和

(b)向管理局发出其认为公正的指示,要求重新审理或以其他方式重新审理被退回重审的全部或部分事项。

(3)重新审理根据第(2)款发回的事项时,管理局须依据法院按第(1)款作出指示的理由以及法庭根据第(2)款作出的指示。

76. 待决上诉的规定

(1)如果对管理局关于限制性贸易行为、消费者福利事项或滥用支配地位的裁决提出上诉,除非法庭另有命令,否则在对上诉作出裁决之前,应遵守管理局作出的停止令或任何其他临时命令或条件。

(2)如果对管理局关于合并的决定提出上诉的,在作出裁决之前,与上诉相关的合并可能不会被最终裁决。

77. 管理局的上诉权

管理局有权就法庭的任何裁决向高等法院提出上诉。

第八部分
财 政 规 定

78. 管理局的资金

(1)管理局的资金应包括——

(a)向管理局提供的任何赠款、捐赠、遗赠或其他捐款;

(b)议会分配给管理局的资金;

(c)管理局收取的费用和罚款;

(d)可退还给管理局的诉讼费用;

(e)就与管理局职能相关的任何事项应向其支付的所有其他款项。

(2)管理局应在年度报告中披露其资金来源的详情。

(3)管理局可以制定规则,规定个人应支付的与管理局流程有关的申请费和其他费用。

79. 财政年度

管理局的财政年度为12个月,至每年6月30日止。

80. 年度预算

（1）管理局应至少在每个财政年度开始前的 3 个月,编制该财政年度管理局的收入和支出的预算。

（2）年度预算应编列管理局在本财政年度的所有预计支出,尤其须规定——

  （a）支付管理局官员、代理人或工作人员的薪酬、津贴和其他费用；

  （b）应付给管理局工作人员的退休金、抚恤金和其他与退休福利相关的费用；

  （c）管理局建筑物和场地的维护费；

  （d）管理局设备和其他财产的维护、修理和更换费用；和

  （e）设立储备基金,以支付退休金、保险、更换建筑物或设备的费用或管理局认为适当的其他事项的未来或或有负债。

（3）年度预算应在相关财政年度开始前由管理局批准,一经批准,预算中规定的金额应提交部长批准。

（4）除非依照根据第(3)款批准的年度预算,或依照经部长和财政部常任秘书事先书面批准的管理局的授权,否则不得为管理局的目的支出任何费用。

81. 账目及审计

（1）管理局应妥善保存管理局的收入、开支、资产和负债的账簿或记录。

（2）在每个财政年度结束后的 3 个月内,管理局应向主计长和审计长提交该年度的管理局账目以及——

  （a）管理局在该财政年度的收支报表；和

  （b）管理局在该财政年度最后一天的资产和负债报表。

（3）管理局的账目应由主计长和审计长根据《公共审计法》(2003 年第 12 号)的规定进行审计和报告。

82. 资金投资

（1）管理局可将管理局的任何资金投资于法律规定可投资的信托基金,或投资于当时的财政部长会批准的任何其他证券。

（2）管理局可在获得当时的财政部长的批准后,将管理局不立即需要的任何款项存入其所确定的一家或多家银行。

第九部分
其 他

83. 年度报告

（1）管理局应在每年 9 月 30 日前,编制一份截至上一年 6 月 30 日的年度报告,并在当年 11 月 30 日前提交给部长。

（2）年度报告应提供有关管理局在其相关年度内的活动和计划的信息,该信息足以准确阐述其活动的性质和范围及其计划和优先事项,包括但不限于——

  （a）管理局关键绩效指标的详情,包括管理局已决定或正在审议的投诉和申请的数量和性质,已完成和正在进行的调查数量和性质,已完成、正在进行或

计划进行的重要研究和报告，以及已完成、正在进行或计划进行的调查数量和性质；

（b）本法或根据本法制定的法规要求管理局在年度报告中包含的信息和其他材料；和

（c）部长以书面形式要求的其他信息或材料。

（3）部长应在收到年度报告后的 2 个月内，将其转交国民议会。

84. 禁止披露的信息

（1）管理局或委员会的成员、总干事、管理局的任何其他雇员，以及被要求或允许出席管理局或委员会的任何会议或根据本法进行调查的其他人，不得公布、传播或以任何其他方式披露该人通过以下方式所知的与任何个人或企业事务有关的任何信息——

（a）行使本法规定的任何权力或履行任何职责；或者

（b）该人出席此类会议或进行此类调查。

（2）第（1）款不适用于在下述情况下披露的信息——

（a）为适当管理或执行本法的目的；

（b）为适当的司法行政；或者

（c）应调查员、主席或有权接收信息的任何其他成员的要求。

85. 工作人员披露私人利益

（1）总干事、调查员或管理局雇用的其他人在管理局调查的任何事项中涉及财务或其他个人利益——

（a）须向理事长披露该利益；和

（b）除非管理局另有指示，否则不得参与或协助调查该事项。

（2）总干事、调查员或管理局雇用的其他人不得使用在履行职责中获得的任何机密信息，为自己或其他人直接或间接获取经济或其他利益。

86. 可展开调查的时间

自侵权行为停止之日起 3 年后，不得对涉嫌违反本法规定的侵权行为进行调查。

87. 妨碍法令的施行

任何人妨碍、反对、阻挠或不适当地影响他人行使本法所赋予其的权力或履行其职责的，即属犯罪。

88. 不遵守传票的规定

任何人——

（a）被正式传唤出席管理局会议，无正当理由不出席的；或者

（b）按规定出席会议，但——

（i）拒绝按照管理局的合法要求宣誓或确认的；

（ii）在宣誓或确认后，拒绝回答管理局依法要求其回答的任何问题，或拒绝提供其明知是虚假的证据的；或者

（iii）未能出示管理局依法要求其出示的为其拥有或控制的任何文件或物品的，

即属犯罪。

89. 不遵从命令

任何违反或不遵守管理局根据本法作出的合法命令的,即属犯罪。

89A. 宽大处理程序

(1)如果企业自愿披露存在本法所禁止的协议或惯例,并与管理局合作调查该协议或惯例,管理局可实施宽大处理程序,则该企业可能不会被处以本法规定的全部或部分罚款。

(2)第(1)款规定的宽大处理程序的详情应在管理局的准则中列出。

[2014年第16号法令,第38条]

90. 其他罪行

任何人——

(a) 在与管理局行使任何权力或履行任何职能有关的事宜上,蓄意作出任何不当影响管理局或成员的行为;

(b) 预测管理局就某项调查作出的任何决定,旨在影响诉讼程序或决定;

(c) 就某项调查作出任何在法庭上会构成藐视法庭的行为;和

(d) 故意向管理局提供虚假信息,

即属犯罪。

91. 一般处罚

犯有本法规定的罪行,但本法未规定相应处罚的,应处以50万先令以下罚款,或3年以下监禁,或两者并罚。

92. 地方法院的管辖权

尽管有其他法律规定,地方法院仍有权实施本法规定的任何处罚。

93. 规则

(1)为更好地实施本法的规定,部长可与管理局协商制定一般性规则。

(2)在不影响第(1)款的一般性情形下,根据本条制定的规则应对本法规定的任何事项作出相应的规定。

[2015年第25号法令,附录]

第十部分
废除、保留和过渡性条款

94. 定义

在本部分中——

"指定日期"是指该法生效的日期;

"部门"是指在指定日期之前存在的财政部的垄断和价格部门。

95. 资产及其他财产

(1)在指定日期之前,以财政部常务秘书长的名义代表该部门持有的所有资产和其他动产和不动产,应根据本条的规定在无须进一步担保的情况下,归管理局所有。

(2)任何有权或有义务执行或修改登记册中与财产有关的任何记录,或签发、修改任何证明财产所有权的证书或其他文件的公职人员,应按照管理局或其代表提出的要求,采取法律规定的一切必要措施,使第(1)款所述财产的转让最终生效。

96. 权利、权力和法律责任等

在指定日期,根据任何法律或其他方式产生的,在指定日期之前由政府或由政府代表部门赋予、授权、施加、强制执行的所有权利、权力、法律责任及义务,均须凭借本条转让给管理局、归属管理局、由管理局施加或强制执行。

97. 法律诉讼

在指定日期及之后,所有由政府或由政府代表部门提起的诉讼或待决法律程序均应由管理局或以管理局为对象进行或检控。

98. 借调至管理局

(1)除第(2)款另有规定外,在指定日期任职的部门专员、高级职员和工作人员应被视为借调至管理局的高级职员和工作人员。

(2)尽管第(1)款有规定,在指定日期后的12个月内,管理局应审查根据该款被视为借调至管理局的所有人员的资格,并可保留那些管理局认为适合聘用的人员,但须遵守以下规定——

(a)该人员选择继续为管理局服务;和

(b)与管理局商定的服务条款和条件(不得损害雇佣者的利益)。

(3)管理局未根据第(2)款聘用的工作人员可以行使其选择权——

(a)从政府部门退休;或者

(b)如果该工作人员未达到退休年龄,则重新安排在公共服务部门工作。

(4)如果工作人员根据第(2)款与管理局达成协议,则其在政府的工作应被视为终止,无权领取遣散费,但不影响其在政府任期终止时应获得的所有薪酬和福利。

(5)本部门在指定日期就该财政年度的预算应被视为管理局在该财政年度剩余时间内的年度预算:

但是管理局可按部长批准的方式修改此类预算。

99. 废除第504章

《限制性贸易行为、垄断和价格控制法》(第504章)特此予以废除。

100. 储蓄

尽管《限制性贸易行为、垄断和价格控制法》(第504章)已废除,但在本法生效前正在进行的任何合并或收购申请、与限制性贸易行为以及与经营者不正当集中有关的调查,均应由管理局接管。

附录

[2017年第11号法令,第8条,附录]
关于管理局的规定

1. 任期

除当然成员外,理事会的任何成员应在符合本附录规定的情况下,按照任命文书中规定的条款和条件,任期3年,但有资格获再度委任,最多可连任两届。

2. 离职

（1）除当然成员外,理事会成员可以——

(a) 随时以书面形式通知部长辞职;

(b) 如该成员有以下情况,部长可将其免职——

(i) 被宣告破产,利用法律救济无力偿债的债务人或为债权人的利益转移成员的报酬;

(ii) 被判处刑事犯罪;

(iii) 按照第4条第(7)款的要求辞职;

(iv) 因健康状况不佳或身心障碍而无法履行职责;

(v) 未经管理局许可,在连续12个月内,未能出席管理局至少三分之二的会议;或者

(vi) 严重违反了根据本法规定管理局应遵守的行为准则。

（2）在罢免成员之前,部长应书面通知该成员,并说明罢免理由。

3. 管理局会议

（1）管理局在每个财政年度内应至少举行4次会议,两次会议间隔时间不得超过4个月。

（2）管理局应按照理事长的指示或经半数以上非当然成员的书面要求召开会议。

（3）在不违反第(1)款和第(2)款规定的情况下,理事长可在与各成员协商后,在其认为适当的时间和地点召开管理局会议。

（4）理事长应主持其出席的所有管理局会议,在理事长缺席的情况下,出席会议的成员可从其中指定一名成员主持会议。

（5）法定人数为4人,包括理事长在内。

（6）所有问题均应由出席并参加表决的成员多数票决定,在票数相等的情况下,主持会议的成员应拥有审议权和决定性表决权。

（7）理事长可决定管理局的特定会议应以电话、闭路电视或理事长认为适当的其他通讯方式举行。

（8）由管理局全体成员签署的决议记录应构成管理局的有效决议,其效力与在管理局有效组成的会议上正式通过的决议相同。

[2017年第11号法令,附录]

4. 利益冲突

（1）就本法而言,如果管理局成员或工作人员获得的任何金钱或其他利益,可能与其作为管理局成员或工作人员适当履行职责相冲突,则该成员或工作人员应被视为存在利益冲突。

（2）如果在任何时候管理局成员与以下事项存在利益冲突——

(a) 提交管理局审议或决定的任何事项;或者

(b) 管理局可以合理预期的可能提交其审议或决定的任何事项。

（3）成员应立即向管理局其他成员披露利益冲突,并不得参与或进一步参与该事项进一步的审议或决定。

（4）如果管理局知悉某成员与管理局处理的任何事项存在利益冲突,管理局应指示该成员避免参与或进一步参与该事项的审议或决定。

(5) 如果理事长有利益冲突,除了遵守本条的其他规定,应以书面方式向部长披露存在的冲突。

(6) 当管理局知悉有任何利益冲突时,应确定该冲突是否会严重影响成员或管理局正确有效履行职能和职责,有利益冲突的成员不得对该决定进行投票。

(7) 如果管理局认为冲突可能会严重影响成员按照第(6)款的规定适当有效地履行职责,则该成员应当辞职,除非其在30日内消除利益冲突以满足管理局的要求。

(8) 管理局应向部长报告其做出的关于可能严重影响上述职能冲突的决定,以及该利益冲突是否已被消除以达到管理局的要求。

(9) 管理局的年度报告应披露报告所涉期间产生的所有利益冲突和决定的详情。

5. 行为准则

(1) 在本法生效后的12个月内,管理局应制定一项行为准则,规定管理局成员和工作人员在履行职责时应遵守的行为标准。

(2) 除第(1)款另有规定外,在通过任何行为准则或对现行行为准则作出任何实质性修改之前,管理局应在公报和全国发行的报纸上公布拟议的准则或修正案,以征求公众意见。

(3) 管理局应在其年度报告中列入一份关于在年度报告所涉期间准则遵守情况的报告。

(4) 根据本条通过或规定的行为准则对管理局及其工作人员具有约束力。

6. 文书的执行

任何合同或文书,如由非法人团体的人订立或执行,则无须盖章,可由管理局一般授权或特别授权的任何人代表管理局订立或执行,以达到目的。

7. 会议记录

管理局应将其所有决议和会议记录记入为此目的备存的簿册内。

第四部
公私合营法（2021年第14号法令）

2021

由全国法律报告委员会经总检察长授权公布

www.kenyalaw.org

2021 年第 14 号法令
公私合营法

［批准日期：2021 年 12 月 7 日］

［施行日期：2021 年 12 月 23 日］

旨在对私营团体通过公私合营关系参与基础设施或开发项目的融资、建设、开发、运营或维护；简化公私合营关系的监管框架；废除 2013 年《公私合营法》及相关目的作出规定的议会法案

［2021 年第 14 号法令］

第一部分
总　　则

1. 简称

本法可称为《公私合营法》(2021)。

2. 释义

在本法中，除非上下文另有规定，否则——

"**负担能力**"是指

（a）缔约方根据项目协议做出的财务承诺是可持续的，不会给缔约方增加不合理的负担，并且可以获取下列经费——

（i）在缔约方现有预算内为其履行与协议有关的职能指定的资金；和

（ii）根据相关的未来预算拨款分配给缔约方的资金；和

（b）缔约方交付与项目有关的设施或服务的费用不会给最终使用者增加不合理的财务负担；

"**内阁秘书**"是指负责与财政有关事务的内阁秘书；

"**委员会**"是指根据第 6 条设立的公私合营委员会；

"**特许权**"是指由项目协议正式确定的合同许可，该许可可能与不动产的单独权益或权利相关联，无论是否向政府支付费用，获得许可的人均有权使用指定的基础设施或承接某一项目并在特许权有效期内收取用户使用费、接收可获得的费用及其他费用；

"**缔约方**"是指——

（a）拟将其职能由私人承担的国家政府层面的国家部门、机构或国有公司；或者

（b）拟将其职能由私人承担的郡级政府层面的郡级政府或郡级公司；

"**缔约方的财产**"包括缔约方的所有动产和不动产以及授予缔约方的知识产权；

"**理事会**"是指根据第 15 条设立的公私合营理事会；

"**可行性研究**"是指为探讨以公私合营伙伴关系的方式承建基础设施或开发设备的技术、

财务、法律、社会和环境可行性而进行的研究；

"**财务结算**"是指项目协议中规定的，满足项目协议项下优先债务首次提取所需的所有先决条件的日期；

"**基金**"是指根据第81条设立的公私合营项目促进基金；

"**本地化**"是指与项目有关的活动通过在当地分配积累的利益，包括通过采购当地现有的劳动力、服务和用品以及系统地发展国家能力和潜能，为肯尼亚经济带来的附加值；

"**私人当事方**"是指与缔约方签订工程协议并根据本法代表缔约方承担工程项目的一方；

"**私人发起的提案**"是指由私人当事方在没有缔约方参与的情况下发起的提案，包含和投标一样能够对提案进行完整评估的信息；

"**项目**"是指新的基础设施、资产或设备的设计、建造、开发或运营，或现有基础设施、资产或设备的修复、现代化、扩建、运营或管理；

"**项目协议**"是指缔约方和私人当事方之间订立的合同，包括双方就协议订立的任何协议附件；

"**项目公司**"是指中标人根据双方签订的项目协议，为承接项目而成立的特殊目的公司；

"**公共债务管理办公室**"是指依据《公共财政管理法》(2012)(2012年第18号)第62条第(1)款设立的公共债务管理办公室；

"**公私合营关系**"是指缔约方和私人当事方之间的合同约定，私人当事方是指——

（a）承诺代表缔约方履行公共职能或提供服务的一方；

（b）以下列资金履行公共职能而获得利益的一方——

　　（i）来自公共基金的补偿；

　　（ii）私人当事方向为其提供服务的用户或消费者收取的费用；或者

　　（iii）此类补偿和此类费用的组合；

（c）根据项目协议条款，对履行职能所产生的风险承担责任的一方；和

（d）将设施移交给缔约方的一方；

"**交易顾问**"是指具有适当技能和经验的人员，可以就与公私合营有关事项向缔约方或董事会提供协助和建议；

"**使用费**"是指为全部或部分使用基础设施或开发设施或服务而征收的费率、通行费或其他费用；和

"**货币价值**"是指在公私合营关系下，私人当事方承担缔约方的公共职能，该缔约方在成本、价格、质量、数量、时效性或风险转移方面所获得的净收益。

3. 法案的目的

本法的目的是——

（a）规定私营部门通过公私合营参与基础设施或开发项目的融资、建设、开发、运营或维护的程序；

（b）为实施公私合营项目而协调制度框架；

（c）实施《宪法》第227条关于公私合营采购的规定；

（d）简化和合理化相关机构的监管、执行和监测任务；和

（e）为促进私营部门的投资，规定透明的项目选择过程、明确的采购程序、减少监管

审批和扩大合约模式。

4. 法案的适用

（1）本法适用于以公私合营方式开展项目融资、设计、建设、修复、运营、装备或维护或者提供公共服务的所有项目协议。

（2）《公共采购和资产处置法》（2015）（2015年第33号）的规定不适用于公私合营。

（3）在不影响第（2）款的一般性规定的情况下，《公共采购和资产处置法》（2015）（2015年第33号）的规定，其适用应遵循以下条件——

　　（a）如果公私合营项目的所有资金均来自私人当事方，则该规定不适用于公私合营项目；

　　（b）如果公私合营项目有对应资金，包括公共资金，则该规定适用于公私合营项目。

5. 法案优先适用

本法规定与其他法律规定相抵触的，本法规定优先适用。

第二部分
公私合营委员会

6. 公私合营委员会

（1）现设立公私合营委员会，该委员会由以下人士组成——

　　（a）国家财政事务部门的首席秘书，担任主席；

　　（b）国家规划事务部门的首席秘书；

　　（c）国家基础设施事务部门的首席秘书；

　　（d）副检察长；

　　（e）郡长理事会提名的2人；

　　（f）通过公报发布公告任命的3名非公职人员；和

　　（g）总干事，担任秘书。

（2）委员会应增选对缔约方负责的首席秘书，负责在会议上讨论公私合营项目。

（3）委员会可增选其知识或经验是正在讨论的公私合营必需的个人或公职人员。

（4）被增选的人不得在会议上投票，只能担任委员会成员，且其任期不超过1年。

（5）第（1）款（a）、（b）、（c）、（d）、（e）和（f）项所述的成员应亲自出席委员会会议，并可书面指定一名官员代表他们参加委员会小组会议。

7. 成员资格和任期

（1）根据第6条第（1）款（f）项，任何人在与公私合营关系相关的事务方面具有至少10年的专业经验，即有资格被任命为委员会成员。

（2）根据第6条第（1）款（f）项，获委任的成员任期为3年，并有资格再连任一届。

（3）根据第6条第（1）款（f）项，应在不同时间任命获委任的人员，以便使其各自的任期在不同时间届满。

8. 委员会的职权

（1）委员会应负责——

(a) 制定公私合营政策；
(b) 监督公私合营合同的执行情况；
(c) 批准标准化的公私合营投标文件；
(d) 批准可行性研究；
(e) 批准私人发起的提案；
(f) 批准议定的合同条款、取消采购或终止项目协议以及更改项目协议；
(g) 监督本法的实施，包括缔约方在根据本法批准的项目上可能产生的或有负债的持续性；和
(h) 履行本法授予的任何其他职能。
（2）委员会应拥有适当履行本法规定职能所需的一切权力。

9. 离职
（1）委员会任命的成员如有以下情况，将被视为离职——
(a) 因精神或身体疾病而无法履行其职务；
(b) 因违反宪法第六章的规定被免职；
(c) 因职业失范被专业机构注销；
(d) 被裁定破产；
(e) 被判犯有刑事罪并被判处不少于6个月的有期徒刑；
(f) 被判犯有本法第84条规定的罪行；
(g) 无正当理由连续三次缺席委员会会议；
(h) 以书面形式向内阁秘书提出辞职；
(i) 没有申报其在委员会正在审议或将要审议的事项中涉及的利益；
(j) 死亡；或者
(k) 被内阁秘书免职。
（2）委员会成员可由于严重不当行为、不称职、因可认定的罪行被定罪或违反宪法而被免职。
（3）在委员会成员被免职之前，应给予该成员发言的机会。
（4）任何人对根据本条作出的将其免职的决定不服的，可就该决定向高等法院提出上诉。

10. 小组委员会
委员会可设立其认为适当履行其职能和行使本法规定的权力所必需的小组委员会。

11. 委员会的授权
委员会可通过一般决议或特定情况下的决议，委托小组委员会或理事会的成员、官员、雇员或代理人行使委员会的任何权力或履行委员会的任何职能。

12. 委员会事务的处理
（1）在符合第（2）款规定的情况下，委员会的业务和事务应按照附录一进行。
（2）除本法另有规定外，委员会可规定自己的程序。
（3）委员会按其决定的方式保存委员会会议的适当记录，包括会议记录。

13. 行为准则
内阁秘书可以制定条例，规定委员会成员和理事会的官员、雇员和代理人行为守则。

14. 报酬
委员会成员的薪酬或津贴应在内阁秘书和工资与薪酬委员会协商确定后支付。

15. 理事会
（1）应设立一个理事会，称为公私合营理事会。
（2）理事会由总干事领导。

16. 总干事
（1）拥有肯尼亚公认大学的高级学位，并且在以下任何领域具备知识和至少10年专业经验的人，有资格被任命为总干事——
  （a）金融；
  （b）经济学；
  （c）法律；
  （d）工程；
  （e）项目管理；或者
  （f）任何其他相关领域。
（2）总干事应由公共服务委员会竞争性招聘和任命。
（3）总干事任期4年，且根据任命条款规定，只能连任一届。

17. 理事会工作人员
根据《委员会公共服务人员法》（2017）第31条和第37条，内阁秘书应与总干事协商，任命理事会工作人员。

18. 借调工作人员到理事会
（1）在与缔约方、郡政府、郡公司或者发展或战略合作伙伴协商后，理事会在可能需要的条件和期限内可以要求从缔约方、郡政府、郡公司或者发展或战略伙伴处借调工作人员。
（2）借调到理事会的工作人员应被视为理事会的工作人员，并在借调期间受理事会的管辖。

19. 理事会的职能
（1）理事会应是实施本法规定的公私合营项目的牵头机构，为此，其应在以下方面负责——
  （a）在公共预算框架内发起、指导和协调公私合营项目的选择、排序和优先排序；
  （b）监督缔约方的评估和开发活动，包括为本法项下项目的实施提供技术专业知识；
  （c）在项目结构、采购和投标评估方面给予缔约方指导和建议；
  （d）领导缔约方进行合同谈判并完成交易；
  （e）自行动议，与缔约方联络，创建和领导项目结构和采购；
  （f）支持国内发展公私合营计划；
  （g）监督本法项下项目的合同管理框架；和
  （h）开展履行理事会的职能所需的任何其他活动。
（2）理事会在履行其职能时，应——
  （a）建立一个公开、高效和公平的管理程序，用于项目的确定、筛选、优先排序、开发、采购、实施和监测。

（b）作为公私合营国家资源中心运作；

（c）为缔约方进行能力建设；

（d）提高公众对公私合营的认识；

（e）在本法项下项目的所有阶段向国家和郡政府的缔约方提供咨询和支持服务；

（f）代表缔约方聘请交易顾问并为此签订协议，以协助缔约方进行项目评估和实施；

（g）审查和批准项目建议书和投标评估报告；

（h）为根据本法实施的项目建立国家登记册；

（i）与相关政府部门合作，监测与公私合营有关的或有负债以及会计和预算问题；和

（j）开展关于公私合营的研究并公布研究结果，以确保公私合营项目持续改进。

（3）理事会应发布标准招标文件，供缔约方使用。

（4）理事会应编制其分配到的任何款项的财务账目和清单，以及根据本法获得的任何财政支持。

第三部分
公 私 合 营

20. 项目协议

（1）拟融资、运营、装备或维护基础设施或者提供公共服务的缔约方可以与符合条件的私人当事方就基础设施的融资、建设、运营、装备或维护或者公共服务的提供，依照本法规定签订项目协议。

（2）根据第（1）款与私人当事方签订项目协议的缔约方，可以在适当的情况下，按照缔约方认为适当的条款和条件指定其财产供私人当事方在涉及项目时和项目持续期间使用。

（3）缔约方应在项目的每个阶段执行理事会的指示。

（4）当一个项目涉及多个缔约方时，理事会应指定其中一个缔约方作为牵头缔约方。

21. 公私合营协议

（1）根据本法的规定，缔约方可以根据附录二与私人当事方签订公私合营协议。

（2）在不影响附录二规定期限的情况下，缔约方不得签订超过30年的公私合营协议。

22. 缔约方的职责

（1）缔约方有义务——

（a）与理事会联络，根据理事会发布的指引确定、筛选和优化项目；

（b）筹备和评估每个项目，以确保其法律、监管、社会、经济和商业可行性；

（c）根据本法进行招标；

（d）提供理事会评估和评价项目所需要的技术专业知识；

（e）监督项目协议的执行情况；

（f）在项目周期内与所有关键利益相关者联络；

(g) 依据项目协议监督项目管理；

(h) 向理事会提交关于项目协议执行情况的年度报告或其他定期报告；

(i) 保存与根据本法执行的项目协议有关的所有文件和协议的记录；

(j) 根据标准文件和理事会发布的其他指引拟定项目协议；

(k) 确保公众参与项目；和

(l) 确保项目协议到期或提前终止时的资产转让符合项目协议中涉及资产转让的条款。

(2) 缔约方须向理事会报告，在履行第(1)款规定的职责时——

(a) 执行理事会的建议；

(b) 遵守理事会发布的指导方针；和

(c) 提交理事会或委员会要求的信息。

23. 公私合营协议期限的确定

(1) 在确定公私合营协议的期限时，缔约方应考虑以下因素——

(a) 本法和其他相关法律的规定；

(b) 本协议项下，拟采取技术的寿命；

(c) 在公私合营协议有效期内，项目协议各方需要维持的投资标准；

(d) 项目的经济和财务可行性以及拟提供设施的经济寿命；

(e) 公私合营协议有效期内，项目资产的折旧；和

(f) 就以下方面合营各方要求的期限——

　　(i) 在公私合营协议的有效期内，保持服务提供标准和投资水平；和

　　(ii) 收回各方的投资。

(2) 理事会可就公私合营协议期限的确定发布指导方针。

(3) 理事会可以根据委员会和总检察长批准的条款和期限延长项目协议的有效期；但延期不得对缔约方或政府施加额外的财政或法定负担。

24. 项目协议的执行

如果缔约方拟建立公私合营关系，则非缔约方的会计主管不得代表缔约方签订有关的项目协议。

25. 项目清单的提交

(1) 除郡政府或郡公司外，缔约方应编制一份其根据本法拟优先承接的项目清单，并提交理事会批准。

(2) 除非项目属于国家发展议程的一部分，否则缔约方不得提交项目清单。

(3) 根据本节编制的项目清单应附有适当的项目概念说明，且此说明应根据理事会发布的指导方针编制。

(4) 理事会应每半年向委员会、内阁秘书和内阁通报其根据本法批准实施的所有项目。

(5) 理事会可以拒绝拟议项目清单中的任何项目，并应书面说明拒绝的理由。

(6) 如果理事会拒绝项目清单中的拟议项目，则应向各缔约方提供必要的指导。

26. 国家清单和优先项目清单

(1) 理事会应建立和维护根据本法第25条和66条批准的最新的国家项目清单。

（2）在符合第（1）款规定的情况下，国家清单应在理事会网站和缔约方网站上公布。

（3）国家清单应保存在理事会主办的可公开访问的数据库中。

（4）理事会应编制国家清单中规定的优先项目清单，以便根据本法实施优先项目。

27. 资格预审程序

缔约方拟与私人当事方订立项目协议，应在签署项目协议前确认该私人当事方具备以下条件——

（a）承担项目的财务能力；

（b）从事类似项目的相关经验；

（c）承担该项目的相关专业知识；和

（d）满足理事会规定的法律、社会和环境尽职调查参数。

28. 政府支持措施

（1）内阁秘书可发布政府支持公私合营的措施，包括——

（a）具有约束力的承诺；

（b）支持函；

（c）信用证；

（d）部分或全部的信用担保；

（e）批准签发部分风险担保和政治风险保险；或者

（f）根据委员会的建议，负责财政事务的内阁秘书确定的任何其他文书：

但该文书应符合有关公共财政管理的法律规定。

（2）内阁秘书只能根据本部分规定发布政府支持措施——

（a）有必要支持一个项目，以降低政治风险类的保费；或者

（b）根据协商的项目协议承保批准的商业风险；

（3）内阁秘书可以根据本部分规定为政府发布支持措施制定指导方针。

29. 成交费用及可回收的项目开发成本

（1）理事会应征收不超过交易总成本1%的成交费，该费用由达成项目财务结算的私人当事方支付。

（2）如果理事会或缔约方因支持项目筹备和采购活动而提供的交易咨询服务或任何其他可收回的项目开发而产生费用，在不考虑通货膨胀调整的情况下，则该费用应从与缔约方订立项目协议的私人当事方处全额收回。

（3）第（2）款规定的成交费用和可回收的项目成本应支付给公私合营项目促进基金。

（4）依据本部分规定，理事会可就可回收项目成本的成本分配和成交费用的支付发布指导方针。

第四部分
项目鉴定和私人当事方的选择

30. 项目鉴定、选择和优先排序

（1）拟根据本法通过公私合营实施项目的缔约方应与理事会协商，负责构思或确定潜在

项目并承担项目的筹备和招标过程。

（2）在根据本法对潜在项目进行构思、鉴定和优先排序时，缔约方应考虑公私合营项目安排的战略和运营利益，而不是缔约方的设施开发或服务提供。

（3）如果缔约方选择实施第 25 条规定的优先项目，则应根据第 32 条评估该项目的可行性。

（4）内阁秘书应与理事会协商，根据本法制定项目构思、鉴定和优先排序的条例。

31. 项目准备和实施

（1）缔约方应在理事会的指导下组成一个项目实施小组，负责监督项目的构建和实施环节，包括——

（a）监督可行性研究的开展；

（b）准备项目的采购；

（c）实施项目招标阶段工作；和

（d）就该项目进行协议谈判。

（2）根据第（1）款组建的项目实施小组应由一名理事会的代表、缔约方与理事会共同确定的缔约方的技术、财务和法律专家组成。

32. 可行性研究

（1）缔约方应在理事会的指导下，对其拟根据本法实施的项目进行可行性研究，以确定该项目的可行性。

（2）缔约方在进行可行性研究时，应当考虑下列因素——

（a）项目的技术要求；

（b）项目各方应满足的法律要求；

（c）项目的社会、经济和环境影响；

（d）项目的可负担性和性价比；和

（e）项目的土地需求和有效且高效启动该项目所需的现场准备活动。

33. 可行性报告的审批

（1）拟通过公私合营实施项目的缔约方应将根据第 32 条编制的可行性报告提交给理事会进行评估。

（2）理事会应连同其提交的评估报告及其提出的建议一起提交给委员会。

（3）委员会应在收到评估报告后 21 天内审议可行性报告，以决定缔约方是否可以根据本法进行项目的采购。

34. 缔约方的技术专长

（1）理事会应评估缔约方的技术专长，以根据本法进行项目的采购、筹备、合同谈判和管理。

（2）如果理事会确定缔约方不具备采购项目的技术专长，缔约方应与理事会协商，任命一名交易顾问，协助缔约方进行项目的筹备、采购、合同谈判和财务结算。

（3）基于公开、透明、平等、成本-效益和机会均等的原则，按照内阁秘书在条例中规定的程序，应根据第（2）款聘请交易顾问。

（4）理事会可以根据第 25 条国家清单中包含的项目，按行业聘请交易顾问。

35. 标准和程序

（1）内阁秘书应根据理事会的建议,规定本法项下项目的识别、选择、可行性研究、投标前批准、投标、谈判、投标后批准、监测和评估的标准和程序。

（2）在不影响第（1）款的一般性规定的情况下,内阁秘书应就下列事项规定标准和程序——

  （a）私人发起的项目采购建议的实践要素;

  （b）本法规定的竞争性招标的实施;

  （c）在缔约方和私人当事方之间的直接谈判过程中应遵守的协议;

  （d）项目各阶段的披露要求;

  （e）订立适用于私人发起的提案的主要分包合同的竞争性采购标准条款,以促进公平的价格厘定和政府资金的高回报;

  （f）基准测试和市场测试的程序;

  （g）私人发起的提案的每个阶段的时间表和程序;

  （h）项目开发阶段的公众参与和利益相关者参与;

  （i）交易顾问的聘请;

  （j）利益冲突的管理;

  （k）标准化的评估标准模板;

  （l）可行性研究;

  （m）项目开发的时间表;和

  （n）为更好地执行本部分条款所需的任何相关事项。

36. 或有负债的限额

（1）内阁秘书应批准委员会可以分配给本法项下项目的或有负债的限额。

（2）委员会应在批准的或有负债限额内,将或有负债分配给本法项下项目。

（3）理事会——

  （a）应至少每6个月一次向内阁秘书通报批准的或有负债组合的分配数量;和

  （b）应通知内阁秘书对超出批准限额的额外或有负债净额的任何要求。

（4）内阁秘书可根据委员会的建议,批准增加或有负债净额,以实现政府公私合营计划的目标。

（5）理事会应编制并向内阁秘书提交有关年度内或有负债分配的年度报告,根据第25条编制的国家项目清单中的项目组合预测未来或有负债的要求。

第五部分
公私合营采购方式

37. 采购方式

（1）缔约方可通过以下方式获得本法项下的公私合营项目——

  （a）直接采购;

  （b）私人发起的提案;或者

(c) 竞标；

(d) 限制性投标。

(2) 在采购公私合营项目时，缔约方应遵循透明、成本-效益和机会均等的原则。

(3) 缔约方应在所有公私合营采购中使用理事会发布的标准招标文件。

(4) 内阁秘书应依据本部分条款规定公私合营采购指南。

直接采购

38. **直接采购**

   如果满足以下任何条件，缔约方可以与理事会协商，采用直接采购方式——

   (a) 私人当事方拥有项目所需的关键方法或技术的知识产权；

   (b) 作品或服务只能从数量有限的私人当事方处获得；

   (c) 特定私人当事方对作品或服务拥有专有权，且没有合理的替代品；

   (d) 基于国家利益、双边或国际合作或对外贸易，缔约方确定存在与特定私人当事方相关的运营和战略优势或原因；

   (e) 在工程项目符合政府批准的拨款条件，而有关结果不会成为公共债务一部分的前提下，私人当事方的直接参与应大幅降低工程或服务的交付成本；

   (f) 迫切需要工程或服务，而任何其他采购方式都不具操作性：

   但此迫切需要是缔约方无法预见的情形，或缔约方拖延行为所致；

   (g) 缔约方已从私人当事方采购货物、设备、技术或服务，出于标准化或与现有货物、设备、技术或服务兼容的需要，决定从私人当事方采购额外供应品，同时考虑以下因素——

   　　(i) 原始采购在满足缔约方需求方面的有效性；

   　　(ii) 与原始采购相比，拟议采购规模的有限性；和

   　　(iii) 所涉商品或服务价格的合理性及其替代品的不适宜性；

   (h) 工程或服务是从公众实体采购的：

   但收购价格应公平合理，并且与已知的工程或服务价格进行了充分的比较；或者

   (i) 内阁秘书可能规定的任何其他原因。

39. **直接采购程序**

   缔约方在直接采购项目期间应遵守以下程序——

   (a) 发布招标文件，作为缔约方准备招标和随后谈判的基础；

   (b) 根据本法颁布的标准和实施程序任命一个评估委员会，用于项目直接采购的谈判；

   (c) 确保已根据本法获得适当的批准；

   (d) 确保产生的项目协议符合本法规定；和

   (e) 内阁秘书可能规定的任何其他程序。

私人发起的提案

40. **私人发起的提案**

   (1) 私人当事方可以向缔约方提交私人发起的提案。

   (2) 如果出现以下情况，缔约方可考虑根据第(1)款提交的私人发起的提案——

(a) 该项目符合国家基础设施优先事项标准,并满足已证实的社会需求;
(b) 项目物有所值;
(c) 项目提案为缔约方提供了充分的资料,供缔约方评估该提案的财务负担能力和可能涉及的或有负债影响;
(d) 项目可以以公平的市场价格交付;
(e) 该项目得到第(3)款所列的所有文件的支持,以实现透明度和问责制;和
(f) 该项目支持公共部门有效转移风险。

(3) 根据第(1)款由私人发起的提案应包含以下信息——
(a) 拟议项目的详细说明,包括参考设计、草图和路线图;
(b) 详细的项目需求分析,包括对社会效益以及与政府基础建设计划一致性的描述;
(c) 对拟议项目的环境和社会特征的描述;
(d) 项目的详细技术说明,包括施工进度计划和业务能力要求;
(e) 项目财务可行性的详细说明,包括成本和收益、初步资金和融资计划,由相关开放性财务模型予以支持;
(f) 拟议项目的初步运营计划;
(g) 对关键项目风险和项目下风险分配的说明;
(h) 披露拟议项目可能需要的任何政府支持措施;
(i) 项目可能需要的非货币政府支持措施的说明;和
(j) 项目不适合公开竞争采购的理由。

(4) 缔约方应将私人发起的提案提交理事会评估和审批。
(5) 内阁秘书可通过公报发布公告,规定根据本部分制定的提交意见书的时间。
(6) 私人当事方应在根据第(1)款提交其私人发起的提案时,向基金会支付不可退还的审查费,审查费按估计项目成本的 0.5% 或 5 万美元(以较低者为准)计算。
(7) 缔约方或理事会不会因第(6)款规定的审查费用而对提案人承担任何责任。
(8) 内阁秘书应与理事会协商,为更好地实施本部分而制定条例。

41. 对私人发起的提案的尽职调查

理事会应与缔约方协调,在开始评估私人发起的提案之前,进行尽职调查,以确认私人当事方——
(a) 未被任何国家或国际组织禁止参与公私合营项目或类似项目;
(b) 没有腐败行为,未从事腐败活动,未因腐败行为被起诉或定罪;
(c) 未资不抵债、被接管或破产,其事务未由法院或司法人员管理,其业务活动未中止,且不受任何现行法律程序的约束;
(d) 在其拥有地税业务的所有司法管辖区和注册母国符合税收规定,并且在其经营和注册管辖区没有拖欠社会保障和就业福利或缴款;和
(e) 在提交提案之前的 5 年内,其董事或高级职员均未被裁定犯有任何与专业行为相关的刑事犯罪,并且未因行政停职或禁止诉讼而被取消资格。

42. 对私人发起的提案的评估

(1) 在评估私人发起的提案以确定其是否适用于公私合营项目的进一步发展时,理事会

应与缔约方协商制定提案的评估标准。

（2）在评估私人发起的提案期间，不得要求私人当事方向缔约方或理事会提交额外的提案。

（3）根据第（1）款制定的评估标准应包括——

  （a）公共利益标准；

  （b）项目可行性标准；

  （c）公私合营适用性标准；和

  （d）负担能力标准。

（4）如果理事会或缔约方要求，私人当事方应以书面形式就私人发起的提案提供任何澄清或补充资料。

（5）理事会和缔约方应在向理事会提交提案之日起 90 天内，与相关政府部门协商，根据评估标准对提案进行评估。

（6）理事会应根据第（1）款规定的评估标准，就私人发起的提案编制详细评估报告，并在评估结束后 5 个工作日内就项目是否可以进入项目开发阶段向委员会提出建议。

（7）委员会应在收到第（6）款规定的报告后 14 个工作日内，确定拟议项目是否可以进入开发阶段，并就适用该项目的采购方法提供指导。

（8）在根据第（7）款作出决定时，委员会应考虑——

  （a）根据第（6）款提交的评估报告；

  （b）理事会的审查和建议；和

  （c）任何基准测试或市场测试结果。

（9）理事会、缔约方或政府不会因批准私人发起的提案而对私人当事方承担任何责任。

43. 私人发起的提案的项目开发

（1）如果委员会批准私人发起提案，该提案应进入项目开发阶段，在此期间，私人当事方应在项目获得批准前准备具体的项目开发活动。

（2）项目开发阶段应在委员会批准之日起 6 个月内完成。

（3）尽管有第（2）款的规定，缔约方可以书面形式向理事会申请延长项目开发阶段的完成时间，说明申请延长时间的理由，并提出新的时间框架和缓解措施，以防止任何进一步的延误。

（4）如果理事会对缔约方根据第（3）款的授权提出的理由满意，则理事会应当批准该申请。

（5）项目开发阶段包括必要的活动，使缔约方和其他适当的决策机构能够在理事会的指导下，在签订合同之前对拟议项目进行详细评估，包括以下活动的开展——

  （a）拟议项目的详细地理、时间和功能范围评估，包括任何通行权或土地征用或人口重新安置计划（如需要）；

  （b）技术可行性研究，包括能够支持定价和社会环境影响评估的技术设计和技术规范时间表；

  （c）财务可行性研究，包括详细的风险评估、财政影响评估或负担能力评估以及资金和财务计划；

(d) 法律可行性研究,包括对法律风险和不确定性的评估;
(e) 社会和环境影响评估(如需要);
(f) 经济可行性研究;
(g) 公私合营适用性评估或性价比评估;
(h) 综合风险矩阵;
(i) 初步的公私合营架构;和
(j) 利益相关者拓展计划,以确保项目的社会可接受性。

(6) 应私人当事方的请求,缔约方可与私人当事方签订项目开发协议,该协议应概述私人当事方开展项目开发活动的条款。

(7) 缔约方与私人当事方之间的项目开发协议应规定——
(a) 项目目标和项目开发协议;
(b) 缔约方和私人当事方协议项下的责任;
(c) 补偿原则规定——
  (i) 如果项目最终被授予私人当事方,则不予补偿;
  (ii) 如果项目被授予另一个私人当事方,提交提案的私人当事方完成项目开发阶段的费用应在财务结算时由该私人当事方支付;和
  (iii) 如项目在开发阶段后没有进展,则政府不承担赔偿责任;
(d) 缔约方与私人当事方之间协调和沟通的方式;
(e) 项目开发的时间表;
(f) 协议终止的条件;
(g) 缔约方和私人当事方的法律或监管义务;
(h) 与透明度和披露、问责制、保密性和利益冲突相关的政策。

(8) 理事会应针对私人发起的提案,为项目开发协议制定标准化的合同文件。

(9) 项目开发阶段产生的所有文件应由缔约方根据第42条规定的评估标准进行评估,理事会应在项目开发阶段完成后20个工作日内向委员会提交建议报告,以供批准。

(10) 缔约方可与理事会协调,聘请外部顾问审查私人当事方对私人发起的提案进行的研究,并提供独立意见。

(11) 根据缔约方的建议,以及委员会在这方面可能征询的任何独立审查结果或意见,委员会可作出以下决定——
(a) 项目符合公共利益、公私合营适用性,项目可行性和可负担性标准,并根据本法批准采购该项目;
(b) 项目不符合公私合营适用性标准,并就项目实施的替代方法提供指导;或者
(c) 项目不符合任何相关标准,应予放弃。

(12) 如果委员会决定根据第(11)款(c)项放弃该项目,缔约方可以选择重组该项目,以满足评估标准,并将项目重新提交委员会以重新确定。

(13) 委员会应在收到第(9)款所指的报告后14天内,根据本部分作出决定。

(14) 根据委员会的决定,缔约方应公布用于评估项目的可行性研究和项目文件,但须遵守目前生效的任何适用的公私合营项目披露指南。

（15）就本条而言——

  （a）"公共利益"是指拟议项目符合国家规定的基础建设需求、政策目标和政府优先事项满足明确的社会需求，并为国家的社会经济议程做出贡献；和

  （b）"项目可行性"是指拟议项目已被确认在技术、财务、社会、环境和法律上可行。

44. 采购设计

（1）在以下情况下，如果委员会确定可以根据第43条第（11）款（a）项进行私人发起的提案的采购，则缔约方须在理事会的协助下，直接与私人当事方就项目提案进行谈判——

  （a）缔约方确定，该提案不会在竞争性采购中产生市场利益；

  （b）提案以独特元素为基础；或者

  （c）出于公共利益的任何其他原因，直接谈判是合理的。

（2）就第（1）款而言，缔约方应为项目的直接谈判制定明确且切合实际的时间表：

但缔约方或私人当事方应承诺在6个月内完成谈判。

（3）直接谈判未在6个月内完成的，谈判终止。

（4）如果缔约方就同一事项收到多个私人当事方发起的提案，且所有提案均进入项目开发阶段，缔约方可采用限制性招标程序，以限制提交提案的私人当事方竞争性的投标行为。

（5）如果由于市场利益或可以向政府提供更高性价比的同等效能的替代技术的存在，缔约方确定项目应以竞争性方式采购，则缔约方可以根据本法选择对该项目进行公开竞争性招标：

但在以下情况下，缔约方可决定是否偿还私人当事方一方承担的费用——

  （a）项目被授予任何其他投标人；

  （b）项目实现财务结算；

  （c）开发费用不超过预估项目成本的0.5%；和

  （d）开发费用由中标人承担。

（6）如果缔约方认为公开招标符合公共利益，则应为招标文件的编制和招标过程的管理制定明确且切合实际的时间表。

（7）在符合第（4）款规定的情况下，缔约方在根据本部分设计采购策略时，应确保平等的投标条件。

限制性投标

45. 限制性招标

（1）如果具备下列条件之一，缔约方可以使用限制性招标——

  （a）由于工程和服务的复杂性或专业性，合同竞争仅限于通过资格预审的投标人；

  （b）审查和评估大量投标书所需的时间和成本与拟采购的工程或服务的价值不成比例；

  （c）有证据表明整个工程或服务市场只有少数几个已知的供应商；

  （d）在适当的情况下，采购实体网站上发布有关于拟通过有限招标进行采购的广告。

（2）缔约方可以按规定的方式通过限制性招标进行采购。

竞争性投标

46. 资格申请

（1）缔约方应在可行性研究报告获得批准后，就拟议项目请合格的投标人提交资格申请。

（2）理事会应就资格申请制定标准，并明确采购和招标管理的实施准则。

（3）缔约方应就第（1）款提出的资格申请明确投标人的资格标准，并可要求每个投标人提供声明或文件，以证明投标人的资格。

（4）缔约方应在采购周期内咨询理事会。

（5）任何对资格申请作出回应的人都应遵守本法的规定和招标文件中对投标人的指示。

（6）如果理事会确定本部分不适用于公私合营项目，理事会应通知缔约方，该项目可以进入招标阶段。

（7）理事会应就根据第（6）款作出的决定发布指导方针。

47. 私人当事方的资格

（1）有意对第46条规定的资格申请作出回应的私人当事方，可以作为私人当事方联合体的一部分予以回应。

（2）如果私人当事方或联合体符合以下条件，则该私人当事方或联合体有资格做出回应——

（a）满足缔约方发出的资格申请中规定的标准；

（b）具备承担拟议项目的技术和财政能力；

（c）具有与缔约方签订项目协议的法律资格；

（d）没有资不抵债、处于接管、破产或正在清算的过程中；和

（e）没有因任何原因被缔约方禁止与缔约方签订项目协议。

48. 资格预审委员会

（1）根据第44条发出通知后，缔约方应成立资格预审委员会，以对投标人进行资格预审。

（2）缔约方认为适当时，可组成项目评审组作为资格预审委员会，以根据第（1）款对投标人进行资格预审。

49. 私人当事方的资格取消

（1）根据第48条组成的资格预审委员会应审查提交给缔约方的资格申请，并编制合格投标人的入围名单。

（2）如果投标人有下列情形，则应在预审环节被取消资格——

（a）提交虚假、不准确或不完整的信息；

（b）串通、纵容或参与任何腐败或不诚实的行为，意图在中标过程中获得对其他投标人不公平的优势；

（c）不符合资格申请中规定的任何合格标准；或者

（d）违反本法或其他任何法律的规定，以便在中标过程中获得对其他投标人不公平的优势。

（3）被取消资格的投标人可以根据第（2）款的规定，在接到取消资格通知的14天内，以规定的形式向申诉委员会提出申请，对其资格被取消提出异议。

（4）申诉委员会须在申请提交后的28天内，听取并裁定根据第（3）款提出的异议。

50. 招标书

（1）缔约方应与理事会协商，在准备合格投标人名单后，编制与项目有关的招标文件，以便邀请合格的投标人投标。

（2）根据第（1）款准备的招标文件应包括以下信息——

- （a）编制和提交标书所需的与项目相关的一般信息；
- （b）项目规范，包括投标人应满足的技术和财务条件；
- （c）成品的规格、服务水平、性能指标和其他必要要求，包括投标人应满足的安全、安保和环境保护要求；
- （d）项目协议的基本条款，包括不可谈判的条件；
- （e）评标时使用的标准和方法；
- （f）需要投标人填写和提交的表格和文件；
- （g）投标人需要提交的投标保证金；
- （h）投标澄清的条件、程序和管理；
- （i）投标人提交投标文件的日期、时间和地点；
- （j）必要时，关于投标前会议的说明；
- （k）任何联合体在其变更允许方面应满足的条件；
- （l）竞争性对话过程中应遵循的程序；和
- （m）项目在招标阶段正常进行所可能需要的任何其他事项。

51. 提交标书

（1）有意根据本法参与项目竞标的投标人应完成并提交技术和财务投标。

（2）投标人应按照缔约方规定的方式，以单独的密封信函提交技术和财务标书。

52. 竞争性对话

（1）经理事会批准，缔约方可与每个入围投标人进行竞争性谈话，以确定项目的技术或财务。

（2）缔约方可以要求每个投标人提交一份不具约束力的技术和财务提案，作为与缔约方竞争性对话的一部分。

（3）竞争性对话应在平等和透明的基础上与每个投标人进行。

（4）竞争性对话期间进行的讨论不得由讨论的任何一方透露给任何人。

（5）在竞争性对话阶段结束时，缔约方可以——

- （a）更改项目规范、风险矩阵或结构；和
- （b）重新对项目进行资格预审。

（6）如果缔约方重新开始资格预审，应邀请参加竞争性对话的每个投标人提交最佳和最终报价，作为评标和授标的依据。

53. 联合体投标

（1）为根据本法进行项目投标而组成的联合体，可以以联合体的名义提交标书。

（2）联合体的投标应附有由联合体成员签署的经公证的具有约束力的协议。

（3）联合体应——

- （a）根据联合体成员承担项目的技术、财务和经验能力，从其成员中任命一个人担

任联合体的牵头成员,代表联合体与缔约方进行交易;和

(b) 向缔约方提交联合体牵头成员的任命通知。

(4) 如果联合体的成员拥有该公司的多数股权或控制其管理,对于联合体的投标,该成员不得直接或间接地,或通过另一个联合体,或通过提交投标的公司提交单独的投标。

(5) 凡违反本部分规定提交投标的联合体,缔约方应取消其投标资格。

(6) 当联合体的成员退出联合体时,缔约方可以——

(a) 取消该联合体参与投标过程的资格;或者

(b) 审查与联合体签订的项目协议的条款。

(7) 如果联合体解雇其牵头成员或者牵头成员退出联合体,缔约方应当取消该联合体的投标资格。

(8) 如果联合体用其他人替换牵头成员以确保该联合体仍有资格参与投标,则第(7)款不适用。

(9) 提交投标的联合体各成员应——

(a) 受项目协议条款的连带约束;和

(b) 共同负责履行本协议项下的义务。

(10) 内阁秘书可与理事会协商,制定条例以更好地实施本部分条款。

54. 提案评审小组

(1) 缔约方应与理事会协商,组成一个提案评审小组,以评估根据本法提交的投标文件。

(2) 提案评审小组应——

(a) 按照招标文件中规定的程序和理事会为此目的发布的任何指导方针开标和评审标书;和

(b) 根据招标文件中规定的评估和授予标准来评估标书。

55. 评标和评标报告

(1) 提案评审小组应在 28 天内按照招标文件中规定的程序和理事会规定的指导方针对技术和财务标书进行评估,并编制评标报告,具体说明——

(a) 评估标准;

(b) 与其他投标人相比,排名第一的投标人如何满足招标文件规定的要求;

(c) 缔约方应考虑的其他必要信息;和

(d) 排名第一的备用投标人。

(2) 提案评审小组应将评审报告及其建议提交给缔约方的会计主管批准。

(3) 如果会计主管对评审委员会的建议不满意,可以将评审报告退回提案评审小组,并提出审核报告的建议。

(4) 评审结束后 7 日内无异议,缔约方应向理事会提交评估报告。

56. 投标人违约

(1) 投标人不符合投标文件规定或根据本法制定的规章时,提案评审小组应当拒绝投标人的投标。

(2) 投标人不符合投标文件规定或根据本法制定的规章时,提案评审小组可以拒绝其提供的所有投标书。

(3) 如果提案评审小组根据本部分拒绝提交提案,该提案评审小组应向会计主管提交一份报告,说明拒绝的原因。

(4) 会计主管应在收到第(3)款规定的报告后 14 日内,将缔约方拒绝投标的决定通知投标人。

(5) 根据本条规定,被拒绝投标的投标人无权获得赔偿。

(6) 根据本部分规定,如果在给定的招标过程中,所有投标均被拒绝,则招标过程应被视为因投标人未能遵守投标要求而终止,缔约方应与理事会协商,确定是否重新启动招标程序。

57. 谈判

(1) 缔约方应与理事会协商,组成一个谈判委员会,该委员会应——

  (a) 根据第 38、40、45 或 46 条与排名第一的投标人进行谈判;

  (b) 对于根据第 46 条进行的谈判,要求排名第二的投标人或招标文件可能表明的任何数量的投标人在与排名第一的投标人完成谈判之前延长其投标的有效期;

  (c) 任命一个由理事会领导的谈判委员会:

但缔约方在理事会的许可下,负责领导流程的特定部分的谈判。

(2) 除其他要素外,谈判委员会与排名第一的投标人之间的谈判——

  (a) 涵盖项目协议的技术、商业、法律、社会、环境、本土化和财务条款;和

  (b) 受招标文件或根据第 44 条颁发的批准中可能明确规定的任何限制约束。

(3) 谈判各方的谈判和决议不得——

  (a) 改变中标的标准;

  (b) 影响招标书中规定的不可协商的条款和条件;

  (c) 改变项目的财务结构;

  (d) 影响适用于私人当事方发起提案的条件;

  (e) 影响投标人在投标书或提案中未提出保留意见的条件。

(4) 尽管有第(3)款的规定,但根据汇率变动或通货膨胀引起的变动而调整投标价格,此种情形不应被视为涨价调整:

但招标文件应明确规定,汇率变动或通货膨胀引起的变动不应被视为涨价调整。

(5) 谈判各方不得修改谈判的条款和评标条款。

(6) 谈判委员会与排名第一的投标人谈判不成功的,谈判委员会应与排名第二的投标人进行谈判。

(7) 第(2)、(3)、(4)、(5)款的规定适用于与排名第二的投标人的谈判。

(8) 谈判委员会应按照理事会规定的指导方针进行谈判,包括委员会与投标人之间谈判期限的指导方针。

58. 项目和风险评估报告

(1) 根据第 57 条结束谈判后,谈判委员会应向缔约方提交项目和财务风险评估报告,其中应详细说明谈判条款、项目的或有负债和委员会的建议。

(2) 如果缔约方对谈判委员会的建议满意,应将项目和财务风险评估报告提交理事会批准。

(3) 如果理事会对谈判委员会的建议不满意,应书面通知缔约方,并说明相应的理由。

（4）如果缔约方已根据第（3）款收到通知,则缔约方应将项目和财务风险评估报告连同理事会根据第（3）款发出的通知一起提交给谈判委员会,并要求委员会审查该报告。

（5）第（1）款和第（2）款经必要修改后,适用于根据第（4）款对报告进行的审查。

59. 委员会审批项目和财务风险评估报告

（1）理事会应将项目和财务风险评估报告和其建议提交委员会审批。

（2）委员会应审议根据第（1）款提交的报告,如果满意,则在收到根据第（1）款提交的报告后的28日内批准缔约方与中标人签署项目协议。

60. 项目审批

（1）委员会应在审批后的30日内将项目和财务风险评估报告的审批书面通知缔约方。

（2）根据第（1）款的通知,缔约方应准备其与投标人之间的项目协议的最终草案,并提交总检察长批准,如果批准,则将其提交给投标人执行。

（3）缔约方应书面通知——

（a）参与委员会决定的投标过程中的所有投标人；和

（b）委员会内阁批准与中标人签订项目协议。

61. 项目协议的执行

（1）根据第60条的规定获得批准后,缔约方应与中标人签订项目协议。

（2）根据第（1）款执行合同的私人当事方应在合同执行之日起12个月内启动项目。

（3）如果私人当事方未能按照第（2）款的规定启动项目,缔约方应终止合同,缔约方或政府不承担任何责任。

62. 投标的取消

（1）如果符合公共利益,缔约方可以在签署项目协议之前的任何时候取消招标过程。

（2）尽管有第（1）款的规定,除非委员会和总检察长批准取消投标,否则缔约方不得取消投标。

（3）根据第（1）款规定进行的取消应通过向投标人发出书面通知的方式进行,并应说明取消的原因。

（4）被取消投标的投标人无权因取消而造成的任何损失获得赔偿。

（5）就本条而言,如果存在以下情况,公共利益将受到损害——

（a）由于重大技术变革或不可抗力事件,该项目已被法律取代或淘汰；

（b）有证据表明,投标明显高于市场价格；

（c）明显发现重大治理问题；

（d）所有已评估的投标书均无响应；

（e）发生内乱、敌对行动或武装冲突,导致项目无法实施；或者

（f）触犯《反腐败和经济犯罪法》（2003）（2003年第3号）或《犯罪所得和反洗钱法》（2009）（2009年第9号）所订罪行的犯罪证据。

63. 待议会审批的协议

根据本法与私人当事方就自然资源开发签订项目协议时,负责合同授权的内阁秘书应根据《宪法》第71条和与自然资源的开发、保护或管理有关的相关法律,将项目提交议会审批。

第六部分
郡政府的公私合营

64. 郡政府项目协议

（1）郡政府可以根据本部分规定与私人当事方签订公私合营协议，以开展公私合营项目。

（2）与私人当事方签订公私合营协议的郡政府应负责项目开发全周期的管理。

（3）拟承接公私合营项目的郡政府应根据第32条对该项目进行详细的可行性研究。

（4）拟开展公私合营项目的郡政府应在项目的每个阶段与理事会联络。

（5）如果根据第(3)款进行的可行性研究表明该项目符合以下条件，则郡政府承办公私合营项目，应当获得负责财务相关事宜的委员会和内阁秘书的书面批准——

  （a）需要政府采取支持措施；或者

  （b）超出郡政府实施该项目的财政能力。

（6）各郡政府应向理事会提交根据第(3)款编制的所有可行性研究报告。

65. 郡议会批准

（1）根据第64条第(5)款，拟开展公私合营项目的各郡政府应在开展项目前，获得各自郡议会的批准。

（2）郡政府的公私合营项目需要政府支持措施的，未经内阁秘书书面批准，郡政府不得承接该项目或签订项目协议。

66. 郡项目清单

（1）拟根据本法实施公私合营项目的郡政府或郡公司应向理事会提交项目清单，以将其纳入第26条下公布的国家项目清单。

（2）除非项目是郡综合发展计划的一部分，否则郡政府或郡公司不得提交项目清单。

67. 第五部分的适用

经必要修改后，第五部分的规定应适用于郡政府的公私合营项目。

第七部分
项目公司，披露和项目协议

68. 项目公司

（1）在签署项目协议时，缔约方和中标人应根据《公司法》(2015)（2015年第17号）成立一家项目公司，以承接项目。

（2）根据第(1)款设立的项目公司——

  （a）可包括一个作为公司少数股东的公共实体；和

  （b）应提供履约保证金，并满足项目协议中规定的条件，以及内阁秘书根据本法制定的条例中规定的条件；

（3）未经缔约方书面批准，项目公司董事不得解散公司、改变其法律结构或减少公司股本,缔约方不得无理拒绝批准。

（4）在缔约方根据项目协议出具工程质量验收书之前,项目公司的大股东不得转让其在项目公司的股份,也不得允许其在项目公司的多数股权被稀释至其失去大股东的地位。

（5）尽管有第(4)款的规定,项目协议的任何一方在内阁秘书的批准下,可根据需要重组项目公司的股权,以确保交易的股权分配：

但项目公司的股权重组不得——

（a）更改项目协议中批准的债务和股权之间的整体分割；和

（b）稀释联合体牵头成员在项目公司股权结构中的控股地位。

（6）尽管有《公司法》(2015)(2015年第17号)的规定,如果股份转让导致项目公司的控制权落入第三方,除非股东已申请并获得缔约方的书面批准,否则转让无效。

（7）除为项目融资外,项目公司不得质押其股份。

（8）在根据本条授予批准时,内阁秘书应根据委员会的建议行事,但如果有合理的理由确定所请求的股权变更会阻碍公共设施或服务的交付保证,内阁秘书也可以拒绝批准。

（9）内阁秘书应与理事会协商,制定条例,以更好地实施本部分。

69. 公布项目协议执行信息

（1）缔约方在签署项目协议时,应在至少两种全国发行的报纸和电子媒体上公布招标结果和下列信息——

（a）项目性质和项目协议的关键条款；

（b）项目下拟开发的工程或拟提供的公共服务；

（c）中标人；

（d）承诺用于该项目的任何公共资金的数额；

（e）项目关税(如适用)；

（f）为项目提供的任何政府支持措施；

（g）项目的社会和经济效益；

（h）项目的持续时间；

（i）项目移交给缔约方时的预期资产质量；和

（j）在项目开展期间对项目进行监测和报告的方式。

（2）理事会可以规定缔约方公布第(1)款指定的信息的方式。

（3）内阁秘书应与理事会协商制定条例,以更好地实施本部分条款。

70. 项目协议各方的最低义务

（1）本法项下项目协议的各方应明确规定各方应履行的如附录三所列最低限度的义务。

（2）尽管有第(1)款的规定,如果项目的收入表现达到并超过根据项目协议商定的目标投资回报率,则每个项目协议都应规定私人当事方与政府之间的收入分享机制和阈值。

（3）内阁秘书可以制定条例,明确项目协议的拟定方式。

71. 适用法律

（1）本法项下的项目协议应遵守肯尼亚法律的规定,项目协议中的任何相反规定均无效。

（2）根据附录三第18条,项目协议各方可同意通过仲裁或项目协议中可能规定的任何其他非司法争议解决手段,解决项目协议项下产生的任何争议。

72. 项目协议的修改和变更

（1）项目协议的一方如果拟就协议中规定的条款和条件、项目的产出或协议中规定的任何豁免条款对协议进行任何修改或变更，可以与另一方就拟议的修改、变更或豁免进行谈判：

但该修改、变更或豁免除非经委员会和总检察长批准，否则不得生效。

（2）根据第（1）款对项目协议的修改、变更或豁免不应获得批准，除非证明该协议经如此修改、变更或豁免，确保——

(i) 该项目继续提供物有所值的服务；

(ii) 如果此类修改、变更或豁免涉及财务问题，经理事会核实，该项目继续进行；

(iii) 继续向私人当事方转移适当的风险；

(iv) 持续提供高效和有效的公共服务；和

(v) 持续保护和维护环境。

（3）根据第（2）款作出的任何批准均须以书面形式作出。

73. 项目管理

（1）作为项目协议一方的缔约方应与行业监管机构一起，在理事会的指导下，为项目协议建立并实施合同管理框架，以达到以下目的——

(a) 监测项目协议的执行情况；

(b) 衡量项目的产出；

(c) 与协议的另一方、设施或服务的用户或其他相关利益相关者联络；

(d) 监督项目协议的管理；

(e) 编制关于项目实施情况的半年度报告；

(f) 向理事会提交项目实施报告；

(g) 实施根据本法发布的相关建议和指导方针；

(h) 提交理事会可能要求的与项目监督有关的信息；和

(i) 提交公共债务管理办公室可能要求的与或有负债管理有关的信息。

（2）项目各方应与理事会协调，任命一名独立专家，根据理事会规定的条款管理项目协议的实施。

（3）根据第（2）款聘请独立专家的费用应构成项目费用的一部分，由私人当事方承担。

（4）涉及私人当事方履行缔约方职能的项目协议不应免除缔约方确保有效和高效履行该职能的责任。

（5）涉及私人当事方使用缔约方资产的项目协议不应免除缔约方确保资产免受没收、盗窃、损失和浪费等可能对资产产生负面影响的因素影响的责任。

（6）理事会应就本法项下每个项目的实施情况对缔约方进行监督并提供必要的指导。

（7）如果理事会根据本部分和第71条确定利益分配时出现不平衡，并且为了促进与项目相关的经济利益持续向肯尼亚公民转移，理事会应与缔约方协商，根据第71条启动项目协议的修改或变更。

（8）行业监管机构应根据内阁秘书依本法制定的条例，监督缔约方和私人当事方在实施本法项下的项目中的表现。

74. 借调缔约方雇员

（1）应项目公司的要求，缔约方可以向公司提供根据本法实施项目所需的雇员。

（2）借调到项目公司的雇员，在借调期间应被视为本公司的雇员，只受该公司的指导和控制。

（3）借调到项目公司的缔约方雇员，在借调期间应按相同或改进的服务条款借调。

75. 申诉委员会

（1）设立一个称为申诉委员会的委员会，该委员会负责听取和裁定有关委员会、理事会或缔约方根据本法作出的任何决定的申诉。

（2）申诉委员会由内阁秘书任命的下列人员组成——

（a）主席，须为符合资格被委任为高等法院法官的人；

（b）具有内阁秘书认为适当的相关知识和经验的其他 4 人；

（c）2 名非郡执行委员会成员，其拥有内阁秘书认为适当的相关知识和经验，由郡长理事会提名。

（3）申诉委员会委员任期 3 年，可以连任一届；

（4）在缴付规定费用后，对理事会、委员会或缔约方关于招标过程或项目协议的决定不服的人可以以规定形式向申诉委员会提交申诉，以复核该决定。

（5）根据本部分提出的申诉应在理事会、委员会或缔约方做出决定之日起 7 日内提出。

（6）申诉委员会应在提交申诉之日起 28 日内听取并裁定申诉。

（7）对委员会的决定不服的人可以在该决定作出后 7 日内以规定的形式向委员会提出复核申请。

（8）对申诉委员会的决定不服的，可在委员会作出决定之日起 14 日内向高等法院提出上诉。

（9）内阁秘书可通过条例规定听取和裁定申诉的程序以及本部分规定的费用。

76. 秘书

（1）内阁秘书应指定一名公职人员担任委员会秘书。

（2）根据第（1）款指定的人员须为肯尼亚高等法院的辩护律师，任期至少 7 年。

77. 报酬

应向委员会成员支付内阁秘书与薪酬委员会协商确定的工资和津贴。

78. 利益冲突

在委员会审议的事项中存在直接或间接利益的委员会成员，应申报利害关系，且不得参与委员会关于该事项的任何程序。

79. 罪行

（1）任何人不得——

（a）无合理理由或合法辩解，阻碍或妨碍、攻击或威胁根据本法行事的委员会成员；

（b）无正当理由，未能提供委员会根据本法要求提供的信息；

（c）无正当理由，未能在合理时间内提供委员会根据本法要求提供的信息；

（d）向委员会提交虚假或误导性信息；

（e）对根据本法行事的委员会成员进行虚假陈述或故意误导；或者

（f）干涉委员会任何成员或对其施加不当影响。

（2）任何人违反第（1）款规定，即属犯罪，一经定罪，可处以不超过 50 万先令的罚款或不超过1年的监禁,或两者并罚。

80. 法令

委员会应发布一项法令,阐明其对特定事项的决定,该法令应以与法院法令相同的方式执行。

第八部分
财 务 规 定

81. 公私合营项目促进基金

(1) 设立公私合营项目促进基金作为本法的融资机制。

(2) 基金的来源应包括——

(a) 归入基金的赠款、礼物、捐赠或其他捐赠;

(b) 可能对项目征收的税款或关税;

(c) 项目公司根据本法支付的成交费用;

(d) 援助拨款;

(e) 根据本法或任何法律可归属或应归属于本基金的款项;和

(f) 内阁秘书可能批准的任何其他来源的资金。

(3) 本基金收到的款项应用于——

(a) 根据本法,在项目准备阶段、招标过程和项目评估中支持缔约方;

(b) 根据本法支持理事会和委员会的活动;和

(c) 将可行性缺口融资扩大到需要但在缺乏政府财政支持的情况下无法实施的项目。

(4) 基金应按照内阁秘书根据《公共财政管理法》(2012)(2012年第18号)制定的规定进行管理。

82. 财务报告、审计和项目执行报告

(1) 项目公司或项目协议的私人当事方应保存和维护与项目有关的适当账簿和记录。

(2) 根据第(1)款保存和维护的账簿应在得到合理通知后,开放供缔约方或理事会审查。

(3) 如果项目有包括公共资金在内的对应资金,审计长应审计项目公司的账目。

(4) 如果一个项目的所有资金都是由私人当事方提供的,项目公司的账目由与国家财政部协商指定的信誉良好的审计公司每年进行审计。

(5) 项目公司或项目协议的私人当事方应在每个财政年度结束后的6个月内,提交经审计的财务账目和缔约方或理事会可能合理要求的任何其他信息。

(6) 项目公司应在项目协议中规定的期限内,在任何情况下,每年至少编制并向缔约方和理事会提交一次项目执行情况报告和监测报告。

第九部分
其 他 规 定

83. 本土化

(1) 项目协议各方在进行与项目有关的活动时——

（a）优先考虑在肯尼亚提供的服务；

（b）优先考虑在肯尼亚制造的符合相关行业规范的供应品；

（c）确保当地的技术转让机制；

（d）优化肯尼亚商品和服务在肯尼亚境外的贸易优惠机会；

（e）促进结构化的企业社会责任方案；和

（f）遵守任何其他肯尼亚现行或适用的法律和政策规定。

（2）委员会应根据理事会的建议，根据肯尼亚经济的优先要求，发布必要的本土化的指导方针、标准和操作说明。

84. 罪行及处罚

（1）任何人有以下行为，即属犯罪——

（a）阻碍或妨碍他人根据本法履行职责或职能或者行使权力；

（b）故意欺骗或误导根据本法履行职责或职能或者行使权力的人员；

（c）无正当理由延误——

（i）超出规定期限开标或评标；

（ii）超出规定期限授予合同；或者

（iii）超出项目协议和履约义务规定的期限向承包商付款；

（d）对评估委员会的任何成员，或者理事会或缔约方的雇员或代理人，或者会计主管施加不当影响或施加压力，以采取有利于或倾向于特定一方的特定行动；

（e）泄露与本法规定的任何机密程序有关的机密信息；

（f）不正当地影响评标；

（g）实施投标文件条款明确禁止的行为；

（h）违反本法或根据其制定的条例签署项目协议或其他标书；

（i）故意违反本法的任何规定；或者

（j）实施欺诈行为。

（2）任何主体被判犯有本条规定的罪行，一经定罪，应承担以下责任——

（a）如果该主体是自然人，则处以不超过200万先令的罚款或不超过5年的监禁，或两者并罚；

（b）如果该主体是法人团体，则处以不超过1 000万先令的罚款。

（3）除第（2）款规定的处罚外——

（a）国家官员或公职人员如被裁定犯有本部分规定的罪行，则应受到纪律处分；

（b）非国家官员或公职人员如被裁定犯有本部分规定的罪行，则禁止其参与本法规定的任何公私合营项目；和

（c）法人团体应被政府禁止参与本法项下的任何公私合营项目。

（4）如果根据本法参与投标程序的个人或其雇员或代理人违反本法的规定，则——

（a）该人、雇员或代理人将被取消签订任何涉及该项目协议的资格；或者

（b）如果已经与该人签订了项目协议，则理事会可以选择撤销该合同。

（5）理事会可向相关专业机构提出申诉，要求对违反本法规定的专业机构成员提起纪律处分。

（6）专业机构根据第（5）款提出的申诉所施加的处罚，应适用于本法项下可能施加的其他任何处罚。

85. 国家官员或公职人员根据本法参与投标

（1）国家官员或公职人员不得直接或间接参与本法项下的任何投标。

（2）本部分适用于利用其配偶、子女或商业伙伴，或其持有股份或以其他方式控制或指示的公司，参与本法项下投标的国家官员或公职人员。

（3）国家官员或公职人员违反本部分规定，即属犯罪，一经定罪，将被处以不超过200万先令的罚款或不超过5年的监禁，或两者并罚。

86. 检查公私合营处所等

私人当事方应根据缔约方或理事会的要求，准予缔约方或理事会的代理人或雇员进入项目场所、现场，和访问存储设施以及记录，以便于根据项目协议的条款进行检查。

87. 2003年第3号第五、六部分的适用

《反腐败和经济犯罪法》（2003）（2003年第3号）第五部分规定的犯罪以及第六部分规定的对不正当利益的赔偿和追偿，经必要修改后应适用于本法。

88. 年度报告

（1）理事会应在每年6月30日之后的3个月内，编制并向委员会提交一份关于肯尼亚公私合营状况的报告。

（2）尽管有第（1）款的一般性规定，年度报告应详述以下内容——

（a）肯尼亚的公私合营状况；

（b）肯尼亚正在实施的公私合营的数量、类型和价值；

（c）在肯尼亚实施公私合营的缔约方；

（d）缔约方已采取的政府支持措施和给予对象；

（e）根据本法被禁止或列入黑名单的私人当事方；

（f）被取消的公私合营投标的数量、类型和价值；

（g）经批准的公私合营企业的或有负债价值（如有）；

（h）已完成和由私人当事方正在运营的项目的财务报告；和

（i）任何其他相关的信息。

（3）内阁秘书应向议会提交年度报告的副本。

89. 条例

（1）为更好地实施本法的规定，内阁秘书一般可以制定条例。

（2）根据第（1）款制定的条例应包括以下内容——

（a）本法项下委员会或理事会职能的执行；和

（b）本法项下基础设施或开发项目的融资、建设、运营、装备和维护。

（3）就宪法第94条第（6）款而言——

（a）根据本部分授权的目的和目标是使内阁秘书能够制定规则，以更好地实施本法的规定；

（b）内阁秘书根据本法制定条例的权限仅限于实施本法的规定和实现本部分规定的目标；

(c) 本部分规则适用的原则和标准是《释义及通则条例》(第2章)和《法定条规法》(2013)(2013年第23号)中规定的原则和标准。

第十部分
救济和过渡性规定

90. 释义

在本部分中,除非上下文另有所指,否则——

(a) "已废除法"是指根据第93条废除的《公私合营法》(2013)(2013年第15号);

(b) "前委员会"是指本法生效前存在的公私合营委员会;

(c) "前申诉委员会"是指本法生效前存在的申诉委员会;和

(d) "前单位"是指本法生效前存在的公私合营单位;

91. 成员及工作人员

(1) 在本法生效前是前委员会成员的人员,在本法生效后,应被视为已根据本法被任命为委员会成员,任期届满。

(2) 在本法生效前是前申诉委员会成员的人员,在本法生效后,应被视为已根据本法被任命为申诉委员会成员,任期届满。

(3) 本法生效前是前单位公职人员的每个人员,在本法生效后,应根据本法生效之前适用的相同合同条款,被视为理事会官员。

92. 救济

(1) 前委员会或前理事会在本法生效前制定或发布的与公私合营有关的任何法规、标准、指南、程序或批准,只要该法规、标准、指南、程序或批准与本法不相抵触,应被视为已根据本法制定或发布。

(2) 向前申诉委员会提交的任何申诉,如果在本法生效时,尚未被审理或裁决,应被视为已根据本法提交,并应得到审理和裁决。

(3) 在本法生效前已由前委员会或内阁批准的项目清单,视情况而定,应被视为已根据本法获得委员会或内阁的批准。

(4) 缔约方和私人当事方根据被废除的法案签订的任何项目协议,应被视为根据本法签订:

但对根据被废除法案签订的任何项目协议的有效性提出质疑的任何申诉,应根据被废除法案的规定进行审理和裁决。

93. 废除

《公私合营法》(2013)(2013年第15号)被废除。

附录一
关于委员会的业务和事务的管理规定
[第12条第(1)款]

1. 会议

(1) 委员会在肯尼亚举行会议的地点由主席决定,会议由主席召集。

（2）委员会在每个财政年度应至少召开4次会议，每2次会议之间的间隔不得超过3个月。

（3）除非四分之三的成员同意，否则理事会总干事应至少提前7天书面通知每位成员参加会议。

（4）主席可自行决定，或应委员会半数以上成员的书面请求并在提出请求后7日内，在其指定的时间和地点召开临时会议。

（5）会议由主席主持，主席缺席时由副主席主持。

（6）委员会成员应从其中选出一名副主席——

（a）在委员会第一次会议上；和

（b）在有必要填补副主席职位的空缺时。

（7）主席或副主席缺席时，由委员会成员从其中推荐一人主持委员会会议。

（8）委员会可邀请任何人出席其会议并参与其审议，但该人对委员会的任何决定均无表决权。

2. 利益冲突

（1）任何人如果在委员会审议的项目、拟议合同或任何事项中拥有个人或信托利益，并且出席了审议该类事项的委员会会议，在会议开始后，该人应在切实可行的情况下，尽快申报该等利益，并不得参与对涉及该等事项的任何问题的审议、讨论或投票。

（2）根据第（1）款作出的利益披露，应记录在作出披露的会议记录内。

（3）委员会应通过行为准则和利益冲突政策，以更好地管理委员会事务。

3. 法定人数

（1）在符合第（2）款规定的情况下，会议的法定人数不得少于委员会成员的一半。

（2）如果出席委员会会议的人未达到本法规定的召开会议所需的法定人数，或由于某成员被排除在会议之外，出席会议的成员人数低于召开会议所需的法定人数，则委员会应推迟对相关事项的审议，直至达到法定人数。

4. 投票表决

委员会提出的问题应由出席并参加表决成员的简单多数决定，在票数相等的情况下，主席有权投决定票。

5. 议事规则和会议记录

委员会须——

（a）确定开展业务的程序规则；和

（b）记录其程序和决定。

附录二
公私合营安排
[第21条]

1. 管理合同，即在不超过10年的规定期限内，由私人当事方负责管理和履行特定义务，并且缔约方保留对所有设施、资本资产和财产的所有权和控制权。

2. 基于绩效合同，在不超过10年的规定期限内由私人当事方负责基础设施的运营、维护和管理,并且缔约方保留设施和资本资产的所有权。

3. 租赁,即私人当事方向缔约方支付租金或特许权使用费,管理、经营和维护设施或将租赁财产用于矿产勘探、生产和开发,并在不超过30年的规定期限内从消费者处收取服务或产品销售的费用和利益。

4. 棕地特许经营权,即缔约方向私人当事方颁发合同许可证,以运营、维护、修复或升级基础设施,收取使用费,并向缔约方支付特许经营费,期限不超过30年。

5. 建设—拥有—运营—转让计划,即由私人当事方设计、建造、融资、运营和维护私人当事方拥有的基础设施,期限不超过30年,或商定的更长期限,之后私人当事方可将设施转让给缔约方。

6. 建设—拥有—运营计划,即私人当事方设计、融资、建造、运营和维护基础设施,并在指定的时间内提供服务。

7. 建设—运营—转让计划,即由私人当事方资助、建设、运营和维护基础设施,并在不超过30年的规定期限结束时将设施转让给缔约方。

8. 建设—租赁—转让,即由缔约方授权私人当事方融资和建设基础设施或开发设施,并在完工后将其出租给缔约方,规定期限不超过30年,期满后设施的所有权自动从私人当事方转让给缔约方。

9. 建设—转让—运营,即由私人当事方建设基础设施,并承担与建设施工相关的成本和风险,完工后将设施的所有权转让给缔约方,并代表缔约方继续运营该设施,期限不超过30年。

10. 建筑转让,即由私人当事方设计、建造和资助公共设施,以换取缔约方在规定期限内的付款,之后在不超过20年的规定期限内自动转让给缔约方。

11. 开发—运营—转让,即通过赋予该私人当事方开发毗邻物业的权利,将拟建基础设施项目私人当事方的外部有利条件纳入安排,并享有双方约定的投资利益,条件是私人当事方在项目开始后不超过30年的期限内将基础设施转让给缔约方,而开发的物业将永远属于私人当事方。

12. 修复—运营—转让,即由私人当事方在不超过30年的规定期限内翻新、运营和维护现有设施,到期后私人当事方将设施转让给缔约方。

13. 修复—拥有—运营,即缔约方将现有设施转让给私人当事方进行翻新和运营,对其所有权没有时间限制,并且私人当事方在设施运营期间应遵守安排的条件。

14. 基于年金的设计、建造、融资和运营,即缔约方授权私人当事方设计、融资、建造、运营或维护公共基础设施,作为交换,私人当事方在不超过30年的规定期限内收到规定的年金款项,期满后设施自动转回缔约方。

15. 合营伙伴关系,即缔约方和私人当事方合作共同开发公共设施,缔约方为项目指定土地等公共资产,并根据具体情况采取各种政府支持措施,私人当事方主要负责公共基础设施的融资、建设和维护,期限不超过30年。

16. 战略伙伴关系,即公共机构根据其可能同意的条款,邀请战略私人当事方共同制定公共投资计划,但根据该协议,包括建设、融资和运营在内的关键项目风险由该私人当事方承担,并且该协议可能有一个确定的结束日期或一组确定的参数,以支持该伙伴关系随时间调整,但不超过30年。

17. 土地交换,即缔约方将现有公共土地或资产转让给私人当事方,以换取私人当事方已开发的资产或设施。

附录三
项目协议中规定的最低合同义务
[第69条]

1. 双方应开展的工程和服务的性质、范围及其实施条件。
2. 缔约方、项目公司(如适用)和贷款人与项目有关的权利,包括贷款人的介入权。
3. 项目协议一方将出资的任何财产的说明。
4. 与项目相关的任何公共设施及其责任的说明。
5. 项目资产的归属,项目场地交接相关各方的义务。
6. 获得授权、许可和批准的责任。
7. 缔约方与私人当事方之间任何收入分配的说明。
8. 相互财务义务及其与融资机制的关系,包括与履约保证金和担保有关的要求。
9. 编制和提交财务报告和其他报告,并进行与项目有关的财务审计。
10. 项目所依据的产品销售价格或服务可用性款项,以及通过增加或减少的方式确定和修正相关规则,以及反映通货膨胀或利率变化的指数化机制(如需要)。
11. 对工程运行、使用和维护的质量保证、质量控制和监督,以及行政、财务和技术监测的手段。
12. 缔约方更改项目条件和对私人当事方施加其他义务的权利范围,以及此类更改命令造成的任何损失的赔偿依据和机制。
13. 项目应投保的保险种类及其操作或使用的风险、签发有利于缔约方的行政担保,以及签发该等担保的规定和程序。
14. 法律变更、不可预见事故、不可抗力或文物发现(视情况而定)的风险分配基础,以及由此产生的赔偿。
15. 合同期限。
16. 在项目协议期满前一方可提前终止合同,及与终止有关的各方权利。
17. 项目协议一方在项目协议期满或终止时,移交项目的过程。
18. 争议解决机制,包括通过仲裁或任何其他友好的争议解决机制解决纠纷。
19. 赔偿事项及赔偿或罚款的支付机制。
20. 承担项目时所需的履约保证金、价值和续约机制。
21. 独立专家的任命。
22. 本土化要求。
23. 直接协议和贷款人权利(如适用)。
24. 项目协议的终止和到期。
25. 缔约各方的义务、承诺和保证。
26. 在私人当事方违约的情况下,缔约方或贷款人紧急介入的情形。

第二编
劳 动 法 规

第五部
就业法（2007年第11号法令）

2023修订版 [2007]

由全国法律报告委员会经总检察长授权公布

www.kenyalaw.org

第一部分
总　则

[批准日期：2007 年 10 月 22 日]

[施行日期：2008 年 7 月 2 日]

旨在废除《就业法》，宣布并界定员工的基本权利，提供雇用雇员的基本条件，规范雇用儿童，并对与上述事宜有关的事项作出规定的议会法案

[2007 年第 11 号法令，2008 年第 61 号法律公告，2014 年第 18 号法令，2015 年第 19 号法令，2017 年第 105 号法律公告，2018 年第 10 号法令，2019 年第 23 号法令，2019 年第 24 号法令，2020 年第 20 号法令，2021 年第 2 号法令，2022 年第 15 号法令]

1. 简称

本法可称为《就业法》(2007)。

2. 释义

在本法中，除非上下文另有规定，否则——

"**授权官员**"是指劳工官员、就业官员或医疗官员；

"**基本工资**"是指雇员的工资总额，不包括津贴和其他福利；

"**委员会**"是指国家劳工委员会；

"**内阁秘书**"是指当时负责有关劳工事务的内阁秘书；

"**临时雇员**"是指其聘用条款规定在每天结束时向其支付报酬且每次聘用时间不超过 24 小时的人；

"**儿童**"是指未满 18 周岁的人；

"**集体协议**"是指工会与雇主、雇主团体或雇主组织之间以书面形式签订的关于雇佣条款和条件的注册协议；

"**服务合同**"是指在一段时间内雇用雇员或担任雇员的口头或书面协议，无论是明示的还是暗示的，包括学徒合同和契约学习合同，但不包括适用本法第十一部分规定的外国服务合同；

"**受抚养人**"是指雇员的家庭成员或主要依赖该雇员生活的亲属；

"**处长**"是指被任命为就业处处长的人；

"**残疾**"是指对一个人的社会和经济参与产生不利影响的身体、感官、精神或其他障碍，包括任何视觉、听觉、学习或身体上的残疾；

"**雇员**"是指为工资或薪金而受雇的人，包括学徒和契约学习者；

"**雇员缴款**"根据 2020 年第 20 号法令附录予以删除；

"**雇员收入**"根据 2019 年第 23 号法令第 52 条予以删除；

"**雇主**"是指签订服务合同雇用任何个人的任何人、公共机构、商号、企业或公司，包括该个人、公共机构、商号、企业或公司的代理人、领班、经理或代理商；

"**雇主供款**"是指雇主向国家住房发展基金缴纳的供款；

"**退出证明**"是指已注册的收养协会给予准养父母将儿童从收养协会的监护下带走的书

面授权；

"**强迫或强制劳动**"是指在任何惩罚的威胁下，包括丧失权利或特权的威胁，由从事该工作或者提供该服务的人非自愿提供的任何工作或服务；

"**HIV**"是指人类免疫缺陷病毒；

"**工业经营**"包括——

（a）矿山、采石场和其他从地表或地表下开采任何物质的工程；

（b）制造、加工或包装原材料的工厂或场所；

（c）任何建筑物、铁路、电车轨道、海港、码头、船坞、运河、内陆水路、道路、隧道、桥梁、高架桥、下水道、排水沟、水井、电报或电话装置、电力工程、燃气工程、供水工程或其他建筑工程的施工、重建、维护、修理、改造或拆除以及任何此类工程或构筑物的地基准备或铺设；或者

（d）通过公路、铁路或内陆水路运输乘客或货物，包括在码头、船坞、船埠和仓库处理货物，但不包括手工运输：

但是——

（i）内阁秘书在考虑到任何工业经营中进行的任何雇佣所涉及的工作性质后，如认为合适，可通过命令宣布该雇佣不受本部分有关工业经营规定的约束，因此，就本部分而言，该雇佣应被视为不属于工业经营中的雇佣；

（ii）仅一部分为工业经营的企业，不得仅因该原因被视为工业经营企业；

"**劳工监察员**"是指被任命为劳工监察员的人；

"**劳工官员**"是指被任命为劳工专员、高级副劳工专员、副劳工专员、助理劳工专员、首席劳资关系官、副首席劳资关系官、高级劳工官、劳资关系官员或劳工官员的人员；

"**停工**"是指雇主关闭工作场所或暂停工作或拒绝雇用任何雇员——

（a）以迫使雇主的雇员接受因贸易纠纷请求提出的要求；和

（b）不以终止雇佣为目的；

"**移民工人**"是指为了受雇于雇主而移居肯尼亚的人，包括任何经常被公认为移民工人的人；

"**采矿**"包括从地表或地下开采某种物质的承揽，不论其为公共或私营；

"**部长**"*根据 2015 年第 19 号法令第 143 条（c）项予以删除；*

"**国家住房发展基金**"*根据 2020 年第 20 号法令附录予以删除；*

"**组织**"包括雇员工会和雇主组织；

"**当事人**"是指服务合同的当事人；

"**计件工作**"是指其报酬由完成的工作量所确定的任何工作，而不计其工作所占用的时间；

"**试用合同**"是指雇佣合同，其期限不超过 12 个月或其中的一部分，采用书面形式订立并明确规定试用期；

"**裁员**"是指雇员非因自身的过错而以非自愿方式丧失就业、职业、工作或事业，包括在人员冗余的情况下，在雇主的倡议下终止雇佣关系，这种做法通常表现为撤销职务、工作或职业以及

失业；

"**注册官**"是指工会注册官；

"**报酬**"是指因雇用该雇员而支付或应付给该雇员的所有货币或实物付款的总价值；

"**罢工**"是指雇员集体停止工作，或一致拒绝或根据员工的共识拒绝继续工作，以迫使其雇主或其雇主所属的雇主组织接受与贸易纠纷有关的任何要求；

"**任务**"是指授权官员认为雇员在正常工作日内可以完成的工作量；

"**工会**"是指主要目的是规范雇员与雇主之间关系的雇员协会，包括雇主组织；

"**妇女**"是指年满18周岁的女性；

"**最恶劣的童工形式**"就未成年人而言，是指他们受雇、从事或被使用从事包含以下内容的任何活动：

(a) 一切形式的奴役或类似奴役的做法，例如买卖儿童、债务奴役或实施农奴制以及强迫或强制招募儿童用于武装冲突；

(b) 利用、诱拐或提供儿童进行卖淫、制作色情制品或进行色情表演；

(c) 利用、诱拐或提供儿童从事非法活动，特别是生产和贩运相关国际条约所界定的毒品；

(d) 根据其性质或开展工作的环境，可能会损害儿童的健康、安全或道德的工作；

"**青少年**"是指年满16周岁但未满18周岁的儿童。

［2015年第19号法令，第143条；2018年第10号法令，第85条；2019年第23号法令，第52条；2020年第20号法令，附录；2021年第2号法令，第2条］

3. 适用

（1）本法适用于任何雇主根据服务合同雇用的所有雇员。

（2）本法不适用于——

(a)《肯尼亚国防法》(2012)中分别定义的肯尼亚国防军或预备役人员；

(b) 肯尼亚警方、肯尼亚监狱管理局或行政警察部队人员；

(ba) 肯尼亚海岸警卫队人员；

(c) 国家青年服务处人员；和

(d) 雇主和雇主的受抚养人，其中受抚养人是家族企业中唯一的雇员。

（3）本法对政府具有约束力。

（4）内阁秘书在与国家劳工委员会协商并考虑到肯尼亚批准的所有相关公约和其他国际文件后，就雇员的实质性特殊问题而言，可以通过命令将该类别雇员排除在本法的全部或部分适用范围之外。

（5）内阁秘书在与国家劳工委员会协商后，就雇佣条款和条件受特殊安排约束的雇员而言，可以通过命令将该类别雇员全部或部分排除在本法的适用范围之外：

但是这些安排提供的保护须等同于或优于本法中被排除在外类别的保护；

（6）根据本法的规定，本法规定的雇佣条款和条件应构成雇员的最低雇佣条款和条件，任何放弃、更改或修改本法条款的协议均无效。

［2015年第19号法令，第144条；第2020年第20号法令，附录］

第二部分
一 般 原 则

4. 禁止强迫劳动

（1）任何人不得利用或协助任何其他人招募、贩卖或使用强迫劳动。

（2）"强迫或强制劳动"不应包括——

（a）根据义务兵役法，为纯粹军事性质的工作而要求的任何工作或服务：但强迫或强制招募儿童用于武装冲突应被视为强迫或强制劳动；

（b）构成肯尼亚正常公民义务一部分的任何工作或服务；

（c）任何人因在法庭上被定罪而被迫从事的任何工作或服务，前提是该工作或服务是在公共当局的监督和控制下进行的，并且该人未受雇于私人、公司或协会或由其支配；

（d）在紧急情况下，例如在发生战争、疾病或灾难威胁，危及全体或部分人口的生存或福祉的任何情况下，所要求从事的任何工作或服务；和

（e）社区成员为该社区的直接利益而提供的小型社区服务，但须征求社区成员或其代表的意见。

（3）任何人违反本条规定，即属犯罪，一经定罪，可处以不超过50万先令的罚款或不超过2年的监禁，或两者并罚。

5. 就业歧视

（1）部长、劳工官员和劳资法庭有责任——

（a）促进就业机会平等，以消除就业歧视；和

（b）促进和保障在肯尼亚境内合法居住的移民工人或移民工人家庭成员的机会平等。

（2）雇主应促进就业机会平等，并努力消除任何就业政策或实践中的歧视。

（3）雇主不得以下列内容为理由直接或间接歧视雇员或潜在雇员、骚扰雇员或潜在雇员——

（a）种族、肤色、性别、语言、宗教、政治或其他观点、国籍、民族或社会出身、残疾、怀孕、婚姻状况或艾滋病毒状况；

（b）有关招聘、培训、晋升、雇佣条款和条件、雇佣终止或因雇佣而产生的其他事项。

（4）下列行为不是歧视——

（a）采取与促进平等或消除工作场所歧视相一致的平权措施；

（b）根据工作内在要求区分、排斥或偏袒任何人；

（c）根据国家就业政策雇用公民；或者

（d）在维护国家安全的必要情况下，限制从事限定类别的工作。

（5）用人单位应当对雇员同工同酬。

（6）雇主违反本条的规定，即属犯罪。

(7) 在涉嫌违反本条的任何诉讼中,雇主应承担举证责任,证明歧视并非如所指称的那样,且歧视行为的不作为并非基于任何本部分规定的理由。

(8) 就本条而言——

(a) "雇员"包括求职者;

(b) "雇主"包括职业介绍所;

(c) "就业政策或实践"包括与招聘程序、广告和选拔标准、任命和任命过程、工作分类和分级、薪酬、就业福利和就业条款和条件、工作分配、工作环境和设施、培训和发展、绩效评估制度、晋升、调动、降级、因纪律措施而终止雇佣关系有关的任何政策或实践。

[2008 年第 1 号修正案;2014 年第 18 号法令,附录]

6. 性骚扰

(1) 如果一名雇员的雇主或该雇主的代表或同事,对该雇员有下列行为,则构成性骚扰——

(a) 直接或间接要求该雇员进行性交、性接触或任何其他形式的性活动,其中包含以下内容的暗示或明示——

(i) 在就业中给予优惠待遇的承诺;

(ii) 在就业中给予不利待遇的威胁;或者

(iii) 对雇员当前或未来就业状况的威胁;

(b) 使用书面或口头的性语言;

(c) 使用涉及性的视觉材料;

(d) 表现出直接或间接使雇员难以接受或冒犯该雇员的具有性性质的身体行为,并且该行为本质上对该员工的就业、工作表现或工作满意度产生不利影响。

(2) 雇用 20 名或以上雇员的雇主应在与雇员或其代表(如有)协商后发布关于性骚扰的政策声明。

(3) 第(2)款要求的政策声明可包含雇主认为适合本条的任何术语,并应包含下列事项——

(a) 第(1)款规定的性骚扰定义;

(b) 声明——

(i) 每个雇员都有权获得不受性骚扰的工作;

(ii) 雇主应采取措施确保没有雇员遭受性骚扰;

(iii) 雇主应采取其认为适当的纪律措施,在雇主指示下惩处对任何雇员实施性骚扰的任何人;

(iv) 解释如何提请雇主注意性骚扰的投诉;

(v) 雇主不应向任何人披露投诉者的姓名或与投诉有关的情况,但为调查投诉或采取与投诉相关的纪律措施而需要披露的情况除外。

(4) 雇主应提请在其指示下的每名人士注意第(2)款要求的政策声明。

第三部分
雇 佣 关 系

7. 服务合同

除非本法另有规定,否则不得以服务合同雇用任何人。

8. 口头和书面合同

本法的规定适用于口头和书面的合同。

9. 服务合同的一般条款

(1) 服务合同——

(a) 为期一段时间或数个工作日,总计相当于 3 个月或以上;或者

(b) 任何指定的工作如果不能合理预期在合计相当于 3 个月的一段时间或数个工作日内完成的,则应采用书面形式。

(2) 作为书面服务合同当事方的雇主应负责起草合同,列明雇佣详情,并根据第(3)款得到雇员的同意。

(3) 为表示同意书面服务合同,雇员可以——

(a) 签署其姓名;或者

(b) 在雇主以外的人在场的情况下,在服务合同上按捺拇指印或其他指印。

(4) 如果雇员不识字或者不能理解合同所用语言或者服务合同条款的语言,雇主应当以劳动者能够理解的语言向劳动者解释合同。

(5) 在招聘方面,雇主不得要求雇员提交任何许可或合规证明,除非该雇主打算与雇员签订服务合同:

但是国家办事处的申请人应在招聘或批准过程中提供可能需要的合规或许可证明。

(6) 签订书面服务合同的雇主可根据《宪法》第六章的规定,要求雇员提交相关实体的强制许可证明。

(7) 尽管有第(6)款的规定,如果雇员不符合第(6)款的要求,雇主可以撤回提供的服务合同。

(8) 相关公共实体应——

(a) 不对根据本部分或任何其他法律颁发的许可证或合规证书收取费用;

(b) 在收到申请后 7 日内向申请人颁发许可证或合规证书,或拒绝该申请。

(9) 就本条而言——

(a) "**雇员**"包括求职者;

(b) "**雇主**"包括职业介绍所;

(c) "**相关实体**"包括为满足《宪法》第六章的要求而颁发许可证的任何公共或私人实体。

[2022 年第 15 号法令,第 2 条]

10. 雇用细则

(1) 第 9 条规定的书面服务合同须列明雇佣详情,在符合第(3)款的规定的情况下,该等雇佣详情可分期提供,但须在雇佣开始后不迟于 2 个月内提供。

(2) 书面服务合同应规定——
　　(a) 雇员的姓名、年龄、永久地址和性别；
　　(b) 雇主姓名；
　　(c) 就业岗位描述；
　　(d) 雇佣开始的日期；
　　(e) 合同的形式和期限；
　　(f) 工作地点；
　　(g) 工作时间；
　　(h) 薪酬、薪酬等级或比率、该薪酬的计算方法以及任何其他福利的详情；
　　(i) 支付报酬的时间间隔；
　　(j) 雇员连续受雇期间开始的日期,应将受雇于前任雇主且计入该期间的任何雇佣纳入考量；和
　　(k) 任何其他规定事项。

(3) 在声明日前不超过 7 日的规定日期或包含声明的分期付款日,本部分所要求的声明还应包含下列细节——
　　(a) 与以下任何一项有关的任何条款和条件——
　　　　(i) 享有年假的权利,包括公共假期和假日工资(所提供的详细信息足以准确计算雇员的权利,包括在终止雇佣关系时获得应计假期工资的权利)；
　　　　(ii) 因生病或受伤而无法工作的条款,包括任何病假工资；
　　　　(iii) 养老金和养老金计划；
　　(b) 雇员有义务发出和有权收到终止雇佣合同的通知期限；
　　(c) 如果雇佣不是无限期的,则该期限是指预期将持续的期限,如果雇佣是固定期限的,则该期限是指持续到终止日期的一段时间；
　　(d) 涉及工作地点,或在要求或允许雇员在不同地点工作的情况下,注明该工作地点和雇主地址；
　　(e) 如果雇主不是一方当事人,任何直接影响雇佣条款和条件的集体协议,包括与他人签订的协议；和
　　(f) 如果雇员被要求在肯尼亚境外工作超过 1 个月——
　　　　(i) 该雇员在肯尼亚境外工作的期间；
　　　　(ii) 该雇员在肯尼亚境外工作时支付报酬的货币；
　　　　(iii) 应支付给雇员的任何额外报酬,以及因雇员在肯尼亚境外工作而应支付给该雇员的任何福利；
　　　　(iv) 与雇员返回肯尼亚有关的任何条款和条件。

(4) 在以下情况下,第(3)款(a)项(iii)目不适用于任何机构或当局的雇员——
　　(a) 雇员的退休金权利取决于根据任何法令包含或生效的条款涉及的退休金计划的条款；和
　　(b) 任何此类条款都要求机构或当局向新雇员提供有关该雇员养老金权利的信息或确定影响这些权利的问题。

(5) 第(1)款规定的事项发生变更时,雇主应与雇员协商,修改合同以反映该变更,并书面通知该雇员。

　　(6) 雇主应在终止雇佣关系后将第(1)款规定的书面雇佣详情保存5年。

　　(7) 如果在任何法律诉讼中,雇主未能出示第(1)款规定的书面合同或书面详情,则雇主须承担证明或反驳合同中规定的雇佣期限的责任。

[2008年第1号修正案]

11. 初步详情说明

　　(1) 就第10条作出的陈述而言,如果没有根据第(2)款(d)项或(j)项或第10条第(2)款或第(3)款的任何其他条文须记入的详情,则该事实应在陈述中说明。

　　(2) 根据第10条作出的陈述,就第10条第(3)款(A)项(ii)目及(iii)目所规定的任何事项的详情,指引雇员查阅其可以合理查阅的任何其他文件的条款。

　　(3) 根据第10条作出的陈述,就第10条第(3)款(e)项所规定的任何事项的详情,指引雇员查阅其可合理查阅的直接影响其雇佣条款及条件的集体协议的条款。

　　(4) 第10条第(2)款和第(3)款要求的详情应包含在一份文件中。

　　(5) 如果在雇员开始受雇后2个月的期限结束之前,雇员将开始在肯尼亚境外工作超过1个月,则第10条规定的声明应在其离开肯尼亚开始工作之前提供。

　　(6) 根据第10条,即使某人的雇佣期限在须作出声明的期限结束之前终止,也应向该人提供声明。

[2008年第1号修正案]

12. 纪律处分声明

　　(1) 根据第10条作出的声明应——

　　　　(a) 规定该雇员适用的纪律处分规则,或指引该雇员查阅其可合理查阅的规定该规则的文件条款;

　　　　(b) 在以下情况下指明雇员可以向谁申请——

　　　　　　(i) 如对与雇员有关的任何纪律处分决定不满意的;和

　　　　　　(ii) 为寻求与受雇有关的任何纠纷之补偿,以及提出申请的方式;和

　　　　(c) 如在任何申请后需要采取进一步措施,指引该雇员查阅其可合理查阅的解释该措施的文件。

　　(2) 第(1)款不适用于与工作中健康或安全相关的规则、纪律处分、申诉或程序。

　　(3) 如在雇员开始工作之日,其雇主雇用的雇员不到50人,则本条不适用。

13. 变更声明

　　(1) 如在重要日期后,第10条及第12条所规定的任何详情有更改,雇主须向雇员提供一份载有更改详情的书面声明。

　　(2) 就第(1)款而言——

　　　　(a) 根据第10条作出的声明中所包括或提及的详情,分期提供的内容除外,关键日期是指该声明所涉及的日期;

　　　　(b) 关于以下事项的详情——

　　　　　　(i) 包括或提述于根据第10条作出的分期提供的声明中,或者

　　　　（ii）按第 11 条第（4）款要求包含在一份文件中，但不包含在根据第 10 条作出的分期提供的声明中，该声明确实包含该规定适用的其他详情，则关键日期是该分期提供所涉及的日期；和

　　（c）就任何其他事项而言，关键日期是指根据第 10 条规定须作出声明的日期。

（3）根据第（1）款作出的声明应尽早作出，并且在任何情况下，不得迟于——

　　（a）相关变更后 1 个月，或者

　　（b）如果该变更是由于雇员被要求在肯尼亚境外工作超过 1 个月，则以雇员离开肯尼亚开始工作的时间起计算。

（4）根据第（1）款作出的声明，可就第 10 条第（3）款 a 项（ii）目及（iii）目及第 12 条第（1）款（a）项及（c）项所指明任何事项的变更，指引雇员查阅其可合理查阅的文件条款。

（5）根据第（1）款作出的声明，可就第 10 条第（3）款（e）项所指明的事项中的任何一项更改，指引雇员了解法律或查阅雇员可合理查阅的直接影响其雇佣条款及条件的任何集体协议。

（6）在雇主根据第 10 条规定向雇员作出声明后——

　　（a）雇主名称变更，但雇主身份未发生任何变化，或者

　　（b）在不破坏雇员受雇连续性的情况下，雇主身份发生变更，且第（7）款适用于该变更，

在变更后立即变为雇主的人无须根据第 12 条向雇员作出声明，但该变更应被视为第（1）款所指的变更。

（7）第（6）款适用于任何变更，前提是该变更不涉及任何事项的变更，但第 10 条和第 11 条规定在第（1）款下的声明中包含或提述的各方名称及详情除外。

（8）根据第（1）款作出的声明，应告知雇员依据第（6）款（b）项所涉变更，并指明雇员连续雇佣期的开始日期。

[2008 年 1 号修正案]

14. 可合理查阅的文件或集体协议

在第 11、12 和 13 条中，凡提及雇员可合理查阅的文件或集体协议是指——

　　（a）雇员在受雇期间有合理的阅读机会；或者

　　（b）雇员可以通过其他方式合理获取。

15. 告知员工其权利

雇主应发布雇员依本法规定享有的权利声明，置于明显处，供所有雇员查阅。

16. 执行

（1）如果雇主没有按照第 10 条、第 12 条或第 13 条的要求向雇员提供声明，或者没有按照第 20 条的要求向雇员提供详细的工资单，雇员可以向劳工官员提出投诉，该投诉应被视为根据第 87 条提出的投诉。

（2）如果由于第 10、12、13 或 20 条引起投诉，劳资法庭裁定应在根据这些条文提供的声明中包含或提及的详情，则雇主应被视为已向雇员提供一份声明，其中包括或提及劳资法庭的裁定中指明的详情。

（3）如果根据第（1）款，劳资法庭必须确定所作出的声明是否符合第 10、13 或 20 条下的声明，则劳资法庭可——

（a）确认雇主提供的声明中包含或提及的详情；

（b）修改该等详情；或者

（c）用劳资法庭认为适当的其他详情代替该等详情，并且该声明应被视为由雇主根据法院的裁决向雇员提供。

（4）任何人未能按照第10、12、13或20条的要求向雇员提供声明，即属犯罪，一经定罪，可处以不超过10万先令的罚款或不超过2年的监禁，或两者并罚。

（5）如果某人违反了第（1）款规定的条款，法院可应雇员或代表该雇员的劳工官员的申请，除第（4）款规定的处罚外，雇员还可申请第（3）款规定的任何补救措施。

[2008年第1号修正案]

第四部分
工 资 保 障

17. 工资、津贴等的支付、处理和收回

（1）根据本法，雇主应以肯尼亚货币支付雇员根据服务合同直接完成的工作所赚取或应付给雇员的全部工资——

（a）用现金；

（b）存入雇员指定的银行或行业协会的账户；

（c）以雇员为受益人的支票、邮政汇票或以雇员为收款人的汇票；或者

（d）在雇员不在的情况下，向雇员以外的人提供，前提是该人经雇员书面正式授权代表雇员领取工资。

（2）雇主应在工作日、工作时间内、在工作地点或附近或雇主与雇员之间可能约定的其他地点向雇员支付工资。

（3）雇主不得在任何出售或随时可供应酒类的地方向雇员支付工资，但受雇在该地方工作的雇员除外。

（4）任何人不得在明示或暗示的条件下要求其他任何人或其受抚养人从事任何工作，也不得向该人提供或承诺任何预付款或任何对价。

（5）如果在服务合同或集体协议中，规定在雇员同意的情况下向雇员支付任何实物津贴，则只有在雇员同意的情况下，且实物津贴满足以下条件才可以支付此种津贴——

（a）用于雇员的个人使用和福利；和

（b）不包含任何酒精或毒品。

（6）尽管有任何现行的法律规定，在执行一项对雇主的财产发出扣押的法令时，法院不得将因执行该命令而实现的收益支付给判令持有人，直到法院就雇员的工资而向雇主发出的法令得到履行，但数额不得超过该雇员6个月的工资。

（7）第（6）款不得妨碍雇员在获偿后，通过正常法律程序追讨应付的余额。

（8）如果附件是针对第8部分所定义的处于破产状态的雇主发出的，在这种情况下，则第（6）款不适用，而应适用该部分的规定。

（9）如果雇主向雇员预付的款额超过雇员1个月工资，或者根据书面服务合同雇用雇员，

预付给该雇员超过其2个月工资的金额,超额款项不得在法庭追讨。

（10）任何人——

  （a）在不违反第19条的情况下,故意不支付雇员根据第(1)款赚取的工资或雇主应付的工资;或者

  （b）违反第(2)、(3)、(4)和(5)款的任何规定,

即属犯罪,一经定罪,可处以不超过10万先令的罚款或不超过2年的监禁,或两者并罚。

（11）雇主不得限制或试图限制雇员以其认为合适的方式处置其工资的权利,也不得通过服务合同或以其他方式试图迫使雇员在雇主拥有直接或间接利益的特定地点或特定目的中处置其工资或部分工资。

[2008年第1号修正案]

18. 工资或薪金到期时

（1）如果签订了一项任务或计件工作的服务合同由雇员执行,则该雇员有权——

  （a）当任务尚未完成时,雇主可选择,在1天结束时依据已完成的工作量按比例支付报酬;或在次日完成任务,在这种情况下,雇员有权在完成任务时获得报酬;或者

  （b）在计件工作的情况下,由其雇主在每个月底依据其在该月完成的工作量按比例支付,或在工作完成时支付,以较早的日期为准。

（2）除第(1)款另有规定外,工资或薪金应被视为到期支付——

  （a）就临时雇员而言,在1天结束时支付;

  （b）如果雇员受雇时间超过1天但不超过1个月,则在该期限结束时支付;

  （c）如果雇员受雇时间超过1个月,则在每个月或不足1个月的月末支付;

  （d）对于受雇期限不确定,或在旅行期间的雇员,分别在每个月或该期限届满时和旅途结束时支付,以较早的日期为准。

（3）如果相关条款比本部分的规定更有利于雇员,则本部分的规定不应影响劳资法庭的命令、判决或裁决,或雇员与其雇主之间的协议。

（4）雇员因合法原因被立即解雇的,应在解雇时向雇员支付截至被解雇之日应得的所有款项、津贴和福利。

（5）服务合同终止后——

  （a）期限届满时,雇主有责任确保向雇员支付其所赚取或雇主应付给雇员的全部工资以及尚未支付的应得的津贴;

  （b）解雇时,雇主应在7日内,向雇员工作所在地区的劳工官员提交书面报告,说明导致解雇的情况和原因,并说明通知期限和雇员在没有被解雇的情况下本应有权获得的工资数额;该报告应列明自雇员被解雇之日起其赚取的任何工资和其他津贴的数额。

（6）在雇员依法被拘留或被判处监禁的服刑期间,不得向雇员支付任何工资。

19. 工资扣除

（1）尽管有第17条第(1)款的规定,雇主可从其雇员的工资中扣除——

  （a）雇员应付的款项,作为雇员已同意提供的公积金或退休金计划或任何经劳工处

处长批准的其他计划的供款；

（b）因雇员故意违约而对雇主合法拥有或保管的任何财产造成的损害或损失的合理金额；

（c）雇员在没有请假或其他合法原因的情况下，整个工作日离开雇主场所或其他适当地点和指定工作的地点应扣除的款项，该数额不超过该工作日1天的工资；

（d）因服务合同特别规定或受托收款、保管和支付款项的雇员的疏忽或不诚实而导致的任何资金短缺的金额；

（e）超过应付给雇员工资的错误支付款项；

（f）当时有效的任何法律、集体协议、工资决定、法院命令或仲裁裁决授权扣除的任何金额；

（g）雇主没有直接或间接利益，以及雇员以书面形式要求雇主从其工资中扣除的任何金额；

（h）雇员根据及按照书面协议的条款应付的到期款项，作为偿还或部分偿还雇主向其提供的贷款，该款项在扣除根据本部分可能应付给该雇员的所有其他款项后，不得超过应付给该雇员工资的50%；和

（i）内阁秘书可能规定的其他金额。

（2）任何雇主不得从应付雇员的工资中扣除款项，作为为雇员提供就业机会或留住雇员的报酬。

（3）在不损害任何追讨到期债务的权利的前提下，尽管有任何其他法律的规定，根据第（1）款的规定，可由雇主在任何时候从其雇员的工资中扣除款项扣除的总额不得超过内阁秘书规定的工资或额外金额或其他金额的三分之二，该规定是一般规定，或就特定雇主或雇员、雇主或雇员群体或任何贸易或行业而言作出的规定。

（4）雇主根据第（1）款（a）、（f）、（g）和（h）项从雇员的薪酬中扣除款项，应按照法律、协议、法院命令或仲裁中规定的期限和其他要求支付扣除的款项（视属情况而定）。

（5）雇主不遵守第（4）款的规定，即属犯罪，一经定罪，可处以不超过10万先令的罚款或不超过2年的监禁，或两者并罚。

（6）如果雇主没有从雇员的薪酬中扣除款项，而根据第（5）款被提起诉讼，法院除了对雇主处以罚款外，还可以命令雇主将从雇员工资中扣除的金额退还给雇员。并用雇主自有资金代表雇员向预期受益人支付。

［2015年第19号法令，第145条］

20. 工资明细表

（1）雇主应在向雇员支付工资或薪金之时或之前向雇员发出书面声明。

（2）第（1）款规定的声明应包含以下内容——

（a）雇员的工资或薪金总额；

（b）任何可变金额，以及根据第22条的规定，从该总额中扣除的任何法定款项以及扣除的目的；和

（c）当净额的不同部分以不同方式支付时，各部分支付的金额和支付方式。

（3）本条不适用于临时雇员、按计件工资或任务工资雇用的雇员或不超过6个月期限雇

用的雇员。

(4) 部长可以将任何类别的雇员或受雇于任何部门的雇员排除在本条的适用范围之外。

21. 法定扣除声明

(1) 在以下情况下,根据第20条发出的工资明细表无须包含单独的法定扣除详情——

 (a) 工资明细表包含法定扣除总额,包括该扣除额;和

 (b) 雇主在提供工资明细表时或之前已向雇员提供第(2)款规定的法定扣除声明。

(2) 法定扣除声明应——

 (a) 为书面形式;

 (b) 就扣除总额内的每项扣除而言,包含以下内容——

  (i) 扣除额;

  (ii) 扣除的时间间隔;和

  (iii) 扣除目的;和

 (c) 根据第(5)款,在支付声明发出之日生效。

(3) 法定扣除声明可通过以下方式修改——

 (a) 增加新的扣除额;

 (b) 详情变更;或者

 (c) 通过书面通知取消现有的扣除,其中须包含雇主向雇员提供的修改详情。

(4) 雇主向雇员提供法定扣除声明,应——

 (a) 自第一份法定扣除声明发出之日起12个月内;和

 (b) 此后每次间隔不超过12个月,以合并的形式重新发布,包含根据第(3)款通知的任何修改。

(5) 就第(2)款(c)项而言,扣除声明——

 (a) 在提供给雇员之日起生效;和

 (b) 在从该日期开始的12个月期间结束时失效,或者,如果根据第(4)款重新发布,则自最后一次重新发布之日起的12个月期间结束时失效。

22. 修改工资条文和扣款声明的权力

内阁秘书可根据委员会的建议——

 (a) 通过在该等条文所列详情中加入项目或删除项目或修订任何该等详情,更改第20条和第21条中关于必须包含在工资声明或法定扣除声明中的详情规定;和

 (b) 更改第21条第(4)款和第(5)款的规定,以缩短或延长这些条款规定的期限,或根据本条规定随时更改的期限。

[2015年第19号法令,第146条]

23. 工资保证金

(1) 部长可要求非在肯尼亚注册或居住的雇主支付相当于雇主雇用或将雇用的所有雇员一个月工资的保证金。

(2) 任何雇主支付的保证金应由部长代表该雇主在一个单独的计息账户中持有,不得出于其他目的使用,除非在该雇主违约的情况下用于支付该雇主的雇员工资和其他权利。

24. 雇员死亡

（1）雇主被通知或知悉雇员因任何原因的死亡时，雇主应在其后尽快以规定的形式向劳工官员发出死亡通知，或者，如果没有劳工官员，则发给雇员受雇地区的地区专员。

（2）雇员在劳动合同期内死亡，雇员的法定代表人经依法证明其行为能力的，有权在提交证明后的 30 日内获得截至死亡之日应支付给该雇员的工资和任何其他报酬及财产。

（3）已故雇员的雇主应在付款后 7 日内，向劳工官员，或在劳工官员缺席时，向地区专员提供付款证据。

（4）在雇员死亡后 3 个月届满时——

（a）没有法定代表人对该雇员的工资或财产提出申索；或者

（b）如果雇主质疑或已拒绝对雇员的工资或财产提出的申索，雇主应将在雇员去世之日应付给雇员的所有工资交给劳工官员或地区专员（视情况而定）并向其交付已故雇员的所有财产，由劳工官员或地区专员根据《继承法》（第 160 章）或适用于处置死者财产的任何其他书面法律以信托方式持有。

（5）如果雇员在受雇期间因伤死亡或丧失工作能力超过 3 日，其雇主应尽快向劳工官员发送一份规定格式的报告，或者，如果没有劳工官员，则应向地区专员发送报告。

25. 被错误扣留或扣除报酬的返还

（1）在不影响违反本部分规定而承担的任何其他法律责任的情况下，违反本部分规定的雇主构成犯罪，一经定罪，可处以不超过 10 万先令的罚款或不超过 2 年的监禁，或两者并罚，并且应被要求偿还任何被错误扣留或扣除的雇员报酬。

（2）雇员可以根据本部分规定——

（a）向劳工官员；

（b）在劳工官员做出涉嫌非法扣除报酬后的 3 年内，提出投诉。

第五部分
就业权利和义务

26. 基本最低的就业条件

（1）本部分和第六部分的规定应构成服务合同的基本最低的条款和条件。

（2）如果由任何条例规定，由集体协议或双方之间的合同商定，或由任何其他法律制定，由劳资法庭的任何判决书或命令裁定的服务合同的条款和条件比本部分和第六部分规定的条款更有利于雇员，那么应适用这种有利的服务条款和条件。

27. 工作时间

（1）根据本法和任何其他法律的规定，雇主应当规范每名员工的工作时间。

（2）尽管有第（1）款的规定，雇员应有权在每 7 日内享有至少 1 个休息日。

28. 年假

（1）雇员有权——

（a）每连续为雇主服务 12 个月后，享有不少于 21 个工作日的带薪休假；

（b）如果在任何 12 个月的带薪休假期内连续服务 2 个月或以上后终止雇佣关系，

则每次服务完 1 个月,可连续享受不少于 1 又 3/4 天的带薪假。

(2)雇主可以在雇员同意的情况下,将第(1)款(a)项规定的最低年假权利分成不同的部分,以在不同的时间间隔给予休假。

(3)除非雇员与雇主之间的协议或集体协议另有规定,且雇员在第(1)款(a)项所指明的任何带薪休假期间的服务年限使该雇员有权享有该假期,否则,第(2)款所议定部分的一部分应至少包括两个不间断工作周。

(4)第(3)款所述的带薪年假的不间断部分应在第(1)款(a)项所述的连续 12 个月服务期间授予和使用,其余的带薪年假应在不迟于第(1)款(a)项所述的休假期结束后的 18 个月内休完,该休假期间是假期权利所涉的期间。

(5)如果在服务合同中雇员有权获得超过第(1)款(a)项规定的最低休假日,雇主和雇员可以就如何利用该休假日达成协议。

29. 产假

(1)女性雇员享有 3 个月的带薪产假。

(2)在第(1)款和第(3)款规定的女性雇员产假期满后,女性雇员有权返回她在产假前的工作岗位或返回一个合理合适的工作岗位,其条件不得低于她未休产假时所适用的条款和条件。

(3)凡——

(a)经雇主同意延长产假;或者

(b)女性雇员在产假结束后恢复其工作岗位之前立即请病假或在雇主同意的情况下请年假、丧假,或任何其他假期,

则第(1)款项下的 3 个月产假应视为在该延长假期的最后一日届满。

(4)女性雇员只有在提前至少 7 日发出通知,才有权享有第(1)、(2)和(3)款中所述的权利,如其打算在特定日期休产假并在随后返回工作岗位,应在合理情况下的更短时间内发出通知。

(5)第(4)款所涉的通知须以书面形式发出。

(6)寻求行使本部分所述任何权利的女性雇员,应在雇主要求的情况下,出示由合格医生或助产士出具的关于其健康状况的证明。

(7)任何女性雇员不得因休产假而丧失第 28 条规定的年假权利。

(8)男性雇员可享有 2 周带薪陪产假。

[2008 年第 1 号修正案]

29A. 收养前休假

(1)如果根据《儿童法》第 157 条,儿童应由根据本法作为雇员的申请人持续照顾和监护,则该雇员有权从安置儿童之日起享受 1 个月的带薪收养前休假。

(2)根据第(1)款有资格休假的雇员,应至少在安置儿童前 14 日内,将收养协会将孩子交由其监护的意向以书面形式通知其雇主。

(3)根据第(2)款发出的通知应附有证明收养协会有意将孩子置于该雇员监护之下的文件,包括该雇员与收养协会之间的监护协议和退出证书。

(4)第 29 条第(2)、(3)和(7)款经必要修改后适用于根据本条有资格休假的雇员。

[2021 年第 2 号法令,第 3 条]

30. 病假

（1）在每连续 12 个月的服务期间，雇员在给其雇主连续服务 2 个月后，有权享有不少于 7 日的带薪病假，其后享有 7 日的半薪病假，但须由雇员出示由具有适当资格的医生或代表该医生行事、负责药房或医疗救助中心的人员签署的无工作能力证明。

（2）对于根据第（1）款有权享受带薪病假的雇员，该雇员应在合理可行的情况下尽快通知或安排通知其雇主其缺勤及缺勤的原因。

（3）就第（1）款和第（2）款而言，"带薪"包括基本工资，不包括根据第 19 条规定的工资扣除。

（4）就第（1）款而言，连续 12 个月的服务应被视为从雇员受雇之日以及随后的受雇周年日开始。

（5）雇主有权将其所有雇员安排在周年纪念日的年度周期内，该日期由雇主决定。

31. 住房

（1）雇主应始终自费在工作地点或其附近为其每位雇员提供合理的住房，或除雇员的工资或薪水外，应向雇员支付足够的款项，如租金，使雇员能够获得合理的住宿。

（2）本条不适用于有如下情况的雇员的服务合同——

  （a）包含一项规定，该规定将雇员打算用作租金的部分合并为雇员基本工资或薪金的一部分，或该规定旨在使雇员能够为自己提供住房；或者

  （b）是（a）项规定的工资合并的集体协议的标的物或已包含在该协议中的其他事项。

（3）内阁秘书可根据委员会在公报刊登的通知所提出的建议，排除本条对某一类雇员的适用，而该类雇员须按该通知所指明的方式对待。

[2015 年第 19 号法令，第 147 条]

31A. 已删除

根据 2020 年第 20 号法令附录予以删除。

31B. 经济适用房征税

（1）尽管有本法第 3 条第（2）款（a）、（b）、（c）和（d）项的规定，每位雇员和雇主都应每月缴纳经济适用住房税款。

（2）经济适用住房税的目的是为经济适用住房开发和相关社会和物质基础设施提供资金，并为肯尼亚人提供经济适用住房融资。

（3）经济适用住房税不得用于除经济适用住房开发和相关社会和物质基础设施以及为肯尼亚人提供经济适用住房融资之外的任何其他目的。

（4）雇主和雇员每月应缴纳的税款应为——

  （a）雇员应缴纳雇员月工资总额的 1.5%；

  （b）雇主应缴纳雇员月工资总额的 1.5%。

[2023 年第 4 号法令，第 84 条]

31C. 雇主的义务

（1）雇主应——

  （a）从雇员的月工资总额中扣除雇员的月薪；

（b）为每位雇员预留出雇主应付的月薪；和

（c）在付款到期当月结束后的9个工作日内，汇出一笔由雇员和雇主支付的款项组成的款额。

（2）未遵守本条规定的雇主可被处以每月未付款项2%的罚款。

[2023年第4号法令，第84条]

32. 水

雇主应在受雇地点以及（视情况而定）在雇主为雇员提供的任何居所的合理距离内，提供足够的卫生饮用水供雇员使用。

33. 食物

（1）如果在签订服务合同时，雇主明确同意提供食物，则其应确保为雇员提供适当的食物，并提供足够和适当的炊具和烹饪工具，费用由雇主承担。

（2）在雇员未经雇主许可或无其他合法理由缺勤期间，本条规定不得被视为对雇主施加的与雇员有关的任何法律责任。

34. 医疗护理

（1）除第（2）款另有规定外，雇主应确保在其雇员生病期间为其雇员提供充足和适当的药物，并在可能的情况下确保在其雇员重病期间提供医疗服务。

（2）雇主应采取一切合理措施，确保在雇员首次患病后在合理可行的范围内尽快将其患病情况告知雇主。

（3）如果雇主证明其不知道雇员患病，并且其采取了所有合理的措施来确保其知悉雇员患病，或者综合全案，证明要求雇主知道雇员生病是不合理的，则诸种情形可以作为对第（1）款所述罪行提出检控的抗辩。

（4）本条不适用于以下情况——

（a）雇员的疾病或伤害是在雇员无合法或正当理由而缺勤期间发生的；

（b）疾病或伤害被证明是自己造成的；

（c）医疗由政府或根据任何法律设立的涵盖雇员的保险计划免费提供。

第六部分
终止和解雇

35. 终止通知

（1）如果服务合同不是执行特定工作的合同，不涉及时间或行程，且在肯尼亚履行，则其应被视为有如下情况——

（a）如果合同是按日支付工资，则任何一方均可在任何一天结束时终止合同，无须通知；

（b）如果合同是按少于1个月的时间间隔定期支付工资，则任何一方均可在发出书面通知后的下一个期限结束时终止合同；或者

（c）如果合同是每隔1个月或超过1个月定期支付工资或薪金，则任何一方均可在发出书面通知后的28日期限结束时终止合同。

（2）第（1）款不适用于其条款规定发出书面终止通知的期限超过本款规定所要求期限的服务合同，否则将适用于该服务合同。

（3）如果收到解雇通知的雇员无法理解该通知，雇主应确保以雇员理解的语言向雇员口头解释该通知。

（4）本条中的任何规定均不影响以下权利——

  （a）服务已被终止的雇员根据第46条的规定对终止的合法性或公平性提出异议；或者

  （b）雇主或雇员因法律认可的任何原因而在未经通知的情况下终止雇佣合同。

（5）根据第（1）款（c）项终止服务合同的雇员有权按工作年限获得服务薪酬，其条款应是固定的。

（6）本条不适用于雇员为以下计划或基金的成员的情况——

  （a）根据《退休福利法》登记的养老金或公积金计划；

  （b）根据集体协议设立的酬金或服务费计划；

  （c）由雇主建立和经营的任何其他计划，其条款比根据本条制定的服务薪酬计划更加优惠；

  （d）全国社会保障基金。

36. 代通知金

第35条第（5）款适用的服务合同的任何一方，在向另一方支付本应由另一方获得的报酬，或在根据该条相应规定要求通知的期限内支付的报酬后，均可终止合同而无须通知。

37. 临时雇佣转换为定期合同

（1）尽管本法另有规定，如果临时雇员——

  （a）工作一段时间或连续数个工作日，总计不少于1个月；或者

  （b）执行合理预期无法在一段时间内完成的工作，或总计相当于3个月或更长的工作时间，

则该临时雇员的服务合同应被视为按月支付工资的合同，第35条第（1）款（c）项应适用于该服务合同。

（2）在计算第（1）款规定的工资及连续工作日时，临时雇员须视为在连续6日的工作期内，有权享有一个带薪休息日，而该休息日或任何公众假期如在有关期间内，均应计算为连续工作日的一部分。

（3）根据第（1）款规定转换服务合同的雇员，以及自受雇之日起连续工作2个月或以上的临时雇员，视为自始不是临时雇员，有权享受本法规定的服务条款和条件。

（4）尽管有本法的任何规定，在劳资法庭就临时雇员的服务条款和条件提出的任何争议中，劳资法庭有权更改临时雇员的服务条款，并可声明雇员按照与本法一致的服务条款和条件受雇。

（5）临时雇员对其雇主根据其雇佣条款和条件所给予的待遇不满，可以向劳工官员提出申诉，应适用本法第87条。

[2008年第1号修正案]

38. 雇主豁免通知

如果雇员发出终止雇佣通知，而雇主豁免全部或部分通知权，则雇主应根据具体情况向雇

员支付相当于雇员未送达通知期间的报酬,除非雇主和雇员另有约定。

39. 旅途中到期的合同可以延期

如果服务合同中规定的期限届满,或者如果雇员在旅行期间寻求终止合同而没有就其期限达成任何协议,则雇主可以为了完成旅行,将服务期延长足够长的时间,但无论如何不得超过1个月,以使雇员能够完成旅行。

40. 因裁员而终止

(1)雇主不得因裁员终止服务合约,除非雇主符合以下条件——

  (a)如果雇员是工会的成员,雇主应在因裁员而计划终止雇佣的日期前不少于1个月,将计划裁员的原因和程度通知该雇员所属的工会和负责该雇员所在地区的劳工官员;

  (b)如果雇员不是工会成员,雇主应以书面形式亲自通知雇员和劳工官员;

  (c)雇主在选择被宣布裁员的雇员时,已适当考虑受裁员影响的特定类别雇员的资历以及每名员工的技能、能力和可靠性;

  (d)雇主与工会之间存在集体协议,其中规定了裁员时应支付的离职福利;雇主没有因雇员是否是工会成员而使雇员处于不利地位;

  (e)如果雇员因被宣布裁员而离职,雇主已用现金支付其离职金;

  (f)雇主已提前1个月向被宣布裁员的雇员通知或支付不少于1个月的代通知金;和

  (g)雇主已按照每满一年不少于15日的标准,向被宣布裁员的雇员支付遣散费。

(2)如雇员的服务因第八部分规定的破产而终止,则第(1)款不适用,在这种情况下,应适用第八部分。

(3)内阁秘书可以制定规则,要求雇用一定最低数量雇员的雇主或任何雇主团体,通过根据法律所确立的既定国家保险计划或任何承保保险业务的经内阁秘书批准的公司所运行的失业保险计划,为其雇员投保裁员风险。

[2008年第1号法令修正案;2015年第19号法令,第148条]

41. 因不当行为被解雇前的通知和听证

(1)除第42条第(1)款另有规定外,雇主应在终止雇用雇员之前,以不当行为、表现不佳或身体无行为能力为理由,以雇员理解的语言,说明雇主解雇的原因,雇员有权在解释过程中让另一名雇员或他选择的车间工会代表在场。

(2)尽管有本部分的任何其他规定,在根据第44条第(3)款或第(4)款终止雇用雇员或立即解雇雇员之前,雇主应听取和考虑雇员可能基于不当行为或表现不佳作出的任何陈述,以及雇员在第(1)款中选择的人(如有)。

42. 试用合同的终止

(1)因雇佣关系终止而终止试用合同的,不适用第41条的规定。

(2)试用期不得超过6个月,但经雇员同意,可以再延长不超过6个月的期限。

(3)雇主根据试用合同雇用雇员不得超过第(2)款规定的总期限。

(4)试用期合同的一方可以提前不少于7日通知终止合同,或者由雇主向雇员支付7日的代通知金。

43. 终止的理由证明

（1）因终止合同而产生的索赔，应当要求雇主证明终止合同的理由，雇主不提供证明的，则合同终止应被视为第45条所指的不公平。

（2）终止合同的理由是指雇主在终止合同时确实认为存在并导致其终止雇员服务的事项。

44. 即时解雇

（1）雇主在没有通知或通知少于雇员根据任何法定条款或合同条款有权获得的通知的情况下终止雇用雇员，则为即时解雇。

（2）根据本条的规定，任何雇主均无权在不通知或通知少于雇员根据任何法定条款或合同条款有权获得的通知的情况下终止服务合同。

（3）根据本法的规定，如果雇员的行为表明他从根本上违反了服务合同规定的义务，雇主可以立即解雇雇员。

（4）下列任何事项均可构成严重不当行为，故雇主可根据合法理由将雇员立即解雇，但列举此类事项或雇主根据第（3）款作出立即解雇雇员的决定，均不妨碍雇主或雇员分别指称或争论导致上述事项的事实或本条未提及的任何其他事项，在下列情况下是否构成解雇的正当或合法理由——

  （a）雇员未经许可或其他合法理由而离开指定的工作地点；
  （b）在工作时间内，雇员因喝酒或醉酒而不愿或无法正常工作；
  （c）雇员故意疏忽履行其有责任履行的任何工作，或者他粗心和不当地履行了根据其合同的性质本应认真和适当地履行的任何工作；
  （d）雇员使用辱骂性或侮辱性语言，或以侮辱性的行为侮辱其雇主或雇主赋予权力的人；
  （e）雇员故意不服从或拒绝服从由其雇主或由其雇主赋予权力的人发布的属于其职责范围内的合法和适当的命令；
  （f）在合法行使根据任何法律赋予的任何逮捕权时，雇员因可判处监禁的可认定的罪行而被捕，并且在14日内未获保释或以其他方式被合法释放；或者
  （g）雇员犯了或有合理及充分理由怀疑其犯了针对其雇主或其雇主财产的刑事罪行，或对其雇主或其雇主财产造成重大损害。

45. 不公平终止

（1）任何雇主不得不公平地解雇雇员。

（2）如果雇主不能证明以下事项，则雇主终止雇佣关系是不公平的——

  （a）终止雇佣的理由是有效的；
  （b）终止的原因是合理的——
    （ⅰ）与员工的行为、能力或兼容性有关；或者
    （ⅱ）基于雇主的运营要求；和
  （c）雇佣关系是按照公平程序终止的。

（3）在终止日期前连续受雇于雇主不少于13个月的雇员，有权投诉雇主对其不公平地解雇。

（4）在以下情况下，就本部分而言，终止雇佣是不公平的——

  （a）终止是由于第46条规定的原因之一；或者

(b) 经查明,在案件的所有情况下,雇主在终止雇用该雇员时均未按照公平和公正的原则行事。

(5) 在决定雇主终止雇用雇员是否公正和公平时,就本部分而言,劳工官员或劳资法庭应考虑——

(a) 雇主在作出解雇雇员的决定时所采用的程序、将该决定传达给雇员的情况以及处理对该决定的任何上诉;

(b) 截至终止之日,雇员的行为和能力;

(c) 雇主遵守与终止雇佣有关的任何法定要求的程度,包括根据第51条签发证书和第41条规定的程序要求;

(d) 雇主在处理导致终止的情况的过往做法;和

(e) 之前向雇员发出的任何警告信函是否存在。

46. 终止或纪律处分的原因

以下不构成解雇或施加纪律处分的合理理由——

(a) 女性雇员怀孕,或与怀孕有关的任何理由;

(b) 雇员正在休假,或雇员提议休其根据法律或合同有权享有的任何假期;

(c) 雇员的会员资格或提议的工会会员资格;

(d) 雇员在工作时间以外,或经雇主同意在工作时间内参与或提议参与工会的活动;

(e) 雇员寻求担任或曾任工会官员或工人代表的职务,或以工会官员或工人代表的身份行事;

(f) 雇员拒绝或提议拒绝加入或退出工会;

(g) 雇员的种族、肤色、部落、性别、宗教、政治观念或派别、民族血统、国籍、社会出身、婚姻状况、艾滋病毒状况或残疾的情况;

(h) 雇员发起或提议发起针对其雇主的投诉或其他法律程序,除非投诉被证明是不负责任且没有根据的;或者

(i) 雇员参与合法罢工。

47. 即时解雇和不公平解雇的申诉

(1) 雇员被即时解雇或者被雇主无正当理由不公平地解除雇佣关系的,雇员可以在被解雇之日起3个月内向劳工官员提出申诉,申诉应作为根据第87条提出的申诉处理。

(2) 根据本条提出索赔的劳工官员应在为雇员和雇主提供一切机会陈述双方的情况后,向双方建议其认为根据第49条的规定解决争议的最佳方式。

(3) 雇员根据本部分提出申诉的权利,是其就同一问题向劳资法庭申诉的权利以及就任何其他侵犯其法定权利的行为提出申诉的权利的补充。

(4) 雇员根据本条提出申诉的权利应是雇员根据集体协议享有的额外权利。

(5) 对于不公平解雇或不当解雇的申诉,证明不公平解雇或不当解雇发生的责任应由该雇员承担,而证明解雇或不当解雇理由的责任则由雇主承担。

(6) 任何在试用合同期间被立即终止服务或被立即解雇的员工不得根据本条提出申诉。

[2008年第1号修正案]

48. 代表

在根据第 47 条提出的任何申诉中，律师不得在诉讼中代表任何一方向劳工官员申诉，但任何一方可由工会官员或雇主组织的官员协助或代表，尽管该官员是律师。

49. 不当解雇和不公平解雇的补救措施

（1）如果劳工官员认为即时解雇或终止合同不合理，其可以建议雇主向雇员支付下列任何或全部费用——

  （a）如果雇员在本法或其服务合同规定的通知期限内获得其有权获得的通知而雇员由此本应获得的工资；

  （b）在应付工资的工作尚未结束前解除合同的，按该雇员工作期间应付工资的比例计算的工资；雇员根据合同有权享有的，因解雇而产生的以及在解雇之日至（a）项所提述的通知期限届满之日之间产生的任何其他损失；或者

  （c）按雇员被解雇时的月工资或薪水总额计算，相当于不超过 12 个月的月工资或薪水。

（2）雇主根据本条支付的任何款项均应进行法定扣除。

（3）如果劳工官员认为雇员的即时解雇或终止雇佣不公平，其可以向雇主建议——

  （a）恢复该雇员的工作，并在各方面视该雇员为未被终止雇佣关系的雇员；或者

  （b）以相同的工资重新聘用该雇员，让其从事与被解雇前受雇的工作相当的工作或其他合理合适的工作。

（4）劳工官员在决定是否推荐第（1）款和第（3）款规定的补救措施时，应考虑以下任何或所有因素——

  （a）雇员的意愿；

  （b）终止发生的情况，包括雇员造成或促成终止的程度（如有）；和

  （c）建议复职或重新聘用的可行性；

  （d）除非在非常特殊的情况下，服务合同不得实际履行的普通法原则；

  （e）雇员服务雇主的年限；

  （f）雇员对其与该雇主的雇佣关系持续的时间长度的合理预期，除非雇佣关系终止；

  （g）雇员在另一雇主处获得同等或合适工作的机会；

  （h）任何依法应支付的遣散费的价值；

  （i）雇员提出索赔的权利或任何未支付的工资、费用或雇员的其他索赔；

  （j）雇员因终止雇佣关系而产生的任何合理费用；

  （k）雇员在一定程度上导致或促成终止雇佣关系的任何行为；

  （l）雇员未能合理减轻因不公平解雇造成的损失；和

  （m）任何由雇主支付并由雇员收取的与终止雇佣有关的补偿，包括特惠金。

50. 须予指导的法院

在根据本法裁定涉及不当解雇或不公平终止雇佣关系的申诉或诉讼时，劳资法庭应遵循第 49 条的规定。

51. 服务证明

（1）雇主应在雇员终止雇佣关系时向其签发服务证明，但雇佣关系持续时间少于连续 4

个星期的除外。

(2) 根据第(1)款签发的服务证书应包含——

(a) 雇主的名称及其邮寄地址；

(b) 雇员姓名；

(c) 雇员开始受雇的日期；

(d) 雇员的受雇性质和通常的工作地点；

(e) 雇员停止受雇的日期；和

(f) 可能规定的其他详情。

(3) 除第(1)款另有规定外，任何雇主均无义务向雇员提供与该雇员的品格或表现有关的证明、推荐信或证书。

(4) 雇主故意或因疏忽未按照第(1)款向雇员提供服务证明，或在服务证明中载有其明知是虚假的陈述，即属犯罪，可处以不超过10万先令的罚款或不超过6个月的监禁，或两者并罚。

第七部分
保 护 儿 童

52. 释义

在本部分中，除非上下文另有规定，否则——

"**雇用**"是指在以下情况下雇用儿童——

(a) 该儿童作为另一人的助手提供劳动，且其劳动被视为该另一人的劳动以支付报酬；

(b) 任何个人或机构利用童工谋取利益，无论儿童是否直接或间接受益；和

(c) 在提供服务的一方是儿童的情况下存在服务合同，无论使用服务的一方是直接还是通过代理使用儿童。

53. 禁止最恶劣的童工形式

(1) 尽管有任何法律规定，任何人不得雇用童工从事任何构成最恶劣的童工形式的活动。

(2) 内阁秘书应与委员会协商制定法规，宣布任何对儿童健康、安全或道德有害的工作、活动或服务合同，并且第(1)款应适用于此类工作、活动或服务合同。

[2015年第19号法令，第149条]

54. 向劳工官员或警察申诉

(1) 任何人如果认为任何儿童受雇于构成最恶劣的童工形式的任何活动，则该人可以向劳工官员或督察及以上级别的警官提出申诉。

(2) 在收到根据第(1)款提出的申诉后，劳工官员或警察，视具体情况而定，应在7日内调查该申诉并将其调查结果提交给申诉者和部长。

(3) 如果劳工官员或警察认为不宜根据第(2)款进行调查，其应以相应书面形式通知当事人和部长，并说明理由。

(4) 尽管有第(2)款的规定，雇用儿童从事任何构成最恶劣的童工形式的工作，应构成可根据第64条或任何其他法律处罚的可审理罪行，但任何人不得因同一犯罪而受到两次处罚。

55. 劳工官员取消和禁止合同的权力

（1）劳工官员可以通过向雇主送达书面通知，终止或取消任何服务合同，其理由是该劳工官员认为雇主是不良分子，或雇佣性质构成最恶劣的童工形式或任何其他法定事由，根据《工业培训法》（第 237 章）的规定由儿童与雇主合法签订的学徒合同或契约学习合同除外。

（2）劳工官员可以通过向任何人送达书面通知，禁止该人雇用儿童从事通知中指定的任何类型或类别的工作，理由是劳工官员认为该人是不良分子，或该雇佣的性质构成最恶劣的童工形式，或出于任何其他可能订明的原因。

（3）根据第（1）款或第（2）款发出的通知应亲自送达雇主或该通知的收件人。

（4）雇主、雇员或个人对根据第（1）款或第（2）款发出的通知不满的，可在该通知送达后 30 日内，针对该通知向劳资法庭提出书面上诉，该法庭可确认或撤销通知，法院的决定为终局裁决。

（5）如在上诉中未撤销根据第（1）款或第（2）款送达雇主或相关人员的通知，雇主或相关人员雇用或继续雇用通知所指的儿童从事该通知所涉及的工作或任何类似工作，或（视属何情况而定）雇用任何儿童从事该通知所涉及的工作或任何类似工作，即属犯罪。

（6）收到根据第（1）款发出的通知的雇主，如在 30 日的上诉限期内，或如已提出上诉，在该上诉结果出来之前，向劳资法庭取得暂停执行劳工官员的通知的决定，在法院决定的期限内，继续雇用通知所指的儿童，均不属犯罪。

56. 禁止雇用 13 岁至 16 岁的儿童

（1）任何人不得在任何企业中雇用未满 13 岁的儿童，无论是否有报酬。

（2）可雇用 13 至 16 岁的儿童从事以下轻体力劳动——

    （a）不可能对儿童的健康或发育有害的；

    （b）不会影响儿童的上学、参加内阁秘书批准的职业指导或培训计划或从所收到的指示中受益的能力的。

（3）内阁秘书可以制定规则，规定可雇用 13 岁至 16 岁儿童从事的轻体力劳动以及该雇用的条款和条件。

[2015 年第 19 号法令，第 150 条]

57. 禁止与 13 至 16 岁儿童签订书面合同

根据《工业培训法》有关学徒合同或契约学习合同的规定，雇用 13 岁至 16 岁的儿童，或使该儿童受雇，或作为父母或监护人或其他当时负责或监护该儿童的人，允许该儿童受雇，除非口头服务合同另有规定，否则即属犯罪，一经定罪，可处以不超过 10 万先令的罚款或不超过 6 个月的监禁，或两者并罚。

58. 限制雇用 13 至 16 岁的儿童从事机械作业

（1）任何人不得在工业企业中雇用 13 至 16 岁的儿童从事机械作业，除非从事《工业培训法》规定的学徒合同或契约学习合同中约定的服务。

（2）任何人不得在通过竖井或坑道进入的任何露天工作区或地下工作区中雇用儿童。

59. 雇用儿童的时间限制

（1）根据第 60 条的规定，任何人不得在下午 6 时 30 分至早上 6 时 30 分期间在工业企业中雇用儿童。

（2）尽管有第（1）款的规定，如遇无法控制或预见的紧急情况，而这些紧急情况会干扰工业企业的正常经营,并且不是非周期性的,则任何人都可以雇佣一名男性青年。

(3)尽管有第(1)款的规定,内阁秘书可在与委员会协商后,以书面形式授权雇主在夜间的特定时段雇用一名年轻人,但应按内阁秘书决定的条件行事。

[2015年第19号法令,第151条]

60. 紧急情况

在重大紧急情况下,当公共利益需要时,内阁秘书可通过公报公告暂停第59条的实施。

[2015年第19号法令,第152条]

61. 儿童就业登记册

(1)雇用儿童的雇主须备存一份登记册,其中载有其雇用的每名儿童的以下详情——

  (a)年龄和出生日期;

  (b)入职和离职的日期;

  (c)可能规定的其他详情。

(2)如果雇主保存此类登记册,则应按照《数据保护法》(2019年第24号)规定的数据保护原则保存登记册。

[2019年第24号法令,附录二]

62. 童工的体检

授权官员可要求受雇儿童在其受雇期间的任何时间接受体检。

63. 年龄的确定

(1)在对本法项下的一项罪行的指控进行审理期间,如有人声称任何人在罪行发生之日超过或低于特定年龄,则审理指控的法院应在其认为必要的调查后,并在听取诉讼任何一方可能提出的任何证据后,为诉讼目的确定该人的年龄,该决定为终局裁决。

(2)法院根据本法作出的定罪、命令或判决不得因任何后续证据证明任何人的年龄未正确地向法院陈述或由法院确定而无效。

(3)根据第(1)款的规定,每当出现关于雇员年龄的任何问题并且没有足够的证据证明该雇员的年龄时,医务人员可以通过其外表或根据任何可用信息估算该雇员的年龄,就本法而言,除非有相反证明,否则如此估算的年龄应被视为雇员的真实年龄。

64. 非法雇用儿童的处罚

(1)任何人违反本部分规定,在工业企业中雇用、聘任或使用儿童,即属犯罪。

(2)任何人利用儿童从事任何构成最恶劣的童工形式的活动,即属犯罪,一经定罪,可处以不超过20万先令的罚款或不超过12个月的监禁,或两者并罚。

(3)被告人证明其确实有理由相信该儿童超过被控年龄的,该理由可以作为抗辩理由。

65. 儿童死亡或受伤的处罚

(1)如果儿童因其雇主违反本部分的任何规定而被杀害、死亡或遭受任何身体伤害,除任何其他处罚外,还应对雇主处以不超过50万先令的罚款或处以不超过12个月的监禁,或两者并罚,罚款的全部或任何部分可用于受伤儿童或其家人的利益,或按照部长的指示用于其他方面。

(2)在以下情况下,雇主无须根据第(1)款承担法律责任——

  (a)对健康造成损害的情况,除非该损害是由该违例事项直接造成的;和

（b）根据本部分就关于造成死亡或伤害的行为或过失对其提出的指控,在伤害发生之前已被审理并被驳回的情况。

第八部分
雇 主 破 产

66. 雇主破产

（1）经雇员或其代表以书面形式向内阁秘书提出申请,内阁秘书确认下列事项——

（a）雇员的雇主无力偿债；

（b）雇员的雇佣关系已终止；和

（c）在适当的日期,雇员有权获得依据本部分全部或部分债务所涉的金额,

根据第69条,内阁秘书应从国家社会保障基金中支付雇员的款项,该金额是内阁秘书认为雇员在债务方面有权获得的金额。

[2015年第19号法令,第153条]

67. 破产的定义

就本部分而言,雇主破产是指——

（a）如果雇主是以下人士——

　（i）已被裁定破产或与其债权人已达成和解或已作安排的；或者

　（ii）已经去世,其遗产将根据《继承法》进行管理的；

（b）如果雇主是公司——

　（i）公司已作出清算令或管理令,或已通过自愿清算决议；或者

　（ii）公司承保的接管人或经理已正式获委任,或已由浮动抵押担保的债券持有人或其代表占有该抵押所包含或受该抵押约束的公司财产。

68. 本部适用的债务

本部分适用于以下债务——

（a）拖欠1个月或1个月以上但不超过6个月或6个月以下的工资；

（b）雇主有责任在第36条规定的通知期限内向雇员支付的任何款项,或因雇主未能按第35条第(1)、(2)和(3)款规定的通知期限向雇员支付的任何金额；

（c）根据第28条有权获得但未休年假的代休假工资；

（d）因不公平解雇而获得的任何基本赔偿；和

（e）以偿还学徒支付的全部或部分费用或以保险费的方式支付的任何合理金额。

69. 根据第68条支付的金额限额

（1）就本部分适用的任何债务向雇员支付的总金额,如果该债务的金额是指某个时期的,则不得超过——

（a）1万先令或月薪的二分之一,以任何1个月应付的较高金额为准；或者

（b）就较短期间而言,按较短期间的比例计算的根据(a)项应付的金额。

（2）内阁秘书可根据委员会的建议,以公报命令的形式更改第(1)款规定的限额。

[2015年第19号法令,第154条]

70. 相关官员的角色

（1）如果已任命或要求任命与雇主破产相关的官员，内阁秘书不得根据第66条就债务进行付款，直到内阁秘书收到相关官员关于该债务金额的声明，表明该债务已在适当日期拖欠雇员，且仍未支付。

（2）应内阁秘书的要求，相关官员应在合理可行的情况下尽快向内阁秘书提供第（1）款所指的声明。

（3）如果内阁秘书确信其不需要根据第（1）款的声明来确定在适当日期拖欠雇员且仍未偿还的债务金额，其可以在未收到声明的情况下就债务进行付款。

（4）就本条而言，相关官员是指——

(a) 根据《破产法》（2015）第三部分任职的破产受托人或临时受托人；

(b) 根据该法第六部分任命的清算人；

(c) 根据该法第八部分任命的管理人；

(d) 破产管理署署长或法院根据该法第三部分第24节批准的债务重组契约中负责监督债务人的其他人员；

(e) 根据该法第九部分或第四部分第1节订立的自愿安排的监事或临时监事；

(f) 由雇主为其债权人签署的信托契约下的受托人。

[2015年第19号法令，第155条]

71. 向劳资法庭申诉

（1）根据第66条申请付款的人可以向劳资法庭申诉——

(a) 内阁秘书未付款；或者

(b) 内阁秘书支付的款项少于本应支付的金额。

（2）劳资法庭不得考虑根据第（1）款提出的申诉，除非该申诉的提出——

(a) 在内阁秘书就申请作出的决定通知到申请人之日起的3个月期限结束之前；或者

(b) 如果在该3个月期限结束前提出申诉是不合理可行的，则该申诉在劳资法庭认为合理的进一步期限内提出。

（3）如果劳资法庭认为内阁秘书应根据第66条支付款项，劳资法庭应——

(a) 为此作出裁决；和

(b) 声明它认为内阁秘书应支付的任何款项。

[2015年第19号法令，第156条]

72. 权利的转让和救济

（1）根据第66条，内阁秘书就本部分适用的债务向雇员支付款项时——

(a) 如果内阁秘书已支付部分债务，在付款时，雇员就债务或部分债务的权利和补救措施应被视为内阁秘书的权利和补救措施；

(b) 劳资法庭要求雇主向雇员支付债务的任何决定有以下效力：内阁秘书已支付的债务或部分债务应由雇主支付给内阁秘书。

（2）根据第（1）款，如果内阁秘书支付了债务或部分债务，则因第（1）款而成为内阁秘书权利的权利包括因债务状态或部分债务作为优先债务而产生的权利。

（3）就第（2）款计算款项时,应优先支付给雇主的其他债权人的总额包括——
(a) 内阁秘书根据第（2）款要求优先支付给雇主的其他债权人的任何索赔；和
(b) 雇员为自己的权利要求获得上述支付的任何索赔,

内阁秘书根据第（2）款要求支付的任何索赔应被视为雇员的索赔。

（4）与雇员相比,内阁秘书就雇员依自己的权利提出的任何索赔向雇员支付相关款项之前,有权就内阁秘书提出的任何索赔获得全额赔偿。

（5）内阁秘书在根据本条行使任何权利或寻求任何补救措施时追回的任何款项应存入国家社会保障基金。

[2015年第19号法令,第157条]

73. 知情权

（1）根据第66条就雇主所欠债务向内阁秘书提出申请时,内阁秘书可要求——
(a) 雇主向其提供合理要求的资料,以决定申请是否有充分理由；和
(b) 保管或控制内阁秘书所要求的相关记录或其他文件的任何人,代表内阁秘书出示任何此类记录或文件以供审查。

（2）根据第（1）款要求提供资料、记录或文件——
(a) 应以书面形式通知需要提供资料或出示记录或文件的人；和
(b) 可通过发出的后续通知更改或撤销。

（3）任何人拒绝或故意不提供本条规定的通知要求其提供或出示的任何资料或记录或文件,即属犯罪,一经定罪,可处以不超过10万先令或不超过6个月的监禁,或两者并罚。

（4）任何人为遵守本条规定的通知要求而故意或过失地作出任何虚假陈述,即属犯罪。

（5）如果法人团体犯下本条规定的罪行,并被查证属实——
(a) 是在以下人员的同意或纵容下犯下的；或者
(b) 可归因于以下人员某方面的疏忽,或任何意图以该等身份行事的人的疏忽：该法人团体的任何董事、经理、秘书或其他类似高级人员,则该人及该法人团体即属犯罪。

（6）法人团体的成员管理该法人团体时,该成员应被视为法人团体的董事,则第（5）款适用于该成员在管理职能方面的作为和失责。

[2015年第19号法令,第158条]

第九部分
就业记录

74. 雇主保存的记录

（1）雇主应保存其雇用的所有雇员的书面记录,根据本法与这些雇员签订合同,该合同应包含以下详细信息——
(a) 根据第6条第（2）款（如适用）作出的政策声明；
(b) 第10条第（3）款的规定；
(c) 第13条的规定；

(d) 第 21 条和第 22 条的规定；

(e) 第 27 条规定的雇员每周休息日；

(f) 第 28 条规定的雇员年假权利、已休天数和到期天数；

(g) 第 29 条规定的产假；

(h) 第 30 条规定的病假；

(i) 如雇主提供住房，提供住房的详情；如工资中不包含住房津贴的，则提供支付给雇员住房津贴的详情；

(j) 食物配给（如适用）；

(k) 第 61 条的规定；

(l) 雇员不当行为的警告记录或其他证据；和

(m) 根据任何法律或内阁秘书可能规定的需要保存的任何其他细节。

(2) 雇主应允许授权官员查阅记录，该授权官员可要求雇主出示与前 36 个月相关的任何期间的记录，以供查阅。

(3) 雇用儿童的雇主根据第 61 条保存登记册，如果登记册载有与每个儿童有关的、依据本条第(1)款雇主应保存的详细信息，则该雇主应被视为已遵守相关规定。

[2008 年第 1 号修正案；2015 年第 19 号法令，第 159 条]

75. 虚假条目等

任何人制作、致使制作或故意允许制作依本法要求保存的其明知在重要事项上属虚假的登记册、记录、簿册或其他文件中的条目，或者向授权官员出示、提供、致使或故意允许出示或提供其明知在重要事项上属虚假的登记册、记录、簿册或其他文件，即属犯罪，一经定罪，可处不超过 10 万先令的罚款或不超过 6 个月的监禁，或两者并罚。

第十部分
就 业 管 理

76. 空缺通知

(1) 本部分适用于雇用 25 名或以上雇员的雇主。

(2) 雇主须将其机构、业务或工作地点的每一空缺，以规定的表格形式通知处长，并提供以下详情——

(a) 雇主的姓名和完整地址；

(b) 空缺职位的详情；

(c) 求职者所需的最低资格；

(d) 工作地点；和

(e) 工作类型，无论是临时合同、永久合同还是定期合同；和

(f) 处长可能要求的其他信息。

(3) 空缺应被视为在以下日期发生——

(a) 雇主设立一个由雇员填补的职位或决定聘用一名雇员的日期；

(b) 雇员终止雇佣关系，或被雇主终止雇佣关系，以及雇主撤销职位的日期。

77. 职位填补或撤销的通知

已通知处长为空缺的职位已被填补或在填补前已被撤销,视情况而定,则雇主应在该职位被填补或撤销后的 2 周内书面通知就业服务办公室。

78. 终止雇佣的通知

雇主终止雇佣或裁减人员,应当在终止雇佣或裁减人员后 2 周内以书面形式通知最近的就业服务办公室。

79. 雇员登记处

雇主应保留一份登记册,在该登记册中填写其每名雇员的全名、年龄、性别、职业、雇佣日期、国籍和教育程度,以及截至 12 月 31 日的每个日历年的雇员申报表,包含该等信息的登记册须于次年 1 月 31 日前送交处长。

80. 豁免

内阁秘书可以豁免任何类别的雇主、任何工业部门或本部分的任何工业,或者本部分的任何条款,或者可以更改第 76 条第(1)款规定的适用范围。

[2008 年第 1 号修正案;2015 年第 19 号法令,第 160 条]

81. 本部分罪行

雇主违反本部分的任何规定,即属犯罪,一经定罪,可处以不超过 10 万先令的罚款或不超过 6 个月的监禁,或两者并罚。

第十一部分
外国服务合同

83. ①格式和认证

外国服务合同应按规定格式,由当事人签字,并经劳工官员认证。

84. 认证前的要求

除非劳工官员确信以下内容,否则不得认证外国服务合同——

(a) 已获得雇员对合同的同意;

(b) 不存在任何欺诈、胁迫或不当影响,以及可能诱使雇员签订合同的任何事实错误或虚假陈述;

(c) 合同符合规定的格式;

(d) 合同中包含的雇佣条款和条件符合本法的规定并为雇员所理解;

(e) 雇员的健康状况适合履行合同规定的职责;和

(f) 雇员在外国服务合同规定的期限内不受任何其他服务合同的约束。

85. 外国服务合同的担保

(1) 当签订外国服务合同的雇主不在肯尼亚境内居住或经营业务时,雇主应当以规定的形式提供担保函,或者如果雇主居住在肯尼亚境内,劳工官员可以要求雇主以规定的形式提供担保函,有一名或多名居住在肯尼亚的担保人,并经劳工官员批准,以劳工官员认为合理的金

---

① 原文无第 82 条。

额适当履行合同以提供担保。

（2）如果雇主在肯尼亚有授权代理人，内阁秘书可要求代理人提供第（1）款规定的担保函，尽管其委托人已披露，代理人仍应受担保函条款的约束。

[2015年第19号法令，第161条]

86. 诱使他人根据非正式合约出国的犯罪

一个人如果——

(a) 雇用、聘用或故意协助雇用或聘用某人，意图在如此受雇或聘用时，该人应在肯尼亚境外从事工作；或者

(b) 诱使或试图诱使雇员在肯尼亚境外工作，

除非他已根据本法与该人或雇员（视情况而定）正式订立外国服务合同，否则即属犯罪，一经定罪，可处以不超过20万先令的罚款或不超过6个月的监禁，或两者并罚。

第十二部分
争议解决程序

87. 劳资纠纷案件的申诉和管辖

（1）根据本法的规定，无论何时——

(a) 雇主或雇员忽视或拒绝履行服务合同；或者

(b) 对任何一方的权利或责任产生任何问题、分歧或争议；或者

(c) 根据任何服务合同，出现涉及任何一方的不当行为、疏忽或虐待，或对任何一方的人身或财产造成任何伤害，

受害方可向劳工官员申诉或在劳资法庭提起申诉或诉讼。

（2）除劳资法庭外，其他法院不得裁决第（1）款提及的任何申诉或诉讼。

（3）第（1）款提述的服务合同或任何其他事项的争议与争议中的主要问题相似或较之次要，则本条不适用于就该争议提起的诉讼。

88. 其他法律规定的一般处罚和犯罪

（1）除儿童外，任何人如违反本法规定，或者违反或不遵守本法任何未明确规定处罚的规定，应处以不超过5万先令的罚款或不超过3个月的监禁，或两者并罚。

（2）本法的任何规定均不得妨碍雇主或雇员因触犯根据任何其他现行法律应予以惩处的罪行而被依法起诉。

（3）任何雇主或雇员不得因同一罪行受到两次处罚。

89. 外国签订服务合同的救济

（1）本法的任何规定都不应妨碍雇主或雇员对在肯尼亚境外签订的合法服务合同违约或不履行时行使各自的权利和补救措施，但对彼此的权利以及对第三方侵权，合同各方在该合同项下的权利可以以与其他合同同样的方式行使。

（2）如果合同已按照本部分执行，则其执行方式应与根据本法签订的合同相同，但由于无书面合同，如果雇员无法阅读和理解合同，则不能按本法规定的合同期限和方式执行；如果该合同已由双方签名，并且对于任何文盲方，应提供如同本法所规定的同等效力的证明。

(3) 合同如果在外国订立的,则该合同应由法官或地方法官鉴证,并加盖法官所属法院的公章。

90. 诉讼时效

尽管有《诉讼时效法》(第 22 章)第 4 条第(1)款的规定,但不得提起基于本法或一般服务合同引起的民事诉讼或法律程序,除非在该法之后的 3 年内由于疏忽或违约提出诉讼,或在持续伤害或损坏的情况下,在其停止后的 12 个月内提起诉讼。

第十三部分
其 他 规 定

91. 规则

(1) 内阁秘书在与委员会协商后,可以制定规则,对本法的所有或任何目的,本法的管理,或为实现本法的目标或目的所必要或有利的规则作出规定,并在不影响上述一般性的情况下,对以下所有或任何目的作出规定——

  (a) 规定根据本法规定的或可能规定的任何事项;
  (b) 雇员的居住或受雇条件,包括卫生设施和供水;
  (c) 在雇主根据服务合同提供食物的情况下,雇员的膳食,包括所提供食物的数量、品种和种类;
  (d) 规范对生病和受伤雇员的照顾;
  (e) 规定由雇主保存和提交的申报表;
  (f) 规定下列——
    (i) 在任何时期内,任何雇员或雇员类别,无论是一般性的还是与任何特定类型的雇佣有关的、可能被要求的最长工作小时数;
    (ii) 允许雇员用餐和休息的时间间隔;
    (iii) 雇员可获准带薪或不带薪的假期或半天假期及差旅费;
    (iv) 与雇员的就业有关的任何其他条件;任何此类条件可能与饮食、住房、医疗、教育、娱乐、纪律或其他方面有关;
  (g) 当一个雇主的雇员超过规定的最高限额时,则应任命劳动监察员;
  (h) 临时雇员的登记和雇用;
  (i) 就业交流的建立和管理,包括通知就业空缺和机会的程序;
  (j) 规定妇女、青年或儿童在任何特定行业或职业中的雇用条件;
  (k) 规定受雇儿童的年龄;
  (l) 要求雇用儿童的雇主提供有关此类儿童或其就业或就业条件的信息并返回给指定官员;
  (m) 由雇主或任何类别的雇主向雇员或任何类别的雇员发放就业卡,无论是一般性的还是与任何特定类型的就业有关的,以及此类卡的形式;
  (n) 规定送达文书中应包含的详情;和
  (o) 规定有关工资以及雇佣条款和条件的通知形式,并就雇佣地点展示该等通知作出规定。

（2）根据本条制定的任何规则可以施加条件，要求执行或完成令授权官员或医疗官员满意的行为或事项，授权任何此类官员以口头或书面形式发布命令，要求执行、完成或禁止执行、完成行为或事项，并且规定期限，在该期限内或之前，应执行或完成该等行为或事情，或满足该等条件。

（3）根据本条制定的任何规则可以区分不同年龄和性别的少年，以及就妇女或少年而言，可以区分不同的地区、职业和环境。

[2015年第19号法令，第162条]

92. 废除第226章和救济条款

（1）废除《就业法》。

（2）除另有规定外，本法的规定是对任何其他法规定的补充，而不是替代或减损。

（3）在本法生效日期后订立的服务合同条款或本法第十一部分适用的外国服务合同，如果提供的服务或就业条件不如本法规定的类似就业条件对雇员有利，则在其不利程度上无效，以及本法所规定的相关雇佣条件应被视为已包含在此类合同或外国服务合同中，视情况而定，构成合同的一部分。

（4）如果——

（a）在《公司与破产法》（2015年）（后续修订）生效之前，内阁秘书根据本法案做出或不做出，或者向内阁秘书做出或不做出的任何行为或事项在上述法令生效之前立即生效；和

（b）在上述法令生效后，内阁秘书根据本法案做出或不做出，或者向内阁秘书做出或不做出该行为或事项

该行为或事项被视为已由内阁秘书做出或未做出，或者已向内阁秘书做出或未向内阁秘书做出。

[2015年第19号法令，第163条]

93. 过渡性条文

根据《就业法》（现已废除）签订的有效服务合同和第十一部分适用的外国服务合同，应在其条款和条件不违反本法规定的范围内继续有效，每一份此类合同均应被视为根据本法规定订立并受其约束的合同，且各方应相应地遵守这些条款规定。

第 207 号法律公告

第三编
税 收 法 规

第六部
所得税法（第 470 章）

所得税（数字服务税）条例（2020）

www.kenyalaw.org

所 得 税 法
（第 470 章）

根据《所得税法》第 130 条和第 3 条第（2A）款的授权，国家财政和规划部内阁秘书制定以下条例——

所得税（数字服务税）条例（2020）

1. 引用与生效

本条例可被称为《所得税（数字服务税）条例》（2020），于 2021 年 1 月 2 日生效。

2. 释义

在本条例中，除非上下文另有规定，否则——

"**数字市场**"的含义见第 3 条第（3）款（ba）项；

"**数字市场提供商**"是指提供数字市场平台的人；

"**数字服务**"是指通过数字市场交付或提供的服务；

"**数字服务提供者**"是指通过数字市场提供数字服务的人；和

"**平台**"是指任何可使数字服务提供商直接或间接连接到服务用户的电子应用程序，包括网站和移动应用程序。

3. 数字服务

（1）应征收数字服务税的数字服务包括——

　　（a）可下载的数字内容，包括可下载的移动应用程序、电子书和电影；

　　（b）OTT 服务，包括流媒体电视节目、电影、音乐、播客和任何形式的数字内容；

　　（c）出售、许可或以任何其他方式处理肯尼亚用户的货币化数据，该数据产生于肯尼亚用户在数字市场的活动；

　　（d）提供数字市场；

　　（e）订阅媒体，包括新闻、杂志和期刊；

　　（f）电子数据管理，包括网站托管、在线数据库、文件共享和云存储服务；

　　（g）线上预约或电子票务服务，包括线上售票；

　　（h）提供搜索引擎和自动桌面服务，包括提供定制的搜索引擎服务；

　　（i）通过预先录制的媒体或电子学习材料进行在线远程培训，包括在线课程和培训；和

　　（j）通过数字市场提供的任何其他服务。

（2）数字服务税不适用于根据本法第 9 条第（2）款或第 35 条征税的收入。

（3）以下服务不属于本条例所规定的数字服务——

　　（a）促进金融工具、商品或外汇的支付、借贷或交易的在线服务，该在线服务由以下单位开展——

　　　　（i）本法附录四规定的金融机构；或者

(ii) 经肯尼亚中央银行授权或批准的金融服务提供商；和

（b）政府机构提供的在线服务。

4. 数字服务税的适用

（1）数字服务税适用于个人在肯尼亚通过在数字市场提供服务而取得的居民或非居民收入。

（2）在肯尼亚设有常设机构的居民或非居民个人缴纳的数字服务税应在其当年收入的应缴税款中抵销。

（3）在肯尼亚没有常设机构的非居民个人缴纳的数字服务税为最终税。

5. 用户位置

（1）如果某人向位于肯尼亚的用户提供或协助提供数字服务，则其应缴纳数字服务税。

（2）如果满足以下条件，则数字服务的用户应被视为位于肯尼亚——

（a）用户从位于肯尼亚的终端接受数字服务，该终端包括电脑、平板电脑和手机；

（b）使用位于肯尼亚的金融机构或公司提供的借记或贷记工具支付数字服务；

（c）数字服务是通过在肯尼亚注册的互联网协议地址或分配给肯尼亚的国际移动电话国家代码获得的；或者

（d）用户在肯尼亚有一个企业、住宅或账单地址。

6. 总交易额

（1）数字服务税应针对数字服务的总交易额征收，该总交易额应——

（a）在提供数字服务的情况下，作为服务对价收到的付款；和

（b）在数字市场的情况下，作为使用平台而支付给数字市场提供商的佣金或费用。

（2）数字服务的总交易额不包括为服务收取的增值税。

7. 登记

（1）在肯尼亚没有常设机构但向肯尼亚用户提供数字服务的非居民个人，可以根据第9条规定的简易税务登记框架进行登记。

（2）肯尼亚居民或在肯尼亚设有常设机构的非居民个人，在肯尼亚提供数字服务，应按规定格式向税务局局长申报数字服务税登记。

8. 任命税务代表（2015 年第 29 号）

在肯尼亚没有常设机构但选择不按照第9条进行登记的非居民个人应根据《税务程序法》（2015）第15A条指定一名税务代表。

9. 简易税务登记

（1）在简易税务登记框架下申请登记的人应通过税务局局长规定的在线登记表办理登记。

（2）根据第（1）款提出的申请应包括以下信息——

（a）申请人的业务名称，包括其交易姓名；

（b）负责税务事宜的联系人姓名；

（c）企业的邮政地址和注册地址及其联系人；

（d）联系人的电话号码；

（e）联系人的电子邮箱；

(f) 申请人开展业务的网站或统一资源定位器；

(g) 申请人在居住国获签发的国家税务识别号码；

(h) 发给申请人企业的公司注册证书；和

(i) 税务局局长可能要求的其他信息。

(3) 申请人可能需要向税务局局长提交必要的文件，以证实根据第(2)款在申请中提供的信息。

(4) 登记后，税务局局长应向申请人发出个人识别号，用于提交申报表和支付数字服务税。

(5) 根据本条例注册的人如停止在肯尼亚提供数字服务，应按规定格式向税务局局长申请注销。

10. 会计和付款

(1) 数字服务税应由以下人员缴纳——

(a) 数字服务提供商或数字市场提供商；或者

(b) 根据第 8 条任命的税务代表。

(2) 第(1)款规定数字服务税的纳税义务人应在提供数字服务的月末至次月 20 日前按规定格式提交申报表并缴纳应缴税款。

11. 申报表修改（2015 年第 29 号）

(1) 根据本条例提交的申报表的修改应符合《税务程序法》(2015)第 31 条的规定。

(2) 如果根据第(1)款进行的修改导致多缴税款，则——

(a) 对于在肯尼亚没有常设机构的非居民个人，多缴的金额应予保留，以抵销后续纳税期间应缴纳的数字服务税；和

(b) 对于肯尼亚居民或在肯尼亚设有常设机构的非居民个人，应根据《税务程序法》(2015)第 47 条退还多付的金额。

12. 记录（2015 年第 29 号）

数字服务税纳税义务人应根据《税务程序法》(2015)第 23 条保留记录。

13. 处罚（2015 年第 29 号）

不遵守本条例规定的人应承担《税收程序法》(2015)规定的相关处罚。

制定于 2020 年 11 月 23 日。

UKUR YATANI

国家财政和规划部内阁秘书

第四编
经济特区法规

第七部
经济特区法（2015 年第 16 号法令）

2023 修订版 [2015]
由全国法律报告委员会经总检察长授权公布

www.kenyalaw.org

2015 年第 16 号法令
经济特区法

[批准日期：2015 年 9 月 11 日]

[施行日期：2015 年 12 月 15 日]

旨在设立经济特区、促进和便利全球和当地投资者的投资并为此类投资的开发和管理提供有利环境及相关目的作出规定的议会法案

[2015 年第 16 号法令，2016 年第 38 号法令，2023 年第 4 号法令]

第一部分
总　　则

1. 简称及生效

本法可称为《经济特区法》(2015)，自发布之日起 90 天届满后生效。

2. 释义

在本法中，除非上下文另有规定，否则——

"**农业区**"是指根据第 4 条规定旨在促进农业及其服务和相关活动的经济特区；

"**管理局**"是指根据第 10 条设立的经济特区管理局；

"**理事会**"是指根据第 12 条设立的管理局的理事会；

"**商业流程外包**"是指为特定业务功能或流程向企业提供外包服务，例如人力资源、财务、会计和采购等后台支持服务；

"**商业服务园区**"是指根据第 4 条为促进服务提供而规定的经济特区，包括但不限于区域总部、业务流程外包中心、呼叫中心、共享服务中心、管理咨询及顾问服务及其他相关服务；

"**商业服务许可证**"是指在经济特区内经营服务的行政许可，不享受本法规定的应得利益；

"**内阁秘书**"是指当时负责有关工业化事务的内阁秘书；

"**公司**"具有《公司法》(第 468 章)第 2 条赋予的含义，包括在肯尼亚境外成立但根据该法在肯尼亚注册的公司；

"**海关管制**"是指根据《东非共同体海关管理法》(2004)规定的法律和法规而采取的措施；

"**海关监管区**"是指企业开展特定海关监管业务的经济特区；

"**关税区**"是指乌干达共和国、肯尼亚共和国和坦桑尼亚联合共和国以及根据《东非共同体成立条约》第 3 条成为东非共同体成员的任何其他国家所在区域，但不包括经济特区；

"**关税**"是指《东非共同体海关管理法》规定的关税；

"**出口**"是指货物运出、安排运出关税区或进入经济特区；

"**出口关税**"是指货物出口应缴纳的关税和其他具有同等效力的费用；

"**自由港区**"是指由经济特区或自由港当局管理的指定区域，就进口关税而言，货物在此

区域一般被视为在海关境外；

"**自由贸易区**"是指货物卸货进行转运、储存的经济特区海关监管区，可包括散装、重新包装、分拣、混合、交易或除制造、加工外的其他形式的处理；

"**基金**"指根据第 21 条设立的普通基金；

"**货物**"包括各种货物、物品、商品、动物、物质、行李、商店、材料、货币，并包括除私人信件以外的邮政物品，如果根据本法出售此类货物，则还包括销售该货物的收益；

"**进口**"是指将货物带入海关区域、经济特区；

"**进口税**"是指对进口货物征收的关税和其他具有同等效力的费用；

"**工业园区**"是指根据第 4 条规定的设有综合基础设施，以满足制造业和加工业需求的经济特区；

"**信息通信技术园区**"是指根据第 4 条规定的促进信息通信技术行业及其服务和相关活动的经济特区；

"**基础设施**"是指经济特区发展和经营所必需，并与其特定行业或集群重点相适应的道路、电力、供水、排水、电信、卫生、污水处理厂、网络、建筑物或其他设施；

"**肯尼亚税务局**"是指根据《肯尼亚税务局法》（第 469 章）第 3 条设立的机构；

"**许可证**"是指根据本法颁发的许可证；

"**畜牧区**"是指根据第 4 条规定进行以下活动的经济特区：牲畜编组和检查；牲畜饲养、育肥、屠宰和冷藏；剔骨；增值；兽药制品制造及其他相关活动；

"**制造**"是指通过手工、机械、化学或生物化学方法制作、生产、装配、组装、加工或制造具有独特名称、特性或用途的新产品，包括诸如冷藏、切割、抛光、混合、选矿、再制造和再设计等流程；

"**负面清单**"是指根据肯尼亚法律和东非共同体法律，经济特区企业不得从事的活动清单；

"**适格官员**"是指其权利或职责是执行或要求执行《东非共同体海关管理法》（2004）所涉行为的任何官员；

"**地区总部**"是指从事总部管理活动，通过向关联公司提供管理、监督、共享服务中心和其他支持服务，以监督、管理和控制其当地、区域性和全球业务的经济特区企业；

"**科技园区**"是指根据第 4 条规定为促进科技行业及其服务和相关活动的经济特区；

"**服务**"是指根据 1994 年 4 月 15 日在马拉喀什缔结的《建立世界贸易组织协定》1B 所附的《服务贸易总协定》及其任何后续协定或修正案涵盖的可交易服务；

"**经济特区**"是指根据第 4 条规定为经济特区的地区；

"**经济特区企业**"是指根据本法获得许可的法人团体；

"**经济特区开发商**"是指根据本法从事或计划开发，可能经营或计划经营经济特区的法人团体；

"**经济特区经营者**"是指根据本法规定从事经济特区经营活动的法人团体；和

"**旅游和娱乐中心**"是指根据第 4 条规定为促进旅游和娱乐行业及其服务和相关活动的经济特区。

3. 本法的目的

本法的目的和宗旨如下——

（a）为经济特区各个方面的发展创造有利环境，包括——

（i）综合基础设施的发展；
　　（ii）为指定为经济特区的地区的经济和商业活动制定奖励措施；
　　（iii）为指定为经济特区的地区的企业盈利消除经济或商业活动的障碍；和
　（b）在适当考虑开放、竞争和透明的原则下，对经济特区内的活动进行监管和管理。

第二部分
经 济 特 区

4. 经济特区的宣布

（1）内阁秘书根据管理局的建议，与负责财政事务的内阁秘书协商后，在公报上公告附录一所列的作为经济特区的任何地区。

（2）根据第（1）款宣布的经济特区应——
　（a）界定该区域的界限；和
　（b）在内阁秘书在公报上发布命令并根据管理局的建议予以撤销之前，持续有效。

（3）内阁秘书在收到根据第（1）款提出的建议后，认为在公报刊登经济特区会侵犯公共利益，内阁秘书可将该建议转交管理局，以确保公共利益得以保护。

（4）经济特区应为指定地理区域，可包括海关监管区和非海关监管区，该区域应提供商业扶持政策、综合土地利用和适合行业的现场和场外基础设施和公用事业，或在公共、私营或公私合营基础上有开发的潜力，该区域基础设施开发和海关监管区内引进的货物，依照海关法规定免征关税。

（5）宣布为经济特区的公共土地不得转让给私人使用，但经济特区开发商、经营者、企业或在经济特区内设立的其他机构除外。

（6）根据本条宣布为经济特区的区域可指定为单部门或多部门经济特区，包括但不限于——
　（a）自由贸易区；
　（b）工业园区；
　（c）自由港；
　（d）信息通信技术园区；
　（e）科技园区；
　（f）农业区；
　（g）旅游和娱乐区；
　（h）商业服务园区；
　（i）畜牧区；
　（j）会议和会议设施

　　　［2016年第38号法令，第66条；2023年第4号法令，第100条］

5. 经济特区划定标准

管理局在指定和确定符合许可条件的经济特区项目提案时，应酌情考虑以下因素——
　（a）拟议项目的性质；

(b) 拟建经济特区的预期规模和周围环境；

(c) 可用的土地和未抵押的土地所有权；

(d) 地理位置和地形；

(e) 资源、人口中心和基础设施的毗邻性；

(f) 国家和郡政府对基础设施和其他公用事业的要求，包括水、电力、污水、电信、固体废物和废水管理；

(g) 提供医疗、娱乐、消防安全、海关和行政设施；

(h) 对场外基础设施、公用事业和服务的影响；

(i) 批准土地用途和分区要求以促进经济特区的发展；

(j) 环境标准和要求；和

(k) 条例中可能规定的任何其他标准。

6. 被视为出口和进口到肯尼亚的货物

除非本法或其他法律另有规定，否则——

(a) 从关税区的任何部分运出并带入经济特区的货物，或者从关税区的任何部分向经济特区提供的服务，应被视为从肯尼亚出口；和

(b) 从经济特区运至关税区的任何部分以供在关税区使用的货物，或者从经济特区向关税区的任何部分提供的服务，应被视为进口到关税区。

但是——

(i) 对来自关税区的货物应免征进口关税；

(ii) 按照海关规定的程序，部分成分来自关税区的货物，对其非来自关税区的成分征收进口关税。

[2023年第4号法令，第101条]

7. 经济特区内的商品和服务

在符合第6条规定的情况下——

(a) 海关控制区域内的经济特区，在其内的货物和所提供的服务不得离开该经济特区，除非——

(i) 出口；

(ii) 按照海关条例和程序进入关税区；

(iii) 经适格官员批准并符合可能施加的任何条件，运往任何其他海关控制区；或者

(iv) 经适格官员事先批准并符合可能施加的任何条件，作维修、保养、加工或改装之用；

(b) 凡是在肯尼亚境外制造的货物，应在标签上明确标明该货物的生产国；

(c) 经济特区企业提供的服务可提供给——

(i) 肯尼亚境外的人；

(ii) 经管理局批准的其他经济特区企业，以促进该经济特区企业的出口活动；或者

(iii) 经管理局批准的关税区内的人员。

8. 经济特区货物的运出

（1）根据本法以及适用的东非共同体的海关法，经济特区内的货物可以——

（a）根据本法的规定储存、出售、展示、分解、重新包装、组装、分发、分类、分级、清洁、混合或以其他方式操作或制造；或者

（b）在适格官员的监督下销毁；或者

（c）在适格官员的监督下，以原包装或其他方式从经济特区出口或送往另一个经济特区或保税工厂。

（2）根据本法和东非共同体的海关法，用于特许经济特区企业活动的任何类型的货物均可带入经济特区。

（3）违反本条规定的人即属犯罪，一经定罪，可处以不超过2 000万先令的罚款或不超过3年的监禁，或两者并罚，且根据《东非共同体海关管理法》，该货物将被没收。

（4）经济特区企业还应按照《东非共同体海关管理法》有关规定颁布的具体规定进行经营。

9. 经济特区企业收支情况

除非本法或任何其他法律另有规定，经济特区企业的资金支付和收款应遵守《肯尼亚中央银行法》（第491章）和《银行法》（第488章）的规定。

第三部分
经济特区管理局

10. 管理局的设立

（1）设立一个被称为经济特区管理局的机构。

（2）管理局应为永久存续及具有公章的法人团体，并应以其法人名义能够——

（a）起诉和被起诉；

（b）购买或以其他方式获取、持有、抵押和处置肯尼亚境内外的动产和不动产；

（c）签订合同；

（d）借款或收款，包括拥有自己的基金；和

（e）为适当履行本法规定的职能，而做出或促使做出或执行所有此类应由法人团体依法做出或执行的事项。

11. 管理局的职能

管理局的职能包括——

（a）就经济特区的指定、批准、设立、运营和监管的各个方面向内阁秘书提出建议；

（b）执行政府关于经济特区的政策和方案；

（c）在必要时确定、划定，购买或向开发商和经营者提供将被指定为或已被指定为经济特区的土地区域；

（d）确定投资标准，包括投资门槛；

（e）在必要的情况下，负责或批准在选定经济特区周边或内部对适当的基础设施进行开发、运营或维护以及融资；

（f）审查经济特区开发商、运营商和企业的申请并授予许可证；

（g）向潜在的经济特区开发商、运营商或其他投资者推广和营销经济特区；

　　（h）管理一个"一站式"中心，经济特区企业可以通过该中心办理所有非由管理局直接处理的许可证、批准、执照和设施申请，通过与企业的协议或实施规章的程序或其他规定的程序与其他政府或私营企业进行必要的协调；

　　（i）在规定的时限条件下，专门执行与指定经济特区有关的所有行政业务条例和履行服务职能；

　　（j）保持关于每个经济特区和企业的方案执行情况的最新数据；

　　（k）建立和加强有关国家机构间的合作，确保遵守所有适用的法律、程序和其他相关要求；

　　（l）向内阁秘书提交一份经济特区内禁止活动的负面清单，包括根据该清单制定的法规所限制的一系列额外活动；

　　（m）建议内阁秘书暂停或吊销违反本法、《东非共同体海关管理法》或《增值税法》的经济特区企业或经济特区开发商的许可证；

　　（n）对来自关税区未获得许可的服务提供者的准入进行监管，以便为个别企业提供服务；

　　（o）规范、实施、监测和监督本法规定的经济特区制度的各个方面；

　　（p）保存经济特区内的企业和居民的登记册；和

　　（q）理事会可能指示的任何其他职能。

12. 理事会

　　（1）管理局应由理事会管理，理事会应由以下人员组成——

　　（a）由总统任命的1名理事长；

　　（b）主管工业化和贸易事务的时任部委首席秘书或其指定的候补；

　　（c）财政部的首席秘书或其指定的候补；

　　（d）国家土地委员会主席或其指定的候补；

　　（e）肯尼亚税务局局长或其指定的候补；

　　（f）由内阁秘书从私营部门或任何其他公共机构任命的，具有杰出贡献、相关经验和专业知识的4名理事。

　　（g）作为当然成员的首席执行官。

　　（2）不得根据第（1）款（f）项任命任何人，除非该人符合《肯尼亚宪法》第六章的要求。

13. 理事会的业务和事务处理

　　（1）理事会业务和事务的运行和监管应符合附录二的规定。

　　（2）除附录二另有规定外，委员会可规范其程序。

14. 理事会的权力

　　（1）理事会应拥有适当履行本法规定的管理局职能所需的一切权力。

　　（2）在不影响上述一般性的情况下，理事会有权——

　　（a）以最能达成管理局成立目的的方式控制、监督和管理管理局的资产；

　　（b）决定为管理局的资本支出、经常性支出以及储备金拨备的款项；

　　（c）接受任何赠款、赠与、捐款或捐赠，并从中进行合法支出；

（d）根据需要，为管理局的资金开立银行账户；

（e）以第 25 条规定的方式将管理局未立即用于其目的的任何资金进行投资；

（f）执行可能附带或有助于实现或履行本法规定的管理局任何职能的所有其他行为或开展任何活动。

15. 理事酬金

管理局须根据内阁秘书的意见向其理事支付确定的酬金、费用或津贴。

16. 首席执行官

（1）管理局须有一名首席执行官，由理事会以竞争方式任命。

（2）不得根据本条任命任何人，除非该人——

（a）拥有机构认可的相关学位，并在与工业、贸易、法律、金融、经济、管理、企业或工程方面具有至少 10 年的工作经验；

（b）符合《宪法》第六章的要求。

（3）首席执行官应——

（a）担任理事会秘书；和

（b）根据理事会的指示，负责理事会事务和人员的日常管理。

17. 管理局工作人员

管理局可以根据理事会确定的服务条款和条件，并根据薪酬委员会的建议，直接或通过一站式中心，任命适当履行本法规定的职能所需的官员和其他工作人员。

18. 管理局授权

理事会通过一般或特定情况的决议，授权任何委员会或理事会的任何成员、官员、雇员或代理人行使根据本法或任何法律规定的权力或履行管理局的任何职能或职责。

19. 个人责任免除

（1）管理局的工作人员在履行或将履行根据本法规定的任何职责或行使任何权力时，对根据管理局或理事会的指示做出的善意行为，不承担个人责任。

（2）第（1）款所规定的人员在任何法院就其在本法项下根据理事会的指示做出或声称做出的任何行为，其被提起的诉讼中所产生的任何费用，如果法院认为该行为是善意的，则费用应从基金中支付，除非该费用由他在该诉讼或起诉中收回。

（3）本条的规定不得免除管理局在侵权或合同中的责任，即因行使根据本法或其他法律授予的任何权力而对任何人、其财产或其任何利益造成的损害向他人支付赔偿或损害赔偿。

20. 公章

（1）管理局的公章须按理事会的指示妥善保管，除非得到理事会的命令，否则不得使用。

（2）加盖管理局的公章须经主席和首席执行官的签名认证以及法律不要求加盖公章的文件认证，理事会的所有决定均可由主席和首席执行官的签名进行认证。

（3）尽管有第（2）款的规定，在主席或首席执行官在某一特定事项上缺席的情况下，理事会应提名一名成员代表主席或首席执行官认证该印章。

（4）管理局的公章加盖在文件上并经过正式认证后，须在司法上予以通知，除非有相反证明,否则理事会根据本条做出的任何命令或授权须推定为正式发出。

第四部分
财 务 规 定

21. 基金会的设立
(1) 管理局设立基金会,称为普通基金会,归属于管理局并由理事会管理。
(2) 应向基金会支付——
 (a) 议会为此目的提供的款项,用于支付管理局在根据本法行使其权力或履行其职能时产生的支出;
 (b) 管理局在根据本法或其他法律行使其权力或履行其职能的过程中可能产生或归属于管理局的费用、款项或资产;和
 (c) 提供、捐赠或借给管理局的任何其他来源的所有款项。
(3) 应从管理局的资金中支付管理局在行使、履行本法规定的目标、职能和职责时所产生的必要费用。
(4) 在财政年度结束时,管理局的资金余额应按财政部的指示使用。

22. 财政年度
管理局的财政年度为 12 个月,至每年 6 月 30 日止。

23. 年度预算
(1) 在每个财政年度开始前至少 3 个月,理事会须安排拟定管理局该年度的收支预算。
(2) 年度预算应为管理局在该财政年度的所有预算支出作出规定,该预算应特别在以下方面作出规定——
 (a) 支付理事的津贴和费用,以及管理局工作人员的薪金、津贴和其他费用;
 (b) 支付管理局职员的退休金、酬金和其他费用;
 (c) 对管理局的建筑物和场地的适当维护;
 (d) 管理局设备和其他财产的维护、修理和更换;
 (e) 设立此类储备基金,以应付与退休福利、保险或更换建筑物或设备有关的未来或或有负债,或其他理事会认为需要的事项;
 (f) 为经济特区的推广和营销提供资金;
 (g) 为管理局的培训、研究和发展活动提供资金;和
 (h) 管理局在行使、履行本法的职能时产生的任何其他支出。
(3) 年度预算应在与其相关的财政年度开始前由理事会批准,并应提交内阁秘书批准,在内阁秘书批准后,未经内阁秘书同意,理事会不得更改年度预算。

24. 账目和审计
(1) 理事会应保存有关管理局所有收入、资产的账簿和记录。
(2) 在每个财政年度结束后的 3 个月内,理事会应向审计长或根据本节任命的审计员提交管理局的账目以及——
 (a) 管理局在该年度的收支表;和

（b）管理局在该年最后一天公布的资产负债表。

但是——

(i) 对来自关税区的货物应免征进口关税；和

(ii) 按照海关规定的程序，部分成分来自关税区的货物，对其非来自关税区的成分征收进口关税。

（3）管理局的账目应根据《公共审计法》(2003)（2003年第12号）进行审计和报告。

（4）管理局应在财政年度结束后的4个月内，向内阁秘书提交一份关于该年度管理局运作的报告。

[2023年第4号法令，第102条]

25. 资金投入

管理局可将其资金投资于政府证券，该类证券中临时受托人可依法将其投资于信托基金，或投资于国家财政部为此目的可能不时批准的任何其他证券。

第五部分
监 管 规 定

26. 经济特区经营许可证

任何人不得——

（a）作为经济特区开发商或经营者或企业开展业务；

（b）声称自己在经济特区内提供或维护活动或设施，

除非根据和按照依本法颁发的许可证。

27. 申请及颁发许可证

（1）有意以经济特区开发商、经营者或企业的身份开展业务的人，应按照规定的方式向管理局申请合适的许可证或申请续期。

（2）管理局在收到许可证申请或续期申请后，可根据海关总署署长的建议，并在申请人支付规定的费用后，向申请人颁发合适的许可证或续期许可证。

（3）在评估经济特区开发商、经营者和企业许可证的申请时，管理局应酌情评估申请人提议的经济特区项目的具体工程和财务计划、财务可行性以及环境和社会影响。

（4）管理局应在正式填写的申请表连同相关证明文件一并提交之日起1个月内，根据本法规定迅速作出许可决定。

（5）根据本条颁发的许可证应——

（a）符合规定的方式；

（b）授权被许可人以经济特区开发商、经营者或企业的身份开展业务；

（c）具体说明许可证项下开展的活动；

（d）在管理局规定的期限内有效；

（e）包含管理局认为必要的其他条件。

（6）根据本条颁发的许可证——

（a）当局在认为有必要修改的情况下，可随时书面通知持有人修改；或者

（b）如果持有人未能遵守本法规定或根据本法制定的任何条例规定的持有许可证的条件，管理局可以暂停或吊销许可证，而在此情况下，持有人应采取管理局建议的措施。

（7）内阁秘书应——

（a）在肯尼亚公报上公布所有核准的设立经济特区的申请；和

（b）在本法生效之日起的180天内公布有关经济特区许可的申请、签发、暂停、撤销和上诉程序的规定。

28. 经济特区开发商和经营者资质

经济特区开发商除应符合规定的标准和要求外，还应满足下列要求——

（a）是一家在肯尼亚注册成立的公司，以从事经济特区活动为目的；

（b）具有发展或运营经济特区所需的财务能力、技术和管理专业知识，以及相关开发或运营项目的相关经历；和

（c）根据《经济特区（土地使用）条例》的规定，在本法生效之日起180天内，拥有或租赁经济特区内的土地或房屋。

29. 经济特区企业

（1）本法第六部分规定的利益不得归于任何企业，除非该企业持有由管理局颁发的有效许可证。

（2）如果申请符合本法的目标，且拟议的商业企业符合以下条件，管理局应授予许可——

（a）在肯尼亚注册成立，无论其是否100%为外资所有；

（b）拟在经济特区内从事经济特区企业有资格从事的一项或多项活动；

（c）不对环境产生负面影响，不从事影响国家安全或对健康造成危害的活动；和

（d）依照现行有效的法律开展业务，但本法规定的豁免除外。

30. 许可证登记册

（1）管理局须以其认为适当的形式备存一份根据本法颁发的现行许可证持有人的登记册，其中应包括——

（a）公司名称；和

（b）公司开展业务的实际地址。

（2）凡——

（a）许可证持有人停止经营与许可证有关的业务；或者

（b）需要在许可证持有人登记册中登记的任何事项详情发生变化，

持有人应在有关事件发生后14天内，以规定的格式向管理局提供有关更改的详情。

第六部分
经济特区企业的权利和义务

31. 经济特区内允许的活动

根据第5条规定，管理局应通知肯尼亚税务局关于根据本法获得许可的经济特区开发商、经营者或企业，具体说明——

（a）企业获得许可的活动；和
（b）许可证所附的条件。

32. 经济特区内的设施

（1）考虑到经济特区开发商许可证的一般目的，管理局可要求经济特区开发商在经济特区提供和维护其认为对经济特区适当和有效运作所必需的设施，包括将经济特区与关税区隔开的足够围地。

（2）在未事先给予有关企业听取意见的机会之前，管理局不得发布停止任何活动或转移任何货物的命令。

（3）各经济特区的适格官员应对经济特区的进出境情况进行现场检查。

（4）管理局应负责经济特区内所有规则的监督和执行。

33. 经济区开发商或经营者的权利和义务

（1）经济特区开发商有权——
（a）根据本条第（2）、（3）和（4）款及第 28 条（b）项和其他此类规定可能规定的许可要求，从事或指定经济特区经营者代表其从事对经济特区的管理和行政工作；
（b）将土地或建筑物出租、转租或出售给经许可的经济特区经营者和企业，并就可能提供的其他服务收取租金或费用；
（c）并购、处置或转让经济特区土地或其他资产；
（d）根据适用法律及其许可证，开发、经营和服务经济特区土地和其他资产；
（e）根据其许可在经济特区内提供公共设施和其他服务，并收取此类服务的费用；
（f）根据适用法律在经济特区以外提供公共设施和其他服务；
（g）享受根据本法规定可能产生的利益；
（h）就经济特区土地和其他资产，包括现场和非现场基础设施的开发、运营和服务与私营第三方签订合同；
（i）不受任何法律限制进入和自由参与国际金融市场，以获得资金、信贷、担保和其他金融资源；和
（j）向潜在投资者和服务提供商宣传和推广其持有许可证的经济特区。

（2）经济特区开发商应以下规定的方式——
（a）根据管理局批准的规划，对经济特区场地及其设施进行实体工程开发或改善；
（b）为保护税收，提供足够围地，将经济特区区域与关税地区隔开，并为进出经济特区的人员、交通工具、船只和货物的流动作出适当的规定；
（c）在现场提供或安排提供管理局在其许可证中确定的充分安全保障；
（d）通过和执行经济特区内的规则和条例，以促进安全和高效商业运营；
（e）保存与其活动、就业统计、业务有关的必要和适当的账目和其他记录，并定期或根据管理局的要求向管理局报告特区活动、绩效和发展；和
（f）向管理局登记所有租约。

（3）第（2）款（e）项要求的账目和记录应以官方语言记录。

（4）经济特区开发商或经营者未按照本条规定保存必要和适当的账目和其他要求的记录的，即属犯罪，一经定罪，可处以不超过 30 万先令的罚款或不超过 6 个月的监禁，或两者并罚。

34. 经济特区企业的权利

经许可的经济特区企业应享有——

(a) 充分保护其财产权免受国有化或征用的所有风险的权利;

(b) 有权完全汇回所有资本和利润,不受任何外汇障碍影响的权利;

(c) 保护工业和知识产权的权利,特别是专利、版权、企业名称、工业设计、技术工艺和商标;

(d) 根据东非共同体海关法的规定,进入其已获得许可的经济特区,在关税区内出口和销售所有类别或种类的商品和服务的权利;

(e) 与一个非经济特区企业进行交易和经营的权利;

(f) 与多个非经济特区企业进行交易和经营的权利;

(g) 与任何其他企业签订合同,购买、出售、出租、转租或以其他方式运用、管理或转让经济特区内的土地或建筑物的权利,但该企业应拥有其财产权;

(h) 与任何其他企业签订合同,购买、出售、出租、转租或以其他方式运用、管理或转让经济特区内的土地或建筑物的权利,但须符合《东非共同体海关管理法》的规定和有关此类企业在经济特区内活动的适用法规;

(i) 对在其获得许可的经济特区区内或区外销售的任何商品或服务价格作出决定的权利;

(j) 在国家范围内开放、自由、有竞争力的投资环境的权益,包括有权自由地在其获得许可的经济特区内参与本法未禁止的任何商业、贸易、制造或服务活动的权利;和

(k) 本法授予经许可的经济特区企业的其他权利和利益。

35. 经济特区企业、开发商和经营者的权益

(1) 所有经许可的经济特区企业、开发商和经营者应享受相应税法规定的税收优惠。

(2) 在符合第(1)款规定的情况下,经许可的经济特区企业、开发商和经营者应获得以下情形的豁免——

(a) 执行与经济特区企业、开发商和经营者的商业活动有关的文书而产生的印花税;

(b) 《外国投资和保护法》(第518章)有关获批企业证书的规定;

(c) 《统计法》(2006)(2006年第4号)的规定;

(d) 支付各郡政府财政法案征收的广告费和商业服务许可费;

(e) 《酒精饮料控制法》(2010)(2010年第4号)规定下的一般酒类许可证和酒店酒类许可证;

(f) 《茶叶法》(第343章)规定下的生产许可证;

(g) 《未加工贵金属贸易法》(第309章)规定下的未加工贵金属交易许可证;

(h) 《电影和舞台剧法》(第222章)规定下的拍摄许可证;

(i) 《业主和租户(商店、酒店和餐饮场所)法》(第301章)规定下实施的租金或租赁管制;和

(j) 与内阁秘书就该事项协商后,根据本法通过在公报上发布公告可能授予的其他

豁免。

（3）经许可的经济特区企业、开发商和经营者有权获得最多占其全职雇员20%的工作许可；

（4）尽管有第（3）款的规定，根据管理局的建议，特殊部门可以获得额外的工作许可。

[2016年第38号法令，第67条]

第七部分
其他规定

36. 内阁秘书的权力

内阁秘书可不时指示管理局以规定的形式提供有关管理局工作和活动的报表、账目和任何其他信息。

37. 争议解决

（1）如果经济特区开发商、经营者或企业与管理局或政府之间关于经济特区企业发生争议，应尽一切努力在30天内通过谈判和相互协商友好解决争端。

（2）如果第（1）款下的争议未获解决，当事人可以通过双方共同约定的下列任何一种方式将其提交仲裁——

(a) 根据联合国国际贸易法委员会、巴黎国际商会或国际投资争端解决中心为仲裁制定的程序规则；或者

(b) 根据政府和投资者所属国家共同加入的双边或多边投资保护协议的框架；或者

(c) 根据《仲裁法》(1995)（1995年第4号）。

（3）如果当事双方未能在14天内就第（2）款（a）项和（b）项规定的争议解决机制达成一致，则适用《仲裁法》。

38. 印花税的豁免

管理局应免除根据《印花税法》（第480章）就土地交易征收的任何印花税。

39. 条例

（1）内阁秘书应根据管理局的建议，就本法要求规定的任何事项或授权制定条例的事项制定条例。

（2）在不影响第（1）款一般性的情况下，条例可以——

(a) 确定所有经济特区的指定和公告标准；

(b) 明确指定经济特区的申请流程、标准、条件、条款和程序，以及经济特区开发商、经营者和企业的许可；

(c) 确定根据本法颁发的许可证形式，以及修改和撤销许可证的程序；

(d) 确定进入经济特区人员的一般条件；

(e) 要求经济特区开发商、运营商和企业提供信息；

(f) 确定有关经济特区一站式中心的建立、运作、运营和程序有关的规则；

(g) 确定经济特区的投资规则；

(h) 确定经济特区的土地使用规则、开发和建筑管制以及公共设施供应和运营的规

定；和

(ⅰ) 确定根据本法征收的费用。

40. 过渡

法人团体在本法生效时，如有以下情形，应被视为经济特区开发商——

(a) 经内阁秘书批准，以公共、私营或公私合营的方式从事综合基础设施的开发或管理；和

(b) 采取重大步骤开始开发或管理综合基础设施。

附录一

[第4条]

经济特区的类型

1. 管理局应批准多个部门或单一部门的经济特区，包括但不限于——

　　(a) 自由贸易区(FTZ)

　　(b) 工业园区

　　(c) 自由港

　　(d) 信息通信技术园区(ICT园区)

　　(e) 科技园区

　　(f) 农业区

　　(g) 旅游和娱乐区

　　(h) 商业服务园区

附录二

[第13条]

关于理事会业务和事务处理的规定

1. 任期

　　除本附录的规定外，主席或除当然成员外的理事应按照任命文书中规定的条款和条件任职3年，但可以连任一届。

2. 离任

　　非当然成员的理事可以——

　　(a) 随时以书面形式通知内阁秘书辞职；

　　(b) 如果理事有以下情形，根据理事会的建议由内阁秘书将其免职——

　　　　(ⅰ) 未经理事会同意连续3次缺席理事会会议；

　　　　(ⅱ) 根据肯尼亚法律，被判构成重罪的刑事犯罪；

　　　　(ⅲ) 因长期身体或精神疾病而丧失行为能力超过6个月；

　　　　(ⅳ) 违反《宪法》第六章的规定；或者

　　　　(ⅴ) 在其他方面不能或不适合履行其职能。

3. 会议

　　(1) 理事会应在每个财政年度举行不少于4次会议，且两次会议的日期之间间隔不超过

4个月。

(2) 尽管有第(1)款的规定,理事长可根据至少3名董事的书面请求,随时召开理事会特别会议,以处理理事会的事务。

(3) 除非理事会全体成员中的四分之三同意,否则每次理事会会议应至少提前14日书面通知每位理事会成员。

(4) 理事会开展业务的法定人数为包括理事长或主持人在内的理事总数的一半。

(5) 理事长应主持理事会的每次会议,若理事长缺席,则出席会议的理事应从出席理事中选出一人主持会议,当选者在该会议和所处理的事务方面享有主席的一切权力。

(6) 除非达成一致决定,否则理事会对任何事项的决定应以出席并参加表决的理事的多数票为准,在票数相等的情况下,理事长或主持人应投决定性的一票。

(7) 除第(4)款另有规定外,理事会的任何程序不得仅因理事一人空缺而无效。

(8) 根据本附录的规定,理事会可以决定其本身的程序以及理事会任何委员会的程序和其他人出席会议的程序,并可以就此制定常规指令。

4. 理事会委员会

(1) 理事会可设立其认为合适的委员会,以履行其可能决定的职能和职责。

(2) 理事会应从其理事中任命根据第(1)款设立的委员会的理事长。

(3) 理事会可在其认为适当的情况下,增选任何人参加其任何委员会的审议。

(4) 根据第(1)款任命的委员会所作出的所有决定均须经理事会批准。

5. 利益披露

(1) 出席会议的理事如果与任何协议或其他事项有利害关系,应在会议上并在会议开始后在合理可行的情况下尽快披露该事实,并且不得参与审议或讨论,不得就有关协议或其他事项的任何问题进行投票,不得在审议该事项期间被计入会议的法定人数。

(2) 根据第(1)款作出的利益披露应记录在相关会议记录中。

(3) 理事违反第(1)款,即属犯罪,一经定罪,可处以不超过20万先令的罚款。

6. 合同和文本

任何合同或文本,如果由非法人团体的主体订立或签署,则无须加盖印章,可由任何人代表理事会订立或签署,或由任何获理事会为此目的一般或特别授权的人代表理事会签署。

第五编
反商业贿赂法规

第八部
反腐败和经济犯罪法（2003年第3号法令）

2023修订版[2003]

由全国法律报告委员会经总检察长授权公布

www.kenyalaw.org

2003 年第 3 号法令
反腐败和经济犯罪法

［批准日期：2003 年 4 月 30 日］

［施行日期：2003 年 5 月 2 日］

旨在对预防、调查和惩罚腐败、经济犯罪和相关犯罪以及与
之相关的事项作出规定的议会法案

［2003 年第 3 号法令、2007 年第 7 号法令、2010 年第 10 号法令、2011 年第 22 号法令、
2012 年第 12 号法令、2014 年第 18 号法令、2016 年第 47 号法令、2023 年第 10 号法令］

第一部分
总　　则

1. 简称

本法可称为《反腐败和经济犯罪法》。

2. 释义

（1）在本法中，除非上下文另有规定，否则——

"**咨询理事会**"是指根据第三部分设立的肯尼亚反腐败咨询理事会；

"**助理理事**"是指委员会的助理理事；

"**利益**"是指任何馈赠、贷款、费用、奖励、任命、服务、好处、宽容、承诺或其他对价或利益；

"**委员会**"是指根据《宪法》第 79 条，《道德与反腐败委员会法》（2011 年第 22 号）第 3 条下设立的道德与反腐败委员会；

"**腐败**"是指——

　（a）第 39、44、46、47 条所规定的任何罪行；

　（b）贿赂；

　（c）欺诈；

　（d）贪污或挪用公款；

　（e）滥用职权；

　（f）违反信托；或者

　（g）涉及不诚实的罪行——

　　（i）与根据任何法案征收的任何税收、税率或税款相关的行为；或者

　　（ii）根据相关法律规定的有关选举公职人员的行为；

"**理事**"*根据 2014 年第 18 号法令附录予以删除*；

"**经济犯罪**"是指——

　（a）第 45 条规定的罪行；或者

(b) 任何维持或保护公共收入的法律规定的涉及不诚实的罪行;

(c) 涉及为腐败所得进行洗钱的罪行。

"调查员"是指理事根据第 23 条对其授权代表委员会进行调查的人;

"部长"是指负责廉正事务的部长;

"私人机构"是指任何非公共机构的个人或组织,包括志愿组织、慈善组织、公司、合伙企业、俱乐部及任何其他机构或组织,不论其如何组成;

"公共机构"是指——

(a) 政府,包括内阁,或政府的任何部门、公共事业机构或企业;

(b) 国民议会或议会服务机构;

(c) 地方当局;

(d) 任何公司、理事会、董事会、委员会或其他机构,其有权根据任何与地方政府、公共卫生或公共事业或其他有关的法律行事,以管理属于政府或由政府授予的资金或根据任何此类法律通过税率、税款或收费筹集的资金;或者

(e) 一家公司,其全部或多数股份为个人或实体所拥有,该个人或实体根据本定义的前述任何条款规定属于公共机构;

"公职人员"是指公共机构的官员、雇员或成员,包括无薪、兼职或临时的人员;

"秘书"是指根据《道德与反腐败法》(2011 年第 22 号)第 16 条任命的委员会秘书;

"不明资产"是指以下人员的资产——

(a) 在该人被合理怀疑涉嫌腐败或经济犯罪时或前后获得的资产;和

(b) 其价值与该人当时或前后的已知收入来源不成比例,并且没有令人满意的解释。

(2) 就本法而言,如果任何记录、财产、信息或其他物品在其控制之下,则该人应被视为占有这些物品。

[2007 年第 7 号法令,附录;2011 年第 22 号法令,第 36 条;2014 年第 18 号法令,附录;
2023 年第 10 号法令,附录]

第二部分
特别法官的委任

3. 任命特别法官的权力

(1) 首席大法官可以通过在肯尼亚公报上的通知,为一个或多个地区、为一个案件或一类案件指定尽可能多的特别法官以审理以下罪行,即——

(a) 腐败、贿赂和经济犯罪及相关犯罪;和

(b) 串谋实施或企图实施或教唆(a)项规定的任何罪行。

(2) 任何人除非担任或曾经担任首席法官或主要法官或至少 10 年的律师,否则没有资格根据本法被任命为特别法官。

[2007 年第 7 号法令,附录;2016 年第 47 号法令,第 26 条]

4. 由特别法官审理的案件

(1) 尽管《刑事诉讼法》(第 75 章)或任何其他现行法律中有任何规定,本法规定的罪行

只能由特别法官审理。

（2）本法规定的每项罪行均应由犯罪地区的特别法官审理，或视情况由为案件指定的特别法官审理，或在该地区的特别法官多于一人的情况下，由首席大法官为此指定的其中一人审判。

（3）在审理任何案件时，除本法所指明的罪行外，特别法官也可根据《刑事诉讼法》（第75章）审理被告在同一审判中被控的罪行。

（4）尽管《刑事诉讼法》（第75章）有任何规定，特别法官应在切实可行的范围内，对犯罪行为进行日常审判，直至完成。

[2007年第7号法令，附录]

5. 特别法官的程序和权力

（1）为取得本应直接或间接参与或知悉罪行的人的证据，特别法官可赦免该人，只要该人在其所知道的范围内全面和真实地披露与该罪行有关的全部情况，并对犯下罪行的其他有关人员给予赦免，无论该人是主犯还是教唆者，此赦免即为《宪法》第77条第（6）款所称的赦免。

（2）《刑事诉讼法》（第75章）和《治安法院法》（第10章）的规定，在不违反本法的情况下，应适用于特别法官审理的诉讼程序；就上述规定而言，特别法官的法院应被视为法院，而在特别法官面前进行起诉的人应被视为检察官。

（3）依据法律的授权，特别法官可对任何被其定罪的人判处刑罚，以惩罚该人所犯的罪行。

第三部分
肯尼亚反腐败委员会和咨询理事会

A—肯尼亚反腐败委员会

6. 根据2011年第22号法令第37条予以废除。
7. 根据2011年第22号法令第37条予以废除。
8. 根据2011年第22号法令第37条予以废除。
9. 根据2011年第22号法令第37条予以废除。
10. 根据2011年第22号法令第37条予以废除。
11. 根据2011年第22号法令第37条予以废除。
12. 根据2011年第22号法令第37条予以废除。
13. 根据2011年第22号法令第37条予以废除。
14. 根据2011年第22号法令第37条予以废除。
15. 根据2011年第22号法令第37条予以废除。

B—肯尼亚反腐败咨询理事会

16. 咨询理事会的成立

（1）肯尼亚反腐败咨询理事会以此方式成立。

（2）咨询理事会应是一个非法人团体，由以下人员组成——

（a）由以下各方提名的1名成员——

（i）肯尼亚律师协会；

（ii）肯尼亚注册会计师协会；

（iii）国际女律师联合会（FIDA）肯尼亚分会；

（iv）肯尼亚制造商协会；

（v）第(3)款所述的宗教组织联合论坛；

（vi）肯尼亚雇主联合会；

（vii）肯尼亚银行家协会；

（viii）中央工会组织；

（ix）东非专业协会；

（x）肯尼亚建筑协会；

（xi）肯尼亚工程师协会；和

（xii）肯尼亚医学协会；和

（b）理事。

（3）第(2)款(a)项(v)目所述的宗教组织联合论坛应由以下代表组成——

（a）肯尼亚穆斯林最高委员会；

（b）肯尼亚主教团；

（c）肯尼亚全国教会理事会；

（d）肯尼亚福音派团契；和

（e）肯尼亚印度教理事会。

（4）附表二适用于咨询理事会及其成员。

17. 咨询理事会的职能

（1）咨询理事会的主要职能是就委员会根据本法行使权力和履行职能向委员会提供一般性建议。

（2）咨询理事会应具有本法可能授予的或者本法规定的其他职能。

18. 咨询理事会的独立性

在履行其职能时，咨询理事会不受任何其他人或当局的指示或控制，仅对议会负责。

19. 根据2014年第18号法令附录予以删除。

20. 主席、副主席

（1）咨询理事会应提名其提名的一名成员为咨询理事会主席，另一名其提名成员为副主席。

（2）上述提名的成员应由总统分别委任。

（3）除非提前辞职或终止，主席和副主席应各司其职，直至其作为咨询理事会成员的任期届满为止。

21. 咨询理事会秘书

根据《道德和反腐败法》第16条任命的委员会秘书应为咨询理事会秘书。

[2014年第18号法令,附录]

22. 咨询理事会的程序

（1）咨询理事会的业务和事务应当根据附录三的规定执行。

（2）除附录三规定外,咨询理事会可规范其程序。
（3）咨询理事会的7名提名成员应构成处理委员会任何事务的法定人数。
（4）咨询理事会可邀请任何人出席其任何会议并参与其审议,但该受邀人不得对理事会的任何决定拥有投票权。

第四部分
调　查

23. 调查员

（1）秘书或秘书授权的人可以代表委员会进行调查。

（2）除非本部分另有规定,为调查的目的,本部分授予委员会的权力可由秘书或调查员行使。

（3）为调查的目的,秘书或调查员除根据本部分拥有的任何其他权力外,还应具有警官的权力、特权和豁免权。

（4）《刑事诉讼法》(第75章)、《证据法》(第80章)、《警察法》(第84章)以及赋予警察侦查、预防和调查与腐败和经济犯罪有关的罪行所必需的权力、特权和豁免权的任何其他法律的规定,只要不违反本法或任何其他法律的规定,前述对于警察的规定,同样适用于秘书和调查员。

[2007年第7号法令,附录;2014年第18号法令,附录]

24. 调查员的身份证明

（1）委员会应向调查员签发身份证明文件,该身份证明文件应证明被签发对象是调查员。

（2）委员会签发的身份证明文件应由秘书签字。

[2014年第18号法令,附录]

25. 未调查的投诉

如果委员会收到有关任何人腐败行为的投诉,并且委员会拒绝调查或在调查结束前停止调查,委员会应将其决定及其理由书面通知投诉人。

25A. 停止调查

（1）委员会可在与部长和总检察长协商后,以部长规定的形式作出承诺,不对任何涉嫌犯有本法项下罪行的人发起或继续调查。

（2）如果委员打算采取第（1）款规定的行动,则应在日报上发布通知,邀请利害关系人在通知规定的期限内就该项承诺与其联系。

（3）根据本条作出的承诺仅在嫌疑人有以下情况下时作出——

　　(a) 全面、真实地披露与过去腐败或经济犯罪有关的所有重要事实;

　　(b) 通过委员会,向所有受影响的人支付或退还任何非法获得的财产或金钱,或将其存入委员会,并按部长规定的利率计息;

　　(c) 向任何受其腐败行为影响的人作出赔偿;

　　(d) 赔偿因其腐败行为造成的所有公共财产损失。

（4）委员会应至少在两份全国发行的报纸上以通知公布其作出该项承诺的意图——

（a）说明该承诺的拟议受益人的姓名；
　　（b）说明该人涉嫌犯下的罪行；
　　（c）确认该人已满足第(2)款规定的所有条件；和
　　（d）邀请对提议的承诺有异议的任何人在通知规定的期限内向委员会提出异议。
（5）受侵害的人可以基于以下理由反对提议的承诺——
　　（a）嫌疑人未完全满足第(2)款规定的条件；或者
　　（b）嫌疑人有任何其他与本节相关的证据，该证据可能会影响委员会关于该承诺的决定。
（6）委员会应考虑提交的所有反对意见，并应根据情况采取适当的行动。
（7）委员会不得对涉及导致危害公共安全、法律和秩序情形的腐败或经济犯罪作出任何承诺。
（8）根据本条作出承诺的委员会中的任何人，将被取消担任公职的资格。

[2007年第7号法令,附录]

26. 嫌疑人财产陈述

（1）如果在调查任何罪行的过程中，秘书认为可以协助或加快此类调查时，则秘书可通过书面通知要求被合理怀疑有腐败或经济犯罪的人，出于该通知中说明的原因，须在通知指明的合理时间内，就秘书指明的任何财产提供书面说明，且就该指明的财产——
　　（a）列举嫌疑人的财产和获得财产的时间；和
　　（b）就涉嫌腐败或经济犯罪时或前后获得的任何财产，说明该财产是通过购买、赠与、继承还是以其他方式获得的，以及以何种对价（如有）获得了该项财产。
（2）忽视或不遵守本条规定的人，即属犯罪，一经定罪，可处以不超过30万先令的罚款或不超过3年的监禁，或两者并罚。
（3）本条规定的委员会权力只能由秘书行使。

[2007年第7号法令,附录；2014年第18号法令,附录]

27. 提供信息的要求等

（1）委员会可单方面向法院申请命令，要求嫌疑人的关联人在命令指定的合理时间内提供书面声明，说明秘书指定的任何财产，无论该财产是通过购买、赠与、继承或其他方式获得的，以及获得该财产的对价（如有）。
（2）在第(1)款中，"**嫌疑人的关联人**"是指调查员有理由相信可能与涉嫌腐败或经济犯罪的人有交易的人，无论其是否涉嫌腐败或经济犯罪。
（3）委员会可以书面通知要求任何人在通知规定的合理时间内提供该人持有的与涉嫌腐败或经济犯罪的人有关的任何信息或文件。
（4）忽视或不遵守本条规定的人，即属犯罪，一经定罪，可处以不超过30万先令的罚款或不超过3年的监禁，或两者并罚。
（5）本部分不要求披露受辩护律师特权保护的任何内容，包括受《证据法》（第80章）第134条或137条保护的任何内容。

[2007年第7号法令,附录；2014年第18号法令,附录]

28. 提供记录和财产

（1）委员会可以在通知所涉当事人的情况下，向法院申请命令——

（a）要求任何人,无论其是否涉嫌腐败或经济犯罪,出示其持有的调查中可能需要的特定记录;和

（b）要求该人或任何其他人在其所知范围内,就该记录提供解释或信息,无论这些记录是否由其本人制作。

（2）第（1）款（b）项的要求可能包括亲自出席提供解释和信息的要求。

（3）第（1）款的要求可要求个人在不超过6个月的一段时间内持续出示记录或提供解释和信息。

（4）第（3）款中的6个月期限并不妨碍委员会提出进一步的时间要求,只要每项要求所涉及的期限不超过6个月。

（5）在不影响第30条实施的情况下,委员会可以复制或摘录根据本条要求制作的任何记录。

（6）根据本条出示以电子形式存储的记录的要求是——

（a）将记录缩减为硬拷贝并出示;和

（b）如有特别要求,以电子形式出示记录副本。

（7）在本条中,"**记录**"包括账簿、报表、银行账户或其他账户、报告、法律或商业文件和信函,但严格个人性质的信函除外。

（8）委员会可通过书面通知要求某人在通知规定的合理时间内出示该人拥有的任何财产以供检查,该财产属于合理涉嫌腐败或经济犯罪人的财产。

（9）忽视或不遵守本条规定的人,即属犯罪,一经定罪,可处以不超过30万先令的罚款或不超过3年的监禁,或两者并罚。

（10）本部分不要求披露受辩护律师特权保护的任何内容,包括受《证据法》(第80章)第134条或137条保护的任何内容。

[2007年第7号法令,附录;2014年第18号法令,附录]

29. 搜查住所

（1）委员会可凭执行令进入和搜查在该处所内有合理嫌疑的任何记录、财产或其他物品,而这些物品并未由任何人根据本部分上述条文下的要求提供。

（2）本条赋予的权力是对第23条第（3）款或本部分任何其他规定所赋予权力的补充,而非缩小或者限制。

30. 提供或发现物品的可接受性

如果通知是针对被调查人或被指控犯有腐败或经济犯罪的人,则根据该通知提供的任何陈述、记录或资料,不得在任何刑事诉讼中作为不利于该人的证据,除非该人被控明知或罔顾后果提供虚假信息。

[2007年第7号法令,附录]

31. 旅行证件的交还

（1）在以下情况下,法院可以应委员会的单方面申请发布命令,要求某人将其旅行证件交回委员会——

（a）该人合理涉嫌腐败或经济犯罪;和

（b）相关的腐败或经济犯罪正在调查中。

（2）如果某人根据第（1）款的命令交出其旅行证件，委员会——

  （a）如不提起刑事诉讼，则须在相关腐败或经济犯罪的调查完成后退回文件；和

  （b）可自行决定在有条件或无条件的情况下退回文件，以确保该人出庭。

（3）第（1）款中的命令针对的人可向法院申请，解除、更改该命令或命令归还其旅行证件，并且法院可在听取各方意见后解除或更改命令、命令退回旅行证件或驳回申请。

（4）如果某人没有按照第（1）款的命令归还其旅行证件，该人可能会被逮捕并被移交法院，除非法院确信该人没有任何旅行文件，否则法院应当命令拘留该人，直至对有关腐败或经济犯罪的调查结束。

（5）根据第（4）款的命令被拘留的人应在以下情况下获释——

  （a）该人向委员会交出其旅行证件；

  （b）该人向法庭证明其没有任何旅行证件；或者

  （c）对有关腐败或经济犯罪的调查已完成，法院确信不会提起刑事诉讼。

（6）根据第（4）款的命令被拘留的人，应至少每8日或按法院可能命令的更短间隔被移交法院，以确定是否应根据第（5）款释放该人。

32. 逮捕人

在不影响第23条第（3）款的一般性原则下，与警察执法相同，秘书和调查员有权逮捕任何人并指控其犯罪，并为调查目的拘留他们。

［2014年第18号法令，附录］

33. 可能影响调查的披露

（1）除非得到理事许可或有其他合法理由，否则任何人不得披露根据本法进行的调查细节，包括被调查人的身份。

（2）任何人违反本条，即属犯罪，一经定罪，可处以不超过30万先令的罚款或不超过3年的监禁，或两者并罚。

34. 冒充调查员

（1）除调查员外，任何人不得自称是调查员或以调查员的身份行事。

（2）任何人违反本条，即属犯罪，一经定罪，可处以不超过30万先令的罚款或不超3年的监禁，或两者并罚。

35. 调查报告

（1）调查后，委员会应向检察长报告调查结果。

（2）委员会的报告应包括委员会可能提出的关于某人涉嫌腐败或经济犯罪被起诉的任何建议。

［2012年第12号法令，附录］

36. 季度报告

（1）委员会应编制季度报告，说明根据第35条向检察长提交的报告数量以及委员会认为适当的与这些报告有关的其他统计信息。

（2）季度报告应说明委员会提出的腐败或经济犯罪起诉某人的建议是否被接受。

（3）委员会应向总检察长提供每份季度报告的副本。

（4）总检察长应将每份季度报告的副本提交国民议会。

（5）委员会应安排在公报上公布每份季度报告。

[2012年第12号法令,附录]

37. 检控年度报告

（1）检察长应就腐败或经济犯罪的起诉编制年度报告。

（2）年度报告涵盖的年度截至12月31日。

（3）每年的年度报告应包括一年内该年度每次起诉所采取的措施摘要以及在该年年终时每个起诉的状态。

（4）年度报告还应说明委员会提出的起诉腐败或经济犯罪人的建议是否被接受,并简要说明不接受该建议的原因。

（5）如果上一年最终结案的起诉已列入前一年的年度报告中,则年度报告不需要包括该起诉。

（6）在年度报告所涉年份结束后的前10个会议日内,总检察长应向国民议会提交年度报告。

（7）本条实施后的第一份年度报告涵盖期间应从本条实施日起至次年的12月31日止。

[2012年第12号法令,附录]

第五部分
罪　行

38. "代理人"和"委托人"的含义

（1）在本部分中——

"代理人"是指以任何身份,无论是在公共部门还是在私营部门,受雇于他人或代表他人行事的人;

"委托人"是指无论是在公共部门还是私营部门,其雇用代理人或代理人为其行事或代表其行事的人。

（2）如某人根据《宪法》或法律拥有权力,而根据法律不清楚该人是否是代理人或哪个公共机构是代理人的委托人,则就本部分而言,该人应被视为政府的代理人,而该权力的行使应被视为与政府的业务或事务有关。

（3）就本部分而言——

（a）内阁部长应被视为内阁和政府的代理人;和

（b）担任指定职务或职位的人应被视为指定的委托人的代理人。

（4）为第（3）款（b）项的目的,根据本法制定的规章可以规定公职、职位和负责人。

39. 根据2016年第47号法令第23条予以删除。

40. 建议的秘密引诱

（1）本条适用于因向某人提供建议作为诱因或奖励的利益,或因其他原因而获得的利益。

（2）如果某人有以下情形,则该人犯了罪行——

（a）接受或索取,或同意接受或索取本条适用的利益,且该人打算将该利益对接受建议者保密;或者

(b) 给予或提供,或同意给予或提供本条适用的利益,且该人打算将该利益对接受建议者保密。

(3) 在本条中,"**提供建议**"包括提供信息。

41. 欺骗委托人

(1) 代理人明知某项陈述在任何重大方面具有虚假或误导性,而向其委托人作出该陈述而损害其委托的,即属犯罪。

(2) 代理人使用或向其委托人提供其明知在任何重大方面包含任何虚假或误导内容的文件,而对其委托人造成损害的,即属犯罪。

42. 利益冲突

(1) 如果代理人在其委托人将作出的决定中具有直接或间接的私人利益,则代理人在以下情况下的行为即属犯罪——

(a) 代理人知道或有理由相信委托人不知道该利益而代理人未披露该利益;和

(b) 代理人对委托人的决定投票或参与诉讼。

(2) 私人机构可以授权其代理人投票或参与该私人机构的诉讼,并且获授权的代理人的投票或参与不违反第(1)款规定。

(3) 公共机构的代理人明知而直接或间接地在源自公共机构或与公共机构有关的任何合同、协议或投资中获得或持有私人利益,即属犯罪。

(4) 第(3)款不适用于代理人的雇佣合同、相关或类似的合同或协议或任何规定的合同、协议或投资。

43. 受托人委任的不当利益

(1) 本条适用于因委任某人为财产受托人或参与或协助该任命而作为诱因或奖励的利益。

(2) 根据第(3)款的规定,某人在以下情况下的行为属于犯罪——

(a) 从财产受托人处接受或索取,或同意接受或索取本部分适用的利益;或者

(b) 给予或提供,或同意给予或提供给财产受托人本条适用的利益。

(3) 第(2)款不适用于经每位有权享有该财产的人的知情同意或根据法院的命令所做出的任何事情。

(4) 在本条中,"**财产受托人**"包括——

(a) 被任命处理财产的执行人或管理人;

(b) 根据授权或委任,对财产享有权力的人;和

(c) 代表身体虚弱或精神丧失能力的人管理,或者被任命或受雇管理财产的人或委员会成员。

44. 投标操纵等

(1) 本条适用于作为以下诱因或报酬的利益——

(a) 不提交标书、建议书、报价或投标;

(b) 撤回或更改标书、建议书、报价或投标;或者

(c) 提交标书、建议书、报价或投标,其中规定了价格或任何规定的包含或排除。

(2) 如果某人有以下情形,即属犯罪——

(a) 接受或索取或者同意接受或索取本条适用的利益;或者

(b) 给予或提供或者同意给予或提供本条适用的利益。

45. 公共财产和税收保护等

（1）任何人如以欺诈或其他方式非法从事以下活动，即属犯罪——

  （a） 获取公共财产或公共服务或利益；

  （b） 抵押或处置任何公共财产；

  （c） 损害公共财产，包括使计算机或任何其他电子机器执行任何功能，直接或间接导致损失或对任何公共收入或服务产生不利影响；

  （d） 未能向任何公共机构支付任何税款或费用、征税或收费，或在支付任何此类税款、费用、征税或收费时获得任何豁免、减免。

（2）其职能涉及公共税收或公共财产的任何部分的行政、保管、管理、收取或使用的官员或个人如果有以下情形，即属犯罪——

  （a） 从公共税收中欺诈支付或超额支付——

    （i） 不合格或有缺陷的商品；

    （ii） 未提供或未足额提供的商品；或者

    （iii） 未提供或未充分提供的服务，

  （b） 出于故意或疏忽，不遵守与财产的采购、分配、销售或处置、合同投标、资金管理或支出有关的任何法律或适用程序和准则；或者

  （c） 在没有事先计划的情况下从事项目。

（3）在本条中，"**公共财产**"是指公共机构的或由公共机构控制、托管的不动产或动产，包括金钱。

46. 滥用职权

任何人利用其职务为自己或他人提供不当利益，即属犯罪。

47. 可疑财产的处理

（1）任何人处理其认为或有理由相信是在腐败行为过程中或因腐败行为而获得的财产，即属犯罪。

（2）就本条而言，如果某人有以下情形，则其行为是处理财产——

  （a） 持有、接收、隐匿或使用该财产或导致该财产被使用；

  （b） 就该财产订立交易或促使该交易的订立。

（3）在本条中，"**腐败行为**"是指——

  （a） 构成腐败或经济犯罪的行为；

  （b） 在本法实施之前发生的行为，并且该行为——

    （i） 当时构成犯罪；和

    （ii） 如果发生在本法实施后，将构成腐败或经济犯罪。

47A. 企图、阴谋等

（1）任何人企图实施腐败或者经济犯罪的，即属犯罪。

（2）就本条而言，如果某人出于犯罪的意图，做或不做旨在实施该犯罪的事情，但没有达到将该意图实现到足以实施该犯罪的程度，则该人即属企图实施腐败或经济犯罪。

（3）与他人合谋实施腐败或经济犯罪，即属犯罪。

（4）任何人煽动他人做出任何作为或不作为，如果就其性质而言，该作为或不作为构成腐败或经济犯罪，即属犯罪。

[2007年第7号法令，附录]

48. 对本部分所订罪行的处罚
（1）被判犯本部所订罪行的人，可处以——
- （a）不超过100万先令的罚款，或不超过10年的监禁，或两者并罚；和
- （b）如果由于犯罪行为，该人获得了可量化的利益或任何其他人遭受了可量化的损失，则可对其处以额外的强制罚款。

（2）第（1）款（b）项所述的强制罚款应按以下方式确定——
- （a）强制罚款应等于第（1）款（b）项所述的利益或损失金额的两倍；
- （b）如果犯罪行为导致第（1）款（b）项所述的利益和损失，则强制罚款应等于利益和损失金额之和的两倍。

49. 惯例不作为抗辩理由
在指控本部分所犯罪行时，接受、索取、给予或提供任何利益是任何业务、事业、职位、专业或职业的惯例，不得作为抗辩理由。

50. 不可能，无意图等不作为辩护理由
如果对本部分所订罪行的指控，涉及作为或不作为的诱因或报酬的利益，则以下内容不得作为抗辩理由——
- （a）该作为或不作为不在某人的权力范围内，或者该人无意作出该作为或不作为；或者
- （b）该作为或不作为并未发生。

第六部分
不当利益的赔偿和追回

51. 赔偿责任
任何人做出任何构成腐败或经济犯罪的行为，都要对任何因此遭受损失的任何人承担赔偿责任，该赔偿数额将是所遭受损失的全部赔偿。

52. 不正当利益的责任
任何人如收取利益而构成第39、40或43条所订的罪行，就该利益的价值而言，该人须对以下人员负法律责任——
- （a）如果该行为构成第39条所涉的罪行，须向代理人的委托人负责；
- （b）如果该行为构成第40条所涉的罪行，须向接受建议者负责；或者
- （c）如果该行为构成第43条所涉的罪行，须向有权享有该财产的有关人员负责。

53. 责任——其他规定
（1）根据第51条或52条须支付规定款项的人还应负责按规定利率支付相应利息。

（2）第51条或52条的任何规定并不影响任何人可能承担的任何其他责任。

（3）某人根据第51条或第52条须向公共机构承担的款项可由公共机构或委员会代表其

收回。

（4）为进一步明确，《政府诉讼法》（第40章）中的规定不得阻止委员会根据第（3）款提起民事诉讼以追回款项。

（5）如果某人是腐败或经济犯罪的当事方，或该人的相关行为也构成了腐败或经济犯罪，则该人无权根据第51条或第52条获得与特定腐败或经济犯罪有关的任何款项。

54. 定罪赔偿令

（1）法院判定任何人犯有任何腐败或经济犯罪，应在定罪时或在其后提出申请时，命令该人——

　　（a）根据第51条或第52条，支付其可能应承担的任何款项；和

　　（b）将在构成腐败或经济犯罪的行为中获得的财产或与该财产价值相当的财产给予合法所有人。

（2）如果没有或无法确定第（1）款（b）项所述的合法所有人，法院应下令没收该财产或等值款项给政府。

（3）在根据本条作出命令时，法院可以量化任何金额或可以决定如何量化该金额。

（4）根据本条作出的命令，可由该命令的受益人强制执行，如同在民事诉讼中作出的命令。

55. 没收来源不明资产

（1）在本条中，"**腐败行为**"是指——

　　（a）构成腐败或经济犯罪的行为；

　　（b）在本法实施之前发生的行为——

　　　　（i）当时构成犯罪；和

　　　　（ii）如果发生在本法实施后，将构成腐败或经济犯罪。

（2）在以下情况下，委员会可以根据本条对某人提起诉讼——

　　（a）经调查，委员会确信该人拥有来源不明的资产；和

　　（b）在委员会行使其调查或其他权力的过程中，该人获得了合理的机会来解释有关资产与其已知合法收入来源之间不成比例，而委员会对这种不成比例的充分解释不满意。

（3）根据本条提起的诉讼应以原诉传票的方式在高等法院提起。

（4）在根据本条进行的诉讼中——

　　（a）委员会应举证证明该人拥有来源不明的资产；

　　（b）资产有争议的人应有机会盘问任何被传唤的证人，并对委员会提出的任何证据提出质疑，并在符合本条规定的情况下，享有并可以行使在民事诉讼中通常赋予被告人的权利。

（5）如果委员会在引证该人拥有来源不明的资产的证据后，法院在权衡可能性的基础上，根据迄今为止提出的证据，认为该人确实拥有来源不明的资产，则可以要求该人通过法院认为充分的证词和其他证据，使法院确信资产是非因腐败行为而获得的。

（6）如果在作出上述解释后，法院不认同所有有关资产是非因腐败行为而获得的，可命令该人向政府支付与来源不明的财产价值相等的款项，但该款项并非由于腐败行为而取得的。

（7）为本条项下诉讼的目的,资产有争议的人的资产应被视为包括法院认定的另一人的任何资产,该资产——

　　（a）以信托方式为资产有争议的人持有或以其他方式代表该人持有;或者

　　（b）在没有适当对价的情况下,以赠与或贷款的形式,从其资产有争议的人处获得。

（8）本条规定的诉讼记录可作为任何其他诉讼的证据,包括对腐败或经济犯罪的任何起诉。

（9）本条应具有追溯效力。

[2007年第7号法令,附录]

56. 保留可疑财产的命令等

（1）根据委员会的单方面申请,如果高等法院有合理的理由怀疑有关财产是通过腐败行为而获得的,可以下令禁止转让、处置或以其他方式处理该财产。

（2）根据本条的规定,法院可对涉嫌腐败或随后获得财产的人发出命令。

（3）根据本条发出的命令有效期为6个月,并且法院可以应委员会的申请延长有效期。

（4）根据本条收到命令的人,可在命令送达后15日内,向法院申请撤销或变更该命令,法院可在听取各方意见后撤销、变更命令或驳回申请。

（5）法院只有在权衡各种可能性后,确信撤销或变更命令所涉及的财产非因腐败行为而获得,才可以撤销或变更根据第（4）款作出的执行命令。

（6）收到根据本条发出的命令而违反该命令的人,即属犯罪,一经定罪,可处以不超过200万先令的罚款或不超过10年的监禁,或两者并罚。

（7）在本条中,"**腐败行为**"是指——

　　（a）构成腐败或经济犯罪的行为;或者

　　（b）在本法实施之前发生的行为,且该行为——

　　　　（i）在当时构成犯罪;和

　　　　（ii）如果发生在本法生效后,将构成腐败或经济犯罪。

[2016年第47号法令,第24条]

56A. 任命接管人

（1）委员会可在获得法院许可的情况下,随时为委员会怀疑通过腐败行为获得的财产任命接管人。

（2）根据上述第（1）款接管人的任命须由理事或助理理事以书面签署。

（3）接管人有权管理、控制和占有其获任命接管的财产。

（4）委员会或接管人应在任命时或此后不久,向拥有或可能拥有财产保管权或控制权的人送达通知,并且如果任何法律要求对该财产进行登记,则应向相关登记官发出类似的通知:

如果财产位于肯尼亚境外,则无须发出通知,但委员会有权就财产的没收、管理、控制和遣返事宜与外国政府、政府部门和国际机构联络。

（5）除非得到法院命令的授权,否则根据前款规定收到通知的人不得以任何不符合接管人指示的方式处理财产。

（6）任何人违反第（5）款,即属犯罪,对于首次犯罪,可处以不超过200万先令的罚款或不超过10年的监禁,或两者并罚;对于同一财产的后续犯罪,可处以不超过10年的监禁,但不得选择罚款。

（7）为免生疑问，任何种类的财产，无论是有形财产或无形财产、动产或不动产，包括建筑物、收入、债务、银行存款、商业机构、股票和其他财产，均可根据本条任命接管人。

（8）接管人应保存适当的账簿并向委员会提交季度报告，还可以从其获任命接管的财产中获取接管费用。

（9）对根据本条任命接管人不服的人可以书面请求委员会撤销任命，以换取一些合理的保证金，或者可以基于以下理由向高等法院申请撤销或变更任命——

(a) 其向委员会提供了一份合理的担保，但委员会并未接受；或者

(b) 其有证据表明，根据可能性的平衡，其获得该财产不是通过犯罪或民事过错行为。

（10）根据第（9）款向高等法院提出的申请应在各方之间进行审理，委员会有权对申请人进行交叉质询并提出反驳的证据。

[2007年第7号法令，附录]

56B. 庭外和解

（1）在本法或任何其他法律授权委员会提起民事诉讼或申请的任何事项中，委员会可以合法向拟被起诉者发出通知或信函，并且可以在该通知或信函中，告知该人针对其的申索，并进一步通知该人可以在提起诉讼前的指定时间内解决该申索。

（2）委员会可与其拟向法院或已实际向法院提起民事诉讼或申请的任何人谈判并达成和解。

（3）委员会可以书面承诺不对以下人员提起刑事诉讼——

(a) 已全面真实披露与其本人或他人过去的腐败和经济犯罪有关的所有重要事实；和

(b) 自愿支付、存入或退还其通过腐败或经济犯罪获得的所有财产；

(c) 已赔偿其腐败行为对公共财产造成的所有损失。

（4）根据本条达成的和解或承诺应在法院登记。

[2007年第7号法令，附录]

56C. 资金和其他资产的追回

（1）委员会追回的任何资金应存入综合基金。

（2）尽管本法或其他法律有任何规定，在调查过程中或在调查结束时，在诉讼开始时或诉讼中（无论该诉讼是民事诉讼或刑事诉讼）或在该等诉讼结束后，追回的任何资产或财产，无论是动产还是不动产，均应移交给财政部常任秘书长。

[2010年第10号法令，第78条]

第七部分
证　据

57. 作为证据的来源不明资产等

（1）法院可以将来源不明的资产作为被控腐败或经济犯罪的人获得利益的证据。

（2）就本条而言，被告人的资产应被视为包括法院认定的另一人的资产，该资产——

(a) 以信托方式为被告人持有，或以其他方式为被告人持有或其代表持有；或者

（b）在没有适当对价的情况下从被告人处获得。

58. 有行为证明的腐败推定

如果某人被指控犯有第五部分所述的罪行，其一项要件是腐败行为所为，被告人被证明做了该行为，则除非有相反证据证明，否则该人须被推定为以腐败方式做出该作为。

59. 证明财产价值的证书等

（1）在对腐败或经济犯罪的起诉或根据本法进行的诉讼中，除非有相反的证据证明，否则估价官发出的关于利益或财产价值的证书是可以接受的，并且该证书是该价值的证明。

（2）在没有相反证据的情况下，法院应推定，声称是估价官发出的证书即为该证书。

（3）在本条中，"估价官"是指由委员会或政府任命、雇用或授权对财产进行估价的人，其任命、雇用或授权须通过公报通知。

60. 与共犯有关的规则等

就任何要求证实共犯的证据规则或惯例而言，任何人不得仅因为以下情形而被指控为犯有第五部分所涉罪行的共犯——

（a）该人接受、索取或同意向被告人收取或索取利益；或者

（b）该人给予、提供或同意给予或提供给被告人利益。

61. 职位证明及补偿

（1）在对腐败或经济犯罪的起诉或根据本法进行的诉讼中，机构官员关于某人在该机构中的职位或赔偿的证书是可以接受的，并且在没有相反证据的情况下，该证书是该职位或赔偿的证明。

（2）在没有相反证据的情况下，法院应推定声称是机构官员作出的证书即为该证书。

第七A部分
执　　行

61A. 针对委员会的执行

尽管法律有任何相反规定，凡判决或命令委员会作出损害赔偿或其他方式付款的——

（a）不得针对委员会或委员会的资产、债务或银行存款签发任何性质的执行或扣押；

（b）除非有人对该判决或命令提出上诉或申请，否则理事须安排根据该法令支付委员会款项给有权获得该款项的人，而该款项已在年度预算中予以明确规定；

（c）未经理事事先书面许可，任何依法有权扣押财产的人不得扣押或拿走委员会的财产。

［2007年第7号法令，附录］

第八部分
其　　他

62. 因被指控犯有腐败或经济犯罪被停职

（1）被指控犯有腐败或经济犯罪的公职人员或国家官员应从指控之日起至案件审结，被

处以半薪停职：

但案件应在24个月内审结。

（2）领取半薪的停职公职人员将继续领取全额津贴。

（3）如果针对公职人员的诉讼被终止或其被宣告无罪，则对该公职人员的停职应终止。

（4）任何法律规定的可将公职人员停薪停职或者解雇的任何权力或要求不因本条而减损；

（5）以下规定适用于非由总检察长或在其指示下提起诉讼中的指控——

（a）除非法院或总检察长批准起诉或诉讼程序由总检察长接管，否则本条不适用于指控；和

（b）如果起诉获批准或诉讼程序被接管，就本条而言，起诉日期应被视为获批准或诉讼程序被接管的日期。

（6）如果《宪法》限制或规定了罢免该职位持有人的理由或该职位必须空缺的情况，则本条不适用于该职位。

（7）本条不适用于本法生效之前提出的指控。

[2014年第18号法令，附录]

63. 因被判腐败或经济犯罪而停职等

（1）因腐败或经济犯罪被定罪的公职人员自定罪之日起，在上诉结果未决之前，应被停薪停职。

（2）如果定罪在上诉中被推翻，则该公职人员将不再被停职。

（3）在以下情况下，该公职人员应被解雇——

（a）提出上诉的期限届满而相关的定罪仍未上诉；

（b）上诉维持原判的。

（4）如果《宪法》限制或规定了罢免该职位持有人的理由或该职位必须空缺的情况，则本条不适用于该职位。

（5）本条不适用于本法生效之前发生的定罪。

64. 因被判腐败或经济犯罪而被取消资格

（1）因腐败或经济犯罪被定罪的人，自定罪之日起10年内，丧失选举或被任命为公职人员的资格。

（2）如果《宪法》规定了选举产生的职位的任职资格，则本条不适用于该职位。

（3）本条不适用于本法生效之前发生的定罪。

（4）委员会应至少每年一次将根据本条被取消资格的所有人员的姓名在公报上公布。

65. 对举报人的保护

（1）不得就以下事项对某人提起或维持任何诉讼或程序，包括纪律处分——

（a）该人向委员会或调查员提供协助的；或者

（b）该人向委员会或调查员披露信息的。

（2）如果作出陈述的人不相信该陈述的真实性，则第（1）款不适用于该陈述。

（3）在对腐败或经济犯罪的起诉或根据本法提起的诉讼中，对于曾协助委员会或调查员或曾向其披露信息的人，不得要求证人识别或提供可能导致识别该人的信息。

（4）在对腐败或经济犯罪的起诉或根据本法提起的诉讼中,对于曾协助委员会或调查员或曾向其披露信息的人,法院应确保从与程序有关的制作或检查的任何文件中,删除或隐藏可识别或可能导致识别该人的信息。

（5）第（3）款和第（4）款不适用于能够确保法院裁定充分公正所必要的范围。

66. 妨碍根据本法行事的人等

（1）任何人不得——

（a）无正当理由或合法辩解,妨碍或阻碍,或者攻击或威胁根据本法行事的人；

（b）欺骗或故意误导委员会或根据本法行事的人；

（c）销毁、更改、隐藏或删除该人认为或有理由相信可能与根据本法进行的调查或诉讼有关的文件、记录或证据；或者

（d）向委员会或根据本法行事的人提出虚假指控。

（2）任何人违反第（1）款,即属犯罪,一经定罪,可处以不超过50万先令的罚款或不超过5年的监禁,或两者并罚。

67. 在肯尼亚境外的行为——犯罪

肯尼亚公民在肯尼亚境外发生的行为,如果该行为发生在肯尼亚境内将构成本法项下的犯罪,则构成本法项下的犯罪。

68. 法规

部长一般可以制定法规以更好地执行本法的规定。

第九部分
废除、过渡和修订

69. 释义

在本部分中——

"**前咨询理事会**"指已废除的法案下的咨询理事会；

"**废除法**"是指根据第70条予以废除的《防止腐败法》(第65章)。

70. 废除第65章

《防止腐败法》(第65章)被予以废除。

71. 废除法下的罪行

（1）本节适用于在本法生效前根据废除法所犯的罪行或涉嫌犯罪。

（2）除第五部分外,本法经任何必要修改后适用于第（1）款所述的犯罪,为此,此类犯罪应被视为腐败或经济犯罪。

（3）为了更加明确,本部分——

（a）不适用于发生时不属于犯罪的任何作为或不作为；和

（b）不应被解释为授权施加根据《宪法》第77条第（4）款不能施加的惩罚。

72. 临时理事等

（1）在委员会成立前,曾担任肯尼亚警察部队反腐败部门负责人的人将在委员会成立后成为委员会临时理事。

（2）根据本法任命一名理事后,第(1)款规定的临时理事将不再担任临时理事。

（3）为更加明确,第(1)款下的临时理事应拥有并可以行使和履行理事的所有权力和职能,直到理事获任命为止,并可为第8条第(3)款的目的而参加咨询理事会的任何审议。

73. 移交自肯尼亚警察部队反腐败部门

（1）肯尼亚警察部队反腐败部门所有正在进行的行动,包括所有正在进行的调查,应在本法生效之日起移交给委员会。

（2）自本法生效之日起,肯尼亚警察部队反腐败部门的所有资产均应成为委员会的资产。

（3）在不限制第(2)款一般性规定的情况下,成为委员会资产的资产应包括电子文件在内的所有文件,该文件与肯尼亚警察部队反腐败部门正在进行或过去的行动相关,也包括正在进行或过去的调查。

（4）肯尼亚警察部队应根据委员会的要求向委员会提供协助,以根据本条促进肯尼亚警察部队反腐败部门的业务和资产向委员会移交。

（5）为了更加明确,本节不会导致任何工作人员从肯尼亚警察部队反腐败部门调到委员会,但委员会可能会接受其认为适合借调的工作人员。

74. 对第22章第42条的修订

《诉讼时效法》第42条经修订,在第(h)项末尾插入"或"一词,并在第(h)项之后立即插入以下新项——

(i) 对某人追回一定数额的诉讼程序是根据《反腐败和经济犯罪法》(2003)第51条或第52条的规定或根据该法第55条或第56条提起的诉讼。

附录一

[2007年第7号法令,第8条,附录]

关于委员会工作人员的规定

1. 理事或助理理事任职资格

（1）获任命为理事或助理理事的人员,必须具备以下资格——

(a) 该人必须至少对以下其中一项了解或有其中一项的经验——

(i) 法律；

(ii) 公共行政；

(iii) 会计和财政事项；

(iv) 欺诈调查；和

(b) 此人必须非常诚实和正直。

（2）咨询理事会不得推荐不符合本条规定的人。

2. 职位空缺,代理助理

（1）如果理事或助理理事的职位出现空缺,咨询理事会应在3个月内推荐人选填补空缺。

（2）在助理理事生病、缺席或职位空缺期间,咨询理事会可任命委员会的一名工作人员担任代理助理理事。

（3）咨询理事会可随时撤销根据第(2)款作出的任命,并任命委员会的另一名工作人员为助理理事。

3. 理事或助理理事的任期

（1）理事或助理理事的任期为 5 年；但助理理事的任期可能为 4 年，以避免助理理事的任期在理事任期届满时或前后届满。

（2）曾任理事、助理理事的人员，可连任，但不得连任两届以上理事，或者不得连任两届以上助理理事。

（3）理事除因死亡、辞职或根据第 5 条停止任职而导致职位空缺外，应继续任职，直到其被重新任命或由根据该法任命的新理事接替为止。

［2007 年第 7 号法令，附录］

4. 理事或助理理事辞职

（1）理事或助理理事可以向总统递交书面辞呈辞职。

（2）辞呈自总统或总统授权的人收到之日起生效。

5. 理事或助理理事的免职

（1）理事或助理理事的任命只有在符合本条规定的情况下才可终止。

（2）根据咨询理事会的建议，总统可以在以下情况下终止某人的理事或助理理事的任命——

（a）违反本附录第 6 条第（1）款；

（b）被判定破产；或者

（c）被判犯有《刑法》或本法规定的罪行或涉及不诚实的罪行。

（3）如果根据本条设立的特别法庭发现理事和助理理事有以下情形，总统可以中止对理事和助理理事的任命——

（a）因精神障碍或身体虚弱无法履行其职务；或者

（b）涉及腐败交易。

（4）如果咨询理事会认为理事或助理理事有以下情形，咨询理事会可要求首席大法官组建一个法庭——

（a）可能因精神障碍或身体虚弱而无法履行其职务；或者

（b）可能涉及腐败交易。

（5）咨询理事会应在向首席大法官提出请求的同时，将根据第（4）款提出的请求书副本提交给总统，并且总统可以暂停理事或助理理事的职务，直至最终决议事项审结。

（6）在收到根据第（4）款提出的请求后，首席大法官应立即任命一个由 3 名成员组成的法庭，并指定其中一名为主席。

（7）法庭的每名成员均应是有资格被任命为高等法院或上诉法院法官的人。

（8）法庭应按照其可能裁定的程序进行调查。

（9）法庭的程序应符合自然正义的规则。

（10）在结束调查后 30 日内，法庭应——

（a）公开宣布其调查结果和理由；和

（b）向总统提交报告。

6. 员工活动的限制

（1）在获任命后，委员会的任何工作人员，包括理事或助理理事，不得——

（a）受雇从事任何其他工作或业务；

（b）担任任何其他公职；或者

（c）积极参与任何政党的事务或支持竞选公职的任何候选人。

（2）担任公职并被借调到委员会的人不会仅仅因为继续担任该公职而违反第（1）款，只要该人在借调到委员会期间不履行该公职的职责。

7. 纪律守则

（1）理事应为委员会发布一份守则，规定其员工的纪律。

（2）守则可就可能有争议的事项进行调查和作出决定，包括通过听证会。

（3）守则可规定最高至解雇的处罚，并可能包括对因委员会财产损失或损坏而产生的费用追偿的规定。

8. 其他人员的免职

除了根据本法可将委员会工作人员（不是理事或助理理事）免职的任何其他理由外，该成员可由理事免职，理由是该成员违反了根据本附录第7条的规定，或理事不再对该成员的诚信有信心：

但是，除非工作人员事先得到合理的机会来说明其不应该被免职的理由，否则任何工作人员不得根据本条被免职。

9. 个人责任保护

（1）不得就本法项下理事、助理理事、调查员或委员会的任何工作人员善意的作为或不作为提起赔偿或损害赔偿诉讼。

（2）本款不应免除委员会的任何责任。

附录二

［2007年第7号法令，第22条，附录］

关于咨询理事会成员的规定

1. 提名成员的任命

（1）本款规定了咨询理事会成员的任命由机构根据第16条第（2）款（a）项提名。

（2）提名机构应向部长提交2名被提名人的姓名。

（3）部长应收到被提名人姓名的7个工作日内将姓名提交给国民议会以供批准。

（4）国民议会应在收到被提名人姓名的第一次会议后14日内——

（a）考虑被提名人并批准其中1名被提名人或拒绝2名被提名人；和

（b）通知部长其根据（a）项规定作出的批准或拒绝。

（5）如果国民议会批准1名被提名人，部长应在收到国民议会通知后14日内将被提名人的姓名提交给总统，总统应在收到该提名后14日内任命被提名人为咨询理事会成员。

（6）如果国民议会拒绝提名机构提交的2名被提名人，则部长应在收到国民议会通知后的14日内，要求提名机构向部长提交新提名，第（3）、（4）和（5）款以及本款经必要修改后适用于该新被提名人。

（7）在提名和批准咨询理事会成员时，提名机构和国民议会应考虑——

（a）该人的诚实和正直以及该人的知识和经验；和

（b）在咨询理事会中代表肯尼亚多样性的重要性。
　　（8）在咨询理事会成员职位出现空缺后7日内,部长应要求提名机构根据第（2）款提交被提名人,提名机构应在被要求提交后的21日内提交。
　　（9）以下规定适用于本法生效后对咨询理事会的初次任命——
　　　　（a）每个提名机构应在本法生效后21日内提交其初始被提名人；
　　　　（b）部长应等到有足够的被提名人获得批准以达到法定人数后,再根据第（5）款提交已获批准的被提名人姓名；
　　　　（c）在任命足够数量的咨询理事会成员以达到法定人数后15日内,部长应召集咨询理事会会议,以提名初始主席和副主席。

2. 成员任期
　　（1）咨询理事会每名被提名成员的任期为5年。
　　（2）咨询理事会成员的任期不得超过两届。
　　（3）咨询理事会成员,除非其职位因其死亡、辞职或根据第4款停止任职而空缺,否则应继续任职,直到其被重新任命或由根据该法任命的新成员接替为止。

[2007年第7号法令,附录]

3. 辞职
　　（1）咨询理事会的被提名成员可以向总统递交书面辞呈辞职。
　　（2）辞呈自总统或总统授权的人收到之日起生效。

4. 终止任命
　　咨询理事会成员只有在以下情况下,总统才可以根据咨询理事会的建议终止对其的任命——
　　　　（a）因精神或身体疾病而无法履行其职务；
　　　　（b）被判定破产；
　　　　（c）被判犯有《刑法》（第63章）或本法规定的罪行,或犯有不诚实的罪行；或者
　　　　（d）连续三次无故缺席咨询理事会会议。

5. 个人利益的披露
　　（1）在咨询理事会正在审议或将要审议的事项中拥有直接或间接个人利益的咨询理事会成员,应在其知道有关该事项的相关事实后,在合理可行的范围内尽快向咨询理事会披露其利益的性质。
　　（2）对某一事项的利益披露应记录在咨询理事会会议记录中,在咨询理事会处理该事项时,该成员不得在场,不得参加任何审议或就此事投票。

6. 津贴
　　委员会应向咨询理事会成员支付津贴和费用,该津贴和费用由财政部部长与国民议会为此目的指定的国民议会委员会协商确定。

7. 个人责任保护
　　（1）不得对咨询理事会成员或咨询理事会授权的任何其他人就本法项下善意的作为或不作为而提起任何诉讼或要求损害赔偿。
　　（2）本款不应免除咨询理事会的任何责任。

附录三

[第21条]

关于商业行为及咨询理事会事务的规定

1. 会议

（1）咨询理事会应在每个财政年度至少召开4次会议，并且两次会议的间隔不超过4个月。

（2）会议由主席召集，主席缺席时由副主席召集。

（3）除非四分之三的成员另有约定，否则应至少提前14日通知每位成员参加会议。

（4）会议应由主席主持，或在主席缺席的情况下由副主席主持，在双方均缺席的情况下，由咨询理事会在会议上为此目的选出的人主持。

2. 投票

咨询理事会的决定应由出席并参与表决的成员的过半数作出，在票数相等的情况下，主持会议的人应投第二票或决定票。

3. 会议记录

所有会议记录均应保存并记入为此目的而保存的簿册中。

GROUP ONE
INVESTMENT LAWS AND REGULATIONS

TITLE ONE
FOREIGN INVESTMENTS PROTECTION ACT
(CHAPTER 518)

Revised Edition 2017 [1990]

Published by the National Council for Law Reporting
with the Authority of the Attorney-General

www.kenyalaw.org

CHAPTER 518
FOREIGN INVESTMENTS PROTECTION ACT

[*Date of assent: 11th December, 1964.*]
[*Date of commencement: 15th December, 1964.*]

An Act of Parliament to give protection to certain approved foreign investments and for matters incidental thereto

[Act No. 35 of 1964, Act No. 6 of 1976, Act No. 7 of 1988, Act No. 6 of 1994, Act No. 8 of 2009.]

1. Short title

This Act may be cited as the Foreign Investments Protection Act.

2. Interpretation

(1) In this Act, unless the context otherwise requires—

"**approved**" in relation to any enterprise, foreign currency, period, sum or amount means any enterprise, currency, period, sum or amount specified in the relevant certificate issued under section 3;

"**foreign assets**" includes foreign currency, credits, rights, benefits or property, any currency, credits, rights, benefits or property obtained by the expenditure of foreign currency, the provision of foreign credit, or the use or exploitation of foreign rights, benefits or property, and any profits from an investment in an approved enterprise by the holder of a certificate issued under section 3 in relation to that enterprise;

"**foreign national**" means a person who is not a citizen of Kenya, and includes a body corporate not being a body incorporated in Kenya;

"**the Minister**" means the Minister for the time being responsible for finance.

(2) For the avoidance of doubt it is hereby declared that assets shall not cease to be foreign assets by reason of their being assets in some other part of the Commonwealth, and that currency shall not cease to be foreign currency by reason of it being in Kenya as well as in some place outside Kenya, so long as, in the case of currency, the relevant sum originates from outside Kenya.

[Act No. 6 of 1976, Sch.]

3. Foreign investors may apply for and be granted certificates

(1) A foreign national who proposes to invest foreign assets in Kenya may apply to the Minister for a certificate that the enterprise in which the assets are proposed to be invested is an approved enterprise for the purposes of this Act.

(2) The Minister shall consider every application made under subsection (1) and in any case in which he is satisfied that the enterprise would further the economic development of, or would be of benefit to Kenya, he may in his discretion issue a certificate to the

applicant.
  (3) *Deleted by Act No. 7 of 1988, s. 3.*
  (4) Every certificate shall state—
    (a) the name of the holder;
    (b) the name and a description of the enterprise;
    (c) the amount of the foreign assets invested or to be invested by the holder of the certificate in the enterprise divided as between—
      (i) capital, being deemed to be a fixed amount representing the equity of the holder in the enterprise for the purposes of this Act and which shall be expressed in the certificate in, and shall for the purposes of this Act be in, either Kenya currency or the relevant foreign currency; and
      (ii) any loan, which may be expressed in, and may for the purposes of this Act be in, either Kenya currency or the relevant foreign currency;
    (d) the foreign currency invested or to be invested;
    (e) *deleted by Act No. 7 of 1988, s. 3;*
    (f) such other matters as may be necessary or desirable for the purposes of this Act.
  (5) If the foreign assets have not yet been invested a conditional certificate shall be issued stating, in addition to the details specified in subsection (3), the period in which they shall be invested.

[Act No. 6 of 1976, Sch., Act No. 7 of 1988, s. 3.]

4. Amendment of certificate

The Minister may amend a certificate granted under section 3—
  (a) in any case in which he is satisfied that some other foreign national has succeeded to the interest in the enterprise of the holder of the certificate, by substituting for the name of the holder the name of his successor:

  Provided that the Minister shall not substitute the name of any person who has acquired the interest of the holder by the expenditure, directly or indirectly, of assets other than foreign assets;
  (b) in any case where an interest in the enterprise passes to any other person on the death of the holder;
  (c) in any case where the name of the enterprise is altered, by substituting the name as so altered;
  (d) in any case in which new foreign assets are invested or are to be invested in the enterprise by the holder, or the holder has withdrawn or been paid, in accordance with this Act, any part of his investment by varying the approved amount in either Kenya currency or the relevant foreign currency in accordance therewith;
  (e) in any case where the investment consists of the acquisition of shares or stock of a body corporate, and new shares or stock are acquired otherwise than by the investment of assets which are not foreign assets, by amending the number or

amount and the description thereof;

(f) with the written consent of the holder of the certificate, by varying the approved foreign currency;

(g) by extending the period during which foreign assets are to be invested; and

(h) subject to these foregoing provisions and to the written consent of the holder, in such other manner as may be necessary or desirable.

[Act No. 6 of 1976, Sch., Act No. 7 of 1988, s. 4.]

5. Foreign assets to be brought in during approved period

If, at the time at which a certificate is issued under this Act, any foreign assets or part thereof to which the certificate relates have not been invested in the approved enterprise, they shall be so invested within the approved period, and, if not so invested within that period, the certificate shall be deemed to have been revoked.

6. *Repealed by Act No. 6 of 1994, s. 74.*

7. Transfer of profits, etc.

Notwithstanding the provisions of any other law for the time being in force, the holder of a certificate may, in respect of the approved enterprise to which such certificate relates, transfer out of Kenya in the approved foreign currency and at the prevailing rate of exchange—

(a) the profits, including retained profits which have not been capitalized, after taxation, arising from or out of his investment in foreign assets:

Provided that any increase in the capital value of the investment arising out of the sale of the whole or any part of the capital assets of the enterprise or revaluation of capital assets shall not be deemed to be profit arising from or out of the investment for the purposes of this Act;

(b) the capital specified in the certificate as representing and being deemed to be the fixed amount of the equity of the holder of the certificate in the enterprise for the purpose of this Act:

Provided that—

(i) where any amendment or variation is made in the amount of the said capital under the provisions of section 4, the amended or varied amount shall be substituted for the original amount; and

(ii) no additional amount or sum shall be added to the capital specified in the certificate (as amended or varied) to represent any increase in the capital value of the investment since the issue of the certificate or since the last amendment or variation of the certificate; and

(c) the principal and interest of any loan specified in the certificate.

[Act No. 6 of 1976, Sch., Act No. 7 of 1988, s. 5, Act No. 6 of 1994, s. 74.]

8. Compulsory acquisition

No approved enterprise or any property belonging thereto shall be compulsorily taken possession of, and no interest in or right over such enterprise or property shall be compulsorily acquired, except in accordance with the provisions concerning compulsory taking of possession and acquisition and the payment of full and prompt payment of compensation contained in section 75 of the Constitution and reproduced in the Schedule to this Act.

8A. *Repealed by Act No. 6 of 1994, s. 74.*

8B. Special arrangement for investment promotion and protection

(1) The Minister for Finance may, from time to time, by notice in the *Gazette* declare that the arrangement specified in the notice, being arrangements made with the Government of any country with a view to promoting and protecting the investments of that country in Kenya, shall have effect according to its tenor.

(2) A notice under this section may be amended or revoked by a subsequent notice and an amendment or revoking notice may contain such transitional provision or termination date as the Minister may consider necessary or expedient.

[Act No. 8 of 2009, s. 66.]

9. Regulations and directions

The Minister may make regulations or give directions generally for the better carrying out of the purposes of this Act and prescribing the manner in which applications shall be made for certificates under this Act, and the information which shall accompany those applications.

SCHEDULE
[Section 8.]
THE CONSTITUTION OF KENYA

75. Protection from deprivation of property

(1) No property of any description shall be compulsorily taken possession of, and no interest in or right over property of any description shall be compulsorily acquired, except where the following conditions are satisfied, that is to say—

(a) the taking of possession or acquisition is necessary in the interests of defence, public safety, public order, public morality, public health, town and country planning or the development or utilization of any property in such manner as to promote the public benefit; and

(b) the necessity therefore is such as to afford reasonable justification for the causing of any hardship that may result to any person having an interest in or right over the property; and

(c) provision is made by a law applicable to that taking of possession or acquisition for the prompt payment of full compensation.

(2) Every person having an interest or right in or over property which is compulsorily taken possession of or whose interest in or right over any property is compulsorily acquired shall have a right of direct access to the High Court for—

(a) the determination of his interest or right, the legality of the taking of possession or acquisition of the property, interest or right, and the amount of any compensation to which he is entitled; and

(b) the purpose of obtaining prompt payment of that compensation:

Provided that if Parliament so provides in relation to any matter referred to in paragraph (a) the right of access shall be by way of appeal (exercisable as of right at the instance of the person having the right or interest in the property) from a tribunal or authority, other than the High Court, having jurisdiction under any law to determine that matter.

(3) The Chief Justice may make rules with respect to the practice and procedure of the High Court or any other tribunal or authority in relation to the jurisdiction conferred on the High Court by subsection (2) or exercisable by the other tribunal or authority for the purposes of that subsection (including rules with respect to the time within which applications or appeals to the High Court or applications to the other tribunal or authority may be brought).

(4) *Deleted by Act No. 13 of 1977, s. 3.*

(5) *Deleted by Act No. 13 of 1977, s. 3.*

(6) Nothing contained in or done under the authority of any law shall be held to be inconsistent with or in contravention of subsection (1) or (2)—

(a) to the extent that the law in question makes provision for the taking of possession or acquisition of any property—

(i) in satisfaction of any tax, duty, rate, cess or other impost;

(ii) by way of penalty for breach of the law, whether under civil process or after conviction of a criminal offence under the law of Kenya;

(iii) as an incident of a lease, tenancy, mortgage, charge bill of sale, pledge or contract;

(iv) in the execution of judgments or orders of a court in proceedings for the determination of civil rights or obligations;

(v) in circumstances where it is reasonably necessary so to do because the property is in a dangerous state or injurious to the health of human beings, animals or plants;

(vi) in consequence of any law with respect to the limitation of actions; or

(vii) for so long only as may be necessary for the purposes of any examination, investigation, trial or inquiry or, in the case of land, for the purposes of the carrying out thereon of work of soil conservation or the conservation of other natural resources or work relating to agricultural development or improvement (being work relating to such development or improvement that the owner or occupier of the land has been required, and has without reasonable excuse refused or failed, to carry out);

and except so far as that provision or, as the case may be, the thing done under the authority thereof is shown not to be reasonably justifiable in a democratic society; or

(b) to the extent that the law in question makes provision for the taking of possession or acquisition of—
  (i) enemy property;
  (ii) property of a deceased person, a person of unsound mind or a person who has not attained the age of eighteen years, for the purpose of its administration for the benefit of the persons entitled to the beneficial interest therein;
  (iii) property of a person adjudged bankrupt or a body corporate in liquidation, for the purpose of its administration for the benefit of the creditors of the bankrupt or body corporate and, subject thereto, for the benefit of other persons entitled to the beneficial interest in the property; or
  (iv) property subject to a trust, for the purpose of vesting the property in persons appointed as trustees under the instrument creating the trust or by a court or, by order of a court, for the purpose of giving effect to the trust.

(7) Nothing contained in or done under the authority of any Act of Parliament shall be held to be inconsistent with or in contravention of this section to the extent that the Act in question makes provision for the compulsory taking possession of any property or the compulsory acquisition of any interest in or right over property where that property, interest or right is vested in a body corporate, established by law for public purposes, in which no moneys have been invested other than moneys provided by Parliament.

TITLE TWO
THE INVESTMENT PROMOTION ACT
(NO. 6 OF 2004)

Revised Edition 2014 [2004]

Published by the National Council for Law Reporting

with the Authority of the Attorney-General

www.kenyalaw.org

NO. 6 OF 2004
INVESTMENT PROMOTION ACT

[*Date of assent: 31st December, 2004.*]
[*Date of commencement: 3rd October, 2005.*]

An Act of Parliament to promote and facilitate investment by assisting investors in obtaining the licences necessary to invest and by providing other assistance and incentives and for related purposes

[Act No. 6 of 2004, Legal Notice 123 of 2005, Act No. 6 of 2005, Act No. 19 of 2014.]

PART I
PRELIMINARY

1. Short title

This Act may be cited as the Investment Promotion Act, 2004.

2. Definitions

In this Act, unless the context otherwise requires—

"**Authority**" means the Kenya Investment Authority continued under section 14;

"**foreign investor**" means—

  (a) a natural person who is not a citizen of Kenya;
  (b) a partnership in which the controlling interest is owned by a person or persons who are not citizens of Kenya; or
  (c) a company or other body corporate incorporated under the laws of a country other than Kenya.

"**investment**" means the contribution of local or foreign capital by an investor, including the creation or acquisition of business assets by or for a business enterprise and includes the expansion, restructuring, improvement or rehabilitation of a business enterprise;

"**investment certificate**" means an investment certificate issued under this Act;

"**licence**" includes a registration, permit, approval or authorization required by law regardless of how it is described;

"**local investor**" means—

  (a) a natural person who is a citizen of Kenya;
  (b) a partnership in which the partnership controlling interest in owned by a person who is a citizen of Kenya;
  (c) a company incorporated under the laws of Kenya, in which the majority of shares are held by a person who is a citizen of Kenya; or
  (d) a trust or trust corporation established under the Laws of Kenya, in which the

majority of trustees and beneficiaries are citizens of Kenya.

"Minister" means the Minister responsible for matters relating to Investment.

PART II
INVESTMENT CERTIFICATES – APPLICATION AND ISSUE, ETC.

3. Applications

(1) A local investor may apply to the Authority for an investment certificate.

(2) A foreign investor who intends to invest in Kenya may apply to the Authority for an investment certificate.

(3) An application for an investment certificate shall be in the prescribed form.

(4) The Authority may request clarifications and additional information.

[Act No. 6 of 2005, s. 55.]

4. Entitlement to certificate

(1) An applicant shall be entitled to an investment certificate if—

(a) the application is complete and satisfies the applicable requirements under this Act;

(b) the amount to be invested by a foreign investor is at least one hundred thousand United States of America dollars or the equivalent in any currency;

(c) the amount to be invested by a local investor is at least one million shillings or the equivalent in another currency; and

(d) the investment and the activity related to the investment are lawful and beneficial to Kenya.

(2) In determining whether an investment and the activity related to the investment are beneficial to Kenya for the purposes of subsection (1)(d), the Authority shall consider the extent to which the investment or activity will contribute to the conditions specified in paragraphs (a), (b) and (c), and any or all of the conditions specified in paragraphs (d), (e), (f), (g) and (h)—

(a) creation of employment for Kenyans;

(b) acquisition of new skills or technology for Kenyans;

(c) contribution to tax revenues or other Government revenues;

(d) a transfer of technology to Kenya;

(e) an increase in foreign exchange, either through exports or import substitution;

(f) utilization of domestic raw materials, supplies and services;

(g) adoption of value addition in the processing of local, natural and agricultural resources;

(h) utilization, promotion, development and implementation of information and communication technology;

(i) any other factors that the Authority considers beneficial to Kenya.

[Act No. 6 of 2005, s. 56.]

5. Procedures for consideration of application

The procedures set out in the First Schedule shall apply with respect to the consideration of an application for an investment certificate.

6. Issue of certificate

(1) If the Authority decides to issue an investment certificate it shall issue the certificate on the date the applicant requests.

(2) The Authority may issue an investment certificate in the name of a corporation established by the applicant for the purposes of the investment or in the name of any other business organization to be used for the purposes of the investment.

(3) *Deleted by Act No. 6 of 2005, s. 57.*

(4) A local investor who does not hold an investment certificate shall register the investment with the Authority.

[Act No. 6 of 2005, s. 57.]

7. Conditions of certificate

An investment certificate shall be subject to—

(a) such conditions as are prescribed in the regulations; and

(b) such conditions as the Authority may specify at the time the certificate is issued.

8. Transfer

(1) An investment certificate may be transferred only with the written approval of the Authority.

(2) The transfer of an investment certificate is subject to any restrictions prescribed in the regulations.

9. Amendment

At the request of the holder of the certificate, the Authority may amend an investment certificate subject to any restrictions prescribed in the regulations.

10. Revocation

(1) The Authority may revoke an investment certificate on the following grounds—

(a) that the certificate was issued on the basis of incorrect information given by the applicant for the certificate;

(b) that the investment certificate was obtained by fraud; or

(c) that a condition of the investment certificate was breached.

(2) If the Authority proposes to revoke an investment certificate, the Authority shall give the holder of the investment certificate at least thirty days written notice of the grounds for the proposed revocation and shall give the holder an opportunity to make representations as to why the investment certificate should not be revoked.

11. Review of Authority decision

(1) A person who applied for an investment certificate or a person who is or was a holder of an investment certificate may request the Minister to appoint a panel to review a decision of the Authority relating to the application or certificate.

(2) Upon receiving a request under subsection (1), the Minister shall appoint a panel

consisting of—
- (a) a chairman who shall be an advocate of at least ten years standing; and
- (b) two other members each of whom shall be a person who is experienced in law, economics or commerce.

(3) After conducting its review the panel may do any one or more of the following—
- (a) confirm, vary or set aside the decision appealed from;
- (b) direct that the Authority reconsider a matter in accordance with such directions as the panel may make;
- (c) make an order as to the payment of costs.

(4) The Minister may make rules governing the procedure of panels under this section.

(5) Subject to any rules made by the Minister, a panel may govern its own procedure.

(6) A panel shall have the same powers as a court to make orders to secure the attendance of persons, for the production of documents or for the investigation and punishment of contempt.

(7) The Minister shall appoint a secretary to the panel and such other staff as are necessary for the proper discharge of the functions of the panel.

(8) The members of a panel shall be paid such allowances and expenses as are determined by the Minister.

(9) The expenses of the panel, including the allowances and expenses of the members of the panel, shall be paid by the Government.

PART III
INVESTMENT CERTIFICATES – BENEFITS

12. Entitlement to certain licences

(1) An investment certificate shall set out the licences listed in the Second Schedule that are necessary to the proposed investment and to which the holder of the investment certificate would, on application, be legally entitled.

(2) Upon the issue of an investment certificate, the following apply with respect to each licence set out in the certificate under subsection (1)—
- (a) the holder of the investment certificate is entitled to have the licence issued, subject to any conditions set out in the Second Schedule or in the investment certificate, upon application made within twelve months after the investment certificate is issued and upon payment of the applicable fee, if any; and
- (b) until the licence is issued or twelve months elapse after the investment certificate is issued, whichever occurs first, the licence shall be deemed to have been issued, subject to any conditions set out in the Second Schedule or in the investment certificate and subject to the requirement to pay fees under subsection (3).

(3) The holder of an investment certificate shall pay any fees that would be payable

under the relevant legislation for the licences set out in the investment certificate in respect of the time period commencing on the day the investment certificate is issued and such fees shall be paid within six months after the issue of the investment certificate.

(4) The entitlement to licences under subsection (2)(a) is for the initial issue of such licences only and following that initial issue the laws under which the licences are issued apply in the same way as they apply to all licences, including, for greater certainty, with respect to the revocation or renewal of the licences.

(5) The Authority shall facilitate the issue of licences to which the holder of an investment certificate is entitled under this section.

13. Entitlement to entry permits for expatriates

(1) The holder of an investment certificate is entitled to the following entry permits under the Immigration Act (Cap. 172)—

    (a) three class A entry permits for management or technical staff; and

    (b) three class H, I or J entry permits for owners, shareholders or partners.

(2) The initial issue of a permit under this section shall be for a two year period.

(3) The holder of the investment certificate is entitled to have a permit under this section reissued upon its expiry or issued to a different employee, owner, shareholder or partner.

(4) The holder of the investment certificate is not entitled to have a permit issued to a person who is a prohibited immigrant within the meaning of the Immigration Act, (Cap. 172).

(5) A permit under this section is subject to a conditions that the holder of the permit complies with the laws of Kenya.

(6) For each permit under subsection (1) the holder of the investment certificate is entitled to the issue of—

    (a) a dependant's pass for each dependant of the person to whom the permit is issued; and

    (b) such re-entry permits as are required in connection with the permit or with the passes under paragraph (a).

(7) Subsections (4) and (5) apply, with necessary modifications, with respect to passes or re-entry permits under subsection (6).

(8) An entitlement to a permit or pass under this section is conditional upon—

    (a) application being made for the permit or pass;

    (b) the applicable fee, if any, being paid; and

    (c) any security deposit or bond required under the Immigration Act (Cap. 172) being paid or provided.

(9) Notwithstanding subsection (8)(b), no fee is payable for the initial issue of a permit under subsection (1)(b).

(10) If an entry permit described in subsection (1)(a) has already been issued to an employee of the holder of the investment certificate as of the time the investment

certificate was issued, that permit shall be deemed to be one of the permits to which the holder of the certificate is entitled under subsection (1)(a).

(11) If an entry permit described in subsection (1)(b) has already been issued to the holder of the investment certificate or an owner, shareholder or partner of the holder as of the time the investment certificate was issued, that permit shall be deemed to be one of the permits to which the holder of the certificate is entitled under subsection (1)(b).

(12) The Authority shall facilitate the issue of permits and passes that the holder of the investment certificate is entitled to have issued under this section.

(13) For greater certainty, nothing in this section limits the issue, under the Immigration Act (Cap. 172), of other permits or passes in addition to those which the holder of an investment certificate is entitled to have issued under this section.

PART IV
KENYA INVESTMENT AUTHORITY

14. Authority continued as body corporate

The Investment Promotion Centre established under the Investment Promotion Centre Act (Cap. 485) is hereby continued as a body corporate under this Act to be known as the Kenya Investment Authority.

15. Functions

(1) The Authority shall promote and facilitate investment in Kenya.

(2) In promoting and facilitating investment the Authority shall—

  (a) assist foreign and local investors and potential investors by—

    (i) issuing investment certificates;

    (ii) assisting in obtaining any necessary licences and permits;

    (iii) assisting in obtaining incentives or exemptions under the Income Tax Act (Cap. 470), the Customs and Excise Act (Cap. 472), the Value Added Tax Act (Cap. 476) or other legislation; and

    (iv) providing information, including information on investment opportunities or sources of capital.

  (b) promote, both locally and internationally, the opportunities for investment in Kenya;

  (c) review the investment environment and make recommendations to the Government and others, with respect to changes that would promote and facilitate investment, including changes to licensing requirements;

  (d) facilitate and manage investment sites, estates or land together with associated facilities on the sites, estates and land;

  (e) appoint agents within the country and in any other country to carry out certain functions on its behalf, as it may consider necessary;

  (f) carry out such other activities as, in the Authority's opinion, will promote and facilitate investment.

16. Board of Authority

(1) The Authority shall have a board with responsibility for the overall direction and management of the Authority.

(2) The board of the Authority shall consist of the following—
- (a) a Chairman appointed by the President;
- (b) the managing director of the Authority;
- (c) the secretary to the Cabinet;
- (d) the permanent secretaries in the ministries responsible for matters relating to—
  - (i) finance;
  - (ii) trade and Industry;
  - (iii) agriculture;
  - (iv) lands;
  - (v) local authorities; and
  - (vi) planning.
- (e) the chief executive of the Export Processing Zones Authority under the Export Processing Zones Act (Cap. 517);
- (f) the chief executive of the Export Promotion Council; and
- (g) six members appointed by the Minister.

(3) A person shall not be appointed as the Chairman or a member under subsection (2)(g) unless he has distinguished himself in the field of law, economics, commerce, industry or management.

17. Term of office of Chairman, appointed members

The Chairman or a member appointed under section 16(2)(g) shall hold office for a period of three years and shall be eligible for reappointment.

18. Resignation of Chairman, appointed members

(1) The Chairman may resign by written resignation addressed to the President.

(2) A member appointed under section 16(2)(g) may resign by written resignation addressed to the Minister.

19. Removal of Chairman, appointed members

(1) The President may remove the Chairman, and the Minister may remove a member appointed under section 16(2)(g), on a ground set out in subsection (2).

(2) The grounds referred to in subsection (1) are the following—
- (a) the Chairman or member is absent without reasonable excuse from three consecutive meetings of the board of the Authority of which he has had notice;
- (b) the Chairman or member becomes bankrupt;
- (c) the Chairman or member is convicted of an offence involving dishonesty, fraud or moral turpitude;
- (d) the Chairman or member is incapacitated by reason of prolonged physical or mental illness from performing his duties as the Chairman or member; or

(e) the Chairman or member is otherwise unable or unfit to discharge the functions of his office.

20. Allowances of board members

The Authority shall pay the members of the board of the Authority such allowances and expenses as are determined by the Minister.

21. Procedures of the board

(1) The business and affairs of the board of the Authority shall be conducted in accordance with the Third Schedule.

(2) Except as provided in the Third Schedule, the board of the Authority may regulate its own procedure.

22. Secretary of board

The managing director of the Authority shall be the secretary of the board of the Authority.

23. Managing director of Authority

(1) The board of the Authority shall appoint a managing director who shall be the chief executive of the Authority and who, subject to the directions of the board, shall be responsible for the day to day running of the Authority.

(2) The terms and conditions of employment of the managing director shall be determined by the board of the Authority.

(3) A person shall not serve as the managing director for more than eight years.

24. Other staff

(1) The Authority may appoint such other staff in addition to the managing director as the Authority considers advisable.

(2) The terms and conditions of employment of the staff of the Authority, other than the managing director, shall be determined by the Authority.

25. Immunity

No member of the staff of the Authority or member of the board of the Authority or of a committee of the board shall be personally liable for anything done or omitted in good faith under this Act.

PART V
NATIONAL INVESTMENT COUNCIL

26. Council established

The National Investment Council is hereby established as an unincorporated body consisting of the following members—

(a) a Chairman who shall be the President or a Minister designated by the President;

(b) the Ministers responsible for matters relating to—

(i) finance;

(ii) trade and industry;
(iii) agriculture;
(iv) lands;
(v) local authorities;
(vi) planning;
(vii) tourism and information; and
(viii) environment, natural resources and wildlife.
(c) the Governor of the Central Bank of Kenya;
(d) the chairman of the board of the Authority; and
(e) twelve persons appointed by the President to represent the private sector, each of whom has distinguished himself in the field of law, economics, commerce, industry or management.

27. Functions

(1) The functions of the National Investment Council are—
(a) to advise the Government and government agencies on ways to increase investment and economic growth in Kenya; and
(b) to promote co-operation between the public and private sectors in the formulation and implementation of government policies relating to the economy and investment.

(2) In carrying out its functions under subsection (1) the Council shall—
(a) monitor the economic environment to identify impediments to investment and economic growth and to propose incentives to promote investment and economic growth;
(b) monitor economic development in Kenya to identify areas that may not be benefiting from economic development; and
(c) consult with persons from both the public and private sectors to obtain views and suggestions for promoting investment and economic development.

PART VI
MISCELLANEOUS

28. Offence, misleading Authority, etc.

A person who knowingly submits false or misleading information to the Authority for the purposes of obtaining an investment certificate or obtaining any assistance from the Authority is guilty of an offence and is liable, on conviction, to a fine not exceeding one million shillings or to imprisonment for a term not exceeding two years or to both.

29. Offence, improperly divulging information acquired under Act

A person who, without lawful excuse, divulges information acquired in the course of acting under this Act is guilty of an offence and is liable on conviction, to a fine not exceeding one million shillings or to imprisonment for a term not exceeding two years or to both.

30. Regulations

(1) The Minister may make regulations generally for the better carrying out of the provisions of this Act.

(2) Without prejudice to the generality of subsection (1), the Cabinet Secretary may make Regulations for—

(a) amending the Second Schedule;

(b) prescribing the categories of employees to be issued with work permits;

(c) prescribing procedures for the vetting of investors.

[Act No. 19 of 2014, s. 41.]

31. Repeal of Cap. 485

The Investment Promotion Centre Act (Cap. 485) is repealed.

32. General authority, etc. under repealed Act continued

(1) A general authority issued under the Investment Promotion Centre Act before that Act is repealed by section 31 shall be continued as an investment certificate under this Act.

(2) An application for a general authority under the Investment Promotion Centre Act (Cap. 485) before that Act is repealed by section 31 shall be continued as an application for an investment certificate under this Act.

FIRST SCHEDULE
PROCEDURES FOR CONSIDERATION OF APPLICATION FOR INVESTMENT CERTIFICATE

[Section 5.]

1. Definition

In this Schedule—

"**working day**" means a day other than a Saturday, Sunday or public holiday.

2. Report on application

(1) Within ten working days after a completed application is received, the Authority shall prepare a written report on the application.

(2) An application shall be deemed to have been received when any clarifications or additional information required under section 3(3) are received.

3. Decision

Within five working days after the report on the application is prepared, the Authority shall make its decision with respect to the application.

4. Notice of decision

Within five working days after the decision of the Authority is made, the Authority shall give the applicant a written notice of the decision.

5. If the Authority decides to refuse to issue an investment certificate, the Authority shall—

(a) prepare written reasons;

(b) include, with the notice to the applicant under paragraph 4, a copy of the reasons and a copy of the report prepared under paragraph 2; and

(c) give the Minister, within five working days after the decision of the Authority is made, a copy of the application, a copy of the reasons and a copy of the report prepared under paragraph 2.

6. Complaint to Minister if decision is late

(1) If an applicant does not receive a notice of the Authority's decision under paragraph 4 within twenty-five working days after the completed application was given to the Authority, the applicant may make a written complaint to the Minister.

(2) The Minister shall investigate a complaint made under sub-paragraph (1) and shall, within fifteen working days after the complaint was received, inform the applicant of the results of the investigation.

7. Special provisions if environmental, health or security issues

(1) This paragraph applies if an application raises any of the following issues—

(a) an environmental, health or security issue that, in the opinion of the Authority, should be referred to another person or body; or

(b) an issue in relation to which the approval or consent of another person or body is required.

(2) If an application raises an issue described in sub-paragraph (1), the Authority shall refer the issue to the appropriate person or body and shall inform the applicant of that referral.

(3) For the purposes of applying any time periods specified in this Schedule, the time between a referral under sub-paragraph (2) and the response back from the person or body to which the referral was made, shall not be counted.

8. The Authority shall liaise with the appropriate authorities for the purposes of determining whether an applicant for an investment certificate is legally entitled to the licences listed in the Second Schedule that are necessary to the investment.

SECOND SCHEDULE
LICENCES TO WHICH THE HOLDER OF AN INVESTMENT CERTIFICATE MAY BE ENTITLED

[Sections 12, Section 30(2), Sch. 1 Section 8.]

GENERAL

1. Registration under the Industrial Registration Act (Cap. 118).

Condition: That registrable particulars be submitted within six months after the issue of the investment certificate.

2. Licence, including a conditional licence, under the Trade Licensing Act (Cap. 497).

3. Import licence or export licence under the Imports, Exports and Essential Supplies Act (Cap. 502).

4. Registration of premises as a factory under the Factories Act (Cap. 514).

5. Approval of plans under section 69G of the Factories Act (Cap. 514).

6. Licences under the Local Government Act (Cap. 265), including under any by-laws made under that Act.

7. Authority or consent, under the Local Government Act (Cap. 265), including under any by-laws made under that Act, or under the Public Health Act (Cap. 242), to undertake construction of works or premises.

Condition: That the works or premises comply with all design requirements and that the works or premises will not be used until any inspections or certificates required by law are carried out or issued.

8. Development permission under section 33 of the Physical Planning Act, 1996 (No. 6 of 1996) and a certificate of compliance referred to in section 30(7) of that Act.

9. Registration under an order under the Industrial Training Act (Cap. 237).

Condition: That registrable particulars be submitted within six months after the issue of the investment certificate.

10. Private carrier's licence under the Transport Licensing Act (Cap. 404).

11. Permit to use a standardization mark under the Standards Act (Cap. 496).

12. Permit required under section 25 of the Water Act, 2002 (No. 8 of 2002).

13. Licence for a steam vessel under the Lakes and Rivers Act (Cap. 409).

14. Environmental impact licence under the Environmental Management and Co-ordination Act, 1999 (No. 8 of 1999).

HOTEL

15. Hotel licence under the Hotels and Restaurants Act (Cap. 494).

Condition: That the certificate of the medical officer of health required under section 5(4) of that Act be provided.

16. Hotel manager's licence under the Hotels and Restaurants Act (Cap. 494) for the person specified in the investment certificate.

17. Restaurant licence under the Hotels and Restaurants Act (Cap. 494).

Condition: That the certificate of the medical officer of health required under section 5(4) of that Act be provided.

18. Restaurant manager's licence under the Hotels and Restaurants Act (Cap. 494) for the person specified in the investment certificate.

19. General retail liquor licence and hotel liquor licence under the Liquor Licensing Act (Cap. 121).

RESTAURANT

20. Restaurant licence under the Hotels and Restaurants Act (Cap. 494).

Condition: That the certificate of the medical officer of health required under section 5(4) of that Act be provided.

21. Restaurant manager's licence under the Hotels and Restaurants Act (Cap. 494) for the person specified in the investment certificate.

22. Restaurant liquor licence under the Liquor Licensing Act (Cap. 121).

SELLING, PREPARING FOOD, ETC.

23. Licence under the Food, Drugs and Chemical Substances Act (Cap. 254) to use premises to sell, prepare, store or display for sale, any food.

AGRICULTURE – GENERAL

24. Registration under section 22(6) of the Agriculture Act (Cap. 318).

PYRETHRUM GROWING

25. Licence to grow pyrethrum under the Pyrethrum Act (Cap. 340).

SISAL INDUSTRY

26. Registration as a grower under the Sisal Act (Cap. 341).

Condition: That the particulars required under the Sisal Industry.

(Registration) Rules be submitted within six months after the issue of the investment certificate.

27. Licence for a factory under the Sisal Act (Cap. 341).

MILLING OF MAIZE, WHEAT, ETC.

28. Miller's licence under the National Cereals and Produce Board Act (Cap. 338).

TEA FACTORY

29. Manufacturing licence under the Tea Act (Cap. 343).

SUGAR MILL

30. Licence to operate a sugar mill or a jaggery mill under the Sugar Act, 200 (No. 10 of 2001).

COFFEE DEALING

31. Licence to buy, sell, mill, warehouse, export or otherwise deal in or transact business in coffee under the Coffee Act, 2001 (No. 9 of 2001).

32. Movement permit under the Coffee Act, 2001 (No. 9 of 2001).

DAIRY INDUSTRY

33. Registration under Part V of the Dairy Industry Act (Cap. 336).

Condition: That the particulars required under section 32 of that Act be submitted within six months after the issue of the investment certificate.

34. Dairy manager licence under the Dairy Industry Act (Cap. 336) for the person specified in the investment certificate.

35. Retail licence under the Dairy Industry Act (Cap. 336).

36. Registration of premises as a dairy under the Public Health (Milk and Dairies) Rules under the Public Health Act (Cap. 242).

Condition: That the report of the medical officer of health required under the Rules be provided.

37. Licence as a purveyor of milk under the Public Health (Milk and Dairies) Rules under the Public Health Act (Cap. 242).

HIDE, SKIN AND LEATHER DEALING

38. Buyer's licence under the Hide, Skin and Leather Trade Act (Cap. 359).

39. Exporter's licence or importer's licence under the Hide, Skin and Leather Trade Act (Cap. 359).

40. Registration certificate for premises under the Hide, Skin and Leather Trade Act (Cap. 359).

BACON FACTORY

41. Bacon factory licence under the Pig Industry Act (Cap. 361).

42. Licence to slaughter pigs under the Pig Industry Act (Cap. 361).

43. Licence to keep pigs under the Animal Diseases (Control of Pig Diseases) Rules under the Animal Diseases Act (Cap. 364).

SLAUGHTERHOUSE

44. Licence to operate a slaughterhouse under the Meat Control (Local Slaughterhouses) Regulations under the Meat Control Act (Cap. 356).

45. Licence under section 8(1)(a) of the Kenya Meat Commission Act (Cap. 363).

46. Licence to slaughter pigs under the Pig Industry Act (Cap. 361).

47. Licence to keep pigs under the Animal Diseases (Control of Pig Diseases) Rules under the Animal Diseases Act (Cap. 364).

STERILIZING PLANT

48. Licence for a sterilizing plant under the Fertilizers and Animal Foodstuffs Act (Cap. 345).

EXPORT OF MEAT OR SUPPLY OF MEAT TO SHIPS AT MOMBASA

49. Licence under section 8(1)(b) of the Kenya Meat Commission Act (Cap. 363).

STOCK TRADING

50. Stock trader's licence under the Stock Traders Licensing Act (Cap. 498).

FISHERIES

51. Certificate of registration of a vessel under the Fisheries Act (Cap. 378).

52. Licence to catch fish under the Fisheries Act (Cap. 378).

53. Licence for a foreign fishing vessel under the Fisheries Act (Cap. 378).

MANUFACTURING DRUGS

54. Manufacturing licence under the Pharmacy and Poisons Act (Cap. 244).

PHARMACY

55. Registration of premises under the Pharmacy and Poisons Act (Cap. 244).

PEST CONTROL PRODUCTS

56. Licence for premises under the Pest Control Products Act (Cap 346).

MOTOR VEHICLE COMPONENTS OR ACCESSORIES DEALING

57. Licence to deal in motor vehicle components or accessories under the Motor Vehicle Components and Accessories Act (Cap. 520).

SECOND-HAND MOTOR VEHICLE DEALING

58. Licence to carry on business of buying or selling second-hand motor vehicles under the Second-Hand Motor Vehicles Act (Cap. 484).

SCRAP METAL DEALING

59. Licence under the Scrap Metal Act (Cap. 503).

PUBLIC TRANSPORT

60. Public carrier's licence under the Transport Licensing Act (Cap. 404).

Condition: That the licence is subject to any conditions that may be attached to the licence under section 8(2) of that Act.

MINING

61. Prospecting right under the Mining Act (Cap. 306).

62. Exclusive prospecting licence under the Mining Act (Cap. 306) for specified lands.

63. Lease under the Mining Act (Cap. 306) for specified lands.

64. Consent under section 10 of the Wildlife (Conservation and Management) Act (Cap. 376) for specified lands in a National Park.

DEALING IN PRECIOUS METALS

65. Licence to trade in unwrought precious metals under the Trading in Unwrought Precious Metals Act (Cap. 309).

DIAMOND DEALING

66. Diamond dealer's licence under the Diamond Industry Protection Act (Cap. 310).

CINEMA

67. Cinema licence under the Films and Stage Plays Act (Cap. 222).

MAKING OF FILMS

68. Filming licence under the Films and Stage Plays Act (Cap. 222).

69. Authoriation to make a film in a National Park under the Wildlife (Conservation and Management) Act (Cap. 376).

HIRE-PURCHASE BUSINESS

70. Licence to carry on a hire-purchase business under the Hire-Purchase Act (Cap. 507).

AUCTIONEERING

71. Licence under the Auctioneers Act, 1996 (No. 5 of 1996).

THIRD SCHEDULE

PROVISIONS AS TO THE CONDUCT OF BUSINESS AND AFFAIRS OF THE BOARD OF THE AUTHORITY

[Section 21.]

1. Meetings

(1) The board shall have at least four meetings in every financial year and not more than four months shall elapse between one meeting and the next meeting.

(2) Meetings shall be convened by the secretary to the board, on the instructions of the Chairman or upon the requisition of at least five members of the board.

(3) Unless all the members otherwise agree, at least seven days' notice of a meeting shall be given to every member.

(4) A meeting shall be presided over by the Chairman, or in his absence, by a person elected by the board at the meeting for that purpose.

(5) A member described in paragraph (b), (c), (d), (e) or (f) of section 16(2) may

designate one of the following persons as a representative to attend a meeting of the board in the member's absence—

(a) the member's deputy; or

(b) a person who is under the authority of the member and whose rank is the same as or higher than the rank of the member's deputy.

2. Quorum Nine members of the board shall constitute a quorum.

3. Voting A decision of the board shall be by a majority of the members present and voting and, in the case of an equality of votes, the person presiding at the meeting shall have a second or casting vote.

4. Committees

(1) The board may establish committees and delegate to any such committee such of its functions as it considers advisable.

(2) The board may appoint persons who are not members of the board as members of a committee established under sub-paragraph (1).

TITLE THREE
COMPETITION ACT
(NO. 12 OF 2010)

Revised Edition 2019 [2010]

Published by the National Council for Law Reporting

with the Authority of the Attorney-General

www.kenyalaw.org

NO. 12 OF 2010
COMPETITION ACT

[*Date of assent: 30th December, 2010.*]
[*Date of commencement: 1st August, 2011.*]

An Act of Parliament to promote and safeguard competition in the national economy; to protect consumers from unfair and misleading market conduct; to provide for the establishment, powers and functions of the Competition Authority and the Competition Tribunal, and for connected purposes

[Act No. 12 of 2010, L.N. 73/2011, L.N. 23/2011, Act No. 16 of 2014, Act No. 25 of 2015, Act No. 49 of 2016, Act No. 11 of 2017, Act No. 18 of 2 018, Act No. 27 of 2019.]

PART I
PRELIMINARY

1. Short title

This Act may be cited as the Competition Act, 2010.

2. Interpretation

In this Act, unless the context otherwise requires—

"**agreement**" when used in relation to a restricted practice, includes a contract, arrangement or understanding, whether legally enforceable or not;

"**asset**" includes any real or personal property, whether tangible or intangible, intellectual property, goodwill, chose in action, right, licence, cause of action or claim and any other asset having a commercial value;

"**Authority**" means the Competition Authority established by section 7;

"**buyer power**" means the influence exerted by an undertaking or group of undertakings in the position of purchaser of a product or service to—

(a) obtain from a supplier more favourable terms; or

(b) impose a long term opportunity cost including harm or withheld benefit, which, if carried out, would be significantly disproportionate to any resulting long term cost to the undertaking or group of undertakings.

"**competition**" and "**competitor**" have the respective meanings assigned in section 4;

"**concerted practice**" means co-operative or co-ordinated conduct between firms, achieved through direct or indirect contact, that replaces their independent action, but which does not amount to an agreement;

"**consumer**" includes any person who purchases or offers to purchase goods or services otherwise than for the purpose of resale, but does not include a person who purchases any goods or services for the purpose of using them in the production or manufacture of any goods or articles for sale;

"**consumer body**" includes residents' associations and registered consumer groups by whatever name called;

"**County government**" means the county government established by Article 76(1) of the Constitution;

"**customer**" includes any person who purchases or offers to purchase goods or services;

"**Director-General**" means the Director-General appointed under section 12;

"**dominant position in a market**" has the meaning assigned in section 4 and "**dominance**" shall be construed accordingly;

"**enterprise**" means an undertaking;

"**goods**" includes—

    (a) ships, aircraft and vehicles;

    (b) animals, including fish;

    (c) minerals, trees and crops, whether on, under, or attached to land or not; and

    (d) gas, water and electricity;

"**intermediate goods**" means goods used as inputs in manufacturing;

"**licence**" means a licence, permit or authority that allows the licensee to supply or acquire goods or services or to carry on any other activity;

"**local authority**" *deleted by Act No. 49 of 2016, s. 2*;

"**manufacture**" includes any artificial process which transforms goods in order to add value to them for the purpose of resale and any operation of packing or repacking not linked to a form of transportation within a single enterprise;

"**market**" has the meaning provided for in section 4;

"**market power**" means the power of a firm to control prices, to exclude competition or to behave to an appreciable extent, independently of its competitors, customers or suppliers;

"**member**", in connection with the Authority, means the Chairman and any other member of the Authority;

"**merger**" means an acquisition of shares, business or other assets, whether inside or outside Kenya, resulting in the change of control of a business, part of a business or an asset of a business in Kenya in any manner and includes a takeover;

"**Minister**" means the Minister for the time being responsible for finance;

"**person**" includes a body corporate;

"**predatory practice**" means the practice or strategy of seeking to drive competitors out of business or to deter market entry;

"**recognized consumer body**" means a consumer body recognized by the Authority for the purposes of this Act;

"**sale**" includes an agreement to sell or offer for sale, and an "**offer for sale**" shall be deemed to include the exposing of goods for sale, the furnishing of a quotation, whether verbally or in writing, and any other act or notification whatsoever by which willingness to enter into any transaction for sale is expressed;

"**service**" includes any rights (including interests in, and rights in relation to, real or personal property), benefits, privileges or facilities and, without limiting the generality of the foregoing, includes the rights, benefits, privileges or facilities provided, granted or conferred under any contract for or in relation to—

 (a) the performance of work, including work of a professional nature, whether with or without the supply of goods;

 (b) the provision of, or the use or enjoyment of facilities for, amusement, entertainment, transport, broadcasting, tourism, recreation, education or instruction;

 (c) insurance;

 (d) banking;

 (e) the lending of money;

 (f) consultancy;

 (g) private professional practice,

and any right, benefit or privilege for which remuneration is payable in the form of a royalty, tribute, levy or similar charge, but does not include the performance of work or the supply of goods under a contract of employment;

"**state corporation**" has the meaning assigned to it in the State Corporations Act (Cap. 446);

"**supply**"—

 (a) in relation to goods, includes supply or re-supply by way of sale, exchange, lease, hire or hire purchase; and

 (b) in relation to services, includes provide, grant or confer, and "**supplier**" shall be construed accordingly;

"**substantial part of Kenya**" means a part of Kenya which constitutes a district, a town council, a municipal council or a city council;

"**trade**" includes commerce;

"**trade association**" means a body or person (whether incorporated or not) which is formed for the purposes of furthering the interests of its members or persons represented by its members;

"**Tribunal**" means the Competition Tribunal established by section 71;

"**undertaking**" means any business intended to be carried on, or carried on for gain or reward by a person, a partnership or a trust in the production, supply or distribution of goods or provision of any service, and includes a trade association; and

"**unwarranted concentration of economic power**" means the existence of cross directorship between two distinct undertakings or companies producing substantially similar goods or services and whose combined market share is more than forty per cent.

[Act No. 16 of 2014, s. 31, Act No. 49 of 2016, s. 2, Act No. 29 of 2019, s. 2.]

3. Objects of the Act

The object of this Act is to enhance the welfare of the people of Kenya by promoting

and protecting effective competition in markets and preventing unfair and misleading market conduct throughout Kenya, in order to—
> (a) increase efficiency in the production, distribution and supply of goods and services;
> (b) promote innovation;
> (c) maximize the efficient allocation of resources;
> (d) protect consumers;
> (e) create an environment conducive for investment, both foreign and local;
> (f) capture national obligations in competition matters with respect to regional integration initiatives;
> (g) bring national competition law, policy and practice in line with best international practices; and
> (h) promote the competitiveness of national undertakings in world markets.

4. Interpretation of expressions

(1) The following expressions referred to in the Act shall be interpreted in accordance with this section—
> (a) **"competition"** means competition in a market in Kenya and refers to the process whereby two or more persons—
>> (i) supply or attempt to supply to; or
>> (ii) acquire or attempt to acquire from,

the people in that market the same or substitutable goods or services;
> (b) a person is a **"competitor"** of another person if they are in competition with each other or would, but for an agreement to which the two persons are parties, be likely to be in competition with each other;
> (c) **"market"** means a market in Kenya or a substantial part of Kenya and refers to the range of reasonable possibilities for substitution in supply or demand between particular kinds of goods or services and between suppliers or acquirers, or potential suppliers or acquirers, of those goods or services.

(2) In assessing effects on competition or determining whether a person has a dominant position in a market, the following matters, in addition to other relevant matters, shall be taken into account—
> (a) the importation of goods or the supply of services by persons not resident or carrying on business in Kenya; and
> (b) the economic circumstances of the relevant market including the market shares of persons supplying or acquiring goods or services in the market, the ability of those persons to expand their market shares and the potential for new entry into the market.

(3) A person has a dominant position in a market if the person—
> (a) produces, supplies, distributes or otherwise controls not less than one-half of the total goods of any description that are produced, supplied or distributed in

Kenya or any substantial part thereof; or

(b) provides or otherwise controls not less than one-half of the services that are rendered in Kenya or any substantial part thereof.

[Act No. 16 of 2014, s. 32.]

5. Application

(1) This Act shall apply to all persons including the Government, state corporations and local authorities in so far as they engage in trade.

(2) Where there is a conflict between the provisions of this Act and the provisions of any other written law with regard to matters concerning competition, consumer welfare and the powers or functions of the Authority under this Act, the provisions of this Act shall prevail.

(3) If a body charged with public regulation has jurisdiction in respect of any conduct regulated in terms of this Act within a particular sector, the Authority and that body shall—

(a) identify and establish procedures for management of areas of concurrent jurisdiction;

(b) promote co-operation;

(c) provide for the exchange of information and protection of confidential information; and

(d) ensure consistent application of the principles of this Act:

Provided that in all matters concerning competition and consumer welfare, if there is any conflict, disharmony or inconsistency, the determinations, directives, regulations, rules, orders and decisions of the Authority shall prevail.

(4) Notwithstanding the provisions of subsection (1), the Government shall not be liable to any fine or penalty under this Act or be liable to be prosecuted for an offence against this Act.

(5) For the purposes of this section, without affecting the meaning of "**trade**" in other respects—

(a) the sale or acquisition of a business, part of a business or an asset of a business carried on by the Government, a state corporation or a county government constitutes engaging in trade; and

(b) the following do not constitute engaging in trade—

(i) the imposition or collection of taxes;

(ii) the grant or revocation of licences, permits and authorities;

(iii) the collection of fees for licences, permits and authorities;

(iv) internal transactions within the Government, a state corporation or a county government.

[Act No. 49 of 2016, s. 3.]

6. Extra-territorial operation

This Act shall apply to conduct outside Kenya by—

(a) a citizen of Kenya or a person ordinarily resident in Kenya;

(b) a body corporate incorporated in Kenya or carrying on business within Kenya;

(c) any person in relation to the supply or acquisition of goods or services by that person into or within Kenya; or

(d) any person in relation to the acquisition of shares or other assets outside Kenya resulting in the change of control of a business, part of a business or an asset of a business, in Kenya.

PART II
ESTABLISHMENT, POWERS AND FUNCTIONS OF THE AUTHORITY

7. Establishment of the Authority

(1) There is hereby established an Authority to be known as the Competition Authority.

(2) The Authority shall be independent and shall perform its functions and exercise its powers independently and impartially without fear or favour.

(3) The Authority shall be a body corporate with perpetual succession and a common seal and shall, in its corporate name, be capable of—

(a) suing and being sued;

(b) purchasing or otherwise acquiring, holding, charging and disposing of movable and immovable property;

(c) borrowing money; and

(d) doing or performing all other things or acts necessary for the proper performance of its functions under this Act, which may lawfully be done or performed by a body corporate.

8. Conduct of business and affairs of the Authority

(1) The conduct and regulation of the business and affairs of the Authority shall be as provided in the Schedule.

(2) Except as provided in the Schedule, the Authority may regulate its own procedure.

9. Functions of the Authority

(1) The functions of the Authority shall be to—

(a) promote and enforce compliance with the Act;

(b) receive and investigate complaints from legal or natural persons and consumer bodies;

(c) promote public knowledge, awareness and understanding of the obligations, rights and remedies under the Act and the duties, functions and activities of the Authority;

(d) promote the creation of consumer bodies and the establishment of good and proper standards and rules to be followed by such bodies in protecting competition and consumer welfare;

(e) recognize consumer bodies duly registered under the appropriate national laws as the proper bodies, in their areas of operation, to represent consumers before the Authority;

(f) make available to consumers information and guidelines relating to the obligations of persons under the Act and the rights and remedies available to consumers under the Act;

(g) carry out inquiries, studies and research into matters relating to competition and the protection of the interests of consumers;

(h) study government policies, procedures and programmes, legislation and proposals for legislation so as to assess their effects on competition and consumer welfare and publicise the results of such studies;

(i) investigate impediments to competition, including entry into and exit from markets, in the economy as a whole or in particular sectors and publicise the results of such investigations;

(j) investigate policies, procedures and programmes of regulatory authorities so as to assess their effects on competition and consumer welfare and publicise the results of such studies;

(k) participate in deliberations and proceedings of government, government commissions, regulatory authorities and other bodies in relation to competition and consumer welfare;

(l) make representations to government, government commissions, regulatory authorities and other bodies on matters relating to competition and consumer welfare;

(m) liaise with regulatory bodies and other public bodies in all matters relating to competition and consumer welfare;

(n) advise the government on matters relating to competition and consumer welfare.

(2) *Deleted by L.N. 23/2011, Sch.*

[L.N. 23/2011, Sch.]

10. Members of the Authority

(1) The Authority shall consist of the following members—

(a) a chairperson appointed by the President;

(b) the Permanent Secretary in the Ministry for the time being responsible for finance or his representative;

(c) the Permanent Secretary in the Ministry for the time being responsible for trade or his representative;

(d) the Attorney-General or his representative;

(e) the Director-General appointed under section 12; and

(f) five other members appointed by the Minister from among persons experienced in competition and consumer welfare matters, one of whom shall be experienced in consumer welfare matters.

(2) The persons proposed to be members of the Authority under subsection (1)(f) shall,

before their appointment to the Authority, be vetted and approved by Parliament through the relevant Committee of Parliament.

[Act No. 18 of 2018, Sch.]

11. Remuneration of members of the Authority

The members of the Authority shall be paid such remuneration, fees, allowances and disbursements for expenses as may be approved by the Minister.

12. Director-General

(1) There shall be a Director-General of the Authority who shall be appointed by the Authority with the approval of Parliament from persons having knowledge and experience in competition matters.

(2) The Director-General shall hold office on such terms and conditions of employment as the Authority may determine in the instrument of appointment or otherwise in writing from time to time:

Provided that the Director-General shall hold office for a renewable term of five years, subject to a maximum of two terms.

(3) The Director-General shall be an *ex officio* member of the Authority but shall have no right to vote at any meeting of the Authority.

(4) The Director-General shall be the chief executive officer of the Authority and shall, subject to the direction of the Authority, be responsible for the day to day management of the Authority.

13. Staff

(1) The Authority shall employ such staff as it considers appropriate to enable it to perform its functions and exercise its powers.

(2) The Authority may engage consultants and experts, as it considers appropriate, to assist it to perform its functions and exercise its powers.

(3) The Authority shall establish a competitive selection procedure for the appointment of all employees, consultants and experts.

(4) The terms and conditions on which the Authority employs staff and engages consultants and experts shall be as determined by the Authority but shall include the following—

  (a) an employee, consultant or expert shall, without delay, notify the Authority in writing of any conflict of interest as soon as it arises and failure to comply with this requirement, whether wilfully or inadvertently, will be a ground for immediate dismissal;

  (b) where the Authority becomes aware of a conflict of interest, whether as a result of a notification under paragraph (a) or by any other means, the Authority may direct the person not to participate in the consideration of any matter in relation to which the person has the conflict of interest and, in that case, the person shall comply with the direction.

(5) Before employing or engaging any person, the Authority shall obtain from the

person a written declaration of any existing conflict of interest.

(6) Persons employed by the Authority as full-time employees shall not undertake any other paid employment.

(7) The Authority may enter into agreements with government departments and other government authorities and agencies to share the services of particular employees, as it may consider appropriate.

(8) The Authority shall include in its Annual Report a statement of its competitive selection procedure and its employment practices.

14. Common seal

(1) The common seal of the Authority shall be kept in the custody of the Director-General or of such other person as the Authority may direct, and shall not be used except upon the order of the Authority.

(2) The common seal of the Authority, when affixed to a document and duly authenticated, shall be judicially and officially noticed, and unless and until the contrary is proved, any necessary order or authorization by the Authority under this section shall be presumed to have been duly given.

(3) The affixing of the common seal of the Authority shall be authenticated by the signature of the Chairman of the Authority and the Director-General:

Provided that the Authority shall, in the absence of either the Chairman or the Director-General, in any particular matter, nominate one member of the Authority to authenticate the seal of the Authority on behalf of either the Chairman or the Director-General.

15. Delegation by the Authority

(1) The Authority may delegate to any of its members, either generally or otherwise as provided by the instrument of delegation, any of its powers other than—

  (a) duties to make decision under the Act;
  (b) power of delegation itself; and
  (c) the powers to revoke or vary delegation.

(2) A delegated power shall be exercised in accordance with the instrument of delegation.

(3) A delegation may, at any time, be revoked or varied by the Authority.

16. Protection from personal liability

(1) No matter or thing done by a member of the Authority or by any officer, member of staff or agent of the Authority shall, if the matter or thing is done *bona fide* for executing the functions, powers or duties of the Authority, render the member, officer, employee or agent or any person acting on his directions personally liable to any action, claim or demand whatsoever.

(2) No compensation shall be payable to any person for any loss, damage or harm directly or indirectly caused by anything done or intended to be done in good faith by the Authority or any person authorized by the Authority under this Act.

(3) Any expenses incurred by any person in any suit or prosecution brought against

him in any court in respect of any act which is done or purported to be done by him under the direction of the Authority shall, if the court holds that such act was done in good faith, be paid out of the general funds of the Authority, unless such expenses are recovered by him in such suit or prosecution.

17. Liability of the Authority for damages

The provisions of section 16 shall not relieve the Authority of the liability to pay compensation or damages to any person for any injury to him, his property or any of his interests caused by the exercise of any power conferred by this Act or by any other written law or by the failure, whether wholly or partially, of any works.

18. Power to hold inquiries

(1) The Authority may conduct an inquiry or a sectoral study where—
  (a) it considers it necessary or desirable for the purpose of carrying out its functions;
  (b) upon a direction by the Minister in writing to the Authority, requiring it to conduct an inquiry or a sectoral study into a matter specified in the direction.

(2) A direction by the Minister under subsection (1)(b) shall specify a period within which the Authority shall submit its report to the Minister.

(3) In appropriate cases, after conclusion of an inquiry or a sectoral study, the Authority shall in its report to the Minister identify sectors where factors relating to unwarranted concentrations of economic power subsist and give advice regarding measures which may ameliorate such situations.

(4) At the request of a regulatory body, or at its own instance, the Authority may conduct an inquiry into any matter affecting competition abuse of buyer power or consumer welfare and provide a report within a reasonable period.

(5) The Authority shall give notice of an intended inquiry or sectoral study by—
  (a) publishing a notice in the *Gazette* and in at least one daily newspaper of national circulation specifying—
    (i) the subject matter of the intended inquiry;
    (ii) inviting submissions on the subject from members of the public within a specified period; and
    (iii) in the case of an inquiry conducted at the direction of the Minister, the terms of reference issued by the Minister;
  (b) sending written notice of the inquiry, including the information in paragraph (a) to—
    (i) undertakings whose interests the Authority considers likely to be affected by the outcome of the inquiry;
    (ii) industry and consumer organizations which the Authority considers may have an interest in the matter;
    (iii) the Minister.

(6) Every person, undertaking, trade association or body shall be under an obligation to

provide information requested by the Authority in fulfilment of its statutory mandate for conducting an inquiry or sectoral study regulated by this section.

[Act No. 49 of 2016, s. 4, Act No. 27 of 2019, s. 3.]

19. Establishment of divisions of the Authority

(1) The Authority may establish one or more divisions as it may deem appropriate for the proper performance of its functions under this Act.

(2) The Authority shall appoint an employee or employees of the Authority as Directors of the divisions.

(3) Responsibility for running the day to day activities of the Authority and the supervision and allocation of duties to its employees shall vest in the Director-General.

20. Confidentiality

(1) For the purpose of this section, "**material**" includes any information, document or evidence relating to any matter to which this Act applies.

(2) Any person who gives or discloses any material to the Authority, whether under compulsion of law or otherwise, may claim confidentiality in respect of the whole or any part of the material.

(3) The provision of this section shall not be deemed to be breached where material is disclosed to persons outside the Authority any time before a claim for confidentiality is made.

(4) In the case of oral evidence, the claim may be made orally at the time of giving the evidence and in all other cases it shall be in writing, signed by the person making the claim specifying the material and stating the reason for the claim.

(5) If the Authority is satisfied that material is of a confidential nature and—

 (a) its disclosure could adversely affect the competitive position of any person; or

 (b) is commercially sensitive for some other reason,

the Authority shall grant confidentiality for the material.

(6) The Authority shall give notice in writing to a person making a claim for confidentiality of the Authority's decision to grant or not grant confidentiality and, if it has not granted confidentiality, the Authority shall treat the material as confidential for a period of fourteen days after giving such notification.

(7) If a claim for confidentiality—

 (a) is made in relation to material supplied to the Authority voluntarily; and

 (b) the Authority decides not to grant confidentiality in whole or in part for the material,

the person who supplied the material may, within the fourteen days period provided under subsection (6), withdraw the material from the Authority together with other material supplied with it.

(8) Notwithstanding that the Authority has granted a claim for confidentiality under subsection (5), the Authority may disclose the material—

 (a) at any time without notice to any other person if—

(i) the disclosure is made to another person who is also performing a function under this Act;

(ii) the disclosure is made with the consent of the person who gave the material;

(iii) the disclosure is authorised or required under any other law; or

(iv) the disclosure is authorised or required by a court or a tribunal constituted by law; or

(b) if the Authority is of the opinion that—

(i) disclosure of the material would not cause detriment to the person supplying it or the person to whom it relates; or

(ii) although the disclosure of the material would cause detriment to the person supplying it or the person to whom it relates, the public benefit in disclosing it outweighs the detriment,

and the Authority has given fourteen days prior written notice to that person of its intention to disclose the material pursuant to this provision.

(9) Any person who is aggrieved by a decision of the Authority under this section not to grant a claim for confidentiality for material or to disclose confidential material may, at any time while the Authority is obliged by this section to keep the material confidential, appeal to the Tribunal against the decision and the Authority shall continue to treat the material as confidential pending determination of the appeal.

(10) Any person who discloses confidential information otherwise than as authorised by this section, commits an offence.

PART III
RESTRICTIVE TRADE PRACTICES

A – Restrictive Agreements, Practices and Decisions

21. Restrictive trade practices

(1) Agreements between undertakings, decisions by associations of undertakings, decisions by undertakings or concerted practices by undertakings which have as their object or effect the prevention, distortion or lessening of competition in trade in any goods or services in Kenya, or a part of Kenya, are prohibited, unless they are exempt in accordance with the provisions of Section D of this Part.

(2) Agreements, decisions and concerted practices contemplated in subsection (1), include agreements concluded between—

(a) parties in a horizontal relationship, being undertakings trading in competition; or

(b) parties in a vertical relationship, being an undertaking and its suppliers or customers or both.

(3) Without prejudice to the generality of the provisions of subsection (1), that subsection applies in particular to any agreement, decision or concerted practice which—

(a) directly or indirectly fixes purchase or selling prices or any other trading conditions;
(b) divides markets by allocating customers, suppliers, areas or specific types of goods or services;
(c) involves collusive tendering;
(d) involves a practice of minimum resale price maintenance;
(e) limits or controls production, market outlets or access, technical development or investment;
(f) applies dissimilar conditions to equivalent transactions with other trading parties, thereby placing them at a competitive disadvantage;
(g) makes the conclusion of contracts subject to acceptance by other parties of supplementary conditions which by their nature or according to commercial usage have no connection with the subject of the contracts;
(h) amounts to the use of an intellectual property right in a manner that goes beyond the limits of fair, reasonable and non-discriminatory use;
(i) otherwise prevents, distorts or restricts competition.

(4) Subsection (3)(d) shall not prevent a supplier or producer of goods or services from recommending a resale price to a reseller of the goods or a provider of the service, provided—

(a) it is expressly stipulated by the supplier or producer to the reseller or provider that the recommended price is not binding; and
(b) if any product, or any document or thing relating to any product or service, bears a price affixed or applied by the supplier or producer, and the words "recommended price" appear next to the price so affixed or applied.

(5) An agreement or a concerted practice of the nature prohibited by subsection (1) shall be deemed to exist between two or more undertakings if—

(a) any one of the undertakings owns a significant interest in the other or has at least one director or one substantial shareholder in common; and
(b) any combination of the undertakings engages in any of the practices mentioned in subsection (3).

(6) The presumption under subsection (5) may be rebutted if an undertaking or a director or shareholder concerned establishes that a reasonable basis exists to conclude that any practice in which any of the undertakings engaged was a normal commercial response to conditions prevailing in the market.

(7) For the purposes of subsection (5), **"director"** includes—

(a) a director of a company as defined in the Companies Act (Cap. 486);
(b) in relation to an undertaking conducted by a society, a person responsible jointly with others for its management;
(c) a trustee of a trust; or
(d) in relation to an undertaking conducted by an individual or a partnership, the

owner of the undertaking or a partner of the partnership;

(e) in relation to any other undertaking, a person responsible either individually or jointly with others for its management.

(8) Subsection (1) does not apply in respect of an agreement entered into between, or a practice engaged in by—

(a) a company and its wholly owned subsidiary or a wholly owned subsidiary of that subsidiary company; or

(b) undertakings other than companies, each of which is owned or controlled by the same person or persons.

(9) A person who contravenes the provisions of this section commits an offence and shall be liable on conviction to imprisonment for a term not exceeding five years or to a fine not exceeding ten million shillings, or both.

[Act No. 16 of 2014, s. 33.]

B – Restrictive Trade Practices Applicable to Trade Associations

22. Application to practices of trade associations

(1) The following practices conducted by or on behalf of a trade association are declared to be restrictive trade practices—

(a) the unjustifiable exclusion from a trade association of any person carrying on or intending to carry on in good faith the trade in relation to which the association is formed, and in determining whether an exclusion from such an association is unjustifiable, the Authority may examine, in addition to any other matters which it considers relevant, the application of any rules of that association and the reasonableness of those rules;

(b) the making, directly or indirectly, of a recommendation by a trade association to its members or to any class of its members which relates to—

(i) the prices charged or to be charged by such members or any such class of members or to the margins included in the prices or to the pricing formula used in the calculation of those prices; or

(ii) the terms of sale (including discount, credit, delivery, and product and service guarantee terms) of such members or any such class of members and which directly affects prices, profit margins included in the prices, or the pricing formula used in the calculation of prices.

(2) A recommendation by a trade association as described in subsection (1)(b) shall be deemed to be a restrictive trade practice notwithstanding that any statement in the recommendation may or may not be complied with as the members or class of members to whom the recommendation is made think fit.

(3) A recommendation made by any person for the purpose of or having the effect, directly or indirectly, of enabling any trade association to defeat or evade the provisions of this Act shall be deemed to have been made by that trade association.

(4) Where a specific recommendation whether express or implied is made by or on

behalf of a trade association to its members or to any class of its members, concerning the action to be taken or not to be taken by them in relation to any matter affecting the trading conditions of those members, the provisions of this Act shall apply as if membership of the association constituted an agreement under which the members agreed with the association and with each other to comply with the recommendations, notwithstanding anything to the contrary in the constitution or rules of the association.

(5) A member of a trade association who expressly notifies the association in writing that he disassociates himself entirely from an agreement made by that association or, as the case may be, that he will not take action or will refrain from action of a kind referred to in an express or implied recommendation made by that association shall not, in the absence of proof to the contrary, be deemed to be a party to that agreement or, as the case may be, a member of the association who has agreed to comply with the recommendation.

(6) Any person who contravenes the provisions of this section commits an offence and shall be liable on conviction to imprisonment for a term not exceeding five years or to a fine not exceeding ten million shillings, or both.

C – Abuse of Dominant Position

23. Criteria for determining dominant position

(1) For purposes of this section, **"dominant undertaking"** means an undertaking which—
  (a) produces, supplies, distributes or otherwise controls not less than one-half of the total goods of any description which are produced, supplied or distributed in Kenya or any substantial part thereof; or
  (b) provides or otherwise controls not less than one-half of the services which are rendered in Kenya or any substantial part thereof.

(2) Notwithstanding subsection (1), an undertaking shall also be deemed to be dominant for the purposes of this Act where the undertaking—
  (a) though not dominant, controls at least forty per cent but not more than fifty per cent of the market share unless it can show that it does not have market power; or
  (b) controls less than forty per cent of the market share but has market power.

[Act No. 16 of 2014, s. 34.]

24. Abuse of dominant position

(1) Any conduct which amounts to the abuse of a dominant position in a market in Kenya, or a substantial part of Kenya, is prohibited.

(2) Without prejudice to the generality of subsection (1), abuse of a dominant position includes—
  (a) directly or indirectly imposing unfair purchase or selling prices or other unfair trading conditions;
  (b) limiting or restricting production, market outlets or market access, investment, distribution, technical development or technological progress through predatory or other practices;

(c) applying dissimilar conditions to equivalent transactions with other trading parties;

(d) making the conclusion of contracts subject to acceptance by other parties of supplementary conditions which by their nature or according to commercial usage have no connection with the subject-matter of the contracts; and

(e) abuse of an intellectual property right.

(2A) *Deleted by Act No. 27 of 2019, s. 4.*

(2B) *Deleted by Act No. 27 of 2019, s. 4.*

(2C) *Deleted by Act No. 27 of 2019, s. 4.*

(2D) *Deleted by Act No. 27 of 2019, s. 4.*

(3) Any person who contravenes the provisions of this section commits an offence and shall be liable on conviction to imprisonment for a term not exceeding five years or to a fine not exceeding ten million shillings or to both.

[Act No. 49 of 2016, s. 5, Act No. 27 of 2019, s. 4.]

24A. Abuse of buyer power

(1) Any conduct that amounts to abuse of buyer power in a market in Kenya, or a substantial part of Kenya, is prohibited.

(2) Where the Authority establishes that a sector or an undertaking is experiencing or is likely to experience incidences of abuse of buyer power, it may monitor the activities of the sector or undertaking and ensure compliance by imposing reporting and prudential requirements.

(3) The Authority may require industries and sectors, in which instances of abuse of buyer power are likely to occur, to develop a binding code of practice.

(4) In determining any complaint in relation to abuse of buyer power, the Authority shall take into account all relevant circumstances, including—

(a) the nature and determination of contract terms between the concerned undertakings;

(b) the payment requested for access to infrastructure; and

(c) the price paid to suppliers.

(5) Conduct amounting to abuse of buyer power includes—

(a) delays in payment of suppliers without justifiable reason in breach of agreed terms of payment;

(b) unilateral termination or threats of termination of a commercial relationship without notice or on an unreasonably short notice period, and without an objectively justifiable reason;

(c) refusal to receive or return any goods or part thereof without justifiable reason in breach of the agreed contractual terms;

(d) transfer of costs or risks to suppliers of goods or services by imposing a requirement for the suppliers to fund the cost of a promotion of the goods or services;

(e) transfer of commercial risks meant to be borne by the buyer to the suppliers;

(f) demands for preferential terms unfavourable to the suppliers or demanding limitations on supplies to other buyers;

(g) reducing prices by a small but significant amount where there is difficulty in substitutability of alternative buyers or reducing prices below competitive levels; or

(h) bidding up prices of inputs by a buyer undertaking with the aim of excluding competitors from the market.

(6) When investigating abuse of buyer power complaints, the Authority shall be guided by any existing agreement, whether written or not, between a buyer undertaking and supplier undertaking.

(7) An agreement between a buyer undertaking and a supplier undertaking shall include—

(a) the terms of payment;

(b) the payment date;

(c) the interest rate payable on late payment;

(d) the conditions for termination and variation of the contract with reasonable notice; and

(e) the mechanism for the resolution of disputes

(8) The Authority shall publish the code of practice which shall be developed in consultation with the relevant stakeholders, relevant Government agencies and the Attorney-General.

(9) Any person who contravenes the provisions of subsection (1) commits an offence and shall be liable on conviction to imprisonment for a term not exceeding five years or to a fine not exceeding ten million shillings or to both.

[Act No. 27 of 2019, s. 5.]

D – Exemption of Certain Restrictive Practices

25. Grant of exemption for certain restrictive practices

(1) Any undertaking or association of undertakings may apply to the Authority to be exempted from the provisions of Section A or B of this Part in respect of—

(a) any agreement or category of agreements;

(b) any decision or category of decisions;

(c) any concerted practice or category of concerted practices.

(2) An application for an exemption in terms of subsection (1) shall be—

(a) made in the prescribed form and manner;

(b) accompanied by such information as may be prescribed or as the Authority may reasonably require.

(3) The Authority shall give notice by publishing a notice in the *Gazette* of an application received in terms of subsection (1)—

(a) indicating the nature of the exemption sought by the applicant; and

(b) calling upon interested persons to submit to the Authority, within thirty days of the publication of the notice, any written representations which they may wish to make in regard to the application.

26. Determination of application for exemption

(1) After consideration of an application for exemption and any representations submitted by interested persons, the Authority shall make a determination in respect of the application, and may—

(a) grant the exemption;

(b) refuse to grant the exemption, and notify the applicant accordingly with a statement of the reasons for the refusal; or

(c) issue a certificate of clearance stating that in its opinion, on the basis of the facts in its possession, the agreement, decision or concerted practice or the category of agreements, decisions or concerted practices does not constitute an infringement of the prohibitions contained in Section A or B of this Part.

(2) The Authority may grant an exemption if it is satisfied that there are exceptional and compelling reasons of public policy as to why the agreement, decision, concerted practice or category of the same, ought to be excluded from the prohibitions contained in Section A or B of this Part.

(3) In making a decision under subsection (2), the Authority shall take into account the extent to which the agreement, decision or concerted practice, or the category thereof contributes to, or results in, or is likely to contribute to or result in—

(a) maintaining or promoting exports;

(b) improving, or preventing decline in the production or distribution of goods or the provision of services;

(c) promoting technical or economic progress or stability in any industry;

(d) obtaining a benefit for the public which outweighs or would outweigh the lessening in competition that would result, or would be likely to result, from the agreement, decision or concerted practice or the category of agreements, decisions or concerted practices.

(4) The Authority may grant an exemption subject to such conditions and for such period as the Authority may think fit.

27. Revocation or amendment of exemption

(1) If the Authority, at any time after it has granted an exemption or issued a certificate of clearance under section 26, is satisfied that—

(a) the exemption was granted or the certificate of clearance was issued on materially incorrect or misleading information;

(b) there has been a material change of circumstances since the exemption was granted or the certificate was issued;

(c) a condition upon which an exemption was granted has not been complied with, the Authority may revoke or amend the exemption or revoke the certificate of clearance, as the case may be.

(2) If the Authority proposes to revoke or amend an exemption or to revoke a certificate of clearance under subsection (1), it shall—
- (a) give notice in writing of the proposed action to the person to whom the exemption was granted or the certificate of clearance was issued, and to any other person who in the opinion of the Authority is likely to have an interest in the matter; and
- (b) call upon such persons to submit to the Authority, within thirty days of the receipt of the notice, any representations which they may wish to make in regard to the proposed action.

(3) In the event of non-compliance with a condition of an exemption, and irrespective of whether the Authority revokes or amends the exemption on account of the non-compliance, the Authority may make application to the Tribunal for the imposition of a pecuniary penalty in respect of that non-compliance, either with or without any other order.

(4) Any person who does not comply with a condition of exemption commits an offence.

28. Exemption in respect of intellectual property rights

(1) The Authority may, upon application, and on such conditions as the Authority may determine, grant an exemption in relation to any agreement or practice relating to the exercise of any right or interest acquired or protected in terms of any law relating to copyright, patents, designs, trade marks, plant varieties or any other intellectual property rights.

(2) Sections 25, 26 and 27 shall apply, *mutatis mutandis*, to an exemption under this section.

29. Exemption in respect of professional rules

(1) A professional association whose rules contain a restriction that has the effect of preventing, distorting or lessening competition in a market shall apply in writing or in the prescribed manner to the Authority for an exemption in terms of subsection (2).

(2) The Authority may exempt all or part of the rules of a professional association from the provisions of Section A of this Part for a specified period if, having regard to internationally applied norms, any restriction contained in those rules that has the effect of preventing or substantially lessening competition in a market is reasonably required to maintain—
- (a) professional standards; or
- (b) the ordinary function of the profession.

(3) Upon receiving an application in terms of subsection (1), the Authority shall—
- (a) publish a notice of the application in the *Gazette*;
- (b) allow interested parties thirty days from the date of that notice to make representations concerning the application; and
- (c) consult the Government agency or Ministry responsible for the administration of any law governing the profession concerning the application.

(4) After considering the application and any submission or other information received in relation to the application, the Authority shall—
- (a) either grant an exemption or reject the application by issuing a notice in writing to the applicant;
- (b) give written reasons for its decision if it rejects the application; and
- (c) publish a notice of that decision in the *Gazette*.

(5) If the Authority considers that any rules, either wholly or any part thereof, should no longer be exempt under this section, the Authority may revoke the exemption in respect of such rules or the relevant part of the rules, at any time after it has—
- (a) given notice in the *Gazette* of the proposed revocation;
- (b) allowed interested parties thirty days from the date of that notice to make representations concerning the exemption; and
- (c) consulted the responsible Minister referred to in subsection (3)(c).

(6) The exemption of a rule or the revocation of an exemption shall take effect from such date as may be specified by the Authority.

(7) For the purposes of this section, **"professional association"** means the controlling body established or registered under any law in respect of recognized professions, but does not include trade associations and industry lobby institutions or bodies whether incorporated or not.

(8) Any professional association—
- (a) whose rules contain a restriction that has the effect of preventing, distorting or lessening competition in a market in Kenya and which fails to apply for an exemption as required by sub-section (1) and (2); or
- (b) which having applied for exemption under sub-section (1) fails to comply with the Authority's decision rejecting its application, commits an offence, and any official thereof or any person who issues guidelines or rules in contravention of that provision shall be liable, upon conviction, to imprisonment for a term not exceeding five years or to a fine not exceeding ten million shillings, or both.

[Act No. 16 of 2014, s. 35, Act No. 27 of 2019, s. 6.]

30. Notification of grant, revocation or amendment of exemption

(1) The Authority shall, as soon as is practicable, cause to be published in the *Gazette* notice of every exemption granted, and of every exemption revoked together with the reasons thereof, under any provision of this Part.

(2) The Authority may, with the approval of the Cabinet Secretary, by notice in the *Gazette*, exclude any category of decisions, practices or agreements by or between undertakings from the application of the provisions this Part.

[Act No. 16 of 2014, s. 36.]

E – Investigation into Prohibited Practices

31. Investigation by Authority

(1) The Authority may, on its own initiative or upon receipt of information or

complaint from any person or Government agency or Ministry, carry out an investigation into any conduct or proposed conduct which is alleged to constitute or may constitute an infringement of—

(a) prohibitions relating to restrictive trade practices;

(b) prohibitions relating to abuse of dominance; or

(c) prohibitions relating to abuse of buyer power.

(2) If the Authority, having received from any person a complaint or a request to investigate an alleged infringement referred to in subsection (1), decides not to conduct an investigation, the Authority shall inform that person in writing of the reasons for its decision.

(3) *Deleted by L.N. 23/2011, Sch.*

(4) If the Authority decides to conduct an investigation, the Authority may, by notice in writing served on any person in the prescribed manner, require that person—

(a) to furnish to the Authority by writing signed by that person or, in the case of a body corporate, by a director or member or other competent officer, employee or agent of the body corporate, within the time and in the manner specified in the notice, any information pertaining to any matter specified in the notice which the Authority considers relevant to the investigation;

(b) to produce to the Authority, or to a person specified in the notice to act on the Authority behalf, any document or article, specified in the notice which relates to any matter which the Authority considers relevant to the investigation;

(c) to appear before the Authority at a time and place specified in the notice to give evidence or to produce any document or article specified in the notice; and

(d) if he possesses any records considered relevant to the investigation, to give copies of those records to the Authority or alternatively to submit the record to the authority for copying within the time and in the manner specified in the notice.

[L.N. 23/2011, Sch, Act No. 27 of 2019, s. 7.]

32. Entry and search

(1) Where the Authority deems it necessary for its investigations under this Part, the person or persons authorized in writing by it may enter any premises in the occupation or under the control of a trader, manufacturer, producer, commission agent, clearing and forwarding agent, transporter or other person believed to be in possession of relevant information and documents and inspect the premises and any goods, documents and records situated thereon.

(2) Upon entering premises in pursuance of the powers conferred by subsection (1), the person or persons authorized in writing shall, before proceeding to conduct an inspection of the premises, goods, documents and records situated thereon, inform the person present who is or who reasonably appears to be for the time being in charge of the premises of his intention to exercise his powers under this Act.

(3) The authorized persons may use any computer system on the premises, or require

assistance of any person on the premises to use that computer system, to—
- (a) search any data contained in or available to that computer system;
- (b) reproduce any record from that data;
- (c) seize any output from that computer for examination and copying;
- (d) attach and, if necessary, subject to the issuance of a receipt to that effect, remove from the premises for examination and safekeeping anything that has a bearing on the investigation.

(4) The Authority may seek the assistance of police officers and other law enforcement agencies in its execution of the mandate conferred upon it by this section.

33. Power of Authority to take evidence

(1) The Authority may receive in evidence any statement, document, information or matter that may in its opinion assist to deal effectively with an investigation conducted by it, but a statement, document, information or matter shall not be received in evidence unless it meets the requirements for admissibility in a Court of law.

(2) The Authority may take evidence on oath or affirmation from any person attending before it, and for that purpose any member of the Authority may administer an oath or affirmation.

(3) The Authority may permit any person appearing as a witness before it to give evidence by tendering and, if the Authority thinks fit, verifying by oath or affirmation, a written statement.

(4) A person attending before the Authority is entitled to the same immunities and privileges as a witness before the High Court.

34. Proposed decision of Authority

(1) If, upon conclusion of an investigation, the Authority proposes to make a decision that—
- (a) a prohibition or prohibitions under Section A of this Part have been infringed;
- (b) a prohibition or prohibitions under Section B of this Part have been infringed; or
- (c) a prohibition or prohibitions under section C of this Part have been infringed,

it shall give written notice of its proposed decision to each undertaking which may be affected by that decision.

(2) The notice referred to in subsection (1) shall—
- (a) state the reasons for the Authority's proposed decision;
- (b) set out details of any relief that the Authority may consider to impose;
- (c) inform each undertaking that it may, in relation to the Authority's proposed decision or any of the matters contemplated in paragraph (b), within the period specified in the notice—
  - (i) submit written representations to the Authority; and
  - (ii) indicate whether it requires an opportunity to make oral representations to the Authority.

[Act No. 49 of 2016, s. 6.]

35. Hearing conference to be convened for oral representation

(1) If an undertaking indicates that it requires an opportunity to make oral representations to the Authority, the Authority shall—

    (a) convene a conference to be held at a date, time and place determined by the Authority; and

    (b) give written notice of the date, time and place to—

        (i) the undertaking or undertakings concerned;

        (ii) any person who had lodged a complaint with the Authority concerning the conduct which was the subject matter of the Authority's investigation; and

        (iii) any other person whose presence at the conference is considered by the Authority to be desirable.

(2) A person to whom notice has been given of a conference in terms of subsection (1) may be accompanied by any person, including an advocate, whose assistance he may require at the conference.

(3) The proceedings at a conference shall be carried out in as informal a manner as the subject matter may permit.

(4) The Authority shall cause such record of the conference to be kept as is sufficient to set out the matters raised by the persons participating in the conference.

(5) The Authority may terminate the conference if it is satisfied that a reasonable opportunity has been given for the expression of the views of persons participating in the conference.

36. Action following investigation

After consideration of any written representations and of any matters raised at a conference, the Authority may take the following measures—

    (a) declare the conduct which is the subject matter of the Authority's investigation, to constitute an infringement of the prohibitions contained in Section A, B or C of this Part;

    (b) restrain the undertaking or undertakings from engaging in that conduct;

    (c) direct any action to be taken by the undertaking or undertakings concerned to remedy or reverse the infringement or the effects thereof;

    (d) impose a financial penalty of up to ten percent of the immediately preceding year's gross annual turnover in Kenya of the undertaking or undertakings in question; or

    (e) grant any other appropriate relief.

[Act No. 49 of 2016, s. 7.]

37. Interim relief

(1) If the Authority believes, on reasonable grounds, that an undertaking has engaged, is engaging, or is proposing to engage, in conduct that constitutes or may constitute an infringement of the prohibitions contained in section A, B, or C of this Part, and that it is

necessary for the Authority to act as a matter of urgency for the purpose of—
- (a) preventing serious, irreparable damage to any person or category of persons; or
- (b) protecting the public interest,

the Authority may, by order in writing, direct the undertaking or undertakings to stop and desist from engaging in such conduct until the ongoing investigation is concluded.

[Act No. 49 of 2016, s. 8.]

38. Settlement

(1) The Authority may at any time, during or after an investigation into an alleged infringement of the prohibitions contained in this Part, enter into an agreement of settlement with the undertaking or undertakings concerned.

(2) An agreement referred to in subsection (1) may include—
- (a) an award of damages to the complainant;
- (b) any amount proposed to be imposed as a pecuniary penalty.

39. Publication of decision of Authority

(1) The Authority shall cause notice to be given in the *Gazette* of any action taken under section 37 and of any agreement referred to in section 38.

(2) The notice referred to in subsection (1) shall include—
- (a) the name of every undertaking involved; and
- (b) the nature of the conduct that is the subject of the action or the settlement agreement.

40. Appeals to the Tribunal

(1) A person aggrieved by a determination of the Authority made under this Part shall appeal in writing to the Tribunal within thirty days of receiving the Authority's decision.

(2) A party to an appeal under subsection (1) who is dissatisfied with the decision of the Tribunal may appeal to the High Court against that decision within thirty days after the date on which a notice of that decision has been served on him and the decision of the High Court shall be final.

[Act No. 16 of 2014, s. 37.]

PART IV
MERGERS

41. Merger defined

(1) For the purposes of this Part, a merger occurs when one or more undertakings directly or indirectly acquire or establish direct or indirect control over the whole or part of the business of another undertaking.

(2) A merger contemplated in subsection (1) may be achieved in any manner, including—
- (a) the purchase or lease of shares, acquisition of an interest, or purchase of assets of the other undertaking in question;
- (b) the acquisition of a controlling interest in a section of the business of an

undertaking capable of itself being operated independently whether or not the business in question is carried on by a company;

(c) the acquisition of an undertaking under receivership by another undertaking either situated inside or outside Kenya;

(d) acquiring by whatever means the controlling interest in a foreign undertaking that has got a controlling interest in a subsidiary in Kenya;

(e) in the case of a conglomerate undertaking, acquiring the controlling interest of another undertaking or a section of the undertaking being acquired capable of being operated independently;

(f) vertical integration;

(g) exchange of shares between or among undertakings which result in substantial change in ownership structure through whatever strategy or means adopted by the concerned undertakings; or

(h) amalgamation, takeover or any other combination with the other undertaking.

(3) A person controls an undertaking if that person—

(a) beneficially owns more than one half of the issued share capital or business or assets of the undertaking;

(b) is entitled to vote a majority of the votes that may be cast at a general meeting of the undertaking, or has the ability to control the voting of a majority of those votes, either directly or through a controlled entity of that undertaking;

(c) is able to appoint, or to veto the appointment of, a majority of the directors of the undertaking;

(d) is a holding company, and the undertaking is a subsidiary of that company as contemplated in the Companies Act (Cap. 486);

(e) in the case of the undertaking being a trust, has the ability to control the majority of the votes of the trustees or to appoint the majority of the trustees or to appoint or change the majority of the beneficiaries of the trust;

(f) in the case of the undertaking being a nominee undertaking, owns the majority of the members' interest or controls directly or has the right to control the majority of members' votes in the nominee undertaking; or

(g) has the ability to materially influence the policy of the undertaking in a manner comparable to a person who, in ordinary commercial practice, can exercise an element of control referred to in paragraphs (a) to (f).

[Act No. 49 of 2016, s. 9.]

42. Control of mergers

(1) The Authority may, in consultation with the Cabinet Secretary and by notice in the *Gazette*, set the threshold for any merger excluded from the provisions of this Part.

(2) No person, either individually or jointly or in concert with any other person, may implement a proposed merger to which this part applies, unless the proposed merger is—

(a) approved by the Authority; and

(b) implemented in accordance with any conditions attached to the approval.

(3) No merger as described in section 41 carried out in the absence of an authorizing order by the Authority, shall have any legal effect, and no obligation imposed on the participating parties by any agreement in respect of the merger shall be enforceable in legal proceedings.

(4) Payment of the full purchase price by the acquiring undertaking shall be deemed to be implementation of the merger in question for the purposes of this section, and payment of a maximum down payment not exceeding twenty percent of the agreed purchase price shall not constitute implementation.

(5) Any person who contravenes the provisions of this section commits an offence and shall be liable on conviction to imprisonment for a term not exceeding five years or to a fine not exceeding ten million shillings, or both.

(6) The Authority may impose a financial penalty in an amount not exceeding ten percent of the preceding year's gross annual turnover in Kenya of the undertaking or undertakings in question.

[Act No. 49 of 2016, s. 10.]

43. Notice to be given to Authority of proposed merger

(1) Where a merger is proposed, each of the undertakings involved shall notify the Authority of the proposal in writing or in the prescribed manner.

(2) The Authority may, within thirty days of the date of receipt of the notification under subsection (1), request such further information in writing from any one or more of the undertakings concerned.

44. Period for making determination in relation to proposed merger

(1) Subject to subsection (2), the Authority shall consider and make a determination in relation to a proposed merger of which it has received notification in terms of section 43—
   (a) within sixty days after the date on which the Authority receives that notification; or
   (b) if the Authority requests further information under section 43(2), within sixty days after the date of receipt by the Authority of such information; or
   (c) if a hearing conference is convened in accordance with section 45, within thirty days after the date of conclusion of the conference.

(2) Where the Authority is of the opinion that the period referred to in paragraph (a), (b) or (c) of subsection (1) should be extended due to the complexity of the issues involved, it may, before the expiry of that period, by notice in writing to the undertakings involved extend the relevant period for a further period, not exceeding sixty days, specified in the notice.

45. Hearing conference in relation to proposed merger

(1) If the Authority considers it appropriate, it may determine that a conference be held in relation to a proposed merger.

(2) If the Authority determines that a conference is necessary, it shall, before expiry of the period referred to in paragraph (a) or (b) of subsection (1) of section 44 or subsection (2) of that section, as the case may be, give reasonable notice to the undertakings involved

in writing—
- (a) convening the conference;
- (b) specifying the date, time and venue; and
- (c) stipulating the matters to be considered at the conference.

46. Determination of proposed merger

(1) In making a determination in relation to a proposed merger, the Authority may either—
- (a) give approval for the implementation of the merger;
- (b) decline to give approval for the implementation of the merger; or
- (c) give approval for the implementation of the merger with conditions.

(2) The Authority may base its determination in relation to a proposed merger on any criteria which it considers relevant to the circumstances involved in the proposed merger, including—
- (a) the extent to which the proposed merger would be likely to prevent or lessen competition or to restrict trade or the provision of any service or to endanger the continuity of supplies or services;
- (b) the extent to which the proposed merger would be likely to result in any undertaking, including an undertaking not involved as a party in the proposed merger, acquiring a dominant position in a market or strengthening a dominant position in a market;
- (c) the extent to which the proposed merger would be likely to result in a benefit to the public which would outweigh any detriment which would be likely to result from any undertaking, including an undertaking not involved as a party in the proposed merger, acquiring a dominant position in a market or strengthening a dominant position in a market;
- (d) the extent to which the proposed merger would be likely to affect a particular industrial sector or region;
- (e) the extent to which the proposed merger would be likely to affect employment;
- (f) the extent to which the proposed merger would be likely to affect the ability of small undertakings to gain access to or to be competitive in any market;
- (g) the extent to which the proposed merger would be likely to affect the ability of national industries to compete in international markets; and
- (h) any benefits likely to be derived from the proposed merger relating to research and development, technical efficiency, increased production, efficient distribution of goods or provision of services and access to markets.

(3) For the purpose of considering a proposed merger, the Authority may refer the particulars of the proposed merger to an investigator, who may include an employee of the Authority or any other suitable person, for investigation and a report in relation to the criteria referred to in subsection (2), and shall inform the undertakings involved of such referral.

(4) As soon as practicable after a referral in terms of subsection (3), the investigator

concerned shall—
- (a) investigate the proposal so referred; and
- (b) before the date specified by the Authority, furnish the Authority with a report of the investigation.

(5) Any person, including a person not involved as a party in the proposed merger, may voluntarily submit to an investigator or the Authority any document, affidavit, statement or other relevant information in respect of a proposed merger.

(6) The Authority shall—
- (a) give notice of the determination made by the Authority in relation to a proposed merger—
  - (i) to the parties involved in the proposed merger, in writing; and
  - (ii) by notice in the *Gazette*; and
- (b) issue written reasons for its determination—
  - (i) if it prohibits or conditionally approves a proposed merger; or
  - (ii) if it is requested to do so by any party to the merger.

47. Revocation of approval of proposed merger

(1) The Authority may at any time, after consideration of any representations made to it in terms of subsection (2), revoke a decision approving the implementation of a proposed merger if—
- (a) the decision was based on materially incorrect or misleading information for which a party to the merger is responsible; or
- (b) any condition attached to the approval of the merger that is material to the implementation is not complied with.

(2) If the Authority proposes to revoke its decision under subsection (1), it shall give notice in writing of the proposed action to every undertaking involved in the merger, and to any other person who in the opinion of the Authority is likely to have an interest in the matter; and call upon such persons to submit to the Authority, within thirty days of the receipt of the notice, any representations which they may wish to make in regard to the proposed action.

(3) Notwithstanding subsections (1) and (2), the Authority may impose a financial penalty of up to ten percent of the preceding year's annual gross turnover.

(4) Any person who, being a party to a merger—
- (a) gives materially incorrect or misleading information; or
- (b) fails to comply with any condition attached to the approval for the merger,

leading to a revocation of the merger under this section, commits an offence and shall be liable on conviction to a fine not exceeding ten million shillings or to imprisonment for a term not exceeding five years, or to both.

[Act No. 49 of 2016, s. 11.]

48. Review of decisions of Authority by Tribunal

(1) Not later than thirty days after notice is given by the Authority in the *Gazette* in terms of section 46(6) of the determination made by the Authority in relation to a

proposed merger, a party to the merger may apply to the Tribunal, in the form determined by the Tribunal, for review of the Authority's decision.

(1A) Upon receipt of a written decision from the Authority as contemplated under section 46(6), a party may file an appeal to that decision to the Tribunal.

(2) Within thirty days after receiving an application under subsection (1), the Tribunal shall by notice in the *Gazette* give notice of the application for a review, and invite interested parties to make submissions to the Tribunal in regard to any matter to be reviewed within the time and manner stipulated in the notice.

(3) Within four months after the date of the making of an application for a review was made, the Tribunal shall make a determination either—
 (a) overturning the decision of the Authority;
 (b) amending the decision of the Authority by ordering restrictions or including conditions;
 (c) confirming the decision of the Authority; or
 (d) referring the matter back to the Authority for reconsideration on specified terms.

(4) The Tribunal shall—
 (a) give notice of the determination it has made in relation to the review—
  (i) to the Authority and to the parties involved in the proposed merger, in writing; and
  (ii) by notice in the *Gazette*; and
 (b) issue written reasons for that determination to the Authority and the parties involved.

(2) The Tribunal may determine the procedure for a review in terms of this section.

[Act No. 49 of 2016, s. 12.]

49. Compliance with other laws and appeals

(1) Approval of a proposed merger granted by the Authority, or by the Tribunal upon a review, under this Part shall not relieve an undertaking from complying with any other applicable laws.

(2) A party to an appeal under this Part who is dissatisfied with the decision of the Tribunal may appeal to the High Court against that decision within thirty days after the date on which a notice of that decision has been served on him and the decision of the High Court shall be final.

PART V
CONTROL OF UNWARRANTED CONCENTRATION OF ECONOMIC POWER

50. Identifying unwarranted concentration of economic power

(1) The Authority shall keep the structure of production and distribution of goods and

services in Kenya under review to determine where concentrations of economic power exist whose detrimental impact on the economy out-weighs the efficiency advantages, if any, of integration in production or distribution.

(2) The Authority shall investigate any economic sector which it has reason to believe may feature one or more factors relating to unwarranted concentrations of economic power, and for that purpose, the Authority may require any participant in that sector to grant it or any person authorized in writing by it access to records relating to patterns of ownership, market structure and percentages of sales.

(3) The Authority may require any person possessing the records referred to in subsection (2) to provide it with copies of the records.

(4) For the purpose of this Part, an unwarranted concentration of economic power shall be deemed to be prejudicial to the public interest if, having regard to the economic conditions prevailing in the country and to all other factors which are relevant in the particular circumstances, the effect thereof is or would be to—
- (a) unreasonably increase the cost relating to the production, supply, or distribution of goods or the provision of any service; or
- (b) unreasonably increase—
  - (i) the price at which goods are sold; or
  - (ii) the profits derived from the production, supply or distribution of goods or from the performance of any service; or
- (c) lessen, distort, prevent or limit competition in the production, supply or distribution of any goods (including their sale or purchase) or the provision of any service;
- (d) result in a deterioration in the quality of any goods or in the performance of any service; or
- (e) result in an inadequacy in the production, supply or distribution of any goods or services.

51. Hearing conference

(1) If any undertaking in the economic sector under investigation so requests, or the Authority considers it appropriate, it may determine that a hearing be held in relation to a proposed determination regarding unwarranted concentration of economic power.

(2) If the Authority determines that a hearing should be held, it shall give reasonable notice in writing to the undertaking or undertakings involved—
- (a) convening the hearing;
- (b) specifying the date, time and place for the holding thereof; and
- (c) stipulating the matters to be considered thereat.

(3) Where a hearing is contemplated or held, the Authority's determination as to whether or not an unwarranted concentration of economic power exists shall be kept in abeyance pending conclusion of the hearing.

(4) A hearing shall not be deemed inconclusive due to the mere fact of non-cooperation

by concerned undertakings.

52. Orders to dispose of interests

(1) After completion of its investigation, the Authority may make an order directing any person whom it deems to hold an unwarranted concentration of economic power in any sector to dispose of such portion of his interests in production, distribution or the supply of services as it deems necessary to remove the unwarranted concentration.

(2) In addition to subsection (1), the Authority may order, separately or together with the order to dispose of interests made under that subsection, the person in question to observe such other conditions as may be deemed necessary to remove the unwarranted concentration.

(3) A disposal of interest pursuant to an order made under subsection (1) may be accompanied by sale of all or part of a person's beneficial interest in an enterprise, or by the sale of one or more units in a group or chain of manufacturers or distributors or suppliers of services controlled by the person.

(4) No order shall be issued under this section which would have the effect of subdividing a manufacturing facility whose degree of physical integration is such that the introduction of independent management units controlling different components reduces its efficiency and substantially raises production costs per unit of output.

(5) An order made under this section shall allow sufficient time, to be determined by the Authority, for orderly disposal of interests or to comply with any conditions imposed by the Authority so as not to cause undue loss of value to the person to whom the order is addressed.

53. Appeals from the Authority's order

(1) A person aggrieved by an order of the Authority made under this Part may appeal to the Tribunal in the prescribed form.

(2) A party to an appeal under subsection (1) who is dissatisfied with the decision of the Tribunal may appeal to the High Court against that decision within thirty days after the date on which a notice of that decision is served on him and the decision of the High Court shall be final.

54. Offences and penalties

(1) Every person who, whether as principal or agent and whether by himself or his agent—

 (a) having lodged no appeal within the time allocated for appeals against an order of the Authority made under the provisions of this Part, contravenes or fails to comply with such order;

 (b) after the Tribunal has pronounced its decision on the appeal, contravenes or fails to comply with any portion of an order of the Authority made under this Part which is confirmed by the Tribunal or as modified by the Tribunal,

commits an offence.

(2) A party to an appeal under this Part who is dissatisfied with the decision of the

Tribunal may appeal to the High Court against that decision within thirty days after the date of service of the decision on him, and the decision of the High Court shall be final.

(3) Any person who is convicted of an offence under this Part shall be liable to imprisonment for a term not exceeding five years, or to a fine not exceeding ten million shillings, or both.

PART VI
CONSUMER WELFARE

55. False or misleading representations

A person commits an offence when, in trade in connection with the supply or possible supply of goods or services or in connection with the promotion by any means of the supply or use of goods or services, he—

    (a) falsely represents that—
        (i) goods are of a particular standard, quality, value, grade, composition, style or model or have had a particular history or particular previous use;
        (ii) services are of a particular standard, quality, value or grade;
        (iii) goods are new;
        (iv) a particular person has agreed to acquire goods or services;
        (v) goods or services have sponsorship, approval, performance characteristics, accessories, uses or benefits they do not have;
        (vi) the product has a sponsorship, approval or affiliation it does not have;
    (b) makes a false or misleading representation—
        (i) with respect to the price of goods or services;
        (ii) concerning the availability of facilities for the repair of goods or of spare parts for goods;
        (iii) concerning the place of origin of goods;
        (iv) concerning the need for any goods or services; or
        (v) concerning the existence, exclusion or effect of any condition, warranty, guarantee, right or remedy.

56. Unconscionable conduct

(1) It shall be an offence for a person, in trade in connection with the supply or possible supply of goods or services to another person, to engage in conduct that is, in all the circumstances, unconscionable.

(2) Without limiting the matters to which the Authority may have regard for the purpose of determining whether a person has contravened subsection (1) in connection with the supply or possible supply of goods or services to another person (in this subsection referred to as "the consumer"), the Authority may have regard to—

    (a) the relative strengths of the bargaining positions of the person and the consumer;

(b) whether, as a result of conduct engaged in by the person, the consumer was required to comply with conditions that were not reasonably necessary for the protection of the legitimate interests of the person;

(c) whether the consumer was able to understand any documents relating to the supply or possible supply of the goods or services;

(d) whether any undue influence or pressure was exerted on, or any unfair tactics were used against, the consumer or a person acting on behalf of the consumer by the person acting on behalf of the person in relation to the supply or possible supply of the goods or services; and

(e) the amount for which, and the circumstances under which, the consumer could have acquired identical or equivalent goods or services from another supplier.

(3) A person shall not, in the provision of banking, micro-finance and insurance and other services, impose unilateral charges and fees, by whatever name called or described, if the charges and the fees in question had not been brought to the attention of the consumer prior to their imposition or prior to the provision of the service.

(4) A consumer shall be entitled to be informed by a service provider of all charges and fees, by whatever name called or described, intended to be imposed for the provision of a service.

(5) A person shall not be deemed to engage in unconscionable conduct under this section in connection with the supply or possible supply of goods or services to a person by reason only that the person institutes legal proceedings in relation to that supply or possible supply or refers a dispute or claim in relation to that supply or possible supply to arbitration.

(6) For the purpose of determining whether a person has contravened subsection (1) in connection with the supply or possible supply of goods or services to a person—

(a) the Authority shall not have regard to any circumstances that were not reasonably foreseeable at the time of the alleged contravention; and

(b) the Authority may have regard to conduct engaged in, or circumstances existing, before the commencement of this Act.

(7) A reference in this section to goods or services is a reference to goods or services of a kind ordinarily acquired for personal, domestic or household use or consumption.

(8) A reference in this section to the supply or possible supply of goods does not include a reference to the supply or possible supply of goods for the purpose of re-supply or for the purpose of using them up or transforming them in trade.

57. Unconscionable conduct in business transactions

(1) It shall be an offence for a person in trade in connection with—

(a) the supply or possible supply of goods or services to another person; or

(b) the acquisition or possible acquisition of goods or services from another person,

to engage in conduct that is, in all the circumstances, unconscionable.

(2) Without limiting the matters to which the Authority may have regard for the purpose of determining whether a person, being a supplier, has contravened subsection (1)

in connection with the supply or possible supply of goods or services to a business consumer, the Authority may have regard to—
- (a) the relative strengths of the bargaining positions of the supplier and the business consumer;
- (b) whether, as a result of conduct engaged in by the supplier, the business consumer was required to comply with conditions which were not reasonably necessary for the protection of the legitimate interests of the supplier;
- (c) whether the business consumer was able to understand any documents relating to the supply or possible supply of the goods or services;
- (d) whether any undue influence or pressure was exerted on, or any unfair tactics were used against, the business consumer or a person acting on behalf of the business consumer by the supplier or a person acting on behalf of the supplier in relation to the supply or possible supply of the goods or services;
- (e) the amount for which, and the circumstances under which, the business consumer could have acquired identical or equivalent goods or services from a person other than the supplier;
- (f) the extent to which the supplier's conduct towards the business consumer was consistent with the supplier's conduct in similar transactions between the supplier and other like business consumers;
- (g) the requirements of any applicable industry code;
- (h) the requirements of any other industry code, if the business consumer acted on the reasonable belief that the supplier would comply with that code;
- (i) the extent to which the supplier unreasonably failed to disclose to the business consumer—
  - (i) any intended conduct of the supplier that might affect the interests of the business consumer; and
  - (ii) any risks to the business consumer arising from the supplier's intended conduct (being risks that the supplier should have foreseen that would not be apparent to the business consumer);
- (j) the extent to which the supplier was willing to negotiate the terms and conditions of any contract for supply of the goods or services with the business consumer; and
- (k) the extent to which the supplier and the business consumer acted in good faith.

58. Warning notice to public

(1) The Authority shall publish a notice containing one or both of the following—
- (a) a statement that goods of a kind specified in the notice are under investigation to determine whether the goods will or may cause injury to any person;
- (b) a warning of possible risks involved in the use of goods of a kind specified in the notice.

(2) Where an investigation referred to in subsection (1) has been completed, the

Authority shall, as soon as practicable, by notice in writing published in at least one national daily newspaper, announce the results of the investigation, indicating whether, and if so, what action is proposed to be taken in relation to the goods under this Act.

(3) The Authority may delegate to the relevant specialized agencies of the Government its functions as envisaged by this section.

59. Product safety standards and unsafe goods

(1) It shall be an offence for a person, in trade, to supply goods that are intended to be used, or are of a kind likely to be used, by a consumer if the goods are of a kind—

(a) in respect of which there is a prescribed consumer product safety standard and which do not comply with that standard;

(b) in respect of which there is in force a notice under this section declaring the goods to be unsafe goods; or

(c) in respect of which there is in force a notice under this section imposing a permanent ban on the goods.

(2) Where—

(a) the supply of goods by a person constitutes a contravention of this section by reason that the goods do not comply with a prescribed consumer product safety standard;

(b) a person suffers loss or damage by reason of a defect in, or a dangerous characteristic of, the goods or by reason of not having particular information in relation to the goods; and

(c) the person would not have suffered the loss or damage if the goods had complied with that standard,

the person shall be deemed for the purposes of this Act to have suffered the loss or damage by the supplying of the goods.

(3) Where—

(a) the supply of goods by a person constitutes a contravention of this section by reason that there is in force a notice under this section declaring the goods to be unsafe goods or imposing a permanent ban on the goods; and

(b) a person suffers loss or damage by reason of a defect in, or a dangerous characteristic of, the goods or by reason of not having particular information as to a characteristic of the goods,

the person shall be deemed for the purposes of this Act to have suffered the loss or damage by the supplying of the goods.

60. Product information standards

(1) It shall be an offence, in trade, for a person to supply goods that are intended to be used, or are of a kind likely to be used, by a consumer, being goods of a kind in respect of which a consumer product information standard has been prescribed, unless the person has complied with that standard in relation to those goods.

(2) The Authority may, by regulations in respect of goods of a particular kind,

prescribe a consumer product information standard consisting of such requirements as to—
- (a) the disclosure of information relating to the performance, composition, contents, methods of manufacture or processing, design, construction, finish or packaging of the goods; and
- (b) the form and manner in which that information is to be disclosed on or with the goods,

as are reasonably necessary to give persons using the goods information as to the quantity, quality, nature or value of the goods.

(3) Subsection (1) shall not apply to goods that are intended to be used outside Kenya.

(4) If there is applied to goods—
- (a) a statement that the goods are for export only; or
- (b) a statement indicating by the use of words authorised by the regulations to be used for the purposes of this section that the goods are intended to be used outside Kenya,

it shall be presumed for the purposes of this section, unless the contrary is established, that the goods are intended to be so used.

(5) For the purposes of subsection (4), a statement shall be deemed to be applied to goods if—
- (a) the statement is woven in, impressed on, worked into or annexed or affixed to the goods; or
- (b) the statement is applied to a covering, label, reel or thing in or with which the goods are supplied.

(6) A reference in subsection (5) to a covering includes a reference to a stopper, glass, bottle, vessel, box, capsule, case, frame or wrapper and a reference in that paragraph to a label includes a reference to a band or ticket.

(7) A person shall be deemed, for the purposes of this Act, to have suffered the loss or damage by the supplying of the goods where—
- (a) the supplying of goods by a person constitutes a contravention of this section by reason that the person has not complied with a prescribed consumer product information standard in relation to the goods;
- (b) a person suffers loss or damage by reason of not having particular information in relation to the goods; and
- (c) the person would not have suffered the loss or damage if the person had complied with that standard in relation to the goods.

61. Notice to consumers

(1) Where a person (in this section referred to as the "**supplier**"), in trade, supplies, on or after the commencement date of this Act, goods that are intended to be used, or are of a kind likely to be used, by a consumer, and—
- (a) it appears to the Authority that the goods are goods of a kind which will or may cause injury to any person;

(b) the goods are goods of a kind in respect of which there is a prescribed consumer product safety standard and the goods do not comply with that standard; or

(c) the goods are goods of a kind in relation to which there is in force a notice under section 58;

(d) it appears to the Authority that the supplier has not taken satisfactory action to prevent the goods causing injury to any person,

the Authority shall, by appropriate notice, require the supplier to take action in accordance with subsection (2).

(2) The Authority shall, in the circumstances set out in subsection (1), require the supplier to—

(a) recall the goods within a period specified in the notice;

(b) disclose to the public, or to a class of persons specified in the notice, in the matter and within the period specified in the notice, one or more of the following—

(i) the nature of a defect in, or a dangerous characteristic of, the goods identified in the notice;

(ii) the circumstances, being circumstances identified in the notice, in which the use of the goods is dangerous; or

(iii) procedures for disposing of the goods specified in the notice;

(c) inform the public, or a class of persons specified in the notice, in the manner and within the period specified in the notice, that the supplier undertakes to—

(i) repair the goods, except where the notice identifies a dangerous characteristic of the goods, repair the goods;

(ii) replace the goods; or

(iii) refund to a person to whom the goods were supplied (whether by the supplier or by another person) the price of the goods,

within the period specified in the notice.

(3) Prior to the publication by the Authority of the notice mentioned in subsection (1)(c), the Authority shall notify the affected party accordingly and give him an opportunity to be heard as to why such notice should not be published.

(4) The Authority shall consider representations made under subsection (3) and communicate its decision as to publication within a period of twenty-one days.

(5) A person aggrieved by the decision of the Authority under subsection (4) may appeal to the Tribunal.

62. Authority to declare product safety or information standards

(1) The Authority shall notify the public that, in respect of goods of a kind specified in the notice, a particular standard, or a particular part of a standard, prepared or approved by a prescribed association or body, or such a standard or part of a standard with additions or variations specified in the notice, is a consumer product safety standard for the purposes of this Act.

(2) Where a notice has been given, the standard, or the part of the standard, referred to in the notice, or the standard or part of a standard so referred to with additions or variations specified in the notice, as the case may be, shall be deemed to be a prescribed consumer product safety standard for the purposes of this Act.

63. Liability in respect of unsuitable goods

(1) Where—
- (a) an undertaking, in trade, supplies goods manufactured by the undertaking to another person who acquires the goods for re-supply;
- (b) a person (whether or not the person who acquired the goods from the undertaking) supplies the goods, otherwise than by way of sale by auction, to a consumer;
- (c) the goods are acquired by the consumer for a particular purpose that was, expressly or by implication, made known to the corporation, either directly, or through the person from whom the consumer acquired the goods or a person by whom any prior negotiations in connection with the acquisition of the goods were conducted;
- (d) the goods are not reasonably fit for that purpose, whether or not that is a purpose for which such goods are commonly supplied; and
- (e) the consumer or a person who acquires the goods from, or derives title to the goods through or under, the consumer suffers loss or damage by reason that the goods are not reasonably fit for that purpose;

the undertaking shall be liable to compensate the consumer or that other person for the loss or damage and the consumer or that person may recover the amount of the compensation by action against the undertaking in a court of competent jurisdiction.

(2) Subsection (1) shall not apply—
- (a) if the goods are not reasonably fit for the purpose referred to in subsection (1) by reason of—
  - (i) an act or default of any person (not being the undertaking or a servant or agent of the undertaking); or
  - (ii) a cause independent of human control; occurring after the goods have left the control of the undertaking; or
- (b) where the circumstances show that the consumer did not rely, or that it was unreasonable for the consumer to rely, on the skill or judgement of the undertaking.

64. Liability for defective goods

(1) Where a person, in trade supplies goods manufactured by it, and such goods are found to have a defect as a result of which an individual suffers loss or injury, such person is liable to compensate the individual for the loss or injury suffered.

(2) An individual who suffers loss or damage may recover compensation through court action.

65. Unidentified manufacturer

(1) Where a person who wishes to institute an action for compensation does not know who manufactured the goods which are the subject matter of the action, such person may serve on a supplier, or each supplier, of such goods, who is known to him, a written request to give the person particulars identifying—

(a) the person who manufactured the goods; or

(b) the supplier of the goods to the supplier requested.

(2) If, thirty days after the person has made the request or requests under subsection (1), the person still does not know who manufactured the goods, the subject of an action, then the person, or each person, that is a supplier—

(a) to whom a request was made; and

(b) who did not comply with the request,

is taken, for the purposes of the action, to have manufactured the action goods.

66. Defence

(1) In an action under section 64, it shall be a defence to establish that—

(a) the defect in the action goods which is alleged to have caused the loss did not exist at the time of supply of the goods;

(b) they had that defect only because there was compliance with a mandatory standard for them;

(c) the state of scientific or technical knowledge at the time when they were supplied by their actual manufacturer was not such as to enable that defect to be discovered; or

(d) if they were comprised in other finished goods, that defect is attributable only to—

(i) the design of the finished goods; or

(ii) the markings on or accompanying the finished goods; or

(iii) the instructions or warnings given by the manufacturer of the finished goods.

67. Consultations with the Kenya Bureau of Standards

The Authority shall consult with the Kenya Bureau of Standards in all matters involving definition and specification of goods and the grading of goods by quality for the purposes of this Act.

68. Referral of complaints to Government agencies

In appropriate circumstances the Authority shall have powers to refer consumer complaints to specialized agencies of the Government, which agencies shall make apposite determinations and inform the Authority and the complainants accordingly.

69. Notification by Consumer bodies

(1) Recognized consumer bodies shall be entitled to notify the Authority of any alleged infringement of the provisions of this Part.

(2) Upon receipt of a notification by a consumer body, the Authority shall undertake necessary investigations.

(3) A consumer body which gives notification to the Authority shall be required to cooperate with the Authority in its investigation of the alleged infraction of the provisions of this Part.

70. Offences and penalty

A person who contravenes any of the provisions of this Part commits an offence and shall be liable on conviction to imprisonment for a term not exceeding five years, or to a fine not exceeding ten million shillings, or both.

70A. Authority to initiate investigation into complaint

(1) Pursuant to the provisions this Part, the Authority may on its own initiative or upon receipt of information or a complaint from any person, government agency, Ministry, or consumer body, initiate investigations into a consumer complaint.

(2) The provisions of sections 31, 32, 33, 34, 35, 36, 37, 38, 39 and 40 of the Act shall apply *mutatis mutandis* to the investigation of consumer complaints under this section.

[Act No. 49 of 2016, s. 13.]

PART VII
ESTABLISHMENT AND POWERS OF THE COMPETITION TRIBUNAL

71. Establishment of the Competition Tribunal

(1) There is hereby established a Tribunal to be known as the Competition Tribunal which shall exercise the functions conferred upon it by this Act.

(2) The Tribunal shall consist of—
    (a) a chairman, who shall be an advocate of not less than seven years standing; and
    (b) not less than two and not more than four other members, appointed by the Minister.

(3) A member of the Tribunal shall hold office for the period, not exceeding five years, specified in the instrument of his appointment unless, prior to the expiration of that period—
    (a) he resigns his office by written notification under his hand addressed to the Minister; or
    (b) the Minister, being satisfied that the member is unfit by reason of mental or physical infirmity to perform the duties of his office, or that the member has failed to attend at least three consecutive meetings of the Tribunal, revokes his appointment.

(4) The quorum for a meeting of the Tribunal shall be the chairman and two other members.

(5) The members of the Tribunal shall be entitled to receive such fees and allowances as the Minister may determine.

(6) The Minister may, in consultation with the Tribunal, make rules—
    (a) prescribing the manner in which an appeal shall be made to the Tribunal and

the fees to be paid in respect of all appeals;

(b) prescribing the procedure to be adopted by the Tribunal in hearing an appeal and the records to be kept by the Tribunal;

(c) prescribing the manner in which the Tribunal shall be convened and places where and the time at which the sittings shall be held;

(d) generally for the better carrying out of the provisions of this Act relating to the Tribunal and appeals thereto.

72. Procedure on appeals to the Tribunal

In an appeal under this Act—

(a) the appellant shall appear before the Tribunal either in person or by an advocate on the day and at the time fixed for the hearing of the appeal, but if it is proved to the satisfaction of the Tribunal that, owing to absence of the appellant from Kenya, sickness, or other reasonable cause, he is prevented from attending at the hearing of the appeal on the day and at the time fixed for that purpose, the Tribunal may postpone the hearing of the appeal for such reasonable time as it deems necessary; and

(b) the costs of the appeal shall be at the discretion of the Tribunal.

73. Persons entitled to appeal to the Tribunal

The following persons may exercise the right of appeal to the Tribunal conferred under this Act—

(a) any person who, by a determination made by the Authority under this Act—

(i) is directed to discontinue or not to repeat any trade practice;

(ii) is issued with a stop and desist order or any other interim order;

(iii) is permitted to continue or repeat a trade practice subject to conditions prescribed by the order;

(iv) is directed to take certain steps to assist existing or potential suppliers or customers adversely affected by any prohibited trade practices;

(v) is ordered to pay a pecuniary penalty or fine; or

(vi) is aggrieved by a stop and desist order or any other interim order of the Authority;

(b) where any order referred to in paragraph (a) is directed to a class of persons, any person belonging to or representing that class; or

(c) any person who by an order made under section 46 is—

(i) enjoined from proceeding with a proposed merger; or

(ii) authorized to proceed with a proposed merger subject to conditions prescribed by the order.

74. Hearing and determination of appeal

(1) The Tribunal may, in any case, if it considers it in the interest of the parties or of any of them and is not contrary to the interest of other persons concerned or the public interest, order that the hearing or any part of it shall be held *in camera*.

(2) The Tribunal may make an order prohibiting the publication of any report or description of the proceedings or of any part of the proceedings in any appeal before it (whether heard in public or in private), but no such order shall be made prohibiting the publication of the names and descriptions of the parties to the appeal, or of any decision of the Tribunal.

(3) In its determination of any appeal, the Tribunal may confirm, modify, or reverse the order appealed against, or any part of that order.

75. Tribunal to refer appeals back for reconsideration

(1) Notwithstanding anything contained in section 73, the Tribunal may, in any case, instead of determining any appeal under that section, direct the Authority to reconsider, either generally or in respect of any specified matters, the whole or any specified part of the matter to which the appeal relates.

(2) In giving any direction under this section, the Tribunal shall—
- (a) advise the Authority of its reasons for so doing; and
- (b) give to the Authority such directions as it thinks just concerning the rehearing or reconsideration or otherwise of the whole or any part of the matter that is referred back for reconsideration.

(3) In reconsidering the matter referred back under subsection (2), the Authority shall have regard to the Tribunal's reasons for giving a direction under subsection (1) and to the Tribunal's directions under subsection (2).

76. Provisions pending determination of appeal

(1) Where an appeal is brought against a determination by the Authority regarding restrictive trade practices, consumer welfare matters or abuse of dominant positions, the stop and desist order or any other interim order or conditions issued by the Authority shall be observed, unless the Tribunal otherwise orders, pending the determination of the appeal.

(2) Where an appeal is against a determination of the Authority regarding mergers, the merger to which the appeal relates may not be finalised pending the determination of the appeal.

77. Authority's right of appeal

The Authority shall have a right to appeal to the High Court against any decision of the Tribunal.

PART VIII
FINANCIAL PROVISIONS

78. Funds of the Authority

(1) The funds of the Authority shall consist of—
- (a) any grants, donations, bequests or other contributions made to the Authority;
- (b) funds allocated to the Authority by Parliament;
- (c) fees and penalties collected by the Authority;
- (d) litigation costs refundable to the Authority;

(e) all other payments due to the Authority in respect of any matter incidental to its functions.

(2) The Authority shall disclose details of the sources of its funds in the annual report.

(3) The Authority may make rules prescribing filing fees and other fees to be paid by persons in connection with the procedures of the Authority.

79. Financial year

The financial year of the Authority shall be the period of twelve months ending on the thirtieth of June in each year.

80. Annual estimates

(1) At least three months before the commencement of each financial year, the Authority shall cause to be prepared estimates of the revenue and expenditure of the Authority for that financial year.

(2) The annual estimates shall make provision for all estimated expenditure of the Authority for the financial year and in particular, shall provide for—
- (a) the payment of salaries, allowances and other charges in respect of the officers, agents or members of staff of the Authority;
- (b) the payment of pensions, gratuities and other charges in respect of retirement benefits payable to the members of staff of the Authority;
- (c) the maintenance of the buildings and grounds of the Authority;
- (d) the maintenance, repair and replacement of the equipment and other property of the Authority; and
- (e) the creation of such reserve funds to meet future or contingent liabilities in respect of retirement benefits, insurance, replacement of buildings or equipment, or in respect of such other matters as the Authority may deem appropriate.

(3) The annual estimates shall be approved by the Authority before the commencement of the financial year to which they relate and, once approved, the sum provided in the estimates shall be submitted to the Minister for approval.

(4) No expenditure shall be incurred for the purposes of the Authority except in accordance with the annual estimates approved under subsection (3), or in pursuance of an authorisation of the Authority given with prior written approval of the Minister, and the Permanent Secretary to the Treasury.

81. Accounts and audit

(1) The Authority shall cause to be kept proper books and records of accounts of the income, expenditure, assets and liabilities of the Authority.

(2) Within a period of three months after the end of each financial year, the Authority shall submit to the Controller and Auditor-General the accounts of the Authority in respect of that year together with—
- (a) a statement of the income and expenditure of the Authority during that financial year; and
- (b) a statement of the assets and liabilities of the Authority on the last day of that

financial year.

(3) The accounts of the Authority shall be audited and reported upon by the Controller and Auditor-General in accordance with the provisions of the Public Audit Act, 2003 (No. 12 of 2003).

82. Investment of funds

(1) The Authority may invest any of the funds of the Authority in securities in which it may by law invest trust funds, or in any other securities which the Minister for the time being responsible for finance may, from time to time, approve.

(2) The Authority may, subject to the approval of the Minister for the time being responsible for finance, place on deposit with such bank or banks as it may determine, any moneys not immediately required for the purposes of the Authority.

PART IX
MISCELLANEOUS

83. Annual reports

(1) Before thirtieth September each year, the Authority shall prepare an annual report in respect of the year up to the immediately preceding thirtieth June and submit it to the Minister before 30th November in that year.

(2) The annual report shall provide information regarding the activities and plans of the Authority during the year to which it relates sufficient to impart an accurate understanding of the nature and scope of its activities and its plans and priorities and, without limitation, shall include—

    (a) details of the performance of the Authority against its key performance indicators, including the number and nature of complaints and applications the Authority has decided or are under consideration, the number and nature of investigations completed and continuing, significant studies and reports completed, undertaken or planned, and the number and nature of inquiries completed, undertaken or planned;

    (b) such information and other material as the Authority may be required by this Act or regulations made thereunder to include in the annual report; and

    (c) such additional information or other material as the Minister may request in writing.

(3) The Minister shall, within two months after receiving the annual report, transmit it to the National Assembly.

84. Prohibition on disclosure of information

(1) A member of the Authority or of a committee, the Director-General, any other employee of the Authority, and any other person required or permitted to be present at any meeting of the Authority or of a committee or at any investigation in terms of this Act, may not publish or communicate or in any other way disclose any information relating to the affairs of any person or undertaking that has come to such person's knowledge—

(a) in the exercise of any power or performance of any duty or function under this Act; or

(b) as a result of such person's attendance at such meeting or investigation.

(2) Subsection (1) shall not apply to information disclosed—

(a) for the purpose of the proper administration or enforcement of this Act;

(b) for the proper administration of justice; or

(c) at the request of an investigator, the chairman or any other member entitled to receive the information.

85. Disclosure of private interest by staff

(1) The Director-General, an investigator or any other person employed by the Authority who has a financial or other personal interest in any matter which is the subject of an investigation by the Authority—

(a) shall disclose that interest to the chairman; and

(b) unless the Authority otherwise directs, may not participate or assist in the investigation of that matter.

(2) The Director-General, an investigator or any other person employed by the Authority may not use any confidential information obtained in the performance of their functions to obtain, directly or indirectly, a financial or other advantage for himself or herself or any other person.

86. Time within which investigation may be initiated

An investigation into an alleged infringement of the provisions of this Act may not be initiated after three years from the date the infringement has ceased.

87. Hindering administration of Act

A person commits an offence who hinders, opposes, obstructs or unduly influences any person who is exercising a power or performing a duty conferred or imposed on that person by this Act.

88. Failure to comply with summons

Any person who—

(a) having been duly summoned to attend before the Authority, without reasonable excuse fails to do so; or

(b) being in attendance as required—

(i) refuses to take an oath or affirmation as lawfully required by the Authority;

(ii) refuses, after having taken the oath or affirmation, to answer any question to which the Authority may lawfully require an answer or gives evidence which the person knows is false; or

(iii) fails to produce any document or thing in his or her possession or under his or her control lawfully required by the Authority to be produced to it,

commits an offence.

89. Failure to comply with order

Any person who contravenes or fails to comply with a lawful order of the Authority given in terms of this Act commits an offence.

89A. Leniency programme

(1) The Authority may operate a leniency programme where an undertaking that voluntarily discloses the existence of an agreement or practice that is prohibited under this Act and co-operates with the Authority in the investigation of the agreement or practice, may not be subject to all or part of a fine that could otherwise be imposed under this Act.

(2) The details of the leniency programme under subsection (1) shall be set out in the guidelines of the Authority.

[Act No. 16 of 2014, s. 38.]

90. Other offences

Any person who—

(a) does anything calculated to improperly influence the Authority or any member concerning any matter connected with the exercise of any power or the performance of any function of the Authority;

(b) anticipates any decision of the Authority concerning an investigation in a way that is calculated to influence the proceedings or decision;

(c) does anything in connection with an investigation that would constitute contempt of court had the proceedings occurred in a court of law; and

(d) knowingly provides false information to the Authority,

commits an offence.

91. General penalty

A person convicted of an offence under this Act, for which no penalty has been specified under this Act shall be liable to a fine not exceeding five hundred thousand shillings, or to imprisonment for a term not exceeding three years, or both.

92. Jurisdiction of magistrate's courts

Notwithstanding any other law, a magistrate's court has jurisdiction to impose any penalty provided for in this Act.

93. Rules

(1) The Minister may, in consultation with the Authority, make rules generally for the better carrying into effect the provisions of this Act.

(2) Without prejudice to the generality of subsection (1), rules made under this section shall prescribe for anything required to be prescribed under this Act.

[Act No. 25 of 2015, Sch.]

PART X
REPEAL, SAVINGS AND TRANSITIONAL PROVISIONS

94. Definition

In this Part—

"**appointed day**" means the day on which the Act shall come into force; and

"**Department**" means the Monopolies and Prices Department of the Treasury existing immediately before the appointed day.

95. Assets and other property

(1) On the appointed day, all the assets and other property, movable and immovable, which immediately before that day, were held for and on behalf of the Department in the name of the Permanent Secretary to the Treasury shall, by virtue of this section and without further assurance, vest in the Authority.

(2) Every public officer having the power or duty to effect or amend any entry in a register relating to property or to issue or amend any certificate or other document effecting or evidencing title to property, shall, without payment of a fee or other charge and upon request made by or on behalf of the Authority, do all such things as are by law necessary to give final effect to the transfer of the property mentioned in subsection (1).

96. Rights, powers, liabilities, etc

On the appointed day, all rights, powers, liabilities and duties, whether arising under any written law or otherwise, which immediately before the appointed day were vested in, imposed on or enforceable by or against the Government for and on behalf of the Department shall, by virtue of this section, be transferred to, vested in, imposed on or become enforceable by or against the Authority.

97. Legal proceedings

On and after the appointed day, all actions, suits or legal proceedings pending by or against the Government for and on behalf of the Department shall be carried on or prosecuted by or against the Authority.

98. Secondment to Authority

(1) Subject to subsection (2), the Commissioner, officers and servants of the Department in office on the appointed day shall be deemed to be officers and servants on secondment to the Authority.

(2) Notwithstanding the provisions of subsection (1), within twelve months after the appointed day, the Authority shall review the qualifications of all persons deemed to be on secondment to the Authority under that subsection, and may retain those found suitably qualified for employment by the Authority subject to—

 (a) such persons opting to remain in the service of the Authority; and

 (b) such terms and conditions of service (not being to the disadvantage of such persons) as may be agreed with the Authority.

(3) Any employee not retained by the Authority under subsection (2) may exercise his option to either—

 (a) retire from the service of the Government; or

 (b) in cases where the employee has not reached retirement age, be redeployed within the public service.

(4) Where an employee enters into an agreement with the Authority under subsection (2), his service with the Government shall be deemed to be terminated without the right to

severance pay but without prejudice to all other remuneration and benefits payable upon the termination of his appointment with the Government.

(5) The annual estimates for the Department for the financial year in which the appointed day occurs shall be deemed to be the annual estimates of the Authority for the remainder of that financial year:

Provided that such estimates may be varied by the Authority in such manner as the Minister may approve.

99. Repeal of Cap. 504

The Restrictive Trade Practices, Monopolies and Price Control Act (Cap. 504), is hereby repealed.

100. Savings

Notwithstanding the repeal of the Restrictive Trade Practices, Monopolies and Price Control Act (Cap. 504), any applications for mergers or takeovers, any investigations relating to restrictive trade practices and any investigations relating to unwarranted concentrations of economic power ongoing immediately before the commencement of this Act shall be taken over by the Authority.

SCHEDULE

[Section 8, Act No. 11 of 2017, Sch.]

PROVISIONS AS TO THE AUTHORITY

1. Tenure of office

Any member of the Board, other than an *ex officio* member shall, subject to the provisions of this Schedule, hold office for a period of three years, on such terms and conditions as may be specified in the instrument of appointment, but shall be eligible for re-appointment, subject to a maximum of two terms of office.

2. Vacation of office

(1) A member of the Board, other than an *ex officio* member, may—
- (a) at any time resign from office by notice in writing to the Minister;
- (b) be removed from office by the Minister if the member—
  - (i) is declared bankrupt, takes the benefit of any law for the relief of insolvent debtors or assigns the member's remuneration for the benefit of creditors;
  - (ii) is convicted of a criminal offence;
  - (iii) is required by paragraph 4(7) to resign;
  - (iv) is incapable of carrying out his duties because of ill health or physical or mental impairment;
  - (v) fails to attend at least two thirds of all meetings of the Authority, without the Authority's permission, in any period of twelve consecutive months; or
  - (vi) has committed a material breach of a code of conduct to which the Authority is subject under the provisions of this Act.

(2) Before removing a member from office, the Minister shall inform a member in

writing stating the grounds for removal.

3. Meetings of the Authority

(1) The Authority shall meet not less than four times in every financial year and not more than four months shall elapse between the date of one meeting and the date of the next meeting.

(2) The Authority shall convene its meetings as directed by the Chairman or if requested in writing by at least half of the non-*ex officio* members.

(3) Subject to the provisions of sub-paragraphs (1) and (2), the Chairman may convene meetings of the Authority, after consultation with the members, at such times and places as he sees fit.

(4) The chairman shall preside at all meetings of the Authority at which he is present, and in his absence the members present may appoint one from among their number to preside at the meeting.

(5) A quorum will be four members including the Chairman.

(6) All questions shall be decided by a majority of votes of the members present and voting and, in the event of an equality of votes, the presiding member shall have a deliberative and a casting vote.

(7) The Chairman may decide that particular meetings of the Authority should be held by telephone, closed circuit television or other method of communication as the Chairman thinks fit.

(8) A minute of a resolution signed by all members of the Authority shall constitute a valid resolution of the Authority as if it were duly passed at a validly constituted meeting of the Authority.

[Act No. 11 of 2017, Sch.]

4. Conflicts of interest

(1) A member or employee of the Authority shall be considered to have a conflict of interest for the purposes of this Act if he acquires any pecuniary or other interest that could conflict with the proper performance of his duties as a member or employee of the Authority.

(2) If at any time a member of the Authority has a conflict of interest in relation to—

 (a) any matter before the Authority for consideration or determination; or

 (b) any matter the Authority could reasonably expect might come before it for consideration or determination.

(3) The member shall immediately disclose the conflict of interest to the other members of the Authority and refrain from taking part, or any further part, in the consideration or determination of the matter.

(4) Where the Authority becomes aware that a member has a conflict of interest in relation to any matter before the Authority, the Authority shall direct the member to refrain from taking part, or taking any further part, in the consideration or determination of the matter.

(5) If the Chairman has a conflict of interest he shall, in addition to complying with the other provisions of this section, disclose the conflict that exists to the Minister in writing.

(6) Upon the Authority becoming aware of any conflict of interest, it shall make a determination as to whether in future the conflict is likely to interfere significantly with the proper and effective performance of the functions and duties of the member or the Authority and the member with the conflict of interest shall not vote on this determination.

(7) Where the Authority determines that the conflict is likely to interfere significantly with the member's proper and effective performance as provided for in sub-paragraph (6), the member shall resign unless the member has eliminated the conflict to the satisfaction of the Authority within thirty days.

(8) The Authority shall report to the Minister any determination by the Authority that a conflict is likely to interfere significantly with performance as above and whether or not the conflict has been eliminated to the satisfaction of the Authority.

(9) The Annual Report of the Authority shall disclose details of all conflicts of interest and determinations arising during the period covered by the Report.

5. Code of conduct

(1) Within twelve months of the commencement of this Act, the Authority shall adopt a code of conduct prescribing standards of behaviour to be observed by the members and staff of the Authority in the performance of their duties.

(2) Subject to sub-paragraph (1), before adopting any code of conduct or making any substantial amendments to an existing code of conduct, the Authority shall publish the proposed code or amendments in the *Gazette* and in a newspaper circulating nationally, inviting public comment.

(3) The Authority shall include in its Annual Report a report on compliance with the code during the period covered by the Annual Report.

(4) The Code of conduct adopted or prescribed under this section shall be binding on the Authority and its employees.

6. Execution of instruments

Any contract or instrument which, if entered into or executed by a person not being a body corporate, would not require to be under seal, may be entered into or executed on behalf of the Authority by any person generally or specially authorized by the Authority for that purpose.

7. Minutes

The Authority shall cause minutes of all resolutions and proceedings of meetings of the Authority to be entered in books kept for that purpose.

TITLE FOUR
THE PUBLIC PRIVATE PARTNERSHIPS ACT
(NO. 14 OF 2021)

2021

Published by the National Council for Law Reporting with the Authority of the Attorney-General

www.kenyalaw.org

NO. 14 OF 2021
PUBLIC PRIVATE PARTNERSHIPS ACT

[Date of assent: 7th December, 2021.]
[Date of commencement: 23rd December, 2021.]

AN ACT of Parliament to provide for the participation of the private sector in the financing, construction, development, operation or maintenance of infrastructure or development projects through public private partnerships; to streamline the regulatory framework for public private partnerships; to repeal the Public Private Partnerships Act, 2013; and for connected purposes

[Act No. 14 of 2021.]

PART I
PRELIMINARY

1. Short title

This Act may be cited as the Public Private Partnerships Act, 2021.

2. Interpretation

In this Act, unless the context otherwise requires—

"**affordability**" means that—

(a) the financial commitments to be incurred by a contracting authority in terms of a project agreement are sustainable and do not impose an unreasonable burden to the contracting authority and may be met by funds—

   (i) designated within the existing budget of the contracting authority for its function for which the agreement relates; and;

   (ii) assigned to the contracting authority in accordance with its relevant future budgetary allocation; and

(b) the cost of delivering a facility or service in relation to the project by the contracting authority does not impose an unreasonable financial burden on the end users;

"**Cabinet Secretary**" means the Cabinet Secretary responsible for matters relating to finance;

"**Committee**" means the Public Private Partnership Committee established under section 6;

"**concession**" means a contractual licence formalized by a project agreement, which may be linked to a separate interest or right over real property, with or without a fee to Government, entitling a person who is granted the licence to make use of the specified infrastructure or undertake a project and to charge user fees, receive availability payments or both such fees and payments during the term of the concession;

"**contracting authority**", means—
(a) at the national government level, a state department, agency or state corporation which intends to have its functions undertaken by a private party; or
(b) at the county government level, the county government or county corporation which intends to have its functions undertaken by a private party;

"**contracting authority's property**" includes all movable and immovable property belonging to the contracting authority and the intellectual property rights vested in the contracting authority;

"**Directorate**" means the Directorate of Public Private Partnerships established under section 15;

"**feasibility study**" means a study undertaken to explore the technical, financial, legal, social and environmental feasibility of undertaking an infrastructure or development facility as a public private partnership;

"**financial close**" means the date when all conditions precedent required to be met to achieve first draw down on Senior Debt under a project agreement are met, as specified under a project agreement;

"**Fund**" means the Public Private Partnership Project Facilitation Fund established under section 81;

"**local content**" means the added value brought to the Kenyan economy from project-related activities by way of local distribution of accruing benefits including through the procurement of locally available workforce, services and supplies and systematic development of national capacity and capabilities;

"**private party**" means a party that enters into a project agreement with a contracting authority and is responsible for undertaking a project on behalf of the contracting authority under this Act;

"**privately-initiated proposal**" means a proposal that is originated by a private party without the involvement of a contracting authority and may include information that enables the complete evaluation of the proposal as if it were a bid;

"**project**" means the design, construction, development or operation of a new infrastructure, asset or facility or the rehabilitation, modernization, expansion, operation or management of an existing infrastructure, asset or facility;

"**project agreement**" means a contract concluded between a contracting authority and a private party and includes any ancillary agreement entered into by the parties in relation to an agreement;

"**project company**" means a special purpose vehicle company incorporated by a successful bidder for the purpose of undertaking a project in accordance with a project agreement executed by the parties;

"**Public Debt Management Office**" means the Public Debt Management Office established by section 62(1) of the Public Finance Management Act, 2012 (No. 18 of 2012);

"**public private partnership**" means a contractual arrangement between a contracting authority and a private party under which a private party—
- (a) undertakes to perform a public function or provide a service on behalf of the contracting authority;
- (b) receives a benefit for performing a public function by way of—
  - (i) compensation from a public fund;
  - (ii) charges or fees collected by the private party from users or consumers of a service provided to them; or
  - (iii) a combination of such compensation and such charges or fees;
- (c) is generally liable for risks arising from the performance of the function in accordance with the terms of the project agreement; and
- (d) transfers the facility to the contracting authority;

"**transaction advisor**" means a person who has the appropriate skill and experience to assist and advise the contracting authority or the Directorate on matters related to a public private partnership;

"**user fee**" means the rate, toll, fee, or other charge imposed for the use of all or part of an infrastructure or development facility or service; and

"**value for money**" means that the undertaking of a public function of the contracting authority by a private party under a public private partnership results in a net benefit accruing to that contracting authority defined in terms of cost, price, quality, quantity, timeliness or risk transfer.

3. Object of the Act

The object of this Act is to—
- (a) prescribe the procedures for the participation of the private sector in the financing, construction, development, operation or maintenance of infrastructure or development projects through public private partnerships;
- (b) harmonize the institutional framework for the implementation of public private partnership projects;
- (c) give effect to Article 227 of the Constitution on procurement relating to public private partnerships;
- (d) streamline and rationalize the regulatory, implementation and monitoring mandates of relevant agencies; and
- (e) provide for a transparent project selection process, clear procurement procedures, reduced regulatory approvals and expanded contractual models in order to promote private sector investment.

4. Application of Act

(1) This Act shall apply to every project agreement for the financing, design, construction, rehabilitation, operation, equipping or maintenance of a project or provision of a public service undertaken as a public private partnership.

(2) The provisions of the Public Procurement and Asset Disposal Act, 2015 (No. 33 of 2015), shall not apply to a public private partnership.

(3) Without prejudice to the generality of subsection (2), the provisions of the Public Procurement and Assets Disposal Act, 2015 (No. 33 of 2015) shall—

    (a) not apply to a public private partnership project, if all the monies for the project are from the private party;

    (b) apply if there is counterpart funding that is, including public funds, for the public private partnership project.

5. Act to prevail

Where there is a conflict between the provisions of this Act and the provisions of any other written law, the provisions of this Act shall prevail.

PART II
PUBLIC PRIVATE PARTNERSHIP COMMITTEE

6. Public Private Partnership Committee

(1) There is established the Public Private Public Private Partnership Committee which shall consist of—

    (a) the Principal Secretary in the State department responsible for matters relating to finance, who shall be the chairperson;

    (b) the Principal Secretary in the State department responsible for matters relating to planning;

    (c) the Principal Secretary in the State Department responsible for matters relating to infrastructure;

    (d) the Solicitor-General;

    (e) two persons nominated by the Council of County Governors;

    (f) three persons, not being public officers, appointed by notice in the *Gazette* by the Cabinet Secretary; and

    (g) the Director-General, who shall be the secretary.

(2) The Committee shall co-opt the Principal Secretary responsible for the contracting authority whose public private partnership project is the subject of discussion at a meeting.

(3) The Committee may co-opt any person or public officer whose knowledge or experience is necessary for the public private partnership under discussion.

(4) A person who is co-opted shall not vote at a meeting and shall only be a member of the Committee for a period not exceeding one year.

(5) The members referred to under paragraphs (1)(a), (b), (c), (d), (e) and (f) shall attend the Committee's meetings in person and may designate in writing an officer to represent them in sub-committees of the Committee.

7. Qualification and terms of members

(1) A person is qualified to be appointed as a member of the Committee under section 6

(1)(f) if that person has at least ten years' professional experience in matters relevant to public private partnerships.

(2) The members appointed under section 6 (1)(f) shall hold office for a period of three years and may be eligible for re-appointment for one further term.

(3) The persons appointed under section 6 (1)(f) shall be appointed at different times so that the respective expiry dates of their terms of office shall fall at different times.

8. Functions and powers of the Committee

(1) The Committee shall be responsible for—
- (a) formulating policies on public private partnerships;
- (b) overseeing the implementation of public private partnerships contracts;
- (c) approving standardized public private partnership bid documents;
- (d) approving feasibility studies;
- (e) approving privately—initiated proposals;
- (f) approving negotiated contract terms, the cancellation of procurements or termination of project agreements, and the variation of project agreements;
- (g) monitoring the implementation of this Act, including the sustainability of contingent liabilities that may be incurred by a contracting authority for projects approved under the Act; and
- (h) carrying out any other function that may be conferred on it under this Act.

(2) The Committee shall have all the powers necessary for the proper discharge of its functions under this Act.

9. Vacation of office

(1) The office of an appointed member of the Committee shall become vacant if that member—
- (a) is unable to perform the functions of his or her office by reason of mental or physical infirmity;
- (b) is removed from office for breach of the provisions of chapter six of the Constitution;
- (c) is deregistered by a professional body for professional misconduct;
- (d) is adjudged bankrupt;
- (e) is convicted of a criminal offence and sentenced to a term of imprisonment of not less than six months;
- (f) is convicted of an offence under section 84 of this Act;
- (g) is absent, without reasonable cause, from three consecutive meetings of the Committee;
- (h) resigns in writing addressed to the Cabinet Secretary;
- (i) fails to declare his or her interest in any matter being considered or to be considered by the Committee;
- (j) dies; or
- (k) is removed from office by the Cabinet Secretary.

(2) A member of the Committee may be removed from office on the ground of gross misconduct, incompetence, conviction for a cognizable offence, or violation of the Constitution.

(3) Before a member of the Committee is removed from office, that member shall be afforded an opportunity to be heard before such removal.

(4) A person who is aggrieved by the decision to remove that person from office under this section may appeal against the decision to the High Court.

10. Subcommittees

The Committee may establish such subcommittees as it may consider necessary for the proper performance of its functions and exercise of its powers under this Act.

11. Delegation by the Committee

The Committee may, by a resolution either generally or in a particular case, delegate to a subcommittee or to a member, officer, employee or agent of the Directorate, the exercise of any of the powers or performance of any of the functions of the Committee.

12. Conduct of the business of the Committee

(1) Subject to subsection (2), the business and affairs of the Committee shall be conducted in accordance with the First Schedule.

(2) Except as provided in this Act, the Committee may regulate its own procedure.

(3) The Committee shall maintain a proper record of its meetings of the Committee, including minutes, in such manner as it may determine.

13. Code of conduct

The Cabinet Secretary may make Regulations prescribing a code of conduct for Committee's members and officers, employees and agents of the Directorate.

14. Remuneration

There shall be paid to the members of the Committee such remuneration or allowances as the Cabinet Secretary may, in consultation with the Salaries and Remuneration Commission, determine.

15. Directorate

(1) There shall be established a directorate to be known as the Directorate of Public Private Partnerships.

(2) The Directorate shall be headed by the Director-General.

16. Director-General

(1) A person shall be qualified to be appointed as the Director-General if that person holds an advanced degree from a university recognized in Kenya and has knowledge and at least ten years' professional experience in any of the following fields—

(a) finance;

(b) economics;

(c) law;

(d) engineering;

(e) project management; or

(f) any other related and relevant field.

(2) The Director General shall be competitively recruited and appointed by the Public Service Commission.

(3) The Director-General shall hold office for a period of four years, and may only be re-appointed once for a further period of four years, subject to the terms of appointment.

17. Staff of the Directorate

Subject to section 31 and 37 of the Public Service staff of the Commission Act, 2017 the Cabinet Secretary shall, in consultation with the Director General, appoint the staff of the Directorate.

18. Secondment of staff to the Directorate

(1) The Directorate may request the secondment of staff from a contracting authority, county government, county corporation or a development or strategic partner on such terms and for such duration as may, on the consultation with the contracting authority, county government, county corporation or a development or strategic partner, be needed.

(2) The staff seconded to the Directorate shall be deemed to be the staff of the Directorate and fall under the authority of the Directorate for the duration of the secondment.

19. Functions of the Directorate

(1) The Directorate shall be the lead institution in the implementation of a public private partnership project under this Act and, in this regard, shall be responsible for—
  (a) originating, guiding and co-ordinating the selection, ranking and prioritization of public private partnership projects within the public budget framework;
  (b) overseeing appraisal and development activities of contracting authorities including providing technical expertise in the implementation of projects under this Act;
  (c) guiding and advising contracting authorities in project structuring, procurement and tender evaluations;
  (d) leading contracting authorities in contract negotiations and deal closure;
  (e) on its own motion, originating and leading in project structuring and procurement, in liaison with a contracting authority;
  (f) supporting the development of public private partnerships programmes in the country;
  (g) overseeing contract management frameworks for projects under this Act; and
  (h) undertaking any other activity necessary for the fulfilment of any of the functions of the Directorate.

(2) In the performance of its functions, the Directorate shall—
  (a) establish an open, efficient and equitable process for the management of the identification, screening, prioritization, development, procurement, implementation and monitoring of projects;
  (b) serve as the national resource centre on public private partnerships;

(c) conduct capacity-building for contracting authorities;

(d) create public awareness on public private partnerships;

(e) provide advisory and support services to contracting authorities in national and county governments at all stages of a project under this Act;

(f) on behalf of contracting authorities, retain transaction advisors and to enter into agreements for that purpose to assist contracting authorities during project appraisal and implementation;

(g) review and approve project proposals and tender evaluation reports;

(h) establish a national register of projects implemented under this Act;

(i) monitor contingent liabilities and accounting and budgetary issues related to public private partnerships in conjunction with relevant government departments; and

(j) conduct research and publish findings on public private partnerships in order to ensure the continuous improvement of public private partnership projects.

(3) The Directorate shall issue standard bidding documents for use by contracting authorities.

(4) The Directorate shall prepare financial accounts and inventory of any monies allocated to it, and on any financial support received by it under this Act.

PART III
PUBLIC PRIVATE PARTNERSHIPS

20. Project agreements

(1) A contracting authority intending to finance, operate, equip or maintain an infrastructure facility or provide a public service may enter into a project agreement with a qualified private party for the financing, construction, operation, equipping or maintenance of the infrastructure facility or provision of the public service in accordance with the provisions of this Act.

(2) A contracting authority that enters into a project agreement with a private party under subsection (1) may, where it is appropriate, designate its property for the use by a private party, in relation to, and for the duration of, a project on such terms and conditions as the contracting authority shall consider appropriate.

(3) A contracting authority shall implement the directions of the Directorate at every stage of a project.

(4) Where a project involves more than one contracting authority, the Directorate shall designate one of the contracting authorities to be the lead contracting authority.

21. Public private partnership arrangements

(1) Subject to the provisions of this Act, a contracting authority may enter into a public private partnership arrangement with a private party in accordance with the Second Schedule.

(2) Without prejudice to the periods specified under the Second Schedule, a contracting authority shall not enter into a public private partnership arrangement for a period exceeding thirty years.

22. Duties of contracting authorities

(1) A contracting authority has a duty to—
- (a) in liaison with the Directorate, identify, screen and pioritize projects based on a guidance issued by the directorate;
- (b) prepare and appraise each project to ensure its legal, regulatory, social, economic and commercial viability;
- (c) undertake the tendering process in accordance with this Act;
- (d) provide such technical expertise as the Directorate may require to evaluate and appraise a project;
- (e) monitor the implementation of a project agreement;
- (f) liaise with all key stakeholders during the project cycle;
- (g) oversee the management of a project in accordance with the project agreement;
- (h) submit to the Directorate annual or such other periodic reports on the implementation of project agreements;
- (i) maintain a record of all documentation and agreements entered into relating to the implementation of a project agreement under this Act;
- (j) prepare project agreements in accordance with standard documents and other guidance issued by the Directorate;
- (k) ensure there is public participation on a project; and
- (l) ensure that the transfer of assets at the expiry or early termination of a project agreement is consistent with the terms of the project agreement where the project agreement involves a transfer of assets.

(2) In the performance of its duties under subsection (1), a contracting authority shall report to the Directorate and—
- (a) implement the recommendations of the Directorate;
- (b) comply with the guidelines issued by the Directorate; and
- (c) submit such information as may be required by the Directorate or Committee.

23. Determination of the duration of public private partnership agreements

(1) In determining the duration of a public private partnership agreement, a contracting authority shall take into account the following factors—
- (a) the provisions of this Act and any other relevant written law;
- (b) the life span of the technology to be employed under the agreement;
- (c) the investment standards that are required to be maintained by each party to the project agreement throughout the duration of the public private partnership agreement;
- (d) the economic and financial viability of the project and the economic life of the facilities to be provided;

(e) the depreciation of the project assets during the life of the public private partnership agreement; and

(f) the period required by the parties to the partnership to—

(i) maintain service delivery standards and investment levels during the life span of the public private partnership agreement; and

(ii) recoup the parties' investment.

(2) The Directorate may issue guidelines in respect of the determination of the duration of a public private partnership agreement.

(3) The Directorate may extend the tenure of a project agreement on such terms and for such period as may be approved by the Committee and the Attorney-General:

Provided that an extension shall not impose an additional fiscal or statutory burden on the contracting authority or the Government.

24. Execution of project agreements

Where a contracting authority intends to enter into a public private partnership, a person shall not, unless that person is the accounting officer of the contracting authority, enter into a project agreement in relation to that project on behalf of the contracting authority.

25. Submission of project lists

(1) A contracting authority, other than a county government or county corporation, shall prepare a list of projects that it intends to undertake on a priority basis under this Act and submit it to the Directorate for approval.

(2) A contracting authority shall not submit a project list unless the projects are part of the national development agenda.

(3) A project list prepared under this section shall be supported by appropriate project concept notes which shall be prepared in accordance with guidelines issued by the Directorate.

(4) The Directorate shall notify the Committee, the Cabinet Secretary and Cabinet, bi-annually, on all projects it approves for implementation under the Act.

(5) The Directorate may reject any project included in a proposed project list and shall specify the reasons for such refusal in writing.

(6) Where the Directorate rejects a proposed project in a project list, it shall provide the respective contracting authority with the necessary guidance.

26. National list and priority list of projects

(1) The Directorate shall establish and maintain an up-to-date national list of projects that have been approved under sections 25 and 66 of this Act.

(2) Subject to subsection (1), the national list shall be published on the Directorate's website and the contracting authority's website.

(3) The national list shall be maintained in a publicly accessible database hosted by the Directorate.

(4) The Directorate shall prepare a priority list of the projects specified in the National List for implementation under this Act.

27. Prequalification procedures

A contracting authority intending to enter into a project agreement with a private party shall, before the execution of the project agreement, confirm that the private party has—

    (a) the financial capacity to undertake the project;

    (b) the relevant experience in undertaking projects of a similar nature;

    (c) the relevant expertise to undertake the project; and

    (d) satisfied the legal, social and environmental due diligence parameters prescribed by the Directorate.

28. Government support measures

(1) The Cabinet Secretary may issue Government support measures for a public private partnership including—

    (a) a binding undertaking;

    (b) a letter of support;

    (c) a letter of credit;

    (d) a credit guarantee, whether partial or full;

    (e) approval for issuance of partial risk guarantees and political risk insurance; or

    (f) any other instrument that Cabinet Secretary responsible for matters relating to finance may, on the advice of the Committee, determine:

Provided that the instrument shall comply with the provisions of the law relating to public finance management.

(2) The Cabinet Secretary may only issue Government support measures under this section—

    (a) where it is necessary to support a project to lower premiums factored for the profiling of political risks; or

    (b) to underwrite approved commercial risks under a negotiated project agreement.

(3) The Cabinet Secretary may prescribe guidelines for the issuance of Government support measures under this section.

29. Success fees and recoverable project development costs

(1) The Directorate shall impose a success fee not exceeding one per cent of the total project cost of a transaction payable by a private party that achieves financial close on a project.

(2) Where the Directorate or a contracting authority incurs costs for transaction advisory services offered in support of project preparatory and procurement activities or any other recoverable project development costs, such costs shall be recoverable in full, without any inflation adjustment, from the private party that enters into a project agreement with the contracting authority.

(3) Success fees and recoverable project costs under subsection (2) shall be payable into the Public Private Partnership Project Facilitation Fund.

(4) The Directorate may issue guidelines on the allocation of costs and disbursements on success fees imposed under this section in relation to recoverable project costs.

PART IV
PROJECT IDENTIFICATION AND SELECTION OF PRIVATE PARTIES

30. Project identification, selection and prioritisation

(1) A contracting authority intending to implement a project through a public private partnership under this Act shall, in consultation with the Directorate, be responsible for conceptualizing or identifying potential projects and undertaking the preparatory and tendering process of the project.

(2) In conceptualizing, identifying and prioritizing potential projects under this Act, a contracting authority shall consider the strategic and operational benefits of the public private partnership arrangement compared to the development of the facility or, provision of the service by the contracting authority.

(3) Where a contracting authority elects to implement a project prioritized under section 25, it shall appraise the project for viability in accordance with section 32.

(4) The Cabinet Secretary shall, in consultation with the Directorate, make Regulations for the conceptualization, identification and prioritization of projects under this Act.

31. Project preparation and implementation

(1) A contracting authority shall, under the direction of the Directorate, constitute a project implementation team for overseeing the structuring and implementation phases of the project including—

(a) overseeing the conduct of feasibility studies;
(b) preparing the project for procurement;
(c) conducting the tender stage of the project; and
(d) negotiating project agreements for the project.

(2) A project implementation team constituted under subsection (1) shall consist of a representative of the Directorate and such technical, financial and legal experts of the contracting authority as the contracting authority and the Directorate shall determine.

32. Feasibility studies

(1) A contracting authority shall, under the direction of the Directorate, undertake a feasibility study of the project it intends to implement under this Act in order to determine the viability of the project.

(2) The contracting authority shall consider the following matters when undertaking the feasibility study—

(a) the technical requirements of the project;
(b) the legal requirements to be met by the parties to the project;
(c) the social, economic and environmental impact of the project;
(d) the affordability and value for money proposition in the project; and
(e) the project's land requirements and required site preparatory activities necessary for effective and efficient project initiation.

33. Approval of feasibility reports

(1) A contracting authority intending to implement a project through public private partnership shall submit the feasibility report prepared under section 32 to the Directorate for evaluation.

(2) The Directorate shall submit an evaluation report together with its recommendations to the Committee.

(3) The Committee shall within twenty-one days of receipt of the evaluation report consider the feasibility report in determining whether or not the contracting authority may procure a project under this Act.

34. Technical expertise of contracting authorities

(1) The Directorate shall assess the technical expertise of the contracting authority to procure the development, preparation, procurement, contract negotiation and management of a project under this Act.

(2) Where the Directorate determines that the contracting authority does not have the technical expertise to procure the project, the contracting authority shall, in consultation with the Directorate, appoint a transaction advisor to assist the authority in the preparation, procurement, contract negotiations and financial close phases of a project.

(3) The engagement of a transaction advisor under subsection (2) shall be based on the principles of disclosure, transparency, equality, cost-effectiveness and equal opportunity in accordance with the procedure prescribed by the Cabinet Secretary in Regulations.

(4) The Directorate may procure transaction advisors on a sectoral basis based on the projects contained in the National List under section 25.

35. Standards and procedures

(1) The Cabinet Secretary shall, on the recommendation of the Directorate, prescribe the standards and procedures for the identification, selection, feasibility study, pre-tender approval, tendering, negotiation, post-tender approval, monitoring and evaluation of projects under this Act.

(2) Without prejudice to the generality of subsection (1), the Cabinet Secretary shall prescribe standards and procedures—

    (a) on practice elements in the procuring of privately initiated project proposals;

    (b) on the conduct of competitive tender processes under this Act;

    (c) on the protocols to be observed in a direct negotiation process between a contracting authority and a private party;

    (d) on disclosure requirements at every stage of a project;

    (e) on standard contractual clauses applicable to the competitive procurement of principal subcontracts for Privately-Initiated Proposals in the interest of fair price discovery and higher value for money for Government;

    (f) on procedures for benchmarking and market testing;

    (g) on timelines and procedures for every stage of privately-initiated proposals;

    (h) for public participation and stakeholder engagement during project development

stages;
(i) on hiring of transaction advisors;
(j) on the management of conflicts of interest;
(k) on standardised evaluation criteria templates;
(l) on feasibility studies;
(m) on timelines for project development; and
(n) any other relevant matter required for the better implementation of this Part.

36. Limitation of contingent liabilities

(1) The Cabinet Secretary shall approve a limit for contingent liabilities that the Committee may assign to projects under the Act.

(2) The Committee shall assign contingent liabilities to a project approved under this Act within the approved contingent liability limit.

(3) The Directorate—
(a) shall notify the Cabinet Secretary of the allocated quantum of the approved contingent liability portfolio at least once every six months; and
(b) shall notify the Cabinet Secretary of any requirement for additional contingent liability headroom where the approved limit is exceeded.

(3) The Cabinet Secretary may, on the recommendation of the Committee, approve an increased contingent liability headroom to meet the objectives of the public private partnerships programme of the Government.

(4) The Directorate shall prepare and submit to the Cabinet Secretary an annual report on contingent liabilities assigned during the year in question providing projections on future contingent liability requirements based on the projects portfolio in the national list of projects prepared under section 25.

PART V
PUBLIC PRIVATE PARTNERSHIPS PROCUREMENT METHODS

37. Procurement methods

(1) A contracting authority may procure a public private partnership project under this Act through—
(a) direct procurement;
(b) privately-initiated proposals; or
(c) competitive bidding;
(d) restricted biding.

(2) In procuring a public private partnership project, a contracting authority shall be guided by the principles of transparency, cost-effectiveness and equal opportunity.

(3) A contracting authority shall use standard bidding documents issued by the Directorate in all public private partnership procurements.

(4) The Cabinet Secretary shall prescribe guidelines for the procurement of a public

private partnership under this Part.

Direct Procurement

38. Direct procurement

A contracting authority may, in consultation with the Directorate, use direct procurement if any of the following conditions are satisfied—

(a) the private party possesses the intellectual property rights to the key approaches or technologies required for the project;

(b) the works or services are only available from a limited number of private parties;

(c) a particular private party has exclusive rights in respect of the works or services, and no reasonable alternative or substitute is available;

(d) the contracting authority determines that there are operational and strategic advantages and or reasons linked to particular private parties on the basis of national interest, bilateral or international cooperation, or external trade;

(e) the direct engagement of a private party shall significantly lower the cost of delivering the works or services on the basis of the project's qualifying for funding on such terms as the Government shall approve without such outcomes becoming part of the public debt;

(f) there is an urgent need for the works or services, and any other procurement method is impractical:

Provided that the circumstances giving rise to the urgency were not foreseeable by the contracting authority or the result of dilatory conduct by the contracting authority;

(g) the contracting authority, having procured goods, equipment, technology or services from a private party, determines that additional supplies shall be procured from that private party for reasons of standardization or because of the need for compatibility with existing goods, equipment, technology or services, taking into account the—

    (i) effectiveness of the original procurement in meeting the needs of the contracting authority;

    (ii) limited size of the proposed procurement in relation to the original procurement; and

    (iii) reasonableness of the price and the unsuitability of alternatives to the goods or services in question;

(h) the works or services are procured from a public entity:

Provided that the acquisition price shall be fair and reasonable and compare well with known prices of works or services in the circumstances; or

(i) any other reason that may be prescribed by the Cabinet Secretary.

39. Procedure for direct procurement

A contracting authority shall adhere to the following procedures during direct

procurement of projects—
- (a) issue a tender document which shall be the basis of tender preparation by the contracting authority and subsequent negotiations;
- (b) appoint an evaluation committee in accordance with the standards and practice procedures issued under this Act for the negotiation of a direct procurement of a project;
- (c) ensure that appropriate approvals under this Act have been granted;
- (d) ensure that the resulting project agreement complies with this Act; and
- (e) any other procedure that may be prescribed by the Cabinet Secretary.

Privately-Initiated Proposals

40. Privately-initiated proposals

(1) A private party may submit a privately-initiated proposal to a contracting authority.

(2) A contracting authority may consider a privately-initiated proposal submitted under subsection (1) if—
- (a) the project is aligned with national infrastructure priorities and meets a demonstrated societal need;
- (b) the project provides value for money;
- (c) the project proposal provides sufficient information for the contracting authority to assess fiscal affordability and the potential contingent liability implications of the proposal;
- (d) the project can be delivered at a fair market price;
- (e) the project is supported by all documents listed under subsection (3) for purposes of transparency and accountability; and
- (f) the project supports the efficient transfer of risk from the public sector.

(3) The privately-initiated proposal under subsection (1) shall contain the following information—
- (a) a detailed description of the proposed project, including reference designs, sketches and alignment maps;
- (b) detailed project needs analysis, including a description of the benefits to society and alignment with Government's infrastructure plan;
- (c) a description of the environmental and social features of the proposed project;
- (d) a detailed technical description of the project, including a construction schedule and requirements on enabler services;
- (e) a detailed description of the financial viability of the project, including costs and revenues, preliminary funding and financing plan, supported by relevant financial model in open format;
- (f) a preliminary operating plan for the proposed project;
- (g) a description of the key project risks and the risk allocation under the project;
- (h) disclosure of any Government support measures the proposed project may require;

(i) a description of non-monetary Government support measures that the project may require; and

(j) a justification why the project is not suitable for open competitive procurement.

(4) The contracting authority shall submit the privately-initiated proposal to the Directorate for assessment and approval.

(5) The Cabinet Secretary may, by notice in the *Gazette*, prescribe when submissions may be made under this section.

(6) A private party shall pay into the Fund a non-refundable review fee at the time of submitting its privately-initiated proposal under subsection (1), calculated at the rate of zero-point-five per cent of the estimated project cost or fifty thousand United States dollars, whichever is lower.

(7) The review fee paid under subsection (6) shall not create any obligation on the contracting authority or the Directorate towards the proponent.

(8) The Cabinet Secretary shall, in consultation with the Directorate, make Regulations for the better implementation of this section.

41. Due diligence on privately-initiated proposals

The Directorate, in co-ordination with the contracting authority, shall, before commencing an evaluation of a privately-initiated proposal, conduct due diligence to confirm that the private party—

(a) has not been debarred by any country or any international organization from participating in public private partnerships or similar arrangement;

(b) is not corrupt, has not engaged in acts of corruption, and has not been sued or convicted on account of acts of corruption;

(c) is not insolvent, under receivership or bankrupt and its affairs are not being administered by a court or judicial officer, its business activities have not been suspended, and it is not subject to any current legal proceedings;

(d) is tax-compliant in all jurisdictions in which it has local tax presence, and in its home country of registration, and is not at default on payment of social security and employment benefits or contributions in its jurisdictions of operation and registration; and

(e) has not, and its directors or officers have not, been convicted of any criminal offence related to professional conduct within a period of five years preceding the submission of the proposal, and have not otherwise been disqualified pursuant to administrative suspension or debarment proceedings.

42. Evaluation of privately-initiated proposals

(1) The Directorate shall, in consultation with the contracting authority, in evaluating a privately-initiated proposal with a view to determining its suitability for further development as a public private partnership project, establish evaluation criteria for the proposal.

(2) The private party shall not be required to submit additional proposals to the

contracting authority or the Directorate during the evaluation of the privately-initiated proposal.

(3) The evaluation criteria established under subsection (1) shall include—
  (a) public interest criteria;
  (b) project feasibility criteria;
  (c) public private partnership suitability criteria; and
  (d) affordability criteria.

(4) If requested by the Directorate or a contracting authority, the private party shall provide any clarifications or additional information on the privately-initiated proposal in written form.

(5) The Directorate and contracting authority shall, in consultation with relevant government departments, evaluate the proposal against the evaluation criteria within ninety days from the date the proposal is submitted to the Directorate.

(6) The Directorate shall prepare a detailed assessment report on the privately-initiated proposal based on the evaluation criteria established under subsection (1) and make recommendations to the Committee within five working days after concluding the evaluation on whether or not the project can proceed to the project development phase.

(7) The Committee shall, within fourteen working days of receiving the report under subsection (6), determine whether or not the proposed project may proceed to the project development phase, and provide guidance on the procurement method that shall be applied to the said project.

(8) In making its determination under subsection (7), the Committee shall take into consideration—
  (a) the assessment report submitted under subsection (6);
  (b) the review and recommendations of the Directorate; and
  (c) any benchmarking or market testing results.

(9) The approval of a privately-initiated proposal shall not create an obligation on the part of the Directorate, contracting authority or Government toward the private party.

43. Project development of privately-initiated proposals

(1) Where the Committee approves a privately-initiated proposal, the proposal shall proceed to the project development phase, during which a private party shall prepare specific project development activities before the project can be approved.

(2) The project development phase shall be completed within six months from the date of the approval by the Committee.

(3) Despite subsection (2), a contracting authority may apply in writing to the Directorate for the extension of time for the completion of the project development phase, specifying the justification for the application for additional time, and proposing a new timeframe and mitigation measures to prevent any further delays.

(4) Where the Directorate is satisfied with the justifications of the contracting authority under subsection (3), it shall grant the application.

(5) The project development phase consists of the activities necessary to enable the contracting authority and other appropriate decision-making agencies, under the guidance of the Directorate, to undertake a detailed evaluation of the proposed project before contracting, including the development of—

 (a) a detailed geographical, temporal and functional scope of the proposed project, including any right of way or land acquisition or human resettlement plan, where applicable;

 (b) a technical feasibility study, including a technical design and technical specification schedule that is capable of supporting pricing and socio-environmental impact assessments;

 (c) a financial feasibility study, including a detailed risk assessment, fiscal impact assessment or affordability assessment and a funding and financial plan;

 (d) a legal feasibility study, including an assessment of legal risks and uncertainties;

 (e) a social and environmental impact assessment where applicable;

 (f) an economic feasibility study;

 (g) private public partnership suitability assessment or value for money assessment;

 (h) a comprehensive risk matrix;

 (i) a preliminary private public partnership structure; and

 (j) a plan for stakeholder outreach to ensure social acceptability of the project.

(6) At the request of a private party, the contracting authority may enter into a project development agreement with the private party that shall outline the terms under which the private party will undertake project development activities.

(7) A project development agreement between the contracting party and the private party shall provide for the—

 (a) objectives of the project and project development agreement;

 (b) responsibilities of the contracting authority and the private party under the agreement;

 (c) compensation principles specifying that—

  (i) if the project is eventually awarded to the private party, there shall be no compensation;

  (ii) if the project is awarded to another private party, the costs of the private party that submitted the proposal for completing the project development phase, shall be paid by the private party, at financial close; and

  (iii) if the project does not progress beyond the project development phase, there shall be no compensation liability on the part of the Government;

 (d) modalities for coordination and communication between the contracting authority and the private party;

 (e) timelines for project development;

 (f) conditions under which the agreement may be terminated;

(g) legal or regulatory obligations of the contracting authority and the private party; and

(h) policies related to transparency and disclosure, accountability, confidentiality and conflicts of interest.

(8) The Directorate shall develop standardized contract documents for a project development agreement with respect to privately-initiated proposals.

(9) All documents resulting from the project development phase shall be evaluated by the contracting authority in accordance with the evaluation criteria specified in section 42 and the Directorate shall make recommendations thereon to the Committee for approval within twenty working days of completing the project development phase.

(10) The contracting authority, in co-ordination with the Directorate, may hire external advisors to review and provide an independent opinion regarding the studies conducted by the private party regarding the privately-initiated proposal.

(11) The Committee may, on the recommendations of the contracting authority, and any independent reviews or advice that the Committee may solicit in that regard, make a determination that—

(a) the project meets the public interest, public private partnership suitability, project feasibility and affordability criteria, and grant approval for the project to be procured under this Act;

(b) the project does not meet public private partnership suitability criteria and give guidance on alternative methods by which the project may be implemented; or

(c) the project does not meet any of the relevant criteria and should be abandoned.

(12) Where the Committee determines that the project should be abandoned under paragraph (11)(c), the contracting authority may elect to restructure the project to meet the evaluation criteria and resubmit the project to the Committee for a fresh determination.

(13) The Committee shall render its decision under this section within fourteen days of receiving the report under subsection (9).

(14) Following the determination of the Committee, the contracting authority shall publish the feasibility studies and project documentation used to evaluate the project, subject to any applicable disclosure guidelines on public private partnership projects for the time being in force.

(15) For the purposes of this section—

(a) "**public interest**" means the proposed project aligns with stated infrastructure needs, policy objectives and priorities of the Government, addresses a defined societal need, and contributes to the country's socio-economic agenda; and

(b) "**project feasibility**" means the proposed project has been confirmed to be technically, financially, socially, environmentally and legally feasible.

44. Procurement design

(1) Where the Committee determines that the privately-initiated proposal may be procured in terms of section 43 (11)(a), the contracting authority shall, with the

assistance of the Directorate, directly negotiate the project proposal with the private party, if—

    (a) the contracting authority determines that the proposal shall not generate market interest under competitive procurement;

    (b) the proposal is anchored on unique elements; or

    (c) direct negotiations are justified for any other reason in the public interest.

(2) For the purposes of subsection (1), a contracting authority shall establish clear and realistic timelines for the conduct of the direct negotiations on the project:

Provided that the contracting authority or authorities and the private party shall undertake to finalise the negotiations within six months.

(3) Where the direct negotiations are not completed within six months, the negotiations shall be terminated.

(4) Where the contracting authority receives more than one privately-initiated proposal with respect to the same matter and all proposals proceed to the project development stage, the contracting authority may utilize a restricted tendering procedure that limits competitive bidding to the private parties that submitted proposals.

(5) Where a contracting authority determines that the project should be procured competitively because of market interest or the existence of equally competent alternative technologies that could deliver higher value for money to the Government, the contracting authority may elect to subject the project to open competitive tender under this Act:

Provided that the contracting authority may determine whether or not to reimburse the costs incurred by the private party if—

    (a) the project is awarded to any other bidder;

    (b) the project achieves financial close;

    (c) the development costs do not exceed zero-point-five per cent of the estimated project cost; and

    (d) the development costs are borne by the successful bidder.

(6) Where the contracting authority determines that an open tender is in the public interest, it shall establish a clear and realistic timeline for the preparation of tender documentation and the administration of the bidding process.

(7) Subject to subsection (4), the contracting authority shall ensure equal bidding conditions when designing a procurement strategy under this section.

Restricted Bidding

45. Restricted bidding

(1) A contracting authority may use restricted bidding if any of the following conditions are satisfied—

    (a) competition for contract, because of the complex or specialized nature of the works and services is restricted to prequalified tenderers;

    (b) the time and cost required to examine and evaluate a large number of tenders would be disproportionate to the value of the works or services to be procured;

(c) if there is evidence to the effect that there are only a few known suppliers of the whole market of the works or services;

(d) an advertisement is placed, where applicable, on the procuring entity website regarding the intention to procure through limited tender.

(2) A contracting authority may engage in procurement by means of restricted bidding in such manner as may be prescribed.

Competitive Bidding

46. Requests for qualification

(1) A contracting authority shall, on the approval of a feasibility report, invite requests for qualifications from qualified bidders with respect to the proposed project.

(2) The Directorate shall prescribe the standards and specify the practice notes on procurement and tender administration regarding the requests for qualification.

(3) A contracting authority shall, in the request under subsection (1), specify the eligibility criteria of a bidder and may require each bidder to provide statements or documents to prove the bidder's eligibility.

(4) A contracting authority shall consult the Directorate during the procurement cycle.

(5) Any person who responds to a request for qualification shall comply with the provisions of this Act and the instructions to bidders contained in the tender documents.

(6) Where the Directorate determines that this section should not apply to a public private partnership project, the Directorate shall notify the contracting authority and the project may proceed to the bidding stage.

(7) The Directorate shall issue guidelines regarding the making of a determination under subsection (6).

47. Qualification of private parties

(1) A private party intending to respond to a request for qualification under section 46 may do so as part of a consortium of private parties.

(2) A private party or consortium is eligible to respond to a request for qualification if the party or consortium—

(a) satisfies the criteria specified in the request for qualification issued by the contracting authority;

(b) has the technical and financial capacity to undertake the proposed project;

(c) has the legal capacity to enter into a project agreement with the contracting authority;

(d) is not insolvent, in receivership, bankrupt or in the process of being wound up; and

(e) is not for any reason precluded by the contracting authority from entering into a project agreement with the contracting authority.

48. Prequalification committees

(1) The contracting authority shall, upon issuing a notice under section 44, constitute a pre-qualification committee for the purpose of pre-qualifying bidders.

(2) The contracting authority may, where it considers it appropriate, constitute the project appraisal team as the prequalification committee for purpose of prequalifying bidders under subsection (1).

49. Disqualification of private parties

(1) The pre-qualification committee constituted under section 48 shall review the requests for qualification submitted to the contracting authority and prepare a shortlist of qualified bidders.

(2) A bidder shall be disqualified at the prequalification stage if that bidder—
- (a) submits false, inaccurate or incomplete information;
- (b) colludes, connives or is involved in any corrupt or dishonest practice intended to confer an unfair advantage over other bidders in the award of the tender;
- (c) fails to meet any of the eligibility criteria specified in the request for qualification; or
- (d) contravenes the provisions of this Act or any other written law in order to have an unfair advantage over other bidders in the award of the tender.

(3) A disqualified bidder may object to its disqualification under subsection (2) by lodging a petition in the prescribed form with the Petition Committee within fourteen days of being notified of the disqualification.

(4) The Petition Committee shall hear and determine an objection under subsection (3) within twenty-eight days of the petition being lodged.

50. Invitations to bid

(1) A contracting authority shall, in consultation with the Directorate, after the preparation of a short list of prequalified bidders, prepare tender documents in relation to a project for the purpose of inviting bids from eligible bidders.

(2) The tender documents prepared under subsection (1) shall include the following information—
- (a) general information related to the project necessary for the preparation and submission of bids;
- (b) specifications of the project including the technical and financial conditions that should be met by bidders;
- (c) specifications of the final product, level of services, performance indicators and such other requirements as may be necessary including the safety, security and environment preservation requirements to be met by bidders;
- (d) basic terms of the project agreement including non-negotiable conditions;
- (e) the criteria and method to be used in evaluating bids;
- (f) forms and documents that are required to be filled and submitted by bidders;
- (g) the value of the bid security required to be submitted by bidders;
- (h) the conditions, procedures and administration of bid clarifications;
- (i) the date, time and place for the submission of tender documents by bidder;
- (j) instructions regarding pre-bid conferences, where necessary;
- (k) the conditions to be met by any consortiums on permissible changes to a

consortium arrangement;

(1) the procedure to be followed in a competitive dialogue process; and

(m) any other matter that may be necessary for the proper conduct of the tender stage of the project.

51. Submission of bids

(1) A bidder intending to bid for a project under this Act shall complete and submit a technical and financial bid.

(2) The bidder shall submit the technical and financial bid in separate sealed envelopes in the manner prescribed by the contracting authority.

52. Competitive dialogue

(1) A contracting authority may, with the approval of the Directorate, hold a competitive dialogue with each shortlisted bidder for the purpose of defining the technical or financial aspects of the project.

(2) The contracting authority may require each bidder to submit a technical and financial non-binding proposal as part of the competitive dialogue with the authority.

(3) The competitive dialogue shall be held with each bidder on the basis of equality and transparency.

(4) The discussions held during a competitive dialogue shall not be disclosed to any person by any party to the discussions.

(5) At the end of the competitive dialogue stage, the contracting authority may—

(a) alter the project specifications, risk matrix or structure; and

(b) reopen prequalification for the project.

(6) Where the contracting authority reopens prequalification, it shall invite each bidder that participated in the competitive dialogue to submit a best and final offer which shall form the basis for the evaluation of the bids and award of the tender.

53. Bids by consortiums

(1) A consortium constituted for the purpose of bidding for a project under this Act may submit a bid in the name of the consortium.

(2) A bid by a consortium shall be accompanied by a notarised binding agreement executed by the consortium's members.

(3) A consortium shall—

(a) appoint a person from among its members to be the lead consortium member to represent the consortium in its dealings with the contracting authority on the basis of that person's technical, financial and experiential capacity to undertake the project; and

(b) submit a notice of the appointment of the lead consortium member to the contracting authority.

(4) A member of a consortium shall not, with respect to a bid by the consortium, submit a separate bid, whether directly or indirectly, or through another consortium, or through a company which submits a bid if that person owns a majority of the company's shares or has

control over its management.

(5) The contracting authority shall disqualify from the bidding process any consortium that submits a bid in contravention of the provisions of this section.

(6) The contracting authority may, where a member of a consortium withdraws from the consortium—
- (a) disqualify that consortium from participating in the bidding process; or
- (b) review the terms of a project agreement entered into with the consortium.

(7) The contracting authority shall disqualify a consortium from the bidding process if the consortium dismisses its lead consortium member or the lead consortium member withdraws from the consortium.

(8) Subsection (7) shall not apply where the consortium replaces the lead consortium member with another person in a manner that ensures that the consortium remains eligible to participate in the bid.

(9) Each member of a consortium which submits a bid shall be—
- (a) bound jointly and severally by the terms of the project agreement; and
- (b) jointly responsible for the performance of the obligations under the agreement.

(10) The Cabinet Secretary may, in consultation with the Directorate, make Regulations for the better implementation of this section.

54. Proposal evaluation teams

(1) A contracting authority shall, in consultation with the Directorate, constitute a proposal evaluation team for the purpose of evaluating bids submitted under this Act.

(2) The proposal evaluation team shall—
- (a) open and evaluate bids in accordance with the procedure specified in the tender documents and any guidelines issued by the Directorate for that purpose; and
- (b) evaluate the bids by taking into account the evaluation and award criteria prescribed in the tender documents.

55. Evaluation of bids and evaluation reports

(1) The proposal evaluation team shall evaluate the technical and financial bids within twenty-eight days in accordance with the procedure specified in the tender documents and guidelines prescribed by the Directorate and prepare an evaluation report specifying—
- (a) the evaluation criteria;
- (b) the manner in which the first-ranked bidder has satisfied the requirements specified in the tender documents in comparison with the other bidders;
- (c) such other information as the contracting authority shall consider necessary; and
- (d) the first-ranked and reserve bidder.

(2) The proposal evaluation team shall submit the evaluation report together with its recommendations thereon to the accounting officer of the contracting authority for approval.

(3) If the accounting officer is not satisfied with the recommendations of the evaluation committee, the accounting officer may return the evaluation report to the proposal

evaluation team with recommendations for the review of the report.

(4) The contracting authority shall submit than an evaluation report to the Directorate for no objection within seven days of conclusion of the evaluation.

56. Non-compliance by bidders

(1) A proposal evaluation team shall reject a bidder's submission where the bidder fails to comply with the conditions specified in the tender documents or Regulations made under this Act.

(2) A proposal evaluation team may reject all submissions where the bidders fail to comply with the conditions specified in the tender documents or the Regulations made under this Act.

(3) Where a proposal evaluation team rejects a submission under this section, the proposal evaluation team shall submit to the accounting officer a report setting out the reasons for the rejection.

(4) The accounting officer shall inform the bidder of the decision of the contracting authority to reject the bid within fourteen days of receiving the report under subsection (3).

(5) A bidder whose bid has been rejected under this section shall not be entitled to compensation.

(6) Where all bids have been rejected under this section in a given tender process, the tender process shall be deemed to have terminated on account of failure by bidders to comply with tender requirements, and the contracting authority shall, in consultation with the Directorate, determine whether to start the tender process afresh.

57. Negotiations

(1) A contracting authority shall, in consultation with the Directorate, constitute a negotiating committee which shall—

- (a) enter into negotiations with the first-ranked bidder in accordance with sections 38, 40, 45 or 46;
- (b) for negotiations resulting from section 46, request the second-ranked bidder or any number of bidders as the tender documents may have indicated to extend the validity of its or their bids pending the completion of negotiations with the first-ranked bidder;
- (c) appoint a negotiation committee which shall be led by the Directorate:

Provided that the contracting authority may, with the permission of the Directorate, be responsible for leading the negotiations with respect to specific parts of the process.

(2) The negotiations between the negotiating committee and the first-ranked bidder may, among other elements—

- (a) cover the technical, commercial, legal, social, environmental, local content and financial terms of the project agreement; and
- (b) be subject to any limitations that may be expressly set out in the tender documents or in the approvals issued under section 44.

(3) The negotiations and resolutions by the negotiating parties shall not—

(a) alter the criteria on which tender was awarded;
(b) affect the non-negotiable terms and conditions specified in the invitation to tender;
(c) alter the financial structure of the project;
(d) affect the conditions applying to a privately-initiated proposal; and
(e) affect the conditions in respect of which there were no reservations raised by the bidder in the bid or proposal.

(4) Despite subsection (3), adjusting bid prices to account for changes in the foreign exchange rate or changes due to inflation shall not be deemed to be price-increasing adjustments:

Provided that the tender documents shall expressly provide that a change in the exchange rate or a change due to inflation shall not be deemed to be a price-increase adjustment.

(5) The negotiating parties shall not amend the negotiated terms and terms upon which the bid has been evaluated.

(6) Where the negotiations between the negotiating committee and the first-ranked bidder are unsuccessful, the negotiating committee shall enter into negotiations with the second-ranked bidder.

(7) The provisions of subsections (2), (3), (4) and (5) shall apply to the negotiations with the second-ranked bidder.

(8) The negotiating committee shall conduct the negotiations in accordance with the guidelines prescribed by the Directorate, including guidelines on the duration of the negotiations between the committee and the bidder.

58. Project and risk assessment reports

(1) The negotiating committee shall, upon concluding negotiations under section 57, submit to the contracting authority a project and financial risk assessment report which shall specify the negotiated terms, the contingent liability in respect of the project and the committee's recommendations.

(2) If the contracting authority is satisfied with the recommendations of the negotiating committee, it shall submit the project and financial risk assessment report to the Directorate for approval.

(3) If the Directorate is not satisfied with the recommendations of the negotiating committee, it shall notify the contracting authority in writing and specify the reasons thereof.

(4) Where the contracting authority has been notified under subsection (3), it shall refer the project and financial risk assessment report back to the negotiating committee together with the Directorate's notification under subsection (3) and request the committee to review the report.

(5) Subsections (1), and (2) shall apply, with the necessary modifications, to the review of the report under subsection (4).

59. Approval of project and financial risk assessment reports by the Committee

(1) The Directorate shall submit the project and financial risk assessment report and its

recommendations thereon to the Committee for approval.

(2) The Committees shall consider the report submitted to it under subsection (1) and if satisfied, approve the execution of a project agreement between the contracting authority and the successful bidder within twenty-eight days after receiving the report under subsection (1).

60. Approval of projects

(1) The Committee shall notify the contracting authority in writing of the approval of the project and financial risk assessment report within thirty days of the approval.

(2) On the notification under subsection (1), the contracting authority shall prepare a final draft of the project agreement between the contracting authority and the bidder and submit it to the Attorney-General for clearance and if cleared, present it to the bidder for execution.

(3) The contracting authority shall notify in writing—
 (a) all the bidders who participated in the tender process of the decision of the Committee; and
 (b) the Cabinet of the Committee's approval to enter into a project agreement with the successful bidder.

61. Execution of project agreements

(1) On the approval under section 60, the contracting authority shall execute the project agreement with the successful bidder.

(2) A private party that executes a contract under subsection (1) shall commence the project within twelve months from the date of execution of the contract.

(3) If the private party fails to commence the project in accordance with subsection (2), the contracting authority shall terminate the contract and no liability shall attached to the contracting authority or the Government.

62. Cancellation of tenders

(1) A contracting authority may cancel a tender process at any time before the execution of the project agreement if it is in the public interest to do so.

(2) Despite subsection (1), a contracting authority shall not cancel a tender unless the Committee and Attorney-General approve the cancellation.

(3) A cancellation under subsection (1) shall be by notice in writing issued to the bidders and shall specify the reasons for the cancellation.

(4) The bidders in a cancelled tender shall not be entitled to compensation for any losses occasioned by the cancellation.

(5) For purposes of this section, public interest is impaired where the following circumstances exist—
 (a) the project has been overtaken by operation of law or rendered obsolete as a consequence of substantial technological change or by reason of a *force majeure* event;
 (b) there is evidence that the bids are significantly above market prices;

(c) material governance issues have been demonstrably detected;

(d) all evaluated tenders are non-responsive;

(e) civil commotion, hostilities or armed conflict has arisen that renders the implementation of the project impractical; or

(f) evidence of commission of an offence under the Anti-Corruption and Economic Crimes Act, 2003 (No. 3 of 2003) or the Proceeds of Crime and Anti-Money Laundering Act, 2009 (No. 9 of 2009).

63. Agreements to be ratified by Parliament

The Cabinet Secretary responsible for a contracting authority that enters into a project agreement with a private party under this Act in respect of the exploitation of natural resources shall submit the project to Parliament for approval in accordance with Article 71 of the Constitution and the relevant written law relating to the exploitation, conservation or management of the natural resource.

PART VI
PUBLIC PRIVATE PARTNERSHIPS BY COUNTY GOVERNMENTS

64. Project agreements by county governments

(1) A county government may enter into a public private partnership agreement with a private party to undertake a public private partnership project in accordance with this Part.

(2) A county government that enters into a public private partnership agreement with a private party shall be responsible for the administration of the overall project development cycle.

(3) A county government intending to undertake a public private partnership project shall subject the project to a detailed feasibility study in accordance with section 32.

(4) A county government intending to undertake a public private partnership project shall liaise with the Directorate during each phase of the project.

(5) A county government intending to undertake a public private partnership project shall obtain the written approval to undertake the project from the Committee and Cabinet Secretary responsible for matters relating to finance where the feasibility study under subsection (3) shows that the project—

(a) shall require a government support measure; or

(b) exceeds the fiscal ability of the county government to implement the project.

(6) Each county government shall submit to the Directorate all feasibility studies prepared under subsection (3).

65. Approved by county assemblies

(1) Subject to section 64 (5), each county government intending to undertake a public private partnership project shall obtain the approval of the respective county assembly before undertaking the project.

(2) Where a public private partnership project by a county government requires a government

support measure, the county government shall not undertake the project or enter into a project agreement before obtaining the written approval of the Cabinet Secretary.

66. County project lists

(1) A county government or county corporation that intends to implement public private partnership projects under this Act, shall submit a list of the projects to the Directorate for inclusion in the published national list of projects under section 26.

(2) A county government or county corporation shall not submit a project list unless the projects are part of the County Integrated Development Plan.

67. Part V to apply

The provisions of Part V shall apply, with the necessary modifications, to public private partnership projects by county governments.

PART VII
PROJECT COMPANIES, DISCLOSURES AND PROJECT AGREEMENTS

68. Project companies

(1) On the execution of a project agreement, the contracting authority and successful bidder shall establish a project company in accordance with the Companies Act, 2015 (No. 17 of 2015) for the purpose of undertaking the project.

(2) A project company established under subsection (1)—

 (a) may include a public entity as a minority shareholder in the company; and

 (b) shall provide such performance security and fulfil such conditions as may be specified in the project agreement and prescribed by the Cabinet Secretary in accordance with Regulations made under this Act.

(3) The directors of a project company shall not wind up the company, alter the legal structure or reduce the share capital of the company without the written approval of the contracting authority, which approval shall not be unreasonably withheld.

(4) A majority shareholder of a project company shall not transfer any shares held in the project company or permit the dilution of its majority stake in the project company to a point where the shareholder loses such majority standing before the issuance by the contracting authority of a certificate confirming the contracting authority's acceptance of the quality of the project undertaken in accordance with the project agreement.

(5) Notwithstanding subsection (4), any party to a project agreement may, with the approval of the Cabinet Secretary, restructure the project company's shareholding as may be necessary to secure the equity component of a transaction:

Provided that the restructuring of the project company's shareholding shall not—

 (a) alter the overall split between debt and equity approved under the project agreement; and

 (b) dilute the majority position of the lead member of a consortium within the shareholding structures of the project company.

(6) Notwithstanding the provisions of the Companies Act, 2015 (No. 17 of 2015) where the transfer of shares results in the transfer of control of a project company to a third party, the transfer shall not be valid unless the shareholder has applied for, and obtained, the written approval of the contracting authority.

(7) A project company shall not pledge its shares except for the purpose of financing the project.

(8) In granting approvals under this section, the Cabinet Secretary shall, on the recommendation of the Committee, do so, but may also decline to issue an approval if there are reasonable grounds to determine that the requested shareholding alterations would impair the assurance of delivery of the public facility or service.

(9) The Cabinet Secretary shall, in consultation with the Directorate, make Regulations for the better implementation of this section.

69. Publishing information on execution of project agreements

(1) A contracting authority shall, on the execution of a project agreement, publish in at least two newspapers of national circulation and electronic media the results of the tender and the following information—

    (a) the nature of the project and key terms of the project agreement;
    (b) the works to be developed or public services to be performed under the project;
    (c) the successful bidder;
    (d) the amount of any public funds committed to the project;
    (e) the project tariff, if applicable;
    (f) any government support measures provided to the project;
    (g) the social and economic benefits of the project;
    (h) the duration of the project;
    (i) the expected asset quality when the project is handed back to the contracting authority; and
    (j) the manner in which the project will be monitored and reported on during the duration of the project.

(2) The Directorate may prescribe the manner in which the contracting authority shall publish the information specified in subsection (1).

(3) The Cabinet Secretary shall, in consultation with the Directorate, make Regulations for the better implementation of this section.

70. Minimum obligations of parties to a project agreement

(1) The parties to a project agreement under this Act shall specify the minimum obligations to be met by the parties as set out in the Third Schedule.

(2) Notwithstanding subsection (1), every project agreement shall make provision for the revenue sharing mechanisms and thresholds between a private party and the Government, where a project's revenue performance meets and exceeds the target return on investment negotiated under a project agreement.

(3) The Cabinet Secretary may make Regulations specifying the manner in which

project agreements shall be drawn.

71. Applicable law

(1) Project agreements under this Act shall be subject to the provisions of the Laws of Kenya and any provision in a project agreement to the contrary shall be void.

(2) The parties to a project agreement may agree to resolve any disputes arising under the project agreement through arbitration or any other non-judicial means of dispute resolution as may be provided for in the project agreement in accordance with paragraph 18 of the Third Schedule.

72. Amendment and variation of project agreements

(1) A party to a project agreement intending to make any amendment or variation to the agreement in relation to the terms and conditions specified therein, the outputs of a project or any waivers specified in the agreement, may enter into negotiations with the other party on the proposed amendment, variation or waiver:

Provided that the amendment, variation or waiver shall not take effect unless it is approved by the Committee and Attorney-General.

(2) An amendment, variation or waiver to a project agreement under subsection (1) shall not be approved unless it is demonstrated that the agreement, if so amended or varied or provision waived, shall ensure—

    (i) the project shall continue to provide value for money;

    (ii) the project shall continue to be affordable as verified by the Directorate, where such amendment, variation or waiver has financial implications;

    (iii) the continued transfer of appropriate risks to the private party;

    (iv) the continued provision of efficient and effective public services; and

    (v) the continued protection and preservation of the environment.

(3) Any approval under subsection (2) shall be in writing.

73. Project management

(1) A contracting authority that is party to a project agreement shall, together with sector regulators, and with the guidance of the Directorate, establish and implement a contract management framework for the project agreement for the purpose of—

    (a) monitoring the implementation of the project agreement;

    (b) measuring the output of the project;

    (c) liaising with the other party to the agreement, users of the facility or service and other relevant stakeholders;

    (d) overseeing the management of the project agreement;

    (e) preparing bi-annual reports on project implementation;

    (f) submitting reports on project implementation to the Directorate;

    (g) implementing the recommendations and guidelines relevant hereto issued under the Act;

    (h) submitting of such information as may be required by the Directorate with respect to project oversight; and

(i) submitting of such information as may be required by the Public Debt Management Office with respect to contingent liability management.

(2) The project parties shall, in co-ordination with the Directorate, appoint an independent expert to manage the implementation of the project agreement under such terms as the Directorate shall prescribe.

(3) The cost of hiring an independent expert under subsection (2) shall form part of the project cost to be borne by the private party.

(4) A project agreement involving the performance of a function of a contracting authority by a private party shall not divest the contracting authority of the responsibility for ensuring that the function is effectively and efficiently performed.

(5) A project agreement involving the use of a contracting authority's assets by a private party shall not divest the contracting authority of the responsibility of ensuring that the assets are protected against factors which may negatively affect the assets including forfeiture, theft, loss and wastage.

(6) The Directorate shall monitor and provide necessary guidance to contracting authorities on the implementation of each project under this Act.

(7) Where the Directorate determines in accordance with this section and section 71 that there has arisen an imbalance in the distribution of benefits, and for the purpose of promoting the sustained transfer of project-linked economic benefits to the citizens of Kenya, the Directorate shall, in consultation with contracting authority, initiate the amendment or variation of the project agreement in accordance with section 71.

(8) Sector regulatory authorities shall monitor the performance of contracting authorities and private parties in the implementation of projects under this Act in accordance with the Regulations prescribed by the Cabinet Secretary under this Act.

74. Secondment of employees of contracting authority

(1) A contracting authority may, on the request of the project company, second to the company such number of employees as may be necessary for the purposes of the undertaking a project under this Act.

(2) An employee seconded to the project company shall, during the period of secondment, be deemed to be an employee of the company and shall be subject only to the direction and control of the company.

(3) An employee of the contracting authority seconded to the project company shall be seconded on the same or improved terms of service during the period of secondment.

75. Petition Committee

(1) There is established a committee to be known as the Petition Committee which shall hear and determine petitions regarding any decision by the Committee, Directorate or a contracting authority under this Act.

(2) The Petition Committee shall consist of the following persons appointed by the Cabinet Secretary—

(a) the chairperson, who shall be a person qualified to be appointed as a judge of

the High Court;
- (b) four other persons with such relevant knowledge and experience as the Cabinet Secretary shall consider appropriate; and
- (c) two persons, not being a member of county executive committees, and possessing such relevant knowledge and experience as the Cabinet Secretary shall consider appropriate, nominated by the Council of County Governors.

(3) The members of the Petition Committee shall hold office for a term of three years and may be eligible for re-appointment for one further term.

(4) A person who is aggrieved by a decision of the Directorate, Committee or a contracting authority regarding a tender process or project agreement may lodge a petition to review the decision with the Petition Committee in the prescribed form and after paying the prescribed fee.

(5) A petition under this section shall be made within seven days from the date of the decision of the Directorate, Committee or a contracting authority.

(6) The Petition Committee shall hear and determine the petition within twenty-eight days from the date the petition was lodged.

(7) A person aggrieved by the decision of the Committee may, within seven days of the decision, make an application for review to the Committee in the prescribed form.

(8) A person aggrieved by the decision of the Petition Committee may appeal to the High Court within fourteen days from the date of the Committee's decision.

(9) The Cabinet Secretary may, by Regulations, provide for the procedure for hearing and determining a petition and the applicable fees under this section.

76. Secretary

(1) The Cabinet Secretary shall designate a public officer to serve as the Secretary to the Committee.

(2) A person designated under subsection (1) shall be an Advocate of the High Court of Kenya of at least seven years standing.

77. Remuneration

The members of the Committee shall be paid such salaries and allowances as the Cabinet Secretary shall, in consultation with the Salaries and Remuneration Committee, determine.

78. Conflict of interest

A member of the Committee who has a direct or indirect interest in a matter before the Committee shall declare the interest and shall not participate in any proceedings of the Committee on the matter.

79. Offences

(1) A person shall not—
- (a) without reasonable cause or lawful excuse, obstruct or hinder, assault or threaten a member of the Committee acting under this Act;
- (b) without justification, fail to provide information required by the Committee under this Act;

(c) without justification, fail to provide information within reasonable time that is required by the Committee under this Act;

(d) submit false or misleading information to the Committee;

(e) misrepresent to or knowingly mislead a member of the Committee acting under this Act; or

(f) interfere with or exert undue influence on any member of the Committee.

(2) A person who contravenes subsection (1) commits an offence and is liable, on conviction, to a fine not exceeding five hundred thousand shillings or to imprisonment for a term not exceeding one year, or to both.

80. Decree

The Committee shall issue a decree setting out its decision in a particular matter and the decree shall be enforceable in the same manner as a decree of the Court.

PART VIII
FINANCIAL PROVISIONS

81. Public Private Partnership Project Facilitation Fund

There is established the Public Private Partnership Project Facilitation Fund which shall be a financing mechanism for purposes of this Act.

(2) The source of the Fund shall include—

(a) grants, gifts, donations or other endowments accruing to the Fund;

(b) such levies or tariffs as may be imposed on a project;

(c) success fees paid by a project company under this Act;

(d) appropriations-in-aid;

(e) money which may vest in or accrue to the Fund under this Act or any other written law; and

(f) money from any other source as may be approved by the Cabinet Secretary.

(3) The moneys received into the Fund shall be applied to—

(a) support contracting authorities in the preparation phase of a project, the tendering process and project appraisal under this Act;

(b) support the activities of the Directorate and Committee under this Act; and

(c) extend viability gap finance to projects that are desirable but cannot be implemented in the absence of financial support from the Government.

(4) The management of the Fund shall be in accordance with Regulations made by the Cabinet Secretary in accordance with the Public Finance Management Act, 2012 (No. 18 of 2012).

82. Financial reporting, audit and project performance reports

(1) The project company or the private party to a project agreement shall keep and maintain proper books of accounts and records in relation to the project.

(2) The books of account kept and maintained under subsection (1) shall, on reasonable notice, be open for scrutiny by the contracting authority or the Directorate.

(3) The Auditor General shall audit the accounts of a project company, where there is counterpart funding for a project including public funds.

(4) Where all the monies for a project are provided by a private party, the accounts of the project company shall be audited annually by a reputable audit firm, appointed in consultation with the National Treasury.

(5) The project company or the private party to a project agreement shall submit the audited financial accounts and any other information as may reasonably be required by the contracting authority or Directorate within six months after the end of each financial year.

(6) The project company shall prepare and submit project performance reports and monitoring reports to the contracting authority and Directorate within such periods as may be specified in the project agreement and in any case, at least once in each calendar year.

PART IX
MISCELLANEOUS PROVISIONS

83. Local content

(1) The parties to a project agreement shall, in the performance of project-related activities—
   (a) give priority to services provided in Kenya;
   (b) give priority to supplies manufactured in Kenya where the supplies meet the specifications applicable to the related industry;
   (c) ensure mechanisms for technology transfer locally;
   (d) optimise opportunities for trade concessions for Kenyan goods and services outside Kenya;
   (e) promote structured corporate social responsibility programmes; and
   (f) comply with local content requirements provided under any other written law and policy for the time being in force or applicable in Kenya.

(2) The Committee, on the advice of the Directorate, shall issue such guidelines, standards and practice notes on local content as shall be deemed necessary based on the priority requirements of the Kenyan economy.

84. Offences and penalties

(1) A person commits an offence if that person—
   (a) obstructs or hinders a person carrying out a duty or function or exercising a power under this Act;
   (b) knowingly lies to or misleads a person carrying out a duty or function or exercising a power under this Act;
   (c) delays without justifiable cause the—
      (i) opening or evaluation of tenders beyond the prescribed period;
      (ii) awarding of a contract beyond the prescribed period; or
      (iii) payment of contractors beyond the period specified in the project

agreement and performance obligations;
- (d) unduly influences or exerts pressure on any member of an evaluation committee, or employee or agent of the Directorate or contracting authority, or the accounting officer to take a particular action which favours or tends to favour a particular party;
- (e) divulges confidential information relating to any confidential processes under this Act;
- (f) inappropriately influences tender evaluations;
- (g) commits an act that is expressly prohibited under the terms of a tender document;
- (h) signs a project agreement or otherwise a tender in contravention of this Act or Regulations made under it;
- (i) wilfully violates any provision of this Act; or
- (j) commits a fraudulent act.

(2) A person who is convicted of an offence under this section shall be liable upon conviction—
- (a) if the person is a natural person, to a fine not exceeding two million shillings or imprisonment for a term not exceeding five years, or to both;
- (b) if the person is a body corporate, to a fine not exceeding ten millions shillings.

(3) In addition to the penalty prescribed by subsection (2)—
- (a) a State officer or public officer who is convicted of an offence under this section shall be liable to disciplinary action;
- (b) any other person who is not a State officer or public officer who is convicted of an offence under this section shall be barred from participating in any public private partnership project under this Act; and
- (c) a body corporate shall be debarred by the Government and barred from participating in any public private partnership project under this Act.

(4) If a person or an employee or agent of a person participating in a tender process under this Act contravenes the provisions of this Act—
- (a) that person, employee or agent shall be disqualified from entering into any project agreement for the project; or
- (b) if the project agreement has already been entered into with that person, the contract shall be voidable at the option of the Directorate.

(5) The Directorate may lodge a complaint with the relevant professional body for the commencement of disciplinary proceedings against a person who is a member of a professional body who contravenes the provisions of this Act.

(6) The penalties imposed by a professional body pursuant to a complaint lodged under subsection (5) shall apply in addition to any penalties that may be imposed under this Act.

85. Participation of State officers or public officers in tenders under this Act

(1) A State officer or public officer shall not, directly or indirectiy, participate in any

tender under this Act.

(2) This section shall apply to a State officer or public officer who uses the officer's spouse, child, or business associate or a company that officer holds shares in, or otherwise controls or directs to participate in a tender under this Act.

(3) A State officer or public officer who contravenes the provision of this section commits an offence and shall be liable, on conviction, to a fine not exceeding two million shillings or to imprisonment for a term not exceeding five years, or to both.

86. Inspection of public private partnership premises, etc.

A private party shall, on the request of a contracting authority or Directorate, grant to an agent or employee of the contracting authority or Directorate, access to the project premises, site and storage facilities as well as records for the purpose of conducting an inspection in accordance with the terms of a project agreement.

87. Application of Part V and Part VI of No. 3 of 2003

The Offences set out under Part V and the compensation and recovery of improper benefits set out under Part VI of the Anti-Corruption and Economic Crimes Act, 2003 (No. 3 of 2003) shall apply to this Act with the necessary modifications.

88. Annual report

(1) The Directorate shall, not more than three months after the 30th of June in each year, prepare and submit to the Committee a report on the state of public private partnerships in Kenya.

(2) Notwithstanding the generality of subsection (1), the annual report shall detail the following—

- (a) the state of public private partnerships in Kenya;
- (b) the number, types and value of public private partnerships being implemented in Kenya;
- (c) the contracting authorities implementing public private partnerships in Kenya;
- (d) the Government support measures that have been given by contracting authorities and to whom;
- (e) the private parties that have been debarred or blacklisted under the Act;
- (f) the number, types and values of public private partnerships tenders that have been cancelled;
- (g) the value of contingent liabilities, if any, approved for any public private partnership;
- (h) the financial reports of projects which have been completed and are being operated by a private party; and
- (i) any other information that may be relevant.

(3) The Cabinet Secretary shall submit a copy of the annual report to Parliament.

89. Regulations

(1) The Cabinet Secretary may make Regulations generally for the better carrying out of the provisions of this Act.

(2) The Regulations made under subsection (1) shall include regulations on—
  (a) the execution of the Committee's or Directorate's functions under this Act; and
  (b) the financing, construction, operation, equipping and maintenance of infrastructure or development projects under this Act.
(3) For the purpose of Article 94(6) of the Constitution—
  (a) the purpose and objective of the delegation under this section is to enable the Cabinet Secretary to make rules to provide for the better carrying into effect the provisions of this Act;
  (b) the authority of the Cabinet Secretary to make regulations under this Act shall be limited to bringing into effect the provisions of this Act and fulfilment of the objectives specified under this section;
  (c) the principles and standards applicable to the rules made under this section are those set out in the Interpretation and General Provisions Act (Cap. 2) and the Statutory Instruments Act, 2013 (No. 23 of 2013).

PART X
SAVINGS AND TRANSITIONAL PROVISIONS

90. Interpretation

In this Part, unless the context otherwise requires—
  (a) **"repealed Act"** means the Public Private Partnerships Act, 2013 (No. 15 of 2013) repealed under section 93.
  (b) **"former Committee"** means the Public Private Partnership Committee existing immediately before the commencement of this Act;
  (c) **"former Petition Committee"** means the Petition Committee existing immediately before the commencement of this Act; and
  (d) **"former Unit"** means the Public Private Partnership Unit existing immediately before the commencement of this Act.

91. Members and staff

(1) A person who, immediately before the commencement of this Act was a member of the former Committee shall, upon the commencement of this Act, be deemed to have been appointed, as a member of the Committee, under this Act for the remainder of that person's term.

(2) A person who, immediately before the commencement of this Act was a member of the former Petition Committee shall, upon the commencement of this Act, be deemed to have been appointed as a member of the Petition Committee under this Act for the remainder of that person's term.

(3) Every person who, immediately before the commencement of this Act, was a public officer of the former Unit shall, on the commencement of this Act, be deemed to be an officer of the Directorate under the same terms of contract that applied immediately

before the commencement of this Act.

92. Savings

(1) Any Regulations, standards, guidelines, procedures or approvals relating to public private partnership projects made or issued by the former Committee or former Directorate before the commencement of this Act shall be deemed to have been made or issued under this Act in so far as the Regulations, standards, guidelines, procedures or approvals are not inconsistent with this Act.

(2) Any petition that had been lodged with the former Petition Committee that had not been heard or determined at the time this Act came into force shall be deemed to have been lodged under this Act and shall be heard and determined as if it had been lodged under this Act.

(3) Any project lists that had been approved by the former Committee or Cabinet before the commencement of this Act shall be deemed to have been approved by the Committee or Cabinet, as the case may be, under this Act.

(4) Any project agreement that had been entered into by a contracting authority and a private party in accordance with the repealed Act shall be deemed to have been entered into under this Act:

Provided that any petition challenging the validity of any project agreement entered into under the repealed Act shall be heard and determined in accordance with the provisions of the repealed Act.

93. Repeal

The Public Private Partnerships Act, 2013 (No. 15 of 2013) is repealed.

FIRST SCHEDULE

PROVISIONS AS TO THE CONDUCT OF BUSINESS AND AFFAIRS OF THE COMMITTEE

[Section 12(1).]

1. Meetings

(1) The Committee shall meet at such place in Kenya as the chairperson may determine and the meetings shall be convened by the chairperson.

(2) The Committee shall have at least four meetings in every financial year and not more than three months shall elapse between one meeting and the next meeting.

(3) Unless three quarters of the members otherwise agree, at least seven days' notice in writing of a meeting shall be given to every member by the Director-General of the Directorate.

(4) The chairperson may, at his or her discretion or at the written request made by at least half of the members of the Committee and within seven days of the request, convene an extraordinary meeting at such time and place that he or she may appoint.

(5) Meetings shall be presided over by the chairperson or in his or her absence by the vice-chairperson.

(6) The members of a Committee shall elect a vice-chairperson from among themselves—

(a) at the first sitting of the Committee; and

(b) whenever it is necessary to fill the vacancy in the office of the vice chairperson.

(7) Where the chairperson or vice-chairperson is absent, the members shall appoint from among themselves, a person to chair the meeting of the Committee.

(8) The Committee may invite any person to attend any of its meetings and to participate in its deliberations, but such person shall not have a vote in any decision of the Committee.

2. Conflict of interest

(1) If any person has a personal or fiduciary interest in a project, proposed contract or any matter before the Committee, and is present at a meeting of the Committee at which any matter is the subject of consideration, that person shall as soon as is practicable after the commencement of the meeting, declare such interest and shall not take part in any consideration or discussion of, or vote on any question touching such matter.

(2) A disclosure of interest made under subparagraph (1) shall be recorded in the minutes of the meeting at which it is made.

(3) The Committee shall adopt a code of conduct and a conflicts of interest policy for the better administration of the affairs of the Committee.

3. Quorum

(1) Subject to subparagraph (2), the quorum of the meeting shall not be less than half of the members of the Committee.

(2) Where the persons present at a meeting of the Committee do not constitute the quorum necessary to hold a meeting under this Act or where by reason of exclusion of a member from a meeting, the number of members present falls below the quorum necessary to hold a meeting, the Committee shall postpone the consideration of the matter in question until there is a quorum.

4. Voting

A question before the Committee shall be decided by simple majority of the members present and voting and the chairperson shall, in the case of an equality of votes, have a casting vote.

5. Rules of Procedure and minutes

The Committee shall—

(a) determine rules of procedure for the conduct of its business; and

(b) keep minutes of its proceedings and decisions.

SECOND SCHEDULE

PUBLIC PRIVATE PARTNERSHIP ARRANGEMENTS

[Section 21.]

1. Management contract where a private party is responsible for the management and

performance of a specified obligation, within well-defined specifications for a specified period of time not exceeding ten years, and the contracting authority retains ownership and control of all facilities and capital assets and properties.

2. Output performance-based contract where the private party is responsible for the operation, maintenance and management of an infrastructure facility for a specified period of time not exceeding ten years and the contracting authority retains ownership of the facility and capital assets.

3. Lease whereby the private party pays the contracting authority rent or royalties and manages, operates and maintains the facility or utilizes the leased property for the purpose of exploration, production and development of minerals and receives fees, charges or benefits from consumers for the provision of the service or sale of products for specified period of time not exceeding thirty years.

4. Brownfield Concession where contracting authority issues a contractual licence to the private party to operate, maintain, rehabilitate or upgrade an infrastructure facility and to charge a user fee while paying a concession fee to the contracting authority for a specified period of time not exceeding thirty years.

5. Build-Own-Operate-Transfer scheme where the private party designs, constructs, finances, operates and maintains an infrastructure facility owned by the private party for a specified time period not exceeding thirty years, or such longer period as may be agreed, after which the private party transfers the facility to the contracting authority.

6. Build-Own Operate scheme where the private party designs, finances, constructs, operates and maintains the infrastructure facility and provides services for a specified period of time.

7. Build-Operate-and-Transfer scheme where the private party finances, constructs, operates and maintains an infrastructure facility and transfers the facility to the contracting authority at the end of a specified term which shall not exceed thirty years.

8. Build-Lease-and-Transfer where the contracting authority authorizes the private party to finance and construct an infrastructure or development facility and upon its completion lease it to the contracting authority for a specified period not exceeding thirty years and upon the expiry of which the ownership of the facility automatically transfers from the private party to the contracting authority.

9. Build-Transfer-and-Operate where the private party constructs an infrastructure facility and assumes the costs and risks associated with the construction of the building and upon completion, transfers the ownership of the facility to the contracting authority and continues to operate the facility on behalf of the contracting authority for a specified period not exceeding thirty years.

10. Build Transfer where the private party designs, builds, and finances a public facility in exchange for payments by the contracting authority over a specified period of time, after which transfer occurs automatically to the contracting authority for a specified period not exceeding twenty years.

11. Develop-Operate-and-Transfer where favourable conditions external to a proposed infrastructure project by a private party are integrated into the arrangement by giving that private party the right to develop adjoining property, and enjoy the benefits the investment creates as the parties agree on condition that the private party transfers the infrastructure facility to the contracting authority within a period not exceeding thirty years from the commencement of the project and the developed property remain the property of the private party in perpetuity.

12. Rehabilitate-Operate-and-Transfer where the private party refurbishes, operates and maintains for a specified period not exceeding 30 years, an existing facility at the expiry of which the private party transfers the facility to the contracting authority.

13. Rehabilitate-Own-and-Operate where an existing facility is transferred by the contracting authority to the private party to refurbish and operate it with no time limitation imposed on ownership and the private party abides by the conditions of the arrangement during the operation of the facility.

14. Annuity-based Design, Build, Finance and Operate under which a private party is authorized by a contracting authority to design, finance, construct, operate or maintain a public infrastructure facility, in exchange for which the private party receives defined annuity payments over a specified period of time not exceeding 30 years, at the end of which the facility transfers back to the contracting authority automatically.

15. Joint Venture partnerships under which a contracting authority and a private party collaborate in the joint development of a public facility, and under which the contracting authority contributes by designating public assets such as land to the project, and various government support measures as the case may be, and under which the private partner is responsible primarily for financing, construction and maintenance of the public infrastructure facility for a defined period of time not exceeding thirty years.

16. Strategic Partnerships under which a public agency sources strategic private partners to jointly develop a public investment programme under such terms as they may agree, but under which key project risks including construction, financing and operations are held by the private party, and which arrangements may have a defined end date or a defined set of parameters that support relationship adjustment over time but not exceeding thirty years.

17. Land Swap where a contracting authority transfers existing public land or an asset to the private party in consideration of an asset or facility that has been developed by that private party.

THIRD SCHEDULE
MINIMUM CONTRACTUAL OBLIGATIONS REQUIRED
TO BE SPECIFIED IN A PROJECT AGREEMENT
[Section 69.]

1. The nature and scope of works and services that the parties shall carry out and the conditions for their implementation.

2. The rights of a contracting authority, the project company and where applicable, the lender, in relation to the project including step in rights of lenders.

3. A description of any property to be contributed by a party to the project agreement.

4. A description of any utilities to be provided in relation to the project and the responsibility thereof.

5. The ownership of the project assets, the obligations of parties related to the handover and receipt of the project site.

6. The responsibility for obtaining authorizations, permits, and approvals.

7. A description of any sharing of revenue between the contracting authority and the private party.

8. Mutual financial obligations and their relation to the funding mechanism including the requirements relating to performance bonds and guarantees.

9. The preparation and submission of financial and other reports and the carrying out of financial audits in relation to the project.

10. The product sale price or the service availability payment on which the project is based and the rules for its determination and amendment, either by an increase or decrease, as well as the indexation mechanisms to reflect inflation or changes in the interest rate, if required.

11. The means of quality assurance and quality control, and supervision as well as administrative, financial and technical monitoring of the project operation, utilization and maintenance.

12. The extent of the right of the contracting authority to vary the conditions of the project and other obligations imposed on private party, and the basis and mechanisms of compensation for any loss resulting from such variation order.

13. The types of insurance to be taken out on the project, and the risks of its operation or utilization, executive warranties issued in favour of the contracting authority, and provisions and procedures for their release.

14. The basis of risk allocation in respect of a change in the law, unforeseeable accidents, *force majeure*, or discovery of antiquities, as the case may be, and the resultant compensation.

15. The duration of the contract.

16. Early termination events under which a party may terminate the contract prior to the expiry of the project agreement and the rights of the parties in relation to the termination.

17. The process of handing over the project on expiry or on termination of the project agreement by a party to the agreement.

18. Mechanism for dispute resolution including resolution of disputes by way of arbitration or any other amicable dispute resolution mechanism.

19. The events giving rise to compensation and the mechanisms for payment of such compensation or penalties.

20. Performance securities required when undertaking a project, the value and renewal

mechanisms.
21. Appointment of independent experts.
22. Local content requirements.
23. Direct agreements and lenders rights where applicable.
24. Termination and expiry of the project agreement.
25. Obligations of, undertakings and warranties by contracting parties.
26. Cases of emergency step in by either contracting authority or lenders in case of private party default.

GROUP TWO
LABOR LAWS AND REGULATIONS

TITLE FIVE
THE EMPLOYMENT ACT
(NO. 11 OF 2007)

Revised Edition 2023 [2007]

Published by the National Council for Law Reporting

with the Authority of the Attorney-General

www.kenyalaw.org

NO. 11 OF 2007
EMPLOYMENT ACT

[*Date of assent: 22nd October, 2007.*]
[*Date of commencement: 2nd June, 2008.*]

AN ACT of Parliament to repeal the Employment Act, declare and define the fundamental rights of employees, to provide basic conditions of employment of employees, to regulate employment of children, and to provide for matters connected with the foregoing

[Act No. 11 of 2007, Legal Notice 61 of 2008, Act No. 18 of 2014, Act No. 19 of 2015, Legal Notice 105 of 2017, Act No. 10 of 2018, Act No. 23 of 2019, Act No. 24 of 2019, Act No. 20 of 2020, Act No. 2 of 2021, Act No. 15 of 2022.]

PART 1
PRELIMINARY

1. Short title

This Act may be cited as the Employment Act, 2007.

2. Interpretation

In this Act, unless the context otherwise requires—

"authorised officer" means a labour officer, employment officer or medical officer;

"basic salary" means an employee's gross salary excluding allowances and other benefits;

"Board" means the National Labour Board;

"Cabinet Secretary" means the Cabinet Secretary for the time being responsible for matters relating to labour matters;

"casual employee" means a person the terms of whose engagement provide for his payment at the end of each day and who is not engaged for a longer period than twenty-four hours at a time;

"child" means a person who has not attained the age of eighteen years;

"collective agreement" means a registered agreement concerning any terms and conditions of employment made in writing between a trade union and an employer, group of employers or employers' organization;

"contract of service" means an agreement, whether oral or in writing, and whether expressed or implied, to employ or to serve as an employee for a period of time, and includes a contract of apprenticeship and indentured learnership but does not include a foreign contract of service to which Part XI of this Act applies;

"dependent" means a member of an employee's family or a relative who substantially depends on that employee for his livelihood;

"**Director**" means a person appointed as the Director of Employment;

"**disability**" means a physical, sensory, mental or other impairment, including any visual, hearing, learning or physical incapability, which impacts adversely on a person's social and economic participation;

"**employee**" means a person employed for wages or a salary and includes an apprentice and indentured learner;

"**employee contribution**" *deleted by Act No. 20 of 2020, Sch.*;

"**employee earnings**" *deleted by Act No. 23 of 2019, s. 52*;

"**employer**" means any person, public body, firm, corporation or company who or which has entered into a contract of service to employ any individual and includes the agent, foreman, manager or factor of such person, public body, firm, corporation or company;

"**employer contribution**" means the employer's contribution payable into the National Housing Development Fund;

"**exit certificate**" means a written authority given by a registered adoption society to a prospective adoptive parent to take the child from the custody of the adoptive society;

"**forced or compulsory labour**" means any work or service which is extracted from any person under the threat of any penalty, including the threat of a loss of rights or privileges, which is not offered voluntarily by the person doing the work or performing the service;

"**HIV**" means the Human Immune-Deficiency Virus;

"**industrial undertaking**" includes—
  (a) a mine, quarry and other works for the extraction of any substance from the surface or under the surface of the earth;
  (b) a factory or a place where raw materials are manufactured, processed or packaged;
  (c) the construction, reconstruction, maintenance, repair, alteration or demolition of any building, railway, tramway, harbour, dock, pier, canal, inland waterway, road, tunnel, bridge, viaduct, sewer, drain, well, telegraphic or telephone installation, electrical undertaking, gas work, water work or other work of construction, as well as the preparation for or laying of the foundations of any such work or structure; or
  (d) transport of passengers or goods by road, rail, or inland waterway, including the handling of goods at docks, quays, wharves and warehouses, but excluding transport by hand:

Provided that—
  (i) the Cabinet Secretary, if he sees fit so to do, having regard to the nature of the work involved in any employment carried on in any industrial undertaking, may by order declare that the employment shall be excluded from the provisions of this Part relating to industrial undertakings, and

thereupon the employment shall be deemed not to be employment in an industrial undertaking for the purposes of this Part;

(ii) an undertaking of which a part only is an industrial undertaking shall not for that reason alone be deemed to be an industrial undertaking;

"**labour inspector**" means a person appointed as a labour inspector;

"**labour officer**" means a person appointed as the Commissioner of Labour, a Senior Deputy Commissioner of Labour, a Deputy Commissioner of Labour, an Assistant Commissioner of Labour, a Chief Industrial Relations Officer, a Deputy Chief Industrial Relations Officer, a Senior Labour Officer, an Industrial Relations Officer or a Labour Officer;

"**lockout**" means the closing of a place of employment or the suspension of work or refusal by an employer to employ any employees—

(a) for the purpose of compelling the employees of the employer to accept any demand in request of a trade dispute; and

(b) not for the purpose of finally terminating employment;

"**migrant worker**" means a person who migrates to Kenya with a view to being employed by an employer and includes any person regularly admitted as a migrant worker;

"**mine**" includes an undertaking, whether public or private, for the extraction of a substance from the surface, or from under the surface of the earth;

"**Minister**" *deleted by Act No. 19 of 2015, s. 143(c);*

"**National Housing Development Fund**" *deleted by Act No. 20 of 2020, Sch.;*

"**organisation**" includes employees' trade unions and employers organisations;

"**parties**" means the parties to a contract of service;

"**piece work**" means any work the pay for which is ascertained by the amount of work performed irrespective of the time occupied in its performance;

"**probationary contract**" means a contract of employment, which is of not more than twelve months duration or part thereof, is in writing and expressly states that it is for a probationary period;

"**redundancy**" means the loss of employment, occupation, job or career by involuntary means through no fault of an employee, involving termination of employment at the initiative of the employer, where the services of an employee are superfluous and the practices commonly known as abolition of office, job or occupation and loss of employment;

"**Registrar**" means the Registrar of Trade Unions;

"**remuneration**" means the total value of all payments in money or in kind, made or owing to an employee arising from the employment of that employee;

"**strike**" means the cessation of work by employees acting in combination, or a concerted refusal or a refusal under a common understanding of employees to continue to work, for the purpose of compelling their employer or an employers' organization of which their employer is a member, to accede to any demand in respect of a trade dispute;

"**task**" means such amount of work as can, in the opinion of an authorised officer, be performed by an employee in an ordinary working day;

"**trade union**" means an association of employees whose principal purpose is to regulate relations between employees and employers and includes an employer's organisation;

"**woman**" means a female of the age of eighteen years or above;

"**worst form of child labour**" with respect to juveniles, means their employment, engagement or usage in any activity comprising of—

> (a) all forms of slavery or practices similar to slavery, such as the sale and trafficking of children, debt bondage and serfdom and forced or compulsory recruitment of children for use in armed conflict;
>
> (b) the use, procuring or offering of a child for prostitution, for the production of pornography or for pornographic performances;
>
> (c) the use, procuring or offering of a child for illicit activities, in particular for the production and trafficking of drugs as defined in the relevant international treaties;
>
> (d) work which, by its nature or the circumstances in which it is carried out, is likely to harm the health, safety or morals of the child;

"**young person**" means a child who has attained the age of sixteen years but has not attained the age of eighteen years.

[Act No. 19 of 2015, s. 143, Act No. 10 of 2018, s. 85, Act No. 23 of 2019, s. 52, Act No. 20 of 2020, Sch., Act No. 2 of 2021, s. 2.]

3. Application

(1) This Act shall apply to all employees employed by any employer under a contract of service.

(2) This Act shall not apply to—

> (a) the Kenya Defence Forces or the reserve as respectively defined in the Kenya Defence Forces Act, 2012;
>
> (b) the Kenya Police, the Kenya Prisons Service or the Administration Police Force;
>
> (ba) the Kenya Coast Guard Service;
>
> (c) the National Youth Service; and
>
> (d) an employer and the employer's dependants where the dependants are the only employees in a family undertaking.

(3) This Act shall bind the Government.

(4) The Cabinet Secretary may, after consultation with the Board and after taking account of all relevant conventions and other international instruments ratified by Kenya, by order exclude from the application of all or part of this Act limited categories of employees in respect of whom special problems of a substantial nature arise.

(5) The Cabinet Secretary may, after consultation with the Board, by order exclude from the application of all or part of this Act categories of employed persons whose terms

and conditions of employment are governed by special arrangements:

Provided those arrangements afford protection that is equivalent to or better than that part of the Act from which those categories are being excluded.

(6) Subject to the provisions of this Act, the terms and conditions of employment set out in this Act shall constitute minimum terms and conditions of employment of an employee and any agreement to relinquish, vary or amend the terms herein set shall be null and void.

[Act No. 19 of 2015, s. 144, Act No. 20 of 2020 Sch.]

PART II
GENERAL PRINCIPLES

4. Prohibition against forced labour

(1) No person shall use or assist any other person in recruiting, trafficking or using forced labour.

(2) The term **"forced or compulsory labour"** shall not include—

(a) any work or service exacted by virtue of compulsory military service laws for work of a purely military character:

Provided that forced or compulsory recruitment of children for use in armed conflict shall be deemed to be forced or compulsory labour;

(b) any work or service which forms part of the normal civic obligations of the citizens of Kenya;

(c) any work or service exacted from any person as a consequence of a conviction in a court of law, provided that the work or service is carried out under the supervision and control of a public authority and that the person is not hired out to or placed at the disposal of private persons, companies or associations;

(d) any work or service exacted in cases of an emergency, such as in the event of war or disaster or threat of calamity in any circumstance that would endanger the existence or the well-being of the whole or part of the population; and

(e) minor communal services performed by the members of the community in the direct interest of the said community provided the members of the community or their representatives are consulted.

(3) A person who contravenes the provisions of this section commits an offence and shall, on conviction be liable to a fine not exceeding five hundred thousand shillings or to imprisonment for a term not exceeding two years or to both.

5. Discrimination in employment

(1) It shall be the duty of the Minister, labour officers and the Industrial Court—

(a) to promote equality of opportunity in employment in order to eliminate discrimination in employment; and

(b) to promote and guarantee equality of opportunity for a person who, is a migrant worker or a member of the family of the migrant worker, lawfully within Kenya.

(2) An employer shall promote equal opportunity in employment and strive to eliminate discrimination in any employment policy or practice.

(3) No employer shall discriminate directly or indirectly, against an employee or prospective employee or harass an employee or prospective employee—
- (a) on grounds of race, colour, sex, language, religion, political or other opinion, nationality, ethnic or social origin, disability, pregnancy, marital status or HIV status;
- (b) in respect of recruitment, training, promotion, terms and conditions of employment, termination of employment or other matters arising out of the employment.

(4) It is not discrimination to—
- (a) take affirmative action measurers consistent with the promotion of equality or the elimination of discrimination in the workplace;
- (b) distinguish, exclude or prefer any person on the basis of an inherent requirement of a job;
- (c) employ a citizen in accordance with the National employment policy; or
- (d) restrict access to limited categories of employment where it is necessary in the interest of state security.

(5) An employer shall pay his employees equal remuneration for work of equal value.

(6) An employer who contravenes the provision of the section commits an offence.

(7) In any proceedings where a contravention of this section is alleged, the employer shall bear the burden of proving that the discrimination did not take place as alleged, and that the discriminatory act omission is not based on any of the grounds specified in this section.

(8) For the purposes of this section—
- (a) **"employee"** includes an applicant for employment;
- (b) **"employer"** includes an employment agency;
- (c) an **"employment policy or practice"** includes any policy or practice relating to recruitment procedures, advertising and selection criteria, appointments and the appointment process, job classification and grading, remuneration, employment benefits and terms and conditions of employment, job assignments, the working environment and facilities, training and development, performance evaluation systems, promotion, transfer, demotion, termination of employment on disciplinary measures.

[Corr. No. 1 of 2008, Act No. 18 of 2014, Sch.]

6. Sexual harassment

(1) An employee is sexually harassed if the employer of that employee or a representative of that employer or a co-worker—
- (a) directly or indirectly requests that employee for sexual intercourse, sexual

contact or any other form of sexual activity that contains an implied or express—
  (i) promise of preferential treatment in employment;
  (ii) threat of detrimental treatment in employment; or
  (iii) threat about the present or future employment status of the employee;
(b) uses language whether written or spoken of a sexual nature;
(c) uses visual material of a sexual nature; or
(d) shows physical behaviour of a sexual nature which directly or indirectly subjects the employee to behaviour that is unwelcome or offensive to that employee and that by its nature has a detrimental effect on that employee's employment, job performance, or job satisfaction.

(2) An employer who employs twenty or more employees shall, after consulting with the employees or their representatives if any, issue a policy statement on sexual harassment.

(3) The policy statement required under subsection (2) may contain any term the employer considers appropriate for the purposes of this section and shall contain—
  (a) the definition of sexual harassment as specified in subsection (1);
  (b) a statement—
    (i) that every employee is entitled to employment that is free of sexual harassment;
    (ii) that the employer shall take steps to ensure that no employee is subjected to sexual harassment;
    (iii) that the employer shall take such disciplinary measures as the employer deems appropriate against any person under the employer's direction, who subjects any employee to sexual harassment;
    (iv) explaining how complaints of sexual harassment may be brought to the attention of the employer; and
    (v) that the employer will not disclose the name of a complainant or the circumstances related to the complaint to any person except where disclosure is necessary for the purpose of investigating the complaint or taking disciplinary measures in relation thereto.

(4) An employer shall bring to the attention of each person under the employer's direction the policy statement required under subsection (2).

PART III
EMPLOYMENT RELATIONSHIP

7. Contract of service

No person shall be employed under a contract of service except in accordance with the provisions of this Act.

8. Oral and written contracts

The provisions of this Act shall apply to oral and written contracts.

9. General provision of contract of service

(1) A contract of service—

 (a) for a period or a number of working days which amount in the aggregate to the equivalent, of three months or more; or

 (b) which provides for the performance of any specified work which could not reasonably be expected to be completed within a period or a number of working days amounting in the aggregate to the equivalent of three months,

shall be in writing.

(2) An employer who is a party to a written contract of service shall be responsible for causing the contract to be drawn up stating particulars of employment and that the contract is consented to by the employee in accordance with subsection (3).

(3) For the purpose of signifying his consent to a written contract of service an employee may—

 (a) sign his name thereof; or

 (b) imprint thereon an impression of his thumb or one of his fingers in the presence of a person other than his employer.

(4) Where an employee is illiterate or cannot understand the language in which the contract is written, or the provisions of the contract of service, the employer shall have the contract explained to the employee in a language that employee understands.

(5) In respect of recruitment, an employer shall not require an employee to submit any clearance or compliance certificate unless such employer intends to enter into a contract of service with the employee:

Provided that an applicant for a state office shall provide compliance or clearance certificates at such times in the recruitment or approval process as they may be required.

(6) An employer who intends to enter into a written contract of service may, in compliance with chapter six of the Constitution, request an employee to submit mandatory clearance certificates from the relevant entities.

(7) Notwithstanding subsection (6), an employer may, where an employee does not satisfy the requirements under subsection (6), withdraw an offer of contract of service.

(8) A relevant public entity shall—

 (a) not charge a fee for the issuance of a clearance or compliance certificate under this section or any other written law;

 (b) issue an applicant with the clearance or compliance certificate or reject the application within seven days of receipt of the application.

(9) For the purposes of this section—

 (a) "**employee**" includes an applicant for employment;

 (b) "**employer**" includes an employment agency;

 (c) "**relevant entity**" includes any public or private entity that issues clearance certificates for purposes of satisfying the requirements under chapter six of the Constitution.

[Act No. 15 of 2022, s. 2.]

10. Employment particulars

(1) A written contract of service specified in section 9 shall state particulars of employment which may, subject to subsection (3) be given in instalments and shall be given not later than two months after the beginning of the employment.

(2) A written contract of service shall state—

    (a) the name, age, permanent address and sex of the employee;

    (b) the name of the employer;

    (c) the job description of the employment;

    (d) the date of commencement of the employment;

    (e) the form and duration of the contract;

    (f) the place of work;

    (g) the hours of work;

    (h) the remuneration, scale or rate of remuneration, the method of calculating that remuneration and details of any other benefits;

    (i) the intervals at which remuneration is paid;

    (j) the date on which the employee's period of continuous employment began, taking into account any employment with a previous employer which counts towards that period; and

    (k) any other prescribed matter.

(3) The statement required under this section shall also contain particulars, as at a specified date not more than seven days before the statement, or the instalment containing them, is given of—

    (a) any terms and conditions relating to any of the following—

        (i) entitlement to annual leave, including public holidays, and holiday pay, (the particulars given being sufficient to enable the employee's entitlement, including any entitlement to accrued holiday pay on the termination of employment, to be precisely calculated);

        (ii) incapacity to work due to sickness or injury, including any provision for sick pay; and

        (iii) pensions and pension schemes;

    (b) the length of notice which the employee is obliged to give and entitled to receive to terminate his contract of employment;

    (c) where the employment is not intended to be for an indefinite period, the period for which it is expected to continue or, if it is for a fixed term, the date when it is to end;

    (d) either the place of work or, where the employee is required or permitted to work at various places, an indication of that place of work and of the address of the employer;

(e) any collective agreements which directly affect the terms and conditions of the employment including, where the employer is not a party, the person by whom they were made; and

(f) where the employee is required to work outside Kenya for a period of more than one month—

  (i) the period for which that employee is to work outside Kenya;

  (ii) the currency in which remuneration is to be paid while that employee is working outside Kenya;

  (iii) any additional remuneration payable to the employee, and any benefits due to the employee by reason of the employee working outside Kenya; and

  (iv) any terms and conditions relating to the employee's return to Kenya.

(4) Subsection (3)(a)(iii) does not apply to an employee of a body or authority if—

(a) the employee's pension rights depend on the terms of a pension scheme established under any provision contained in or having effect under any Act; and

(b) any such provision requires the body or authority to give to a new employee information concerning the employee's pension rights or the determination of questions affecting those rights.

(5) Where any matter stipulated in subsection (1) changes, the employer shall, in consultation with the employee, revise the contract to reflect the change and notify the employee of the change in writing.

(6) The employer shall keep the written particulars prescribed in subsection (1) for a period of five years after the termination of employment.

(7) If in any legal proceedings an employer fails to produce a written contract or the written particulars, prescribed in subsection (1) the burden of proving or disproving an alleged term of employment stipulated in the contract shall be on the employer.

[Corr. No. 1 of 2008.]

11. Statement of initial particulars

(1) If in the case of a statement under section 10 there are no particulars to be entered under subsection (2)(d) or (j) or under any of the other provisions of section 10(2) or (3), that fact shall be stated in the statement.

(2) A statement under section 10 may refer the employee for particulars of any of the matters specified in section 10(3)(a)(ii) and (iii) to the provisions of any other document which is reasonably accessible to the employee.

(3) A statement under section 10 may refer the employee for particulars of either of the matters specified in section 10(3)(e) to the law or to the provisions of any collective agreement directly affecting the terms and conditions of the employment which is reasonably accessible to the employee.

(4) The particulars required by section 10(2) and (3) shall be included in a single document.

(5) Where before the end of the period of two months after the beginning of an employee's employment the employee is to begin to work outside Kenya for a period of more than one month, the statement under section 10 shall be given to him not later than the time when he leaves Kenya in order to begin work.

(6) A statement shall be given to a person under section 10 even if his employment ends before the end of the period within which the statement is required to be given.

[Corr. No. 1 of 2008.]

12. Statement on disciplinary rules

(1) A statement under section 10 shall—
 (a) specify the disciplinary rules applicable to the employee or refer the employee to the provisions of a document which is reasonably accessible to the employee which specifies the rules;
 (b) specify the person to whom the employee may apply—
  (i) if dissatisfied with any disciplinary decision relating to the employee; and
  (ii) for the purpose of seeking redress of any grievance relating to his employment,
and the manner in which an application shall be made; and
 (c) where there are further steps to be taken consequent to any such application, the steps or refer the employee to the provisions of a document which is accessible to the employee which explains the steps.

(2) Subsection (1) shall not apply to rules, disciplinary decisions, grievances, or procedures relating to health or safety at work.

(3) This section shall not apply where as at the date the employee starts work the employer has employed less than fifty employees.

13. Statement of changes

(1) If, after the material date there is a change in any of the particulars required under sections 10 and 12, the employer shall give to the employee a written statement containing particulars of the change.

(2) For the purposes of subsection (1)—
 (a) in relation to particulars which are included or referred to in a statement given under section 10 otherwise than in instalments, the material date is the date to which the statement relates;
 (b) in relation to a matter particulars of which—
  (i) are included or referred to in an instalment of a statement given under section 10, or
  (ii) are required by section 11(4) to be included in a single document but are not included in an instalment of a statement given under section 10 which does include other particulars to which that provision applies, the material date is the date to which the instalment relates; and
 (c) in relation to any other matter the material date is the date by which a

statement under section 10 is required to be given.

(3) A statement under subsection (1) shall be given at the earliest opportunity and, in any event, not later than—
   (a) one month after the change in question, or
   (b) where that change results from the employee being required to work outside Kenya for a period of more than one month, the time when the employee leaves to start work if that is earlier.

(4) A statement under subsection (1) may refer the employee to the provision of a document which is accessible to the employee for a change in any of the matters specified in section 10(3)(ii) and (iii) and section 12(1)(a) and (c).

(5) A statement under subsection (1) may refer the employee for a change in either of the matters specified in section 10(3)(e) to the law or to the provisions of any collective agreement directly affecting the terms and conditions of the employment which is reasonably accessible to the employee.

(6) Where, after an employer has given to an employee a statement under section 10 either—
   (a) the name of the employer is changed without any change in the identity of the employer, or
   (b) the identity of the employer is changed in circumstances in which the continuity of the employee's period of employment is not broken, and subsection (7) applies in relation to the change,

the person who is the employer immediately after the change is not required to give to the employee a statement under section 12 but the change shall be treated as a change within subsection (1).

(7) Subsection (6) applies in relation to a change if it does not involve any change in any of the matters, other than the names of the parties, particulars of which are required by section 10 and 11 to be included or referred to in the statement under subsection (1).

(8) A statement under subsection (1) which informs an employee of a change referred to in subsection (6)(b) shall specify the date on which the employee's period of continuous employment began.

[Corr. No. 1 of 2008.]

14. Reasonably accessible document or collective agreement

In sections 11, 12 and 13, references to a document or collective agreement which is reasonably accessible to an employee are references to a document or collective agreement which—
   (a) the employee has reasonable opportunities of reading in the course of his employment; or
   (b) is made reasonably accessible to the employee in some other way.

15. Informing employees of their rights

An employer shall display a statement in the prescribed form of the employee's rights under this Act in a conspicuous place, which is accessible to all the employees.

16. Enforcement

(1) Where an employer does not give an employee a statement as required by section 10, 12 or 13 or an itemised pay statement as required by section 20, the employee may file a complaint with the labour officer and the complaint shall be deemed to be complaint filed under section 87.

(2) Where as a result of a complaint arising out of section 10, 12, 13 or 20 the Industrial Court determines particulars which ought to have been included or referred to in a statement given under these sections, the employer shall be deemed to have given to the employee a statement in which those particulars were included or referred to as specified in the decision of the Industrial Court.

(3) Where under subsection (1) the Industrial Court has to determine whether the statement given complies with a statement under section 10, 13 or 20 the Industrial Court may—

 (a) confirm the particulars as included or referred to in the statement given by the employer;

 (b) amend those particulars; or

 (c) substitute other particulars for them as the Industrial Court may determine to be appropriate, and the statement shall be deemed to have been given by the employer to the employee in accordance with the courts decision.

(4) A person who fails to give to an employee a statement as required by section 10, 12, 13 or 20 commits an offence and shall, on conviction be liable to a fine not exceeding one hundred thousand shillings or to imprisonment for a term not exceeding two years or to both.

(5) Where a person contravenes the sections specified in subsection (1), a court, on application of the employee or the labour officer on behalf of the employee may, in addition to the penalty specified in subsection (4) order any remedy specified in subsection (3).

[Corr. No. 1 of 2008.]

PART IV
PROTECTION OF WAGES

17. Payment, disposal and recovery of wages, allowances, etc.

(1) Subject to this Act, an employer shall pay the entire amount of the wages earned by or payable to an employee in respect of work done by the employee in pursuance of a contract of service directly, in the currency of Kenya—

 (a) in cash;

 (b) into an account at a bank, or building society, designated by the employee;

 (c) by cheque, postal order or money order in favour of the employee; or

 (d) in the absence of an employee, to a person other than the employee, if the person is duly authorised by the employee in writing to receive the wages on the employee's behalf.

(2) An employer shall pay wages to an employee on a working day, and during working hours, at or near to the place of employment or at such other place as may be agreed between the employer and the employee.

(3) An employer shall not pay wages to an employee in any place where intoxicating liquor is sold or readily available for supply, except in the case of employees employed to work in that place.

(4) No person shall give or promise to any person any advance of money or any valuable consideration upon a condition expressed or implied that the person or any dependant of that person shall enter upon any employment.

(5) If, in a contract of service or collective agreement, provision is made for the payment of any allowance in kind to an employee with the employees consent the payment may with such consent be made only if, the allowance—

(a) is for the personal use and benefit of the employee; and

(b) does not consist of or include any intoxicating spirit or noxious drug.

(6) Notwithstanding the provisions of any law for the time being in force, whenever an attachment has been issued against the property of an employer in execution of a decree against him, the proceeds realised in pursuance of that execution shall not be paid by the court to a decree-holder until a decree obtained against the employer in respect of the wages of employees has been satisfied to the extent of a sum not exceeding six months' wages of those employees.

(7) Nothing in subsection (6) shall prevent an employee from recovering any balance due after such satisfaction, by ordinary process of law.

(8) Subsection (6) shall not apply if the attachment is issued against an employer undergoing insolvency as defined under Part VIII in which case the provisions under that Part shall apply.

(9) If an employer advances to an employee a sum in excess of the amount of one month's wages of the employee or, in the case of an employee employed under a written contract of service, a sum in excess of the amount of two months' wages of that employee, the excess shall not be recoverable in a court of law.

(10) A person who—

(a) subject to section 19, wilfully fails to make payment of or to tender the wages earned by or payable to an employee in accordance with subsection (1); or

(b) contravenes any of the provisions of subsections (2), (3), (4) and (5),

commits an offence and shall on conviction be liable to fine not exceeding one hundred thousand shillings or to imprisonment for a term not exceeding two years or to both.

(11) No employer shall limit or attempt to limit the right of an employee to dispose of his wages in a manner which the employee deems fit, nor by a contract of service or otherwise seek to compel an employee to dispose of his wages or a portion thereof in a

particular place or for a particular purpose in which the employer has a direct or indirect beneficial interest.

[Corr. No. 1 of 2008.]

18. When wages or salaries due

(1) Where a contract of service entered into under which a task or piece work is to be performed by an employee, the employee shall be entitled—

(a) when the task has not been completed, at the option of his employer, to be paid by his employer at the end of the day in proportion to the amount of the task which has been performed, or to complete the task on the following day, in which case he shall be entitled to be paid on completion of the task; or

(b) in the case of piece work, to be paid by his employer at the end of each month in proportion to the amount of work which he has performed during the month, or on completion of the work, whichever date is the earlier.

(2) Subject to subsection (1), wages or salaries shall be deemed to be due—

(a) in the case of a casual employee, at the end of the day;

(b) in the case of an employee employed for a period of more than a day but not exceeding one month, at the end of that period;

(c) in the case of an employee employed for a period exceeding one month, at the end of each month or part thereof;

(d) in the case of an employee employed for an indefinite period or on a journey, at the expiration of each month or of such period, whichever date is the earlier, and on the completion of the journey, respectively.

(3) The provisions of this section shall not affect an order, judgment or award of the Industrial Court or an agreement between an employee and his employer the relevant terms of which are more favorable to the employee than the provisions of this section.

(4) Where an employee is summarily dismissed for lawful cause, the employee shall, on dismissal be paid all moneys, allowances and benefits due to him up to the date of his dismissal.

(5) Upon the termination of a contract of service—

(a) by effluxion of time, it shall be the duty of the employer to ensure that the employee is paid the entire amount of the wages earned by or payable to the employee and of the allowances due to him as have not been paid;

(b) by dismissal, the employer shall, within seven days, deliver to a labour officer in the district in which the employee was working a written report specifying the circumstances leading to, and the reasons for, the dismissal and stating the period of notice and the amount of wages in lieu thereof to which the employee would, but for the dismissal, have been entitled; and the report shall specify the amount of any wages and other allowance earned by him since the date of the employees dismissal.

(6) No wages shall be payable to an employee in respect of a period during which the

employee is detained in custody or is serving a sentence of imprisonment imposed under any law.

19. Deduction of wages

(1) Notwithstanding section 17(1), an employer may deduct from the wages of his employee—

(a) any amount due from the employee as a contribution to any provident fund or superannuation scheme or any other scheme approved by the Commissioner for Labour to which the employee has agreed to contribute;

(b) a reasonable amount for any damage done to, or loss of, any property lawfully in the possession or custody of the employer occasioned by the wilful default of the employee;

(c) an amount not exceeding one day's wages in respect of each working day for the whole of which the employee, without leave or other lawful cause, absents himself from the premises of the employer or other place proper and appointed for the performance of his work;

(d) an amount equal to the amount of any shortage of money arising through the negligence or dishonesty of the employee whose contract of service provides specifically or his being entrusted with the receipt, custody and payment of money;

(e) any amount paid to the employee in error as wages in excess of the amount of wages due to him;

(f) any amount the deduction of which is authorised by any written law for the time being in force, collective agreement, wage determination, court order or arbitration award;

(g) any amount in which the employer has no direct or indirect beneficial interest, and which the employee has requested the employer in writing to deduct from his wages;

(h) an amount due and payable by the employee under and in accordance with the terms of an agreement in writing, by way of repayment or part repayment of a loan of money made to him by the employer, not exceeding fifty per cent of the wages payable to that employee after the deduction of all such other amounts as may be due from him under this section; and

(i) such other amounts as the Cabinet Secretary may prescribe.

(2) No employer shall make a deduction from the wages payable to an employee as an advance of wages in consideration of, or as a reward for, the provision of employment for that employee, or for retaining the employee in employment.

(3) Without prejudice to any right of recovery of any debt due, and notwithstanding the provisions of any other written law, the total amount of all deductions which under the provisions of subsection (1), may be made by an employer from the wages of his employee at any one time shall not exceed two thirds of such wages or such additional or other

amount as may be prescribed by the Cabinet Secretary either generally or in relation to a specified employer or employee or class of employers or employees or any trade or industry.

(4) An employer who deducts an amount from an employee's remuneration in accordance with subsection (1)(a), (f), (g) and (h) shall pay the amount so deducted in accordance with the time period and other requirements specified in the law, agreement court order or arbitration as the case may be.

(5) An employer who fails to comply with the provisions of subsection (4) commits an offence and shall on conviction be liable to a fine not exceeding one hundred thousand shillings or to imprisonment for a term not exceeding two years or to both.

(6) Where proceedings are brought under subsection (5) in respect of failure by the employer to remit deductions from an employees remuneration, the court may, in addition to fining the employer order the employer to refund to the employee the amount deducted from the employees wages, and pay the intended beneficiary on behalf of the employee with the employer's own funds.

[Act No. 19 of 2015, s. 145.]

20. Itemised pay statement

(1) An employer shall give, a written statement to an employee at or before the time at which any payment of wages or salary is made to the employee.

(2) The statement specified in subsection (1) shall contain particulars of—

(a) the gross amount of the wages or salary of the employee;

(b) the amounts of any variable and subject to section 22, any statutory deductions from that gross amount and the purposes for which they are made; and

(c) where different parts of the net amount are paid in different ways, the amount and method of payment of each part-payment.

(3) This section shall not apply to a casual employee or an employee engaged on piece rate or task rate terms or for any period not exceeding six months.

(4) The Minister may exclude any category of employees or employees employed in any sector from the application of this section.

21. Statement of statutory deductions

(1) A pay statement issued in accordance with section 20 need not contain separate particulars of statutory deductions if—

(a) it contains an aggregate amount of statutory deduction, including that deduction; and

(b) the employer has given to the employee, at or before the time at which the pay statement is given, a statement of statutory deductions specified in subsection (2).

(2) A statement of statutory deductions shall be—

(a) in writing;

(b) contain, in relation to each deduction comprised in the aggregate amount of deductions, particulars of—

(i) the amount of the deduction;

(ii) the intervals at which the deduction is to be made; and

(iii) the purpose for which it is made; and

(c) in accordance with subsection (5), effective at the date on which the pay statement is given.

(3) A statement of statutory deductions may be amended by—

(a) the addition of a new deduction;

(b) a change in the particulars; or

(c) the cancellation of an existing deduction, by notice in writing, containing particulars of the amendment given by the employer to the employee.

(4) An employer who has given to an employee a statement of statutory deductions shall—

(a) within the period of twelve months beginning on the date the first statement of statutory deductions was given; and

(b) at intervals of not more than twelve months afterwards, re-issue it in a consolidated form incorporating any amendments notified in accordance with subsection (3).

(5) For the purposes of subsection (2)(c), a statement of deductions—

(a) becomes effective on the date on which it is given to the employee; and

(b) ceases to be effective at the end of the period of twelve months beginning on that date or, where it is re-issued in accordance with subsection (4), at the end of the period of twelve months beginning with the date of the last re-issue.

22. Power to amend provisions on pay and statements of deductions

The Cabinet Secretary may on the advise of the Board—

(a) vary the provisions of sections 20 and 21 as to the particulars which must be included in a pay statement or a statement of statutory deductions by adding items to, or removing items from, the particulars listed in those sections or by amending any such particulars; and

(b) vary the provisions of section 21(4) and (5) so as to shorten or extend the periods specified in those subsections, or those periods as varied from time to time under this section.

[Act No. 19 of 2015, s. 146.]

23. Security bond for wages

(1) An employer who is not incorporated or resident in Kenya may be required by the Minister to pay a bond assessed at the equivalent of one month's wages for all employees employed or to be employed by the employer.

(2) A bond paid by any employer shall be held by the Minister on behalf of that employer in a separate interest bearing account and shall not be used for any purpose other than paying wages and other entitlements to that employer's employees in the event of default by that employer.

24. Death of an employee

(1) When the death of an employee from any cause whatsoever is brought to the notice

or comes to the knowledge of the employee's employer, the employer shall as soon as practicable thereafter, give notice of the death in the prescribed form to the labour officer or, if there is no labour officer, to the district commissioner of the district in which the employee was employed.

(2) Upon the death of an employee during the term of a contract of service, the legal representatives of the employee shall, upon proof of capacity as required by law, be entitled to be paid wages and any other remuneration and property due to the employee as at the date of death within thirty days of submitting the proof.

(3) The employer of the deceased employee shall, within seven days of such payment provide the labour officer or in his absence the district commissioner with evidence of the payment.

(4) Where on expiry of three months after the employee's death—
  (a) no legal representative has laid claim to the wages or property of the employee; or
  (b) where the employer is in doubt of or has rejected any claim made to the wages or the property of the employee, the employer, shall deliver to the labour officer or district commissioner as the case may be all wages due to the employee at the date of his death and shall deliver to him all property of the deceased employee to be held by the labour officer or the district commissioner in trust subject to the Law of Succession Act (Cap. 160) or any other written law applicable to the disposal of a deceased persons property.

(5) Where an employee is, during the course of his employment killed or incapacitated by injury for a period exceeding three days, his employer shall as soon as practicable, send to the labour officer or, if there is no labour officer to a district commissioner a report in the prescribed form.

25. Repayment of remuneration wrongfully withheld or deducted

(1) Without prejudice to any other liability for a breach of the provisions of this Part, an employer who contravenes the provisions of this Part commits an offence and shall on conviction be liable to a fine not exceeding one hundred thousand shillings or to imprisonment for a term not exceeding two years or to both and shall be required to repay any remuneration wrongfully withheld or wrongfully deducted from the employee.

(2) An employee may file a complaint under this part—
  (a) to a labour officer;
  (b) not later than three years after the allegedly unlawful deduction has been made.

PART V
RIGHTS AND DUTIES IN EMPLOYMENT

26. Basic minimum conditions of employment

(1) The provisions of this Part and Part VI shall constitute basic minimum terms and

conditions of contract of service.

(2) Where the terms and conditions of a contract of service are regulated by any regulations, as agreed in any collective agreement or contract between the parties or enacted by any other written law, decreed by any judgment award or order of the Industrial Court are more favourable to an employee than the terms provided in this Part and Part VI, then such favourable terms and conditions of service shall apply.

27. Hours of work

(1) An employer shall regulate the working hours of each employee in accordance with the provisions of this Act and any other written law.

(2) Notwithstanding subsection (1), an employee shall be entitled to at least one rest day in every period of seven days.

28. Annual leave

(1) An employee shall be entitled—
   (a) after every twelve consecutive months of service with his employer to not less than twenty-one working days of leave with full pay;
   (b) where employment is terminated after the completion of two or more consecutive months of service during any twelve months' leave-earning period, to not less than one and three-quarter days of leave with full pay, in respect of each completed month of service in that period, to be taken consecutively.

(2) An employer may, with the consent of the employee divide the minimum annual leave entitlement under sub-section (1)(a) into different parts to be taken at different intervals.

(3) Unless otherwise provided in an agreement between an employee and an employer or in a collective agreement, and on condition that the length of service of an employee during any leave earning period specified in subsection (1)(a) entitles the employee to such a period, one part of the parts agreed upon under subsection (2) shall consist of at least two uninterrupted working weeks.

(4) The uninterrupted part of the annual leave with pay referred to in subsection (3) shall be granted and taken during the twelve consecutive months of service referred to in subsection (1) (a) and the remainder of the annual leave with pay shall be taken not later than eighteen months from the end of the leave earning period referred to in subsection (1)(a) being the period in respect of which the leave entitlement arose.

(5) Where in a contract of service an employee is entitled to leave days in excess of the minimum specified in subsection (1)(a), the employer and the employee may agree on how to utilize the leave days.

29. Maternity leave

(1) A female employee shall be entitled to three months maternity leave with full pay.

(2) On expiry of a female employee's maternity leave as provided in subsections (1) and (3), the female employee shall have the right to return to the job which she held immediately prior to her maternity leave or to a reasonably suitable job on terms and

conditions not less favourable than those which would have applied had she not been on maternity leave.

(3) Where—
- (a) the maternity leave has been extended with the consent of employer; or
- (b) immediately on expiry of maternity leave before resuming her duties a female employee proceeds on sick leave or with the consent of the employer on annual leave; compassionate leave; or any other leave,

the three months maternity leave under subsection (1) shall be deemed to expire on the last day of such extended leave.

(4) A female employee shall only be entitled to the rights mentioned in subsections (1), (2) and (3) if she gives not less than seven days notice in advance or a shorter period as may be reasonable in the circumstances of her intention to proceed on maternity leave on a specific date and to return to work thereafter.

(5) The notice referred to in subsection (4) shall be in writing.

(6) A female employee who seeks to exercise any of the rights mentioned in this section shall, if required by the employer, produce a certificate as to her medical condition from a qualified medical practitioner or midwife.

(7) No female employee shall forfeit her annual leave entitlement under section 28 on account of having taken her maternity leave.

(8) A male employee shall be entitled to two weeks paternity leave with full pay.

[Corr. No. 1 of 2008.]

29A. Pre-adoptive leave

(1) Where pursuant to section 157 of the Children Act, a child is to be placed in the continuous care and control of an applicant who is an employee under this Act, the employee shall be entitled to one month's pre-adoptive leave with full pay from the date of the placement of the child.

(2) An employee eligible for leave under subsection (1) shall notify the employer in writing of the intention of the adoption society to place the child in the custody of the employee at least fourteen days before the placement of the child.

(3) (3) A notice under subsection (2) shall be accompanied by documentation evidencing the intention of the adoption society to place the child in the custody of the employee, including a custody agreement between the employee and the adoption society and an exit certificate.

(4) Subsections (2), (3) and (7) of section 29 shall, with necessary modifications, apply to an employee eligible to leave under this section.

[Act No. 2 of 2021, s. 3.]

30. Sick leave

(1) After two consecutive months of service with his employer, an employee shall be entitled to sick leave of not less than seven days with full pay and thereafter to sick leave of seven days with half pay, in each period of twelve consecutive months of service, subject to

production by the employee of a certificate of incapacity to work signed by a duly qualified medical practitioner or a person acting on the practitioner's behalf in charge of a dispensary or medical aid centre.

(2) For an employee to be entitled to sick leave with full pay under subsection (1), the employee shall notify or cause to be notified as soon as is reasonably practicable his employer of his absence and the reasons for it.

(3) For the purposes of sub-section (1) and (2) "full pay" includes wages at the basic rate excluding deductions from the wages allowable under section 19.

(4) For purposes of subsection (1), the twelve continuous months of service shall be deemed to commence on the date of the employment of the employee and on such subsequent anniversary dates of employment.

(5) An employer shall have the right to place all his employees on an annual cycle of an anniversary date falling on a day to be determined by the employer.

31. Housing

(1) An employer shall at all times, at his own expense, provide reasonable housing accommodation for each of his employees either at or near to the place of employment, or shall pay to the employee such sufficient sum, as rent, in addition to the wages or salary of the employee, as will enable the employee to obtain reasonable accommodation.

(2) This section shall not apply to an employee whose contract of service—

(a) contains a provision which consolidates as part of the basic wage or salary of the employee, an element intended to be used by the employee as rent or which is otherwise intended to enable the employee to provide himself with housing accommodation; or

(b) is the subject matter of or is otherwise covered by a collective agreement which provides consolidation of wages as provided in paragraph (a).

(3) The Cabinet Secretary may, on the recommendation of the Board by notice in the *Gazette*, exclude the application of this section to a category of employees and such category of employee shall be dealt with as shall be specified in the notice.

[Act No. 19 of 2015, s. 147.]

31A. *Deleted*

Deleted by Act No. 20 of 2020 Sch.

31B. Affordable Housing Levy

(1) Notwithstanding the provisions of section3(2)(a),(b),(c)and(d)of the Act, each employee and employer shall pay a monthly levy to be known as the Affordable Housing Levy.

(2) The purpose of the Affordable Housing Levy shall be to provide funds for the development of affordable housing and associated social and physical infrastructure as well as the provision of affordable home financing to Kenyans.

(3) The Affordable Housing Levy shall not be used for any other purpose other than the development of affordable housing and associated social and physical infrastructure as well

as the provision of affordable home financing to Kenyans.

(4) The monthly levy payable by the employer and employee shall be –
   (a) one point five per centum of the employee's gross monthly salary for the employee;
   (b) one point five per centum of the employee's monthly gross salary for the employer.

[Act No. 4 of 2023, s.84.]

31C. Obligations of the employer

(1) An employer shall—
   (a) deduct an employee's monthly payment from the employee's gross monthly salary;
   (b) set aside the employer's monthly payment for each employee; and
   (c) not later than nine working days after the end of the month in which the payments are due, remit an amount comprising the employee and the employer's payment.

(2) An employer who fails to comply with this section shall be liable to payment of a penalty equivalent to two per cent of the unpaid funds for every month the same remains unpaid.

[Act No. 4 of 2023, s.84.]

32. Water

An employer shall provide a sufficient supply of wholesome water for the use of his employees at the place of employment and, as the case may be, within a reasonable distance of any housing accommodation provided for the employees by the employer.

33. Food

(1) An employer shall, where the provision of food has been expressly agreed to in or at the time of entering into a contract of service, ensure that an employee is properly fed and supplied with sufficient and proper cooking utensils and means of cooking, at the employer's expense.

(2) The provisions of this section shall not be deemed to impose upon an employer any liability in respect of an employee during the time the employee is absent from his place of employment without the permission of the employer or without other lawful excuse.

34. Medical attention

(1) Subject to subsection (2), an employer shall ensure the provision sufficient and of proper medicine for his employees during illness and if possible, medical attendance during serious illness.

(2) An employer shall take all reasonable steps to ensure that he is notified of the illness of an employee as soon as reasonably practicable after the first occurrence of the illness.

(3) It shall be a defence to a prosecution for an offence under subsection (1) if the employer shows that he did not know that the employee was ill and that he took all reasonable steps to ensure that the illness was brought to his notice or that it would have

been unreasonable, in all the circumstances of the case, to have required him to know that the employee was ill.

(4) This section shall not apply where—
    (a) the illness or injury to the employee was contracted during a period when the employee was absent from his employment without lawful cause or excuse;
    (b) the illness or injury is proved to have been self inflicted;
    (c) medical treatment is provided free of charge by the Government or under any insurance scheme established under any written law which covers the employee.

PART VI
TERMINATION AND DISMISSAL

35. Termination notice

(1) A contract of service not being a contract to perform specific work, without reference to time or to undertake a journey shall, if made to be performed in Kenya, be deemed to be—
    (a) where the contract is to pay wages daily, a contract terminable by either party at the close of any day without notice;
    (b) where the contract is to pay wages periodically at intervals of less than one month, a contract terminable by either party at the end of the period next following the giving of notice in writing; or
    (c) where the contract is to pay wages or salary periodically at intervals of or exceeding one month, a contract terminable by either party at the end of the period of twenty-eight days next following the giving of notice in writing.

(2) Subsection (1) shall not apply in the case of a contract of service whose terms provide for the giving of a period of notice of termination in writing greater than the period required by the provision of this subsection which would otherwise be applicable thereto.

(3) If an employee who receives notice of termination is not able to understand the notice, the employer shall ensure that the notice is explained orally to the employee in a language the employee understands.

(4) Nothing in this section affects the right—
    (a) of an employee whose services have been terminated to dispute the lawfulness or fairness of the termination in accordance with the provisions of section 46; or
    (b) of an employer or an employee to terminate a contract of employment without notice for any cause recognised by law.

(5) An employee whose contract of service has been terminated under subsection (1)(c) shall be entitled to service pay for every year worked, the terms of which shall be fixed.

(6) This section shall not apply where an employee is a member of—

(a) a registered pension or provident fund scheme under the Retirement Benefits Act;

(b) a gratuity or service pay scheme established under a collective agreement;

(c) any other scheme established and operated by an employer whose terms are more favourable than those of the service pay scheme established under this section; and

(d) the National Social Security Fund.

36. Payment in lieu of notice

Either of the parties to a contract of service to which section 35(5) applies, may terminate the contract without notice upon payment to the other party of the remuneration which would have been earned by that other party, or paid by him as the case may be in respect of the period of notice required to be given under the corresponding provisions of that section.

37. Conversion of casual employment to term contract

(1) Notwithstanding any provisions of this Act, where a casual employee—

(a) works for a period or a number of continuous working days which amount in the aggregate to the equivalent of not less than one month; or

(b) performs work which cannot reasonably be expected to be completed within a period, or a number of working days amounting in the aggregate to the equivalent of three months or more,

the contract of service of the casual employee shall be deemed to be one where wages are paid monthly and section 35(1)(c) shall apply to that contract of service.

(2) In calculating wages and the continuous working days under subsection (1), a casual employee shall be deemed to be entitled to one paid rest day after a continuous six days working period and such rest day or any public holiday which falls during the period under consideration shall be counted as part of continuous working days.

(3) An employee whose contract of service has been converted in accordance with subsection (1), and who works continuously for two months or more from the date of employment as a casual employee shall be entitled to such terms and conditions of service as he would have been entitled to under this Act had he not initially been employed as a casual employee.

(4) Notwithstanding any provisions of this Act, in any dispute before the Industrial Court on the terms and conditions of service of a casual employee, the Industrial Court shall have the power to vary the terms of service of the casual employee and may in so doing declare the employee to be employed on terms and conditions of service consistent with this Act.

(5) A casual employee who is aggrieved by the treatment of his employer under the terms and conditions of his employment may file a complaint with the labour officer and section 87 of this Act shall apply.

[Corr. No. 1 of 2008.]

38. Waiver of notice by employer

Where an employee gives notice of termination of employment and the employer waives the whole or any part of the notice, the employer shall pay to the employee remuneration equivalent to the period of notice not served by the employee as the case may be, unless the employer and the employee agree otherwise.

39. Contract expiring on a journey may be extended

If the period expressed in a contract of service expires, or if an employee seeks to terminate a contract where no agreement is expressed respecting its duration while the employee is engaged on a journey, the employer may, for the purpose of the completion of the journey, extend the period of service for a sufficient period, but in any case not exceeding one month, to enable the employee to complete the journey.

40. Termination on account of redundancy

(1) An employer shall not terminate a contract of service on account of redundancy unless the employer complies with the following conditions—

(a) where the employee is a member of a trade union, the employer notifies the union to which the employee is a member and the labour officer in charge of the area where the employee is employed of the reasons for, and the extent of, the intended redundancy not less than a month prior to the date of the intended date of termination on account of redundancy;

(b) where an employee is not a member of a trade union, the employer notifies the employee personally in writing and the labour officer;

(c) the employer has, in the selection of employees to be declared redundant had due regard to seniority in time and to the skill, ability and reliability of each employee of the particular class of employees affected by the redundancy;

(d) where there is in existence a collective agreement between an employer and a trade union setting out terminal benefits payable upon redundancy; the employer has not placed the employee at a disadvantage for being or not being a member of the trade union;

(e) the employer has where leave is due to an employee who is declared redundant, paid off the leave in cash;

(f) the employer has paid an employee declared redundant not less than one month's notice or one month's wages in lieu of notice; and

(g) the employer has paid to an employee declared redundant severance pay at the rate of not less than fifteen days pay for each completed year of service.

(2) Subsection (1) shall not apply where an employee's services are terminated on account of insolvency as defined in Part VIII in which case that Part shall be applicable.

(3) The Cabinet Secretary may make rules requiring an employer employing a certain minimum number of employees or any group of employers to insure their employees against the risk of redundancy through an unemployment insurance scheme operated either under an established national insurance scheme established under written law or by any firm

underwriting insurance business to be approved by the Cabinet Secretary.

[Corr. No. 1 of 2008, Act No. 19 of 2015, s. 148.]

41. Notification and hearing before termination on grounds of misconduct

(1) Subject to section 42(1), an employer shall, before terminating the employment of an employee, on the grounds of misconduct, poor performance or physical incapacity explain to the employee, in a language the employee understands, the reason for which the employer is considering termination and the employee shall be entitled to have another employee or a shop floor union representative of his choice present during this explanation.

(2) Notwithstanding any other provision of this Part, an employer shall, before terminating the employment of an employee or summarily dismissing an employee under section 44(3) or (4) hear and consider any representations which the employee may on the grounds of misconduct or poor performance, and the person, if any, chosen by the employee within subsection (1) make.

42. Termination of probationary contracts

(1) The provisions of section 41 shall not apply where a termination of employment terminates a probationary contract.

(2) A probationary period shall not be more than six months but it may be extended for a further period of not more than six months with the agreement of the employee.

(3) No employer shall employ an employee under a probationary contract for more than the aggregate period provided under subsection (2).

(4) A party to a contract for a probationary period may terminate the contract by giving not less than seven days' notice of termination of the contract, or by payment, by the employer to the employee, of seven days' wages in lieu of notice.

43. Proof of reason for termination

(1) In any claim arising out of termination of a contract, the employer shall be required to prove the reason or reasons for the termination, and where the employer fails to do so, the termination shall be deemed to have been unfair within the meaning of section 45.

(2) The reason or reasons for termination of a contract are the matters that the employer at the time of termination of the contract genuinely believed to exist, and which caused the employer to terminate the services of the employee.

44. Summary dismissal

(1) Summary dismissal shall take place when an employer terminates the employment of an employee without notice or with less notice than that to which the employee is entitled by any statutory provision or contractual term.

(2) Subject to the provisions of this section, no employer has the right to terminate a contract of service without notice or with less notice than that to which the employee is entitled by any statutory provision or contractual term.

(3) Subject to the provisions of this Act, an employer may dismiss an employee summarily when the employee has by his conduct indicated that he has fundamentally breached his obligations arising under the contract of service.

(4) Any of the following matters may amount to gross misconduct so as to justify the summary dismissal of an employee for lawful cause, but the enumeration of such matters or the decision of an employer to dismiss an employee summarily under subsection (3) shall not preclude an employer or an employee from respectively alleging or disputing whether the facts giving rise to the same, or whether any other matters not mentioned in this section, constitute justifiable or lawful grounds for the dismissal if: —

(a) without leave or other lawful cause, an employee absents himself from the place appointed for the performance of his work;

(b) during working hours, by becoming or being intoxicated, an employee renders himself unwilling or incapable to perform his work properly;

(c) an employee wilfully neglects to perform any work which it was his duty to perform, or if he carelessly and improperly performs any work which from its nature it was his duty, under his contract, to have performed carefully and properly;

(d) an employee uses abusive or insulting language, or behaves in a manner insulting to his employer or to a person placed in authority over him by his employer;

(e) an employee knowingly fails, or refuses, to obey a lawful and proper command which it was within the scope of his duty to obey, issued by his employer or a person placed in authority over him by his employer;

(f) in the lawful exercise of any power of arrest given by or under any written law, an employee is arrested for a cognizable offence punishable by imprisonment and is not within fourteen days either released on bail or on bond or otherwise lawfully set at liberty; or

(g) an employee commits, or on reasonable and sufficient grounds is suspected of having committed, a criminal offence against or to the substantial detriment of his employer or his employer's property.

45. Unfair termination

(1) No employer shall terminate the employment of an employee unfairly.

(2) A termination of employment by an employer is unfair if the employer fails to prove—

(a) that the reason for the termination is valid;

(b) that the reason for the termination is a fair reason—

(i) related to the employees conduct, capacity or compatibility; or

(ii) based on the operational requirements of the employer; and

(c) that the employment was terminated in accordance with fair procedure.

(3) An employee who has been continuously employed by his employer for a period not less than thirteen months immediately before the date of termination shall have the right to complain that he has been unfairly terminated.

(4) A termination of employment shall be unfair for the purposes of this Part where—

(a) the termination is for one of the reasons specified in section 46; or

(b) it is found out that in all the circumstances of the case, the employer did not act in accordance with justice and equity in terminating the employment of the employee.

(5) In deciding whether it was just and equitable for an employer to terminate the employment of an employee, for the purposes of this section, a labour Officer, or the Industrial Court shall consider—

(a) the procedure adopted by the employer in reaching the decision to dismiss the employee, the communication of that decision to the employee and the handling of any appeal against the decision;

(b) the conduct and capability of the employee up to the date of termination;

(c) the extent to which the employer has complied with any statutory requirements connected with the termination, including the issuing of a certificate under section 51 and the procedural requirements set out in section 41;

(d) the previous practice of the employer in dealing with the type of circumstances which led to the termination; and

(f) the existence of any previous warning letters issued to the employee.

46. Reasons for termination or discipline

The following do not constitute fair reasons for dismissal or for the imposition of a disciplinary penalty—

(a) a female employee's pregnancy, or any reason connected with her pregnancy;

(b) the going on leave of an employee, or the proposal of an employee to take, any leave to which he was entitled under the law or a contract;

(c) an employee's membership or proposed membership of a trade union;

(d) the participation or proposed participation of an employee in the activities of a trade union outside working hours or, with the consent of the employer, within working hours;

(e) an employee's seeking of office as, or acting or having acted in the capacity of, an officer of a trade union or a workers' representative;

(f) an employee's refusal or proposed refusal to join or withdrawal from a trade union;

(g) an employee's race, colour, tribe, sex, religion, political opinion or affiliation, national extraction, nationality, social origin, marital status, HIV status or disability;

(h) an employee's initiation or proposed initiation of a complaint or other legal proceedings against his employer, except where the complaint is shown to be irresponsible and without foundation; or

(i) an employee's participation in a lawful strike.

47. Complaint of summary dismissal and unfair termination

(1) Where an employee has been summarily dismissed or his employer has unfairly

terminated his employment without justification, the employee may, within three months of the date of dismissal, present a complaint to a labour officer and the complaint shall be dealt with as a complaint lodged under section 87.

(2) A labour officer who is presented with a claim under this section shall, after affording every opportunity to both the employee and the employer to state their case, recommend to the parties what in his opinion would be the best means of settling the dispute in accordance with the provisions section 49.

(3) The right of the employee to present a complaint under this section shall be in addition to his right to complain to the Industrial Court on the same issue and to the right to complain of any other infringement of his statutory rights.

(4) The right of an employee to make a complaint under this section shall be in addition to any right an employee may enjoy under a collective agreement.

(5) For any complaint of unfair termination of employment or wrongful dismissal the burden of proving that an unfair termination of employment or wrongful dismissal has occurred shall rest on the employee, while the burden of justifying the grounds for the termination of employment or wrongful dismissal shall rest on the employer.

(6) No employee whose services have been terminated or who has been summarily dismissed during a probationary contract shall make a complaint under this section.

[Corr. No. 1 of 2008.]

48. Representation

In any complaint made under section 47, no advocate shall represent a party in the proceedings before a labour officer, but any party may be assisted or represented by an official of a trade union or an official of an employer's organisation notwithstanding the fact that the official is an advocate.

49. Remedies for wrongful dismissal and unfair termination

(1) Where in the opinion of a labour officer summary dismissal or termination of a contract of an employee is unjustified, the labour officer may recommend to the employer to pay to the employee any or all of the following—

(a) the wages which the employee would have earned had the employee been given the period of notice to which he was entitled under this Act or his contract of service;

(b) where dismissal terminates the contract before the completion of any service upon which the employee's wages became due, the proportion of the wage due for the period of time for which the employee has worked; and any other loss consequent upon the dismissal and arising between the date of dismissal and the date of expiry of the period of notice referred to in paragraph (a) which the employee would have been entitled to by virtue of the contract; or

(c) the equivalent of a number of months wages or salary not exceeding twelve months based on the gross monthly wage or salary of the employee at the time of dismissal.

(2) Any payments made by the employer under this section shall be subject to statutory deductions.

(3) Where in the opinion of a labour officer an employee's summary dismissal or termination of employment was unfair, the labour officer may recommend to the employer to—

    (a) reinstate the employee and treat the employee in all respects as if the employees employment had not been terminated; or

    (b) re-engage the employee in work comparable to that in which the employee was employed prior to his dismissal, or other reasonably suitable work, at the same wage.

(4) A labour officer shall, in deciding whether to recommend the remedies specified in subsections (1) and (3), take into account any or all of the following—

    (a) the wishes of the employee;

    (b) the circumstances in which the termination took place, including the extent, if any, to which the employee caused or contributed to the termination; and

    (c) the practicability of recommending reinstatement or re-engagement;

    (d) the common law principle that there should be no order for specific performance in a contract for service except in very exceptional circumstances;

    (e) the employee's length of service with the employer;

    (f) the reasonable expectation of the employee as to the length of time for which his employment with that employer might have continued but for the termination;

    (g) the opportunities available to the employee for securing comparable or suitable employment with another employer;

    (h) the value of any severance payable by law;

    (i) the right to press claims or any unpaid wages, expenses or other claims owing to the employee;

    (j) any expenses reasonable incurred by the employee as a consequence of the termination;

    (k) any conduct of the employee which to any extent caused or contributed to the termination;

    (l) any failure by the employee to reasonably mitigate the losses attributable to the unjustified termination; and

    (m) any compensation, including *ex-gratia* payment, in respect of termination of employment paid by the employer and received by the employee.

50. Courts to be guided

In determining a complaint or suit under this Act involving wrongful dismissal or unfair termination of the employment of an employee, the Industrial Court shall be guided by the provisions of section 49.

51. Certificate of service

(1) An employer shall issue to an employee a certificate of service upon termination of

his employment, unless the employment has continued for a period of less than four consecutive weeks.

(2) A certificate of service issued under subsection (1) shall contain—

(a) the name of the employer and his postal address;

(b) the name of the employee;

(c) the date when employment of the employee commenced;

(d) the nature and usual place of employment of the employee;

(e) the date when the employment of the employee ceased; and

(f) such other particulars as may be prescribed.

(2) Subject to subsection (1), no employer is bound to give to an employee a testimonial, reference or certificate relating to the character or performance of that employee.

(3) An employer who wilfully or by neglect fails to give an employee a certificate of service in accordance with subsection (1), or who in a certificate of service includes a statement which he knows to be false, commits an offence and shall on conviction be liable to a fine not exceeding one hundred thousand shillings or to imprisonment for a term not exceeding six months or to both.

PART VII
PROTECTION OF CHILDREN

52. Interpretation

In this Part, except where the context otherwise requires—

"**employment**" means employment of a child in a situation where—

(a) the child provides labour as an assistant to another person and his labour is deemed to be the labour of that other person for the purposes of payment;

(b) the child's labour is used for gain by any person or institution whether or not the child benefits directly or indirectly; and

(c) there is in existence a contract for service where the party providing the service is a child whether the person using the services does so directly or by agent.

53. Prohibition of worst forms of child labour

(1) Notwithstanding any provision of any written law, no person shall employ a child in any activity which constitutes worst form of child labour.

(2) The Cabinet Secretary shall, in consultation with the Board, make regulations declaring any work, activity or contract of service harmful to the health, safety or morals of a child and subsection (1) shall apply to such work, activity or contract of service.

[Act No. 19 of 2015, s. 149.]

54. Complaint to the labour officer or police officer

(1) A person may make a complaint to a labour officer or a police officer of the rank of an inspector and above if that person considers any child to be employed in any activity

which constitute worst form of child labour.

(2) On receipt of a complaint under subsection (1), the labour officer or the police officer, as the case may be, shall within seven days investigate the complaint and submit his finding to the person who filed the complaint and to the Minister.

(3) Where the labour officer or the police officer considers it not expedient to conduct an investigation under subsection (2), he shall in writing inform the person and the Minister accordingly, giving reasons thereof.

(4) Notwithstanding subsection (2) employment of a child in any work constituting worst form of child labour shall constitute a cognisable offence punishable under section 64 or any other written law provided that no person shall be punished twice for the same offence.

55. Powers of labour officer to cancel and prohibit contracts

(1) A labour officer may, by notice in writing served upon an employer, terminate or cancel any contract of service, other than a deed of apprenticeship or indentured learnership lawfully entered into under the provisions of the Industrial Training Act (Cap. 237), which has been entered into by a child with the employer, on grounds that, in the opinion of that labour officer, the employer is an undesirable person, or that the nature of the employment constitutes worst forms of child labour or for any other cause which may be prescribed.

(2) A labour officer may, by notice in writing served upon any person, prohibit that person from employing a child in any class or description of employment specified in the notice, on grounds that, in the opinion of the labour officer, that person is an undesirable person, or that the nature of the employment constitutes worst forms of child labour or for any other cause which may be prescribed.

(3) A notice given under subsection (1) or subsection (2) shall be personally served upon the employer or the person to whom it is addressed.

(4) An employer, employee or person who is aggrieved by a notice given under subsection (1) or subsection (2) may, within thirty days after the date of service thereof, appeal in writing against that notice to the Industrial Court which may confirm or set aside the notice and the decision of the court shall be final.

(5) An employer or a person who, having been served with a notice under subsection (1) or subsection (2) which has not been set aside on appeal, employs or continues to employ the child to whom the notice refers in or about the employment to which the notice relates, or any similar employment, or, as the case may be, employs any child in the employment to which the notice relates, or any similar employment, commits an offence.

(6) It shall not be an offence for an employer served with a notice given under subsection (1) to continue to employ the child to whom the notice refers during the period of thirty days limited for appeal or, if an appeal is lodged and subject to obtaining from the Industrial Court a temporary stay of execution of the labour officer's notice within, such period as the court may determine, pending the outcome of that appeal.

56. Prohibition of employment of children between thirteen years and sixteen years of age

(1) No person shall employ a child who has not attained the age of thirteen years whether gainfully or otherwise in any undertaking.

(2) A child of between thirteen years of age and sixteen years of age may be employed to perform light work which is—

(a) not likely to be harmful to the child's health or development; and

(b) not such as to prejudice the child's attendance at school, his participation in vocational orientation or training programmes approved by Cabinet Secretary or his capacity to benefit from the instructions received.

(3) The Cabinet Secretary may make rules prescribing light work in which a child of between thirteen years of age and sixteen years of age may be employed and the terms and conditions of that employment.

[Act No. 19 of 2015, s. 150.]

57. Prohibition of written contracts for child between thirteen and sixteen years of age

Subject to the provisions of the Industrial Training Act relating to contracts of apprenticeship or indentured learnership, a person who employs a child of between thirteen and sixteen years of age, or causes such a child to be employed, or being the parent or guardian or other person having for the time being the charge of or control over the child, allows the child to be employed, otherwise than under a verbal contract of service commits an offence and shall on conviction be liable to a fine not exceeding one hundred thousand shillings or to imprisonment for a term not exceeding six months or to both.

58. Restriction in employing child of between thirteen and sixteen years of age to attend machinery

(1) No person shall employ a child of between thirteen and sixteen years of age, other than one serving under a contract of apprenticeship or indentured learnership in accordance with the provisions of the Industrial Training Act, in an industrial undertaking to attend to machinery.

(2) No person shall employ a child in any opencast workings or sub-surface workings that are entered by means of a shaft or adit.

59. Time restriction in employing a child

(1) Subject to section 60, no person shall employ a child in an industrial undertaking between the hours of 6.30 p.m. and 6.30 a.m.

(2) Notwithstanding the provision of subsection (1), a person may employ a male young person in cases of emergencies which could not have been controlled or foreseen, and which interfere with the normal working of the industrial undertaking and which are not of a periodical nature.

(3) Notwithstanding the provision of subsection (1), the Cabinet Secretary may, after consultation with the Board, authorise an employer in writing to employ a young person for a

specific period of the night subject to such conditions as the Cabinet Secretary may determine.

[Act No. 19 of 2015, s. 151.]

60. Emergencies

In case of a serious emergency, when the public interest demands it, the Cabinet Secretary may, by notice in the *Gazette*, suspend the operation of section 59.

[Act No. 19 of 2015, s. 152.]

61. Registers of child in employment

(1) An employer who employs a child shall keep and maintain a register containing the following particulars of every child he employs—

    (a) age and date of birth;

    (b) date of entry into and of leaving the employment;

    (c) such other particulars as may be prescribed.

(2) Where an employer maintains such a register, the register shall be maintained in accordance with the principles of data protection as set out in the Data Protection Act (No. 24 of 2019).

[Act No. 24 of 2019, 2nd Sch.]

62. Medical examination of a child employee

An authorised officer may require a child in employment to be medically examined at any time during the period of the child's employment.

63. Determination of age

(1) If, during the hearing of a charge for an offence under this Act it is alleged that any person was at the date of the offence of, over or under a particular age, the court hearing the charge shall, after such inquiry as it considers necessary and after hearing any evidence which may be tendered by any party to the proceedings, determine the age of that person for the purposes of the proceedings, and the determination shall be final.

(2) No conviction, order or judgment of a court under this Act shall be invalidated by any subsequent proof that the age of any person has not been correctly stated to, or determined by, the court.

(3) Subject to the provision of subsection (1), whenever any question arises as to the age of an employee and no sufficient evidence is available as to that employee's age, a medical officer may estimate the age of the employee by his appearance or from any available information, and the age so estimated shall, for purposes of this Act, and until the contrary is proved, be deemed to be the true age of the employee.

64. Penalty for unlawful employment of child

(1) A person who employs, engages, or uses a child in an industrial undertaking in contravention of the provisions of this Part, commits an offence.

(2) A person who uses a child in any activity constituting worst form of child labour commits an offence and shall on conviction be liable to a fine not exceeding two hundred thousand shillings or to imprisonment for a term not exceeding twelve months or to both.

(3) It shall be a defence if the accused person proves that he genuinely had reason to

believe that the child was above the age limit, which is the subject of the charge.

65. Penalty in case of death or injury of a child

(1) If a child is killed, dies or suffers any bodily injury in consequence of his employer having contravened any provision of this Part, the employer shall, in addition to any other penalty, be liable to a fine not exceeding five hundred thousand shillings or to imprisonment for a term not exceeding twelve months or to both and the whole or any part of the fine may be applied for the benefit of the injured child or his family or otherwise as the Minister may direct.

(2) An employer shall not be liable under subsection (1)—

    (a) in the case of injury to health, unless the injury was caused directly by the contravention; and

    (b) if a charge against him under this Part in respect of the act or default by which the death or injury was caused has been heard and dismissed before the injury occurred.

PART VIII
INSOLVENCY OF EMPLOYER

66. Insolvency of employer

(1) Where on an application made to him in writing by an employee or his representative the Cabinet Secretary is satisfied that—

    (a) the employer of an employee has become insolvent;

    (b) the employment of the employee has been terminated; and

    (c) on the appropriate date the employee was entitled to be paid the whole or part of any debt to which this Part applies,

the Cabinet Secretary shall, subject to section 69, pay the employee out of the National Social Security Fund, the amount to which, in the opinion of the Cabinet Secretary, the employee is entitled in respect of the debt.

[Act No. 19 of 2015, s. 153.]

67. Definition of insolvency

An employer is insolvent for the purposes of this Part—

    (a) if the employer is a person who—

        (i) has been adjudged bankrupt or has made a composition or arrangement with his creditors; or

        (ii) has died and his estate is to be administered in accordance with the Law of Succession Act;

    (b) if the employer is a company—

        (i) a winding up order or an administration order has been made, or a resolution for voluntary winding up has been passed, with respect to the company; or

(ii) a receiver or a manager of the company's undertaking has been duly appointed, or possession has been taken, by or on behalf of the holders of any debentures secured by a floating charge, of any property of the company comprised in or subject to the charge.

68. Debts to which Part applies

This part applies to the following debts—
- (a) any arrears of wages in respect of one or more months, but not more than six months or part thereof;
- (b) any amount which the employer is liable to pay the employee for the period of notice required by section 36 or for any failure of the employer to give the period of notice required by section 35(1) (ii) and (iii);
- (c) any pay in lieu of leave for annual leave days earned but not taken in accordance with section 28;
- (d) any basic award of compensation for unfair dismissal; and
- (e) any reasonable sum by way of reimbursement of the whole or part of any fee or premium paid by an apprentice.

69. Limitation on amount payable under section 68

(1) The total amount payable to an employee in respect of any debt to which this Part applies, where the amount of the debt is referable to a period of time, shall not exceed—
- (a) ten thousand shillings or one half of the monthly remuneration whichever is greater in respect of any one month payable; or
- (b) in respect of a shorter period an amount proportionate to the shorter period based on the amount payable under paragraph (a).

(2) The Cabinet Secretary may, on the advise of the Board, by Order in the *Gazette*, vary the limit specified in subsection (1).

[Act No. 19 of 2015, s. 154.]

70. Role of relevant officer

(1) Where a relevant officer has been, or is required to be, appointed in connection with an employer's insolvency, the Cabinet Secretary shall not make a payment under section 66 in respect of a debt until the Cabinet Secretary has received a statement from the relevant officer of the amount of that debt which appears to have been owed to the employee on the appropriate date and to remain unpaid.

(2) A relevant officer shall, on the request of the Cabinet Secretary, provide the Cabinet Secretary with a statement for the purposes of subsection (1) as soon as is reasonably practicable.

(3) If the Cabinet Secretary is satisfied that he does not require a statement under subsection (1) in order to determine the amount of a debt which was owed to the employee on the appropriate date and remains unpaid, he may make a payment in respect of the debt without having received the statement.

(4) The following are relevant officers for the purposes of this section—

(a) a bankruptcy trustee or interim trustee holding office under Part III of the Insolvency Act, 2015;

(b) a liquidator appointed under Part VI of that Act;

(c) an administrator appointed under Part VIII of that Act;

(d) the Official Receiver or other person responsible for supervising the debtor under a deed of composition approved by the Court under Division 24 of Part III of that Act;

(e) a supervisor or provisional supervisor under a voluntary arrangement entered into under Part IX or Division 1 of Part IV of that Act;

(f) a trustee under a trust deed for his creditors executed by the employer.

[Act No. 19 of 2015, s. 155.]

71. Complaint to Industrial Court

(1) A person who has applied for a payment under section 66 may present a complaint to the Industrial Court—

(a) that the Cabinet Secretary has failed to make the payment; or

(b) that the payment made by the Cabinet Secretary is less than the amount which should have been paid.

(2) The Industrial Court shall not consider a complaint under subsection (1) unless it is presented—

(a) before the end of the period of three months beginning with the date which the decision of the Cabinet Secretary on the application was communicated to the applicant; or

(b) within such further period as the Industrial Court considers reasonable in a case where it is not reasonably practicable for the complaint to be presented before the end of that period of three months.

(3) Where the Industrial Court finds that the Cabinet Secretary should have made a payment under section 66, the Industrial Court shall—

(a) make an award to that effect; and

(b) declare the amount of any payment which it finds the Cabinet Secretary ought to make.

[Act No. 19 of 2015, s. 156.]

72. Transfer of rights and remedies

(1) Where, in pursuance of section 66, the Cabinet Secretary makes a payment to an employee in respect of a debt to which this Part applies—

(a) on the making of the payment, any rights and remedies of the employee in respect of the debt or, if the Cabinet Secretary has paid only part of it, in respect of that part become rights and remedies of the Cabinet Secretary; and

(b) any decision of the Industrial Court requiring an employer to pay that debt to the employee has the effect that the debt, or the part of it which the Cabinet Secretary has paid, is to be paid to the Cabinet Secretary.

(2) If the Cabinet Secretary has, in accordance with subsection (1), made a payment in respect of a debt, or a part of the debt, the right that become right of the Cabinet Secretary because of subsection (1) include a right arising because of the status of the debt, or that part of it as a preferential debt.

(3) In computing payment for the purposes of subsection (2), the aggregate amount payable in priority to other creditors of the employer in respect of—
> (a) any claim of the Cabinet Secretary to be paid in priority to other creditors of the employer by virtue of subsection (2); and
> (b) any claim by the employee to be so paid made in the employee's own right,

any claim of the Cabinet Secretary to be paid by virtue of subsection (2) shall be treated as if it were a claim of the employee.

(4) The Cabinet Secretary shall be entitled, as against the employee, to be paid in respect of any claim made by the Cabinet Secretary the full amount of the claim before any payment is made to the employee in respect of any claim by the employee to be paid made in the employee's own right.

(5) Any sum recovered by the Cabinet Secretary in exercising any right, or pursuing any remedy, under this section shall be paid into the National Social Security Fund.

[Act No. 19 of 2015, s. 157.]

73. Power to obtain information

(1) Where an application is made to the Cabinet Secretary under section 66 in respect of debt owed by an employer, the Cabinet Secretary may require—
> (a) the employer to provide him with such information as he may reasonably require for the purpose of determining whether the application is well founded; and
> (b) any person having the custody or control of any relevant records or other documents the Cabinet Secretary may require to produce for examination on behalf of the Cabinet Secretary any such records or document.

(2) A request for information, records or a document under subsection (1)—
> (a) shall be made by notice in writing to the person required to furnish the information, or produce the records or document; and
> (b) may be varied or revoked by a subsequent notice so given.

(3) A person who refuses or wilfully neglects to furnish any information or produce any record or document that he has been required to furnish or produce by a notice under this section commits an offence and shall on conviction be liable to a fine not exceeding one hundred thousand shillings or to imprisonment for a term not exceeding six months or to both.

(4) A person who in purporting to comply with a requirement of a notice under this section, knowingly or recklessly makes any false statement commits an offence.

(5) Where an offence under this section is committed by a body corporate and is proved—

(a) to have been committed with the consent or connivance of; or

(b) to be attributable to any neglect on the part of any director, manager, secretary or other similar officer of the body corporate, or any person who was purporting to act in any such capacity, that person and the body corporate commits an offence.

(6) Where a member of a body corporate manages the body corporate, subsection (5) shall apply in relation to the acts and defaults of a member in connection with his functions of management as if he were a director of the body corporate.

[Act No. 19 of 2015, s. 158.]

PART IX
EMPLOYMENT RECORDS

74. Records to be kept by employer

(1) An employer shall keep a written record of all employees employed by him, with whom he has entered into a contract under this Act which shall contain the particulars—

(a) of a policy statement under section 6(2) where applicable;

(b) specified in section 10(3);

(c) specified in section 13;

(d) specified in sections 21 and 22;

(e) of an employee's weekly rest days specified in section 27;

(f) of an employees annual leave entitlement, days taken and days due specified in section 28;

(g) of maternity leave specified in section 29;

(h) of sick leave specified in section 30;

(i) where the employer provides housing, particulars of the accommodation provided and, where the wage rates are deconsolidated particulars of the house allowance paid to the employee;

(j) of food rations where applicable;

(k) specified in section 61;

(l) of a record of warning letters or other evidence of misconduct of an employee; and

(m) any other particulars required to be kept under any written law or as may be prescribed by the Cabinet Secretary.

(2) An employer shall permit an authorised officer who may require an employer to produce for inspection the record for any period relating to the preceding thirty six months to examine the record.

(3) Where an employer who employs a child maintains a register in accordance with section 61, the employer shall be deemed to have complied with this section if the register contains in relation to each child, the particulars required to be kept by the employer under

subsection (1).

[Corr. No. 1 of 2008, Act No. 19 of 2015, s. 159.]

75. False entries etc.

A person who makes, causes to be made or knowingly allows to be made an entry in a register, record, book or other document whatsoever, required by this Act to be kept, which that person knows to be false in a material particular, or produces, furnishes, causes or knowingly allows to be produced or furnished, to an authorised officer, a register, record, book or other document which he knows to be false in a material particular, commits an offence and shall on conviction be liable to a fine not exceeding one hundred thousand shillings or to imprisonment for a term not exceeding six months or to both.

PART X
EMPLOYMENT MANAGEMENT

76. Notification of vacancies

(1) This Part shall apply to an employer who employs twenty-five employees or more.

(2) An employer shall notify the Director of every vacancy occurring in his establishment, business or work place in a prescribed form giving the following details—

(a) the employer's name and full address;

(b) details of the vacant post;

(c) minimum qualification required of the person seeking to be employed;

(d) the place of work; and

(e) the type of work, whether casual, permanent or term contract; and

(f) such other information as the Director may require.

(3) A vacancy shall be deemed to occur on the date—

(a) an employer creates a post to be filled by an employee or decides to engage one;

(b) an employee terminates or has his employment terminated by the employer and the employer abolishes the post.

77. Notification of filling or abolition of post

When a post, which has been notified to the Director as vacant, has been filled or has been abolished before being filled, the employer shall notify the employment service office of this in writing within two weeks of the filling of the post or of its abolition, as the case may be.

78. Notification of termination of employment

An employer shall notify the termination of every employment and of each lay-off of a person in writing to the nearest employment service office within two weeks of the termination or lay-off.

79. Regiser of employees

An employer shall keep a register in which the employer shall enter the full name, age, sex, occupation, date of employment, nationality and educational level of each of his employees and a return of employees for each calendar year, ending on 31st December containing such information shall be sent to the Director not later than 31st January of the following year.

80. Exemptions

The Cabinet Secretary may exempt any category of employers, any sector of industry or any industry from this Part, or any section of this Part or may vary the limit of its application provided under section 76(1).

[Corr. No. 1 of 2008, Act No. 19 of 2015, s. 160.]

81. Offence under Part

An employer who contravenes any of the provisions of this Part commits an offence and shall on conviction be liable to a fine not exceeding one hundred thousand shillings or to imprisonment for a term not exceeding six months or to both.

PART XI
FOREIGN CONTRACTS OF SERVICE

83. Form and attestation

A foreign contract of service shall be in the prescribed form, signed by the parties thereto, and shall be attested by a labour officer.

84. Requirement before attestation

A foreign contract of service shall not be attested unless the labour officer is satisfied—

(a) that the consent of the employee to the contract has been obtained;

(b) of the absence of any fraud, coercion or undue influence, and any mistake of fact, or misrepresentation which might have induced the employee to enter into the contract;

(c) that the contract is in the prescribed form;

(d) that the terms and conditions of employment contained in the contract comply with the provisions of this Act and have been understood by the employee;

(e) that the employee is medically fit for the performance of his duties under the contract; and

(f) that the employee is not bound to serve under any other contract of service during the period provided in the foreign contract.

85. Security in foreign contract of service

(1) When the employer who enters into a foreign contract of service does not reside or carry on business within Kenya, the employer shall, or where the employer resides in Kenya, the labour officer may require the employer to, give security by bond in the prescribed form, with one or more sureties resident in Kenya and approved of by the labour officer for the due performance of the contract in such sums as the labour officer considers reasonable.

(2) Where the employer has an authorised agent resident in Kenya, the Cabinet

Secretary may require that the security bond specified in subsection (1) be given by the agent and the agent shall personally be bound by the terms of the bond notwithstanding the disclosure of his principal.

[Act No. 19 of 2015, s. 161.]

86. Offence to induce person to proceed abroad under informal contract

A person who—

(a) employs, engages, or knowingly aids in the employment or engagement of, a person with the intention that when so employed or engaged that person shall proceed outside the limits of Kenya; or

(b) induces or attempts to induce an employee to proceed outside the limits of Kenya,

unless he has under this Act, duly entered into a foreign contract of service with that person or employee, as the case may be, commits an offence and shall on conviction be liable to a fine not exceeding two hundred thousand shillings or to imprisonment for a term not exceeding six months or to both.

PART XII
DISPUTES SETTLEMENT PROCEDURE

87. Complaint and jurisdiction in cases of dispute between employers and employees

(1) Subject to the provisions of this Act whenever—

(a) an employer or employee neglects or refuses to fulfill a contract of service; or

(b) any question, difference or dispute arises as to the rights or liabilities of either party; or

(c) touching any misconduct, neglect or ill treatment of either party or any injury to the person or property of either party, under any contract of service,

the aggrieved party may complain to the labour officer or lodge a complaint or suit in the Industrial Court.

(2) No court other than the Industrial Court shall determine any complaint or suit referred to in subsection (1).

(3) This section shall not apply in a suit where the dispute over a contract of service or any other matter referred to in subsection (1) is similar or secondary to the main issue in dispute.

88. General penalty and offences under other laws

(1) A person, other than a child, who commits an offence under this Act, or contravenes or fails to comply with any of the provisions of this Act for which no penalty is specifically provided shall be liable to a fine not exceeding fifty thousand shillings or to imprisonment for a term not exceeding three months or to both.

(2) Nothing in this Act shall prevent an employer or employee from being proceeded against according to law for an offence punishable under any other law in force.

(3) No employer or employee shall be punished twice for the same offence.

89. Saving of contracts of service made abroad

(1) Nothing in this Act shall prevent an employer or employee from enforcing their respective rights and remedies for any breach or non-performance of a lawful contract of service made outside Kenya, but the respective rights of the parties under that contract as well against each other as against third parties invading those rights may be enforced in the same manner as other contracts.

(2) Where a contract has been executed in conformity with this Part, it shall be enforced in the same manner as a contract entered into under this Act, but no written contract, tenor and execution of which are not in conformity with this Act shall be enforced as attains an employee who is unable to read and understand the contract and any such contract shall be deemed to be executed in conformity with this Act if it is signed by the names or marks of the contracting parties and bears, as concerns any illiterate parties, an attestation to the like effect as if prescribed by this Act.

(3) Where a contract is made in a foreign country, the contract shall be attested by a judge or magistrate, and shall be authenticated by the official seal of the court to which the judge or magistrate is attached.

90. Limitations

Notwithstanding the provisions of section 4(1) of the Limitation of Actions Act (Cap. 22), no civil action or proceedings based or arising out of this Act or a contract of service in general shall lie or be instituted unless it is commenced within three years next after the act, neglect or default complained or in the case of continuing injury or damage within twelve months next after the cessation thereof.

PART XIII
MISCELLANEOUS PROVISIONS

91. Rules

(1) The Cabinet Secretary may, after consultation with the Board, make rules providing for all or any of the purposes, for the administration of this Act or that may be necessary or expedient for carrying out the objects or purposes of this Act, and, without prejudice to the generality of the foregoing, for all or any of the following purposes—

 (a) prescribing anything which under this Act is to be or may be prescribed;

 (b) the conditions under which employees may be housed or employed, including sanitary arrangements and water supply;

 (c) the feeding of employees in cases where food is to be supplied by the employer under the contract of service, including the quantity, variety and kind of food to be supplied;

 (d) regulating the care of sick and injured employees;

 (e) prescribing books to be kept and returns to be rendered by employers;

 (f) prescribing—

(i) for any period, the maximum number of hours during which any employee or class of employees, whether generally or in relation to any particular kind of employment, may be required to work;

(ii) the intervals to be allowed to them for meals and rest;

(iii) the holidays or half holiday with or without pay and travelling expenses to be allowed to employees;

(iv) any other conditions to be observed in relation to their employment; and any such conditions may relate to feeding, housing, medical attendance, education, recreation, discipline or otherwise;

(g) appointing labour supervisors where employees of one employer exceed the maximum prescribed;

(h) the registration and employment of casual employees;

(i) the establishment and administration of employment exchanges, including the procedure to be adopted for the notification of employment vacancies and opportunities;

(j) prescribing the conditions of the employment of women, young persons or children in any specified trade or occupation;

(k) prescribing the age at which a child may be employed;

(l) requiring employers of children to furnish information and return to any specified officer in respect of such children or their employment or the conditions of their employment;

(j) issue by employer or any class of employers to employees or any class of employees, whether generally or in relation to any particular kind of employment, of employment cards, and the forms of such cards;

(k) prescribing particulars to be included in a certificate of service; and

(l) prescribing the form, and providing for the display in places of employment, of notices relating to wages and the terms and conditions of employment.

(2) Any rules made under this section may impose conditions, require acts or things to be performed or done to the satisfaction of an authorised officer or a medical officer, empower any such officer to issue orders either verbally or in writing requiring acts or things to be performed or done or prohibiting acts or things from being performed or done, and may prescribe periods or dates upon, within or before which such acts or things shall be performed or done or such conditions shall be fulfilled.

(3) Any rules made under this section may distinguish between juveniles of different ages and sexes and, in relation to women or juveniles, between different localities, occupations and circumstances.

[Act No. 19 of 2015, s. 162.]

92. Repeal of Cap. 226 and savings

(1) The Employment Act is repealed.

(2) Except where otherwise provided, the provisions of this Act shall be in addition to,

and not in substitution for or in derogation of, the provisions of any other Act.

(3) A term of contract of service, or foreign contract of service to which Part XI of this Act applies, made after the date of commencement of this Act which provides a condition of service or employment less favourable to an employee than the like condition of employment provided by this Act, shall be void to the extent that it is so less favourable, and the relevant condition of employment provided by this Act shall be deemed to have been included in and to form part of such contract or foreign contract of service as the case may be.

(4) If—

(a) any act or thing that was done or omitted to be done by or to the Cabinet Secretary under this Act before the commencement of the Companies and Insolvency Legislation (Consequential Amendment) Act, 2015, had effect immediately before that commencement; and

(b) that act or thing could be done or be omitted to be done by or to the Cabinet Secretary under this Act after that commencement,

that act or thing is taken to have been done or omitted to be done by or to the Cabinet Secretary.

[Act No. 19 of 2015, s. 163.]

93. Transitional provisions

(1) A valid contract of service, and foreign contract of service to which Part XI applies, entered into in accordance with the Employment Act (now repealed) shall continue in force to the extent that the terms and conditions thereof are not inconsistent with the provisions of this Act, and subject to the foregoing every such contract shall be read and construed as if it were a contract made in accordance with and subject to the provisions of this Act, and the parties thereto shall be subject to those provisions accordingly.

LEGAL NOTICE No. 207

GROUP THREE
TAX LAWS AND REGULATIONS

TITLE SIX
THE INCOME TAX ACT
(*Cap. 470*)

THE INCOME TAX (DIGITAL SERVICE TAX) REGULATIONS, 2020

www.kenyalaw.org

THE INCOME TAX ACT
(Cap. 470)

IN EXERCISE of the powers conferred by section 3 (2A) as read with section 130 of the Income Tax Act, the Cabinet Secretary for the National Treasury and Planning makes the following Regulations—

THE INCOME TAX (DIGITAL SERVICE TAX) REGULATIONS, 2020

1. Citation and commencement

These Regulations may be cited as the Income Tax (Digital Service Tax) Regulations, 2020 and shall come into force on the 2nd January, 2021.

2. Interpretation

In these Regulations, unless the context otherwise requires—

"digital marketplace" has the meaning assigned to it in section 3 (3) (ba);

"digital marketplace provider" means a person who provides a digital marketplace platform;

"digital service" means any service that is delivered or provided over a digital marketplace;

"digital service provider" means a person who provides digital services through a digital marketplace; and

"platform" means any electronic application that allows digital service providers to be connected to users of the services, directly or indirectly, and includes a website and mobile application.

3. Digital services

(1) Digital services for which digital service tax shall apply include—

(a) downloadable digital content including downloadable mobile applications, e-books and films;

(b) over-the-top services including streaming television shows, films, music, podcasts and any form of digital content;

(c) sale of, licensing of, or any other form of monetising data collected about Kenyan users which has been generated from the users' activities on a digital marketplace;

(d) provision of a digital marketplace;

(e) subscription-based media including news, magazines and journals;

(f) electronic data management including website hosting, online data warehousing, file-sharing and cloud storage services;

(g) electronic booking or electronic ticketing services including the online sale of tickets;

(h) provision of search engine and automated held desk services including supply of customised search engine services;

(i) online distance training through pre-recorded media or e-learning including online courses and training; and

(j) any other service provided through a digital marketplace.

(2) Digital service tax shall not apply to income taxed under section 9 (2) or section 35 of the Act.

(3) The following services shall not be digital services for the purposes of these Regulations—

(a) online services which facilitate payments, lending or trading of financial instruments, commodities or foreign exchange carried out by—

(i) a financial institution specified under the Fourth Schedule to the Act; or

(ii) a financial service provider authorised or approved by the Central Bank of Kenya; and

(b) online services provided by Government institutions.

4. Application of digital service tax

(1) Digital service tax shall apply to the income of a resident or non-resident person derived from or accrued in Kenya from the provision of services through a digital marketplace.

(2) Digital service tax paid by a resident or non-resident person with a permanent establishment in Kenya shall be offset against the tax payable by that person for that year of income.

(3) Digital service tax paid by a non-resident person without a permanent establishment in Kenya shall be a final tax.

5. User location

(1) A person shall be subject to digital service tax if that person provides or facilitates the provision of a digital service to a user who is located in Kenya.

(2) A user of a digital service shall be deemed to be located in Kenya if—

(a) the user receives the digital service from a terminal located in Kenya, where terminal includes a computer, tablet and mobile phone;

(b) the payment for the digital service is made using a debit or credit facility provided by a financial institution or company located in Kenya;

(c) the digital service is acquired through an internet protocol address registered in Kenya or an international mobile phone country code assigned to Kenya; or

(d) the user has a business, residential or billing address in Kenya.

6. Gross transaction value

(1) Digital service tax shall be imposed on the gross transaction value of the digital service which shall be—

(a) in the case of the provision of digital services, the payment received as consideration for the services; and

(b) in the case of a digital marketplace, the commission or fee paid to the digital marketplace provider for the use of the platform.

(2) The gross transaction value of a digital service shall not include the value added tax charged for the service.

7. Registration

(1) A non-resident person without a permanent establishment in Kenya who provides a digital service to a user in Kenya may register under the simplified tax registration framework specified in regulation 9.

(2) A resident person, or a non-resident person with a permanent establishment in Kenya, who provides a digital service in Kenya shall be required to apply to the Commissioner for digital service tax registration in the prescribed form.

8. Appointment of a tax representative (No. 29 of 2015.)

A non-resident person without a permanent establishment in Kenya who elects not to register in accordance with regulation 9 shall appoint a tax representative in accordance with section 15A of the Tax Procedures Act, 2015.

9. Simplified tax registration

(1) A person who applies for registration under the simplified tax registration framework shall do so through an online registration form prescribed by the Commissioner.

(2) The application under paragraph (1) shall include the following information—
  (a) the name of the applicant's business including its trading name;
  (b) the name of the contact person responsible for tax matters;
  (c) the postal and registered address of the business and its contact person;
  (d) the telephone number of the contact person;
  (e) the electronic address of the contact person;
  (f) the websites or uniform resource locator of the applicant through which business is conducted;
  (g) the national tax identification number issued to the applicant in the country of residence;
  (h) the certificate of incorporation issued to the applicant's business; and
  (i) any other information that the Commissioner may require.

(3) The applicant may be required to submit to the Commissioner any documents necessary to substantiate the information provided in the application under paragraph (2).

(4) Upon registration, the Commissioner shall issue the applicant with a Personal Identification Number for the purpose of filing returns and payment of the digital service tax.

(5) A person registered under these Regulations who ceases to provide digital services in Kenya shall apply to the Commissioner for deregistration in the prescribed form.

10. Accounting and payment

(1) Digital service tax shall be paid by—
  (a) the digital service provider or digital marketplace provider; or

(b) the tax representative appointed under regulation 8.

(2) A person liable to pay digital service tax under paragraph (1) shall submit a return in the prescribed form and remit the tax due by the twentieth day of the month following the end of the month that the digital service was offered.

11. Amendment of returns (No. 29 of 2015.)

(1) Any amendment to a return submitted under these Regulations shall be in accordance with section 31 of the Tax Procedures Act, 2015.

(2) Where an amendment under paragraph (1) results in the overpayment of tax—

(a) in the case of a non-resident person without a permanent establishment in Kenya, the amount overpaid shall be retained as a credit and offset against the digital service tax payable in the subsequent tax period; and

(b) in the case of a resident person, or a non-resident person with a permanent establishment in Kenya, the amount overpaid shall be refunded in accordance with section 47 of the Tax Procedures Act, 2015.

12. Records (No. 29 of 2015.)

A person liable to digital service tax shall keep records in accordance with section 23 of the Tax Procedures Act, 2015.

13. Penalties (No. 29 of 2015.)

A person who fails to comply with the provisions of these Regulations shall be liable to the relevant penalties prescribed under the Tax Procedures Act, 2015.

Made on the 23rd November, 2020.

UKUR YATANI,
Cabinet Secretary for National Treasury and Planning.

GROUP FOUR
SPECIAL ECONOMIC ZONES
LAWS AND REGULATIONS

TITLE SEVEN
THE SPECIAL ECONOMIC ZONES ACT
(NO. 16 OF 2015)

Revised Edition 2023 [2015]

Published by the National Council for Law Reporting

with the Authority of the Attorney-General

www.kenyalaw.org

NO. 16 OF 2015
SPECIAL ECONOMIC ZONES ACT

[*Date of assent: 11th September, 2015.*]
[*Date of commencement: 15th December, 2015.*]

AN ACT of Parliament to provide for the establishment of special economic zones; the promotion and facilitation of global and local investors; the development and management of enabling environment for such investments, and for connected purposes

[Act No. 16 of 2015, Act No. 38 of 2016, Act No. 4 of 2023.]

PART I
PRELIMINARY

1. Short title and commencement

This Act may be cited as the Special Economic Zones Act, 2015 and shall come into operation upon the expiry of ninety days from the date of its publication.

2. Interpretation

In this Act, unless the context otherwise requires—

"**agricultural zone**" means a special economic zone declared as such under section 4 to facilitate the agricultural sector, its services and associated activities;

"**Authority**" means the Special Economic Zones Authority established under section 10;

"**Board**" means the Board of Directors of the Authority established under section 12;

"**business processing outsourcing**" means the provision of outsourcing services to business for specific business functions or processes such as back office support services in human resources, finance, accounting and procurement amongst other services;

"**business service park**" means a special economic zone declared as such under section 4 to facilitate the provision of services including but not limited to regional headquarters, business processing outsourcing centres, call centres, shared service centres, management consulting and advisory services and other associated services;

"**business service permit**" means an administrative grant of authority to operate services within a special economic zone for which no benefits accruing under this Act are granted;

"**Cabinet Secretary**" means the Cabinet Secretary for the time being responsible for matters relating to industrialization;

"**company**" has the meaning assigned to it by section 2 of the Companies Act (Cap. 486.) and includes a company incorporated outside Kenya but registered in Kenya under that Act;

"**customs control**" means the measures applied to ensure compliance with the laws and regulations under the East African Community Customs Management Act, 2004;

"**customs-controlled area**" means the special economic zone where certain enterprises carry out customs controlled operations;

"**customs territory**" means the geographical area of the Republic of Uganda, the Republic of Kenya and the United Republic of Tanzania and any other country granted membership of the East African Community under Article 3 of the Treaty for the Establishment of the East African Community, but does not include a special economic zone;

"**duty**" means duty as defined under the East African Community Customs Management Act;

"**export**" means to take or cause to be taken out of the customs territory or into a special economic zone;

"**export duties**" means customs duties and other charges having an effect equivalent to customs duties payable on the exportation of goods;

"**Freeport zone**" means a designated area placed at the disposal of the special economic zone or freeport authority where goods introduced into the designated area are generally regarded, in so far as import duties are concerned, as being outside the customs territory;

"**free trade zone**" means a special economic zone customs-controlled area where goods are off-loaded for transhipment, storage and may include bulk breaking, repacking, sorting, mixing, trading or other forms of handling excluding manufacturing and processing;

"**Fund**" means the General Fund established under section 21;

"**goods**" include all kinds of wares, articles, merchandise, animals, matter, baggage, stores, materials, currency and includes postal items other than personal correspondence and where any such goods are sold under this Act, the proceeds of such sale;

"**import**" means to bring or cause to be brought into the customs territory or a special economic zone;

"**import duties**" means any customs duties and other charges of equivalent effect levied on imported goods;

"**industrial park**" means a special economic zone declared as such under section 4 with integrated infrastructure to facilitate the needs of manufacturing and processing industries;

"**information communication technology park**" means a special economic zone declared as such under section 4 to facilitate the information communication technology sector, its services and associated activities;

"**infrastructure**" means roads, power, water, drainage, telecommunication, sanitation or water treatment plants, networks, buildings or other facilities, necessary for the development and operations of special economic zones and appropriate to their particular sector or cluster focus;

"**Kenya Revenue Authority**" means the Authority established by section 3 of the Kenya

Revenue Authority Act (Cap. 469);

"**licence**" means a licence issued under this Act;

"**livestock zone**" means a special economic zone declared as such under section 4, in which the following activities are carried out: livestock marshalling and inspection; livestock feeding or fattening, abattoir and refrigeration; deboning; value addition; manufacture of veterinary products, and other related activities;

"**manufacture**" means to make, produce, fabricate, assemble, process or bring into existence by manual, mechanical, chemical or biochemical methods into a new product having a distinctive name, character or use and includes processes such as refrigeration, cutting, polishing, blending, beneficiation, re-making and re-engineering;

"**negative list**" means a list of activities not allowed to be undertaken by special economic zone enterprises under the laws of Kenya and those of the East African Community;

"**proper officer**" means any officer whose right or duty is to perform or require the performance of the acts referred to in the East African Community Customs Management Act, 2004;

"**regional headquarters**" means a special economic zone enterprise engaged in headquarters management activities to oversee, manage and control their local, regional and global operations by providing managerial, supervisory, shared services centre and other support services to affiliate companies;

"**science and technology park**" means a special economic zone declared as such under section 4 to facilitate the science and technology sector, its services and its associated activities;

"**services**" means tradable services which are covered under the General Agreement on Trade in Services annexed as 1B to the Agreement establishing the World Trade Organisation concluded at Marrakesh on the 15th day of April, 1994 and any successor agreements or amendments thereto;

"**special economic zone**" means a zone declared as such under section 4;

"**special economic zone enterprise**" means a corporate body which has been licensed under this Act;

"**special economic zone developer**" means a corporate body which is engaged in or plans on developing, and which may or may not also operate or plan to operate, a special economic zone under this Act;

"**special economic zones operator**" means a corporate body engaged in the management of a special economic zone and designated as such under the provisions of this Act; and

"**tourist and recreation centre**" means a special economic zone declared as such under section 4 to facilitate tourism and recreation sector, its services and associated activities.

3. Object and purpose of Act

The object and purpose of this Act is to provide for—

(a) an enabling environment for the development of all aspects of special economic zones

including—
- (i) development of integrated infrastructure facilities;
- (ii) creation of incentives for economic and business activities in areas designated as special economic zones;
- (iii) removal of impediments to economic or business activities that generate profit for enterprises in areas designated as special economic zones; and

(b) the regulation and administration of activities within the special economic zones with due regard to the principles of openness, competitiveness and transparency.

PART II
THE SPECIAL ECONOMIC ZONES

4. Declaration of special economic zones

(1) The Cabinet Secretary shall, on the recommendation of the Authority, and in consultation with the Cabinet Secretary responsible for matters relating to finance declare, by notice in the *Gazette*, any area as a Special Economic Zone as set out in the First Schedule.

(2) A declaration of a special economic zone under subsection (1) shall—
- (a) define the limits of the zone; and
- (b) remain in force until revoked by an order in the *Gazette* by the Cabinet Secretary and on the recommendation of the Authority.

(3) Where upon receipt of a recommendation under subsection (1), the Cabinet Secretary considers that gazettement of a special economic zone would infringe upon the public interest, the Cabinet Secretary may refer the recommendation back to the Authority to ensure the protection of that public interest.

(4) A special economic zone shall be a designated geographical area which may include both customs controlled area and non-customs controlled area where business enabling policies, integrated land uses and sector-appropriate on-site and off-site infrastructure and utilities shall be provided, or which has the potential to be developed, whether on a public, private or public-private partnership basis, where development of zone infrastructure and goods introduced in customs-controlled area are exempted from customs duties in accordance with customs laws.

(5) Any public land declared as a special economic zone shall not be alienated for private use except to special economic zone developers, operators or enterprises or other bodies established within a special economic zone.

(6) An area declared as a special economic zone under this section may be designated as a single sector or multiple sector special economic zone, and may include, but not limited to—
- (a) free trade zones;
- (b) industrial parks;

(c) free ports;
(d) information communication technology parks;
(e) science and technology parks;
(f) agricultural zones;
(g) tourist and recreational zones;
(h) business service parks;
(i) livestock zones;
(j) convention and conference facilities.

[Act No. 38 of 2016, s. 66, Act No. 4 of 2023, s. 100.]

5. Criteria for designating special economic zones

The Authority shall, in designating and determining the special economic zone project proposals that qualify for licensing, take into account the following considerations as may be appropriate—

(a) nature of the proposed project;
(b) intended size and perimeter of the proposed special economic zone;
(c) availability of land and unencumbered land titles;
(d) geographical location and topography;
(e) proximity to resources, population centres and infrastructure;
(f) infrastructure and other utility requirements from national and county governments including water, power, sewage, telecommunication, solid waste and waste water management;
(g) provision of medical, recreational, security fire safety, customs, and administrative facilities;
(h) impact on off-site infrastructure, utilities and services;
(i) approvals of land uses and zoning requirements to facilitate the special economic zones;
(j) environmental standards and requirements; and
(k) any other criteria as may be prescribed in the regulations.

6. Goods to be considered as exported and imported into Kenya

Unless otherwise provided under this Act, or any other written law—

(a) goods which are taken out from any part of the customs territory and brought into the special economic zone or services provided from part of the customs territory to a special economic zone shall be deemed to have been exported from Kenya; and
(b) goods which are brought out of a special economic zone and taken into any part of the customs territory for use therein or services provided from a special economic zone to any part of the customs territory shall be deemed to be imported into the customs territory.

Provided that —

(i) goods whose content originates from the customs territory shall be exempt from payment of import duties;

  (ii) goods whose content partially originates from the customs territory shall pay import duties on the non-originating component subject to the customs procedures.

[Act No. 4 of 2023, s.101.]

7. Goods and services within a special economic zone

Subject to section 6—

(a) goods and services within a special economic zone, which shall constitute a customs controlled area, shall not be taken out of the zone except—

  (i) for export;

  (ii) for entry into the customs territory, subject to the regulations and procedures on customs;

  (iii) for removal to any other customs controlled area with the approval of the proper officers, and subject to any conditions as may be imposed; or

  (iv) for repair and maintenance or processing or conversion with prior approval of the proper officer and subject to any conditions as may be imposed;

(b) where goods are manufactured outside Kenya, such goods shall be clearly labelled as products of the country where such goods were manufactured;

(c) services provided by a special economic zone enterprise may be provided to—

  (i) persons outside Kenya;

  (ii) other special economic zone enterprises in furtherance of the export activities of such enterprises subject to approval of the Authority; or

  (iii) persons in the customs territory subject to approval of the Authority.

8. Removal of goods from a special economic zone

(1) Subject to this Act as well as applicable customs laws of the East African Community, goods within a special economic zone may be—

(a) stored, sold, exhibited, broken up, repackaged, assembled, distributed, sorted, graded, cleaned, mixed, or otherwise manipulated or manufactured in accordance with the provisions of this Act; or

(b) destroyed under the supervision of the proper officer; or

(c) removed, under the supervision of the proper officer from the special economic zone for export or sent into another special economic zone or bonded factory, either in its original package or otherwise.

(2) Subject to this Act and the customs laws of the East African Community, goods of any description which would be used in the activities of a licensed special economic zone enterprise may be brought into a special economic zone.

(3) A person who contravenes this section commits an offence and is liable to a fine not exceeding twenty million shillings or imprisonment for a term not exceeding three years or both and the goods shall be forfeited under the East African Community Customs Management Act.

(4) The special economic zone enterprise shall also operate in conformity with the specific regulations issued under the relevant provisions of the East African Community Customs Management Act.

9. Receipts and payments of special economic zone enterprises

Unless otherwise provided under this Act or any other applicable law, payments and receipt of funds by a special economic zone enterprise shall be subject to the provisions of the Central Bank of Kenya Act (Cap. 491) and the Banking Act (Cap. 488).

PART III
THE SPECIAL ECONOMIC ZONES AUTHORITY

10. Establishment of the Authority

(1) There is established a body to be known as the Special Economic Zones Authority.

(2) The Authority shall be a body corporate, with perpetual succession and a common seal, and shall, in its corporate name, be capable of—

   (a) suing and being sued;
   (b) purchasing or otherwise acquiring, holding, charging and disposing of movable and immovable property in and out of Kenya;
   (c) entering into contracts;
   (d) borrowing or receiving money including having its own Fund; and
   (e) doing or causing to be done or performing all such things or acts for the proper performance of its functions under this Act, as may be lawfully done or performed by a corporate body.

11. Functions of the Authority

The functions of the Authority shall be to—

   (a) make recommendations to the Cabinet Secretary on all aspects of designation, approval, establishment, operation and regulation of special economic zones;
   (b) implement the policies and programmes of the Government with regard to special economic zones;
   (c) identify, map and, where necessary, procure or avail to developers and operators the areas of land to be, or which have been, designated as special economic zones;
   (d) determine investment criteria including investment threshold;
   (e) undertake or approve the development, operation or maintenance, as well as finance, appropriate infrastructure up to the perimeter of, or within, select special economic zones, as and when deemed necessary;
   (f) review applications and grant licences to special economic zone developers, operators and enterprises;
   (g) promote and market special economic zones to potential special economic zone developers, operators, or other investors;

(h) administer a "one-stop" centre through which special economic zone enterprises can channel all their applications for permits, approvals, licences and facilities not handled directly by the Authority, coordinating with such other Government or private entities as may be necessary through agreements with the entities or procedures defined in implementing regulations or such other prescribed procedures;

(i) exclusively perform under time-bound conditions as may be prescribed, all administrative business regulations and services functions in relation to the designated special economic zones;

(j) maintain current data on the performances of the programme in each individual special economic zone and enterprise;

(k) establish and enhance inter-agency collaboration among relevant State agencies to ensure compliance with all applicable laws, procedures and other applicable requirements;

(l) recommend to the Cabinet Secretary a negative list of activities that are prohibited in the special economic zones including an additional set of, restricted activities under the regulations made thereunder;

(m) recommend to the Cabinet Secretary to suspend or cancel the licences of a special economic zone enterprise or a special economic zone developer which is in the violation of this Act, the East African Community Customs Management Act or the Value Added Tax Act;

(n) regulate the access of non-licensed service providers from the customs territory as may be required in order to service individual enterprises;

(o) regulate, implement, monitor and supervise all aspects of the special economic zones regime set forth in this Act;

(p) maintain a register of enterprises and residents domiciled in the special economic zones; and

(q) any other functions as may be directed by the Board.

12. Board of Directors

(1) The Authority shall be administered by a Board of Directors which shall consist of—

(a) a Chairperson to be appointed by the President;

(b) the Principal Secretary of the ministry for the time being responsible for matters relating to industrialization and trade or his designated alternate;

(c) the Principal Secretary to the treasury or his designated alternate;

(d) the Chairperson of the National Land Commission or his designated alternate;

(e) the Commissioner General of the Kenya Revenue Authority or his designated alternate;

(f) four other directors appointed by the Cabinet Secretary, from the private sector or any other public institution being persons who have distinguished service, relevant experience, and expertise.

(g) the Chief Executive Officer who shall be an *ex officio* member.

(2) No person shall be appointed under subsection (1) (f) unless such person satisfies the requirements of Chapter Six of the Constitution of Kenya.

13. Conduct of business and affairs of the Board

(1) The conduct and regulation of the business and affairs of the Board shall be as set out in the Second Schedule.

(2) Except as provided in the Second Schedule, the Board may regulate its own procedure.

14. Powers of the Board

(1) The Board shall have all powers necessary for the proper performance of the functions of the Authority under this Act.

(2) Without prejudice to the generality of the foregoing, the Board shall have power to—

(a) control, supervise and administer the assets of the Authority in such manner as best promotes the purpose for which the Authority is established;

(b) determine the provisions to be made for capital and recurrent expenditure and for the reserves of the Authority;

(c) receive any grants, gifts, donations or endowments and make legitimate disbursements therefrom;

(d) open such banking accounts for the funds of the Authority as may be necessary;

(e) invest any of the funds of the Authority not immediately required for its purposes in the manner provided in section 25;

(f) perform all such other acts or undertake any activity as may be incidental or conducive to the attainment or fulfilment of any of the functions of the Authority under this Act.

15. Remuneration of directors

The Authority shall pay its directors such remuneration, fees or allowances as it may determine upon the advice of the Cabinet Secretary.

16. Chief Executive Officer

(1) There shall be a Chief Executive Officer of the Authority who shall be appointed competitively by the Board.

(2) No person shall be appointed under this section unless such person—

(a) possesses a relevant degree from a recognized institution and has at least ten years working experience in matters relating to industry, trade, law, finance, economics, management, entrepreneurship or engineering;

(b) satisfies the requirements of Chapter Six of the Constitution.

(3) The Chief Executive Officer shall—

(a) be the secretary to the Board; and

(b) subject to the directions of the Board, be responsible for the day to day management of the affairs and staff of the Board.

17. Staff of the Authority

The Authority may appoint such officers and other staff as are necessary for the proper discharge of its functions under this Act, whether directly or through one-stop shops, upon such terms and conditions of service as the Board may determine and on the advice of the Salaries and Remuneration Commission.

18. Delegation by the Authority

The Board may, by resolution either generally or any particular case, delegate to any committee or to any member, officer, employee or agent of the Board, the exercise of any of the powers or the performance of any of the functions or duties of the Authority under this Act or under any other written law.

19. Protection from personal liability

(1) The staff of the Authority shall not be personally liable for an act which is done or purported to be done in good faith on the direction of the Authority or the Board in the performance or intended performance of any duty or in the exercise of any power under this Act.

(2) Any expenses incurred by a person referred to in subsection (1) in any suit or prosecution brought against him before any court in respect of any act which is done or purported to be done by him under this Act on the direction of the Board shall, if the court holds that that act was done in good faith be paid out of the Fund, unless the expenses are recovered by him in that suit or prosecution.

(3) The provisions of this section shall not relieve the Authority of the liability in tort or contract, to pay compensation or damages to any person for any injury to him, his property or any of his interests caused by the exercise of any power conferred by this Act, or any other written law.

20. Common seal

(1) The common seal of the Authority shall be kept in such custody as the Board may direct and shall not be used except on the order of the Board.

(2) The affixing of the common seal of the Authority shall be authenticated by the signature of the Chairperson and the Chief Executive Officer and any document not required by law to be made under seal and all decisions of the Board may be authenticated by the signatures of both the Chairperson and the Chief Executive Officer.

(3) Notwithstanding the provisions of subparagraph (2), the Board shall, in the absence of either the Chairperson or the Chief Executive Officer in a particular matter, nominate one member to authenticate the seal on behalf of either the Chairperson or the Chief Executive Officer.

(4) The common seal of the Authority when affixed to a document and duly authenticated shall be judicially noticed and unless the contrary is proved, any necessary order or authorization by the Board under this section shall be presumed to have been duly given.

PART IV
FINANCIAL PROVISIONS

21. Establishment of the Fund

(1) There is established a Fund of the Authority to be known as the General Fund which shall vest in the Authority and shall be administered by the Board.

(2) There shall be paid into the Fund—
- (a) monies provided by Parliament for that purpose, towards expenditure incurred by the Authority in the exercise of its powers or the performance of its functions under this Act;
- (b) such fees, monies or assets as may accrue to or vest in the Authority in the course of the exercise of its powers or the performance of its functions under this Act or under any written law; and
- (c) all monies from any other source provided for or donated or lent to the Authority.

(3) There shall be paid out of the funds of the Authority all such sums of money required to defray the expenditure incurred by the Authority in the exercise, discharge and performance of its objectives, functions and duties under this Act.

(4) The balance of the funds of the Authority at the end of the financial year shall be utilized as directed by the National Treasury.

22. Financial year

The financial year of the Authority shall be the period of twelve months ending on the thirtieth of June in each year.

23. Annual estimates

(1) At least three months before the commencement of each financial year, the Board shall cause to be prepared estimates of the revenue and expenditure of the Authority for that year.

(2) The annual estimates shall make provisions for all the estimated expenditure of the Authority for the financial year and in particular the estimates shall provide for—
- (a) the payment of allowances and the charges in respect of the directors and the salaries, allowances and other charges in respect of staff of the Authority;
- (b) the payment of pensions, gratuities and other charges in respect of staff of the Authority;
- (c) the proper maintenance of the buildings and grounds of the Authority;
- (d) the maintenance, repair and replacement of the equipment and other property of the Authority;
- (e) the creation of such reserve funds to meet future or contingent liabilities in respect of retirement benefits, insurance or replacement of buildings or equipment, or in respect of such other matters as the Board may deem appropriate;

(f) the funding of promotion and marketing of special economic zones;

(g) the funding of training, research and development activities of the Authority; and

(h) any other expenditure incurred by the Authority in the exercise, discharge, and performance of its functions this Act.

(3) The annual estimates shall be approved by the Board before the commencement of the financial year to which they relate and shall be submitted to the Cabinet Secretary for approval and after the Cabinet Secretary's approval, the Board shall not vary the annual estimates of the Authority without the consent of the Cabinet Secretary.

24. Accounts and audit

(1) The Board shall cause to be kept all proper books and records of income, assets of the Authority.

(2) Within a period of three months from the end of each financial year, the Board shall submit to the Auditor-General or to an auditor appointed under this section the account of the Authority together with—

(a) a statement of the income and expenditure of the authority during that year; and

(b) a balance sheet of the Authority on the last day of that year.

Provided that —

(i) goods whose content originates from the customs territory shall be exempt from payment of import duties; and

(ii) goods whose content partially originates from the customs territory shall pay import duties on the non-originating component subject to customs procedures.

(3) The accounts of the Authority shall be audited and reported upon in accordance with the Public Audit Act, 2003 (No. 12 of 2003).

(4) The Authority shall within four months of the closure of the financial year, submit to the Cabinet Secretary, a report on the operations of the Authority during that year.

[Act No. 4 of 2023, s. 102.]

25. Investment of funds

The Authority may invest its funds in government securities, in which for the time being trustees may by law invest in trust funds, or in any other securities which the National Treasury may, from time to time, approve for that purpose.

PART V
REGULATORY PROVISIONS

26. Licence to operate in special economic zone

A person shall not—

(a) carry on business as a special economic zone developer or operator or enterprise;

(b) hold himself out as providing or maintaining activities or facilities within a special economic zone,

except under and in accordance with a licence issued under this Act.

27. Application and issue of licence

(1) A person who, intends to carry on business as a special economic zone developer, operator or enterprise, shall apply in the prescribed form to the Authority for an appropriate licence or for a renewal of the licence.

(2) On receiving an application for licence or for a renewal of a licence, the Authority, may on the recommendation of the Commissioner of Customs and upon payment of the prescribed fee, issue to the applicant the appropriate licence or renew the licence.

(3) In evaluating applications for special economic zone developer, operator and enterprise licences, the Authority shall assess the specific engineering and financial plans, financial viability, and environmental and social impact of the applicant's proposed special economic zone project, as appropriate.

(4) The Authority shall expeditiously render its decisions on licensing under this Act within one month from the date on which the duly completed application form is submitted together with relevant supporting documents.

(5) A licence issued under this section shall—
   (a) be in the prescribed form;
   (b) authorize the licensee to carry on business as a special economic zone developer, operator or enterprise;
   (c) be specific with regard to the activity to be carried out under the licence;
   (d) be valid for such period as the Authority may prescribe;
   (e) contain such other conditions as the Authority deems necessary.

(6) A licence issued under this section may—
   (a) be amended at any time on written notice to the holder by the authority, if in its opinion the amendment is necessary; or
   (b) be suspended or revoked by the Authority if the holder fails to comply with the conditions contained in the licence laid down in this Act or in any regulations made thereunder and where a licence is suspended or revoked, the holder shall take such steps as may be recommended by the Authority.

(7) The Cabinet Secretary shall—
   (a) publish in the Kenya *Gazette* all approved applications to establish a special economic zone; and
   (b) within one hundred and eighty days of the coming into force of this Act, publish regulations on the application, issuance, suspension, revocation and appeal process on licensing of special economic zones.

28. Qualifications of a special economic zone developer and operator

A special economic zone developer shall, in addition to such other criteria and requirements as may be prescribed—

   (a) be a company incorporated in Kenya, for the purpose of undertaking special economic zone activities;

(b) have the financial capacity, technical and managerial expertise, and associated track record of relevant development or operational projects, required for developing or operating the special economic zone; and

(c) own or lease land or premises within the special economic zone as stipulated under the Special Economic Zones (Land Use) Regulations to be enacted within one hundred and eighty days of the coming into force of this Act.

29. Special economic zone enterprises

(1) The benefits prescribed in Part VI of this Act shall not accrue to any enterprise unless it holds a valid licence issued by the Authority.

(2) The Authority shall grant a licence if the application meets the objectives of this Act, and if the proposed business enterprise—

(a) is incorporated in Kenya whether or not it is one hundred per cent foreign owned;

(b) proposes to engage in any activity or activities eligible to be undertaken by a special economic zone enterprise in the special economic zone;

(c) does not have a negative impact on the environment or engage in activities impinging on national security or presenting a health hazard; and

(d) conducts business in accordance with the laws for the time being in force save for any exemptions under this Act.

30. Register of licences

(1) The Authority shall keep in a form as it considers appropriate, a register of the holders of current licences issued under this Act, which shall include—

(a) the company name; and

(b) the physical address at which the company carries on its business.

(2) Where—

(a) the holder of the licence ceases to carry on the business to which the licence relates; or

(b) a change occurs in any particulars which are required to be entered in the register of licence holders with respect to the holder of a licence,

the holder shall within fourteen days of the occurrence of the event concerned give to the Authority particulars of the change in the prescribed form.

PART VI
RIGHTS AND OBLIGATIONS OF SPECIAL ECONOMIC ZONE ENTITIES

31. Activities permitted within a special economic zone

The Authority shall, subject to section 5, give notice to the Kenya Revenue Authority of every special economic zone, developer, operator or enterprise licensed under this Act specifying—

(a) the activities in respect of which the enterprise is licensed; and

(b) any conditions attached to the licence.

32. Facilities within a special economic zone

(1) Taking into account the general intent of the special economic zone developer licence, the Authority may require the special economic zone developer to provide and maintain in a special economic zone such facilities including adequate enclosure to separate a special economic zone from the customs territory, as it may consider necessary for the proper and efficient function of the zone.

(2) The Authority shall not issue an order for cessation of any activities or removal of any goods without first giving the concerned enterprise an opportunity of being heard.

(3) The proper officers in each special economic zone shall offer on-site inspection to the special economic zone for imports into, and exports out of, the special economic zone.

(4) The Authority shall be responsible for the monitoring and enforcement of all rules, within special economic zones.

33. Rights and obligations of an economic zone developer or operator

(1) A special economic zone developer shall have the right to—

(a) act or appoint a special economic zone operator to undertake management and administration of the special economic zone on its behalf subject to subsections (2), (3) and (4) of this section, section 28 (b) and such other licensing requirements as may be prescribed;

(b) lease, sub-lease or sell land or buildings to licensed special economic zone operators and, enterprises, and charge rent or fees for other services that may be provided;

(c) acquire, dispose or transfer special economic zone lands or other assets;

(d) develop, operate and service special economic zone lands and other assets in conformity with applicable law and its licence;

(e) provide utilities and other services in the special economic zone, in accordance with its licence, and to charge fees for such services;

(f) provide utilities and other services outside the special economic zone in conformity with applicable law;

(g) enjoy the benefits that may accrue under the provisions of this Act;

(h) enter into contracts with private third parties for the development, operation, and servicing of special economic zone lands and other assets, including on-site and off-site infrastructure;

(i) enter and freely participate in international financial markets, without any legal impediments or restrictions, to obtain funds, credits, guarantees and other financial resources; and

(j) advertise and promote the special economic zone for which it holds a licence to potential investors and service providers.

(2) A special economic zone developer shall, in such manner as may be prescribed—

(a) perform such physical development works or make such improvements to the special economic zone site and its facilities as may be required according to the plans approved by the Authority;

(b) provide adequate enclosures to segregate the zone area from the customs territory for the protection of revenue together with suitable provisions for the movement of persons, conveyances, vessels and goods entering or leaving the zone;

(c) provide or cause to be provided, adequate security on the site, as may be determined by the Authority in its licence;

(d) adopt and enforce such rules and regulations within the special economic zone that promote safe and efficient business operations;

(e) maintain adequate and proper accounts, and other records in relation to its activities, employment statistics, business and report on zone activities, performance and development to the Authority on a periodic basis or as required by the Authority; and

(f) register all leases with the Authority.

(3) The accounts and records required under paragraph (e) of subsection (2) shall be maintained in any of the official languages.

(4) A special economic zone developer or a special economic zone operator who fails to maintain adequate and proper accounts and other records as required by this section commits an offence and is liable to a fine not exceeding three hundred thousand shillings or to imprisonment for a term not exceeding six months or both.

34. Rights of special economic zone enterprises

A licensed special economic zone enterprise shall enjoy—

(a) the full protection of its property rights against all risks of nationalization or expropriation;

(b) the right to fully repatriate all capital and profits, without any foreign exchange impediments;

(c) the right of protection of industrial and intellectual property rights, in particular patents, copyrights, business names, industrial designs, technical processes and trademarks;

(d) the right to admit into the special economic zone for which it is licensed, to export and sell in the customs territory all classes or kinds of goods and services in accordance with the custom laws of the East African Community;

(e) the right to transact and carry on business with a non-special economic zones enterprise;

(f) the right to transact and carry on business with non-special economic zone enterprises;

(g) the right to contract with any other enterprise, to buy, sell, lease, sub-let or otherwise exercise, manage, or transfer land or buildings within a special economic zone, subject to the said enterprise's own property rights;

(h) the right to contract with any other enterprise, to buy, sell, lease, sub-let or otherwise exercise, manage or transfer land or buildings within a special economic zone subject to the provisions of the East African Community Customs Management Act and applicable regulations in respect of the activities of such enterprise within the special economic zone;

(i) the right to determine the prices of any of its goods or services sold inside or outside the special economic zone for which it is licensed;

(j) the benefits in the national context of an open, free, competitive investment environment including the right to freely engage with the special economic zone for which it is licensed in any business, trade, manufacturing or service activity not prohibited by this Act; and

(k) all other rights and benefits granted to licensed special economic zones enterprises under this Act.

35. Benefits accruing to special economic zone enterprises, developers and operators

(1) All licensed special economic zone enterprises, developers and operators shall be granted tax incentives as specified in the respective tax laws.

(2) Subject to subsection (1), the licensed special economic zone enterprises, developers and operators shall be granted the following exemptions from—

(a) stamp duty on the execution of any instrument relating to the business activities of special economic zone enterprises, developers and operators;

(b) the provisions of the Foreign Investments and Protection Act (Cap. 518) relating to certificate for approved enterprise;

(c) the provisions of the Statistics Act, 2006 (No. 4 of 2006);

(d) the payment of advertisement fees and business service permit fees levied by the respective County Governments' finance Acts;

(e) general liquor licence and hotel liquor licence under the Alcoholic Drinks Control Act, 2010 (No. 4 of 2010);

(f) manufacturing licence under the Tea Act (Cap. 343);

(g) licence to trade in unwrought precious metals under the Trading in Unwrought Precious Metals Act (Cap. 309);

(h) filming licence under the Films and Stages Plays Act (Cap. 222);

(i) rent or tenancy controls under the Landlord and Tenant (Shops, Hotels and Catering establishments) Act (Cap. 301); and

(j) any other exemption as may be granted under this Act in consultation with the Cabinet Secretary for that matter, by notice in the *Gazette*.

(3) The licensed special economic zone enterprises, developers and operators shall be entitled to work permits of up to twenty per cent of their full-time employees;

(4) Despite subsection (3), on the recommendation of the Authority, additional work permits may be obtained for specialised sectors.

[Act No. 38 of 2016, s. 67.]

PART VII
MISCELLANEOUS PROVISIONS

36. Powers of the Cabinet Secretary

The Cabinet Secretary may from time to time direct the Authority to furnish in such form as may be prescribed returns, accounts and any other information with respect to the work and activities of the Authority.

37. Dispute resolution

(1) Where a dispute arises between a special economic zone developer, operator or enterprise and the Authority or the Government in respect of the special economic zone entity, all efforts shall be made to settle the dispute through negotiations and mutual agreement for an amicable settlement within thirty days.

(2) Where a dispute under subsection (1) is not settled, the parties may submit it to arbitration in accordance with any of the following methods as may be mutually agreed by the parties—

    (a) in accordance with the rules of procedure set forth for arbitration by the United Nations Commission on International Trade Law, the International Chamber of Commerce in Paris or the International Center for Settlement of Investment Disputes Resolution; or

    (b) within the framework of any bilateral or multilateral agreement on investment protection to which the Government and the country of which the investor is a national are parties; or

    (c) in accordance with the Arbitration Act, 1995 (No. 4 of 1995).

(3) If the parties do not agree to the mechanisms of settlement of dispute under subsection 2 (a) and (b) within fourteen days, the Arbitration Act shall apply.

38. Exemption from Stamp duty

The Authority shall be exempt from payment of any stamp duty chargeable under the Stamp Duty Act (Cap. 480) for land transactions.

39. Regulations

(1) The Cabinet Secretary shall, upon the recommendation by the Authority, make regulations in respect of any matter required by this Act to be prescribed or in respect of which regulations are authorized to be made.

(2) Without prejudice to the generality of subsection (1), the regulations may—

    (a) determine criteria for the designation and gazetting of all special economic zones;

    (b) determine the application process, criteria, conditions, terms and procedures for designation of special economic zones and licensing of special economic zone developers, operators and enterprises;

    (c) determine the form of licences to be issued under this Act and the procedures from amendment and revocation of the licences;

(d) determine the general conditions of entry of persons into a special economic zone;

(e) require information from special economic zone developers, operators and enterprises;

(f) determine the rules pertaining to the establishment, functioning, operations and procedures for the special economic zones one-stop-shops;

(g) determine the investment rules for special economic zones;

(h) determine the land use rules for special economic zones, development and building controls as well as utility provisions and operations; and

(i) determine the fees to be levied under this Act.

40. Transition

A corporate body shall be deemed to be a special economic zone developer on the commencement of this Act if it has—

(a) been approved by the Cabinet Secretary to engage in the development or management of integrated infrastructure facilities on public, private or public-private partnership basis; and

(b) undertaken significant steps to commence development or management of the integrated infrastructure facilities.

FIRST SCHEDULE
[Section 4]
TYPES OF SPECIAL ECONOMIC ZONES

1. The Authority shall permit multiple sector or single sector Special Economic Zones including but not limited to the following—

(a) Free Trade Zones (FTZ)

(b) Industrial Parks

(c) Free Ports

(d) Information Communication and Technology Parks (ICT Parks)

(e) Science and Technology Parks

(f) Agricultural Zones

(g) Tourist and Recreational Zones

(h) Business Service Parks

SECOND SCHEDULE
[Section 13]
PROVISIONS AS TO THE CONDUCT OF BUSINESS AND AFFAIRS OF THE BOARD

1. Tenure of office

The Chairperson or a director other than an *ex-officio* member shall, subject to the provisions of this Schedule, hold office for a period of three years, on such terms and conditions as may be specified in the instrument of appointment, but may be eligible for re-appointment for one further term.

2. Vacation of office

A director other than an ex officio member may—
 (a) at any time resign from office by notice in writing to the Cabinet Secretary;
 (b) be removed from office by the Cabinet Secretary on recommendation of the Board if the director—
  (i) has been absent from three consecutive meetings of the Board without its permission;
  (ii) is convicted of a criminal offence that amounts to a felony under the laws of Kenya;
  (iii) is incapacitated by prolonged physical or mental illness for a period exceeding six months;
  (iv) contravenes Chapter Six of the Constitution; or
  (v) is otherwise unable or unfit to discharge his functions.

3. Meetings

(1) The Board shall meet not less than four times in every financial year and not more than four months shall elapse between the date of one meeting and the date of the next meeting.

(2) Notwithstanding subparagraph (1), the Chairperson may, and upon requisition in writing by at least three directors, convene a special meeting of the Board at any time for the transaction of the business of the Board.

(3) Unless three quarters of the total members of the Board otherwise agree, at least fourteen days' written notice of every meeting of the Board shall be given to every member of the Board.

(4) The quorum for the conduct of the business of the Board shall be half of the total directors including the Chairperson or the person presiding.

(5) The Chairperson shall preside at every meeting of the Board but the directors present shall elect one of their number to preside whenever the Chairperson is absent, and the person so elected shall have all the powers of the Chairperson with respect to that meeting and the business transacted.

(6) Unless a unanimous decision is reached, a decision on any matter before the Board shall be by a majority of the votes of the directors present and voting, and in case of an equality of votes, the Chairperson or the person presiding shall have a casting vote.

(7) Subject to subparagraph (4), no proceedings of the Board shall be invalid by reason only of a vacancy among the directors thereof.

(8) Subject to the provisions of this Schedule, the Board may determine its own procedure and the procedure for any committee of the Board and for the attendance

of other persons at its meetings and may make standing orders in respect thereof.

4. Committees of the Board

(1) The Board may establish such committees as it may deem appropriate to perform such functions and responsibilities as it may determine.

(2) The Board shall appoint the chairperson of a committee established under subparagraph (1) from amongst its directors.

(3) The Board may, where it deems appropriate, co-opt any person to attend the deliberations of any of its committees.

(4) All decisions by the committees appointed under subsection (1) shall be ratified by the Board.

5. Disclosure of interest

(1) A director who has an interest in any contract, or other matter present at a meeting shall at the meeting and as soon as reasonably practicable after the commencement, disclose the fact thereof and shall not take part in the consideration or discussion of, or vote on, any questions with respect to the contract or other matter, or be counted in the quorum of the meeting during consideration of the matter.

(2) A disclosure of interest made under subparagraph (1) shall be recorded in the minutes of the meeting at which it is made.

(3) A director who contravenes subparagraph (1) commits an offence and is liable to a fine not exceeding two hundred thousand shillings.

6. Contracts and instruments

Any contract or instrument which, if entered into or executed by a person not being a body corporate, would not require to be under seal may be entered into or executed on behalf of the Board by any person or executed on behalf of the Board by any person generally or specially authorized by the Board for that purpose.

GROUP FIVE
ANTI-CORRUPTION AND ECONOMIC CRIMES LAWS AND REGULATIONS

TITLE EIGHT
ANTI-CORRUPTION AND ECONOMIC CRIMES ACT
(NO. 3 OF 2003)

Revised Edition 2023 [2003]

Published by the National Council for Law Reporting
with the Authority of the Attorney-General

www.kenyalaw.org

NO. 3 OF 2003
ANTI-CORRUPTION AND ECONOMIC CRIMES ACT

[*Date of assent: 30th April, 2003.*]
[*Date of commencement: 2nd May, 2003.*]

An Act of Parliament to provide for the prevention, investigation and punishment of corruption, economic crime and related offences and for matters incidental thereto and connected therewith

[Act No. 3 of 2003, Act No. 7 of 2007, Act No. 10 of 2010, Act No. 22 of 2011, Act No. 12 of 2012, Act No. 18 of 2014, Act No. 47 of 2016, Act No. 10 of 2023.]

PART I
PRELIMINARY

1. Short title

This Act may be cited as the Anti-Corruption and Economic Crimes Act.

2. Interpretation

(1) In this Act, unless the context otherwise requires—

"**Advisory Board**" means the Kenya Anti-Corruption Advisory Board established under Part III;

"**Assistant Director**" means an Assistant Director of the Commission;

"**benefit**" means any gift, loan, fee, reward, appointment, service, favour, forbearance, promise or other consideration or advantage;

"**Commission**" means the Ethics and Anti-Corruption Commission established under section 3 of the Ethics and Anti-Corruption Commission Act, (No. 22 of 2011), pursuant to Article 79 of the Constitution;

"**corruption**" means—

    (a) an offence under any of the provisions of sections 39, 44, 46 and 47;

    (b) bribery;

    (c) fraud;

    (d) embezzlement or misappropriation of public funds;

    (e) abuse of office;

    (f) breach of trust; or

    (g) an offence involving dishonesty—

        (i) in connection with any tax, rate or impost levied under any Act; or

        (ii) under any written law relating to the elections of persons to public office;

"**Director**" *deleted by Act No. 18 of 2014, Sch.;*

"**economic crime**" means—
- (a) an offence under section 45; or
- (b) an offence involving dishonesty under any written law providing for the maintenance or protection of the public revenue;
- (c) an offence involving the laundering of the proceeds of corruption.

"**investigator**" means a person authorized by the Director under section 23 to conduct an investigation on behalf of the Commission;

"**Minister**" means the Minister responsible for integrity issues;

"**private body**" means any person or organisation not being a public body and includes a voluntary organisation, charitable organisation, company, partnership, club and any other body or organisation howsoever constituted;

"**public body**" means—
- (a) the Government, including Cabinet, or any department, service or undertaking of the Government;
- (b) the National Assembly or the Parliamentary Service;
- (c) a local authority;
- (d) any corporation, council, board, committee or other body which has power to act under and for the purposes of any written law relating to local government, public health or undertakings of public utility or otherwise to administer funds belonging to or granted by the Government or money raised by rates, taxes or charges in pursuance of any such law; or
- (e) a corporation, the whole or a controlling majority of the shares of which are owned by a person or entity that is a public body by virtue of any of the preceding paragraphs of this definition;

"**public officer**" means an officer, employee or member of a public body, including one that is unpaid, part-time or temporary;

"**Secretary**" means the Secretary of the Commission appointed under section 16 of the Ethics and Anti-Corruption Act, (No. 22 of 2011);

"**unexplained assets**" means assets of a person—
- (a) acquired at or around the time the person was reasonably suspected of corruption or economic crime; and
- (b) whose value is disproportionate to his known sources of income at or around that time and for which there is no satisfactory explanation.

(2) For the purposes of this Act, a person shall be deemed to be in possession of any record, property, information or other thing if the possession of it is under his control.

[Act No. 7 of 2007, Sch., Act No. 22 of 2011, s. 36, Act No. 18 of 2014, Sch., Act No. 10 of 2023, Sch.]

PART II
APPOINTMENT OF SPECIAL MAGISTRATES

3. Power to appoint special magistrates

(1) The Chief Justice may, by notification in the Kenya *Gazette*, appoint as many special Magistrates as may be necessary for such area or areas or for such case or group of cases as may be specified in the notification to try the following offences, namely—

(a) corruption, bribery and economic crimes and related offences; and

(b) any conspiracy to commit or any attempt to commit or any abetment of any of the offences specified in paragraph (a).

(2) A person shall not be qualified for appointment as a special Magistrate under this Act unless he is or has been a chief magistrate or a principal magistrate or an advocate of at least ten years standing.

[Act No. 7 of 2007, Sch., Act No. 47 of 2016, s. 26.]

4. Cases triable by special Magistrates

(1) Notwithstanding anything contained in the Criminal Procedure Code (Cap. 75), or in any other law for the time being in force, the offences specified in this Act shall be tried by special Magistrates only.

(2) Every offence specified in this Act shall be tried by the special Magistrate for the area within which it was committed, or, as the case may be, by the special Magistrate appointed for the case, or where there are more special Magistrates than one for such area, by one of them as may be specified in this behalf by the Chief Justice.

(3) When trying any case, a special Magistrate may also try any offence, other than an offence specified in this Act, with which the accused may, under the Criminal Procedure Code (Cap. 75), be charged at the same trial.

(4) Notwithstanding anything contained in the Criminal Procedure Code (Cap. 75), a special Magistrate shall, as far as practicable, hold the trial of an offence on a day-to-day basis until completion.

[Act No. 7 of 2007, Sch.]

5. Procedure and powers of special Magistrates

(1) A special Magistrate may, with a view to obtaining the evidence of any person supposed to have been directly or indirectly concerned in, or privy to, an offence, tender a pardon to such person on condition of his making a full and true disclosure of the whole circumstance within his knowledge relating to the offence and to every other person concerned, whether as principal or abettor, in the commission thereof and any pardon so tendered shall be a pardon for purposes of section 77 (6) of the Constitution.

(2) The provisions of the Criminal Procedure Code (Cap. 75) and the Magistrates' Courts Act (Cap. 10) shall, so far as they are not inconsistent with this Act, apply to

the proceedings before a special Magistrate; and for the purposes of the said provisions, the Court of the special Magistrate shall be deemed to be a court and the person conducting a prosecution before a special Magistrate shall be deemed to be a public prosecutor.

(3) A special Magistrate may pass upon any person convicted by him any sentence authorized by law for the punishment of the offence of which such person is convicted.

PART III
KENYA ANTI-CORRUPTION COMMISSION AND ADVISORY BOARD

A—Kenya Anti-Corruption Commission

6. *Repealed by Act No. 22 of 2011, s. 37.*
7. *Repealed by Act No. 22 of 2011, s. 37.*
8. *Repealed by Act No. 22 of 2011, s. 37.*
9. *Repealed by Act No. 22 of 2011, s. 37.*
10. *Repealed by Act No. 22 of 2011, s. 37.*
11. *Repealed by Act No. 22 of 2011, s. 37.*
12. *Repealed by Act No. 22 of 2011, s. 37.*
13. *Repealed by Act No. 22 of 2011, s. 37.*
14. *Repealed by Act No. 22 of 2011, s. 37.*
15. *Repealed by Act No. 22 of 2011, s. 37.*

B—Kenya Anti-Corruption Advisory Board

16. Establishment of Advisory Board

(1) The Kenya Anti-Corruption Advisory Board is hereby established.

(2) The Advisory Board shall be an unincorporated body consisting of—
  (a) one member nominated by each of the following—
    (i) the Law Society of Kenya;
    (ii) the Institute of Certified Public Accountants of Kenya;
    (iii) the International Federation of Women Lawyers (FIDA) Kenya Chapter;
    (iv) the Kenya Association of Manufacturers;
    (v) the joint forum of religious organizations described in subsection (3);
    (vi) the Federation of Kenya Employers;
    (vii) the Kenya Bankers Association;
    (viii) the Central Organisation of Trade Unions;
    (ix) the Association of Professional Societies in East Africa;
    (x) the Architectural Association of Kenya;
    (xi) the Institution of Engineers of Kenya; and
    (xii) the Kenya Medical Association; and
  (b) the Director.

(3) The joint forum of religious organizations referred to in subsection (2)(a)(v) shall

consist of representatives of—
- (a) the Supreme Council of Kenya Muslims;
- (b) the Kenya Episcopal Conference;
- (c) the National Council of Churches of Kenya;
- (d) the Evangelical Fellowship of Kenya; and
- (e) the Hindu Council of Kenya.

(4) The Second Schedule shall apply in respect of the Advisory Board and its members.

17. Functions of Advisory Board

(1) The principal function of the Advisory Board is to advise the Commission generally on the exercise of its powers and the performance of its functions under this Act.

(2) The Advisory Board shall have such other functions as may be conferred on it by or under this Act.

18. Independence of Advisory Board

In the performance of its functions, the Advisory Board shall not be subject to the direction or control of any other person or authority and shall be accountable only to Parliament.

19. *Deleted by Act No. 18 of 2014, Sch.*

20. Chairman and Vice-chairman

(1) The Advisory Board shall nominate one of its nominated members to be the Chairman of the Advisory Board and another of its nominated members to be its Vice-chairman.

(2) The members so nominated shall be appointed to their respective offices by the President.

(3) Subject to an earlier resignation or termination, the Chairman and Vice-chairman shall each hold office until his current term as a member of the Advisory Board expires.

21. Secretary to Advisory Board

The Secretary of the Commission appointed under section 16 of the Ethics and Anti-Corruption Act shall be the Secretary to the Advisory Board.

[Act No. 18 of 2014, Sch.]

22. Procedures of the Advisory Board

(1) The business and affairs of the Advisory Board shall be conducted in accordance with the Third Schedule.

(2) Except as provided in the Third Schedule, the Advisory Board may regulate its own procedure.

(3) Seven nominated members of the Advisory Board shall constitute a quorum for the transaction of any business of the Board.

(4) The Advisory Board may invite any person to attend any of its meetings and to participate in its deliberations, but such an invitee shall not have a vote in any decision of the Board.

PART IV
INVESTIGATIONS

23. Investigators

(1) The Secretary or a person authorized by the Secretary may conduct an investigation on behalf of the Commission.

(2) Except as otherwise provided by this Part, the powers conferred on the Commission by this Part may be exercised, for the purposes of an investigation, by the Secretary or an investigator.

(3) For the purposes of an investigation, the Secretary and an investigator shall have the powers, privileges and immunities of a police officer in addition to any other powers the Secretary or investigator has under this Part.

(4) The provisions of the Criminal Procedure Code (Cap. 75), the Evidence Act (Cap. 80), the Police Act (Cap. 84) and any other law conferring on the police the powers, privileges and immunities necessary for the detection, prevention and investigation of offences relating to corruption and economic crime shall, so far as they are not inconsistent with the provisions of this Act or any other law, apply to the Secretary and an investigator as if reference in those provisions to a police officer included reference to the Secretary or an investigator.

[Act No. 7 of 2007, Sch., Act No. 18 of 2014, Sch.]

24. Identification for investigators

(1) The Commission shall issue identification documentation to an investigator and such identification shall be evidence that the person to whom it is issued is an investigator.

(2) The identification documentation issued by the Commission shall be signed by the Secretary.

[Act No. 18 of 2014, Sch.]

25. Complaint not investigated

If the Commission receives a complaint concerning corrupt conduct on the part of any person and the Commission declines to investigate or discontinues its investigation before the investigation is concluded, the Commission shall inform the complainant in writing of its decision and of the reasons for its decision.

25A. Cessation of investigations

(1) The Commission may, in consultation with the Minister and the Attorney-General, tender an undertaking in a form prescribed by the Minister, not to institute or continue with investigations against any person suspected of an offence under this Act.

(2) Where the Commissioner intends to take action as specified in subsection (1), it shall by notice in the daily newspapers invite interested persons to approach it for such an undertaking within a period specified in the notice.

(3) An undertaking under this section shall only be made in cases where the suspected

person—
- (a) makes a full and true disclosure of all material facts relating to past corruption or economic crime;
- (b) through the Commission, pays or refunds to, or deposit with, the Commission for, all persons affected, any property or money irregularly obtained, with interest thereon at a rate prescribed by the Minister;
- (c) makes reparation to any person affected by his corrupt conduct; and
- (d) pays for all loss of public property occasioned by his corrupt conduct.

(4) The Commission shall publish its intention to make the undertaking by notice in at least two newspapers of national circulation—
- (a) stating the name of the proposed beneficiary of the undertaking;
- (b) stating the offence of which the person is suspected;
- (c) confirming that the person has fulfilled all the conditions set out in subsection (2); and
- (d) inviting any person with an objection to the proposed undertaking to forward their objections to the Commission within a period specified in the notice.

(5) An aggrieved person may object to the proposed undertaking on the grounds that—
- (a) the suspected person has not fully satisfied the conditions set out in subsection (2); or
- (b) he has any other evidence relevant under this section which may affect the Commission's decision regarding the undertaking.

(6) The Commission shall consider all objections submitted and shall take such action as may be appropriate in the circumstances.

(7) The Commission shall not make any undertaking in respect of corrupt conduct or economic crime which leads to circumstances which cause a danger to public safety, law and order.

(8) Any person in respect of whom the Commission makes an undertaking under this section shall be disqualified from holding public office.

[Act No. 7 of 2007, Sch.]

26. Statement of suspect's property

(1) If, in the course of investigation into any offence, the Secretary is satisfied that it could assist or expedite such investigation, the Secretary may, by notice in writing, require a person who, for reasons to be stated in such notice, is reasonably suspected of corruption or economic crime to furnish, within a reasonable time specified in the notice, a written statement in relation to any property specified by the Secretary and with regard to such specified property—
- (a) enumerating the suspected person's property and the times at which it was acquired; and
- (b) stating, in relation to any property that was acquired at or about the time of the suspected corruption or economic crime, whether the property was acquired by

purchase, gift, inheritance or in some other manner, and what consideration, if any, was given for the property.

(2) A person who neglects or fails to comply with a requirement under this section is guilty of an offence and is liable on conviction to a fine not exceeding three hundred thousand shillings or to imprisonment for a term not exceeding three years, or to both.

(3) The powers of the Commission under this section may be exercised only by the Secretary.

[Act No. 7 of 2007, Sch., Act No. 18 of 2014, Sch.]

27. Requirement to provide information, etc.

(1) The Commission may apply *ex parte* to the court for an order requiring an associate of a suspected person to provide, within a reasonable time specified in the order, a written statement stating, in relation to any property specified by the Secretary, whether the property was acquired by purchase, gift, inheritance or in some other manner, and what consideration, if any, was given for the property.

(2) In subsection (1), **"associate of a suspected person"** means a person, whether or not suspected of corruption or economic crime, who the investigator reasonably believes may have had dealings with a person suspected of corruption or economic crime.

(3) The Commission may by notice in writing require any person to provide, within a reasonable time specified in the notice, any information or documents in the person's possession that relate to a person suspected of corruption or economic crime.

(4) A person who neglects or fails to comply with a requirement under this section is guilty of an offence and is liable on conviction to a fine not exceeding three hundred thousand shillings or to imprisonment for a term not exceeding three years, or to both.

(5) No requirement under this section requires anything to be disclosed that is protected by the privilege of advocates including anything protected by section 134 or 137 of the Evidence Act (Cap. 80).

[Act No. 7 of 2007, Sch., Act No. 18 of 2014, Sch.]

28. Production of records and property

(1) The Commission may apply, with notice to affected parties, to the court for an order to—

(a) require a person, whether or not suspected of corruption or economic crime, to produce specified records in his possession that may be required for an investigation; and

(b) require that person or any other to provide explanations or information within his knowledge with respect to such records, whether the records were produced by the person or not.

(2) A requirement under subsection (1)(b) may include a requirement to attend personally to provide explanations and information.

(3) A requirement under subsection (1) may require a person to produce records or provide explanations and information on an ongoing basis over a period of time, not

exceeding six months.

(4) The six month limitation in subsection (3) does not prevent the Commission from making further requirements for further periods of time as long as the period of time in respect of which each requirement is made does not exceed six months.

(5) Without affecting the operation of section 30, the Commission may make copies of or take extracts from any record produced pursuant to a requirement under this section.

(6) A requirement under this section to produce a record stored in electronic form is a requirement—

(a) to reduce the record to hard copy and produce it; and

(b) if specifically required, to produce a copy of the record in electronic form.

(7) In this section, **"records"** includes books, returns, bank accounts or other accounts, reports, legal or business documents and correspondence other than correspondence of a strictly personal nature.

(8) The Commission may by notice in writing require a person to produce for inspection, within a reasonable time specified in the notice, any property in the person's possession, being property of a person reasonably suspected of corruption or economic crime.

(9) A person who neglects or fails to comply with a requirement under this section is guilty of an offence and is liable on conviction to a fine not exceeding three hundred thousand shillings or to imprisonment for a term not exceeding three years, or to both.

(10) No requirement under this section requires anything to be disclosed that is protected by the privilege of advocates including anything protected by section 134 or 137 of the Evidence Act (Cap. 80).

[Act No. 7 of 2007, Sch., Act No. 18 of 2014, Sch.]

29. Search of premises

(1) The Commission may, with a warrant, enter upon and search any premises for any record, property or other thing reasonably suspected to be in or on the premises and that has not been produced by a person pursuant to a requirement under the foregoing provisions of this Part.

(2) The power conferred by this section is in addition to, and does not limit or restrict, a power conferred by section 23(3) or by any other provision of this Part.

30. Admissibility of things produced or found

Where the notice is directed at a person under investigation or a person who has been charged with an offence of corruption or an economic crime, any statement, record or information, given pursuant to such notice, shall not be given in evidence against such person in any criminal proceedings except where such person is charged with knowingly or recklessly giving false information.

[Act No. 7 of 2007, Sch.]

31. Surrender of travel documents

(1) On the *ex parte* application of the Commission, a court may issue an order requiring a person to surrender his travel documents to the Commission if—

(a) the person is reasonably suspected of corruption or economic crime; and

(b) the corruption or economic crime concerned is being investigated.

(2) If a person surrenders his travel documents pursuant to an order under subsection (1), the Commission—

(a) shall return the documents after the investigation of the corruption or economic crime concerned is completed, if no criminal proceedings are to be instituted; and

(b) may return the documents, at its discretion, either with or without conditions to ensure the appearance of the person.

(3) A person against whom an order under subsection (1) is made may apply to the court to discharge or vary the order or to order the return of his travel documents and the court may, after hearing the parties, discharge or vary the order, order the return of the travel documents, or dismiss the application.

(4) If a person fails to surrender his travel documents pursuant to an order under subsection (1), the person may be arrested and brought before the court and the court shall, unless the court is satisfied that the person does not have any travel documents, order that the person be detained pending the conclusion of the investigation of the corruption or economic crime concerned.

(5) A person who is detained pursuant to an order under subsection (4) shall be released if—

(a) he surrenders his travel documents to the Commission;

(b) he satisfies the court that he does not have any travel documents; or

(c) the investigation of the corruption or economic crime concerned is completed and the court is satisfied that no criminal proceedings are to be instituted.

(6) A person who is detained pursuant to an order under subsection (4) shall be brought before the court at least every eight days or at such shorter intervals as the court may order, to determine if the person should be released under subsection (5).

32. Arrest of persons

Without prejudice to the generality of section 23(3), the Secretary and an investigator shall have power to arrest any person for and charge them with an offence, and to detain them for the purpose of an investigation, to the like extent as a police officer.

[Act No. 18 of 2014, Sch.]

33. Disclosure that may affect investigation

(1) No person shall, except with leave of the Director or with other lawful excuse, disclose the details of an investigation under this Act, including the identity of anyone being investigated.

(2) A person who contravenes this section is guilty of an offence and is liable on conviction to a fine not exceeding three hundred thousand shillings or to imprisonment for a term not exceeding three years, or to both.

34. Impersonating investigator

(1) No person other than an investigator shall represent himself to be or act as an

investigator.

(2) A person who contravenes this section is guilty of an offence and is liable on conviction to a fine not exceeding three hundred thousand shillings or to imprisonment for a term not exceeding three years, or to both.

35. Investigation report

(1) Following an investigation the Commission shall report to the Director of Public Prosecutions on the results of the investigation.

(2) The Commission's report shall include any recommendation the Commission may have that a person be prosecuted for corruption or economic crime.

[Act No. 12 of 2012, Sch.]

36. Quarterly reports

(1) The Commission shall prepare quarterly reports setting out the number of reports made to the Director of Public Prosecutions under section 35 and such other statistical information relating to those reports as the Commission considers appropriate.

(2) A quarterly report shall indicate if a recommendation of the Commission to prosecute a person for corruption or economic crime was not accepted.

(3) The Commission shall give a copy of each quarterly report to the Attorney-General.

(4) The Attorney-General shall lay a copy of each quarterly report before the National Assembly.

(5) The Commission shall cause each quarterly report to be published in the *Gazette*.

[Act No. 12 of 2012, Sch.]

37. Annual report on prosecutions

(1) The Director of Public Prosecutions shall prepare an annual report with respect to prosecutions for corruption or economic crime.

(2) The year covered by an annual report shall be the year ending on December 31st.

(3) The annual report for a year shall include a summary of the steps taken, during the year, in each prosecution and the status, at the end of the year, of each prosecution.

(4) The annual report shall also indicate if a recommendation of the Commission to prosecute a person for corruption or economic crime was not accepted and shall set out succinctly the reasons for not accepting the recommendation.

(5) The annual report for a year need not include the status of a prosecution that has been finally concluded in a previous year if that status was included in a previous annual report.

(6) The Attorney-General shall lay each annual report before the National Assembly within the first ten sitting days of the National Assembly following the end of the year to which the report relates.

(7) The first annual report following the coming into operation of this section shall cover the period from the coming into operation of this section to the following December 31st.

[Act No. 12 of 2012, Sch.]

PART V
OFFENCES

38. Meaning of "agent" and "principal"

(1) In this Part—

"**agent**" means a person who, in any capacity, and whether in the public or private sector, is employed by or acts for or on behalf of another person;

"**principal**" means a person, whether in the public or private sector, who employs an agent or for whom or on whose behalf an agent acts.

(2) If a person has a power under the Constitution or an Act and it is unclear, under the law, with respect to that power whether the person is an agent or which public body is the agent's principal, the person shall be deemed, for the purposes of this Part, to be an agent for the Government and the exercise of the power shall be deemed to be a matter relating to the business or affairs of the Government.

(3) For the purposes of this Part—
   (a) a Cabinet Minister shall be deemed to be an agent for both the Cabinet and the Government; and
   (b) the holder of a prescribed office or position shall be deemed to be an agent for the prescribed principal.

(4) The regulations made under this Act may prescribe offices, positions and principals for the purposes of subsection (3)(b).

39. *Deleted by Act No. 47 of 2016, s. 23.*

40. Secret inducements for advice

(1) This section applies with respect to a benefit that is an inducement or reward for, or otherwise on account of, the giving of advice to a person.

(2) A person is guilty of an offence if the person—
   (a) receives or solicits, or agrees to receive or solicit, a benefit to which this section applies if the person intends the benefit to be a secret from the person being advised; or
   (b) gives or offers, or agrees to give or offer, a benefit to which this section applies if the person intends the benefit to be a secret from the person being advised.

(3) In this section, "**giving advice**" includes giving information.

41. Deceiving principal

(1) An agent who, to the detriment of his principal, makes a statement to his principal that he knows is false or misleading in any material respect is guilty of an offence.

(2) An agent who, to the detriment of his principal, uses, or gives to his principal, a document that he knows contains anything that is false or misleading in any material respect is guilty of an offence.

42. Conflicts of interest

(1) If an agent has a direct or indirect private interest in a decision that his principal is to make the agent is guilty of an offence if—

(a) the agent knows or has reason to believe that the principal is unaware of the interest and the agent fails to disclose the interest; and

(b) the agent votes or participates in the proceedings of his principal in relation to the decision.

(2) A private body may authorize its agent to vote or participate in the proceedings of the private body and the voting or participation of an agent as so authorized is not a contravention of subsection (1).

(3) An agent of a public body who knowingly acquires or holds, directly or indirectly, a private interest in any contract, agreement or investment emanating from or connected with the public body is guilty of an offence.

(4) Subsection (3) does not apply with respect to an employment contract of the agent, or a related or similar contract or agreement or to any prescribed contract, agreement or investment.

43. Improper benefits to trustees for appointments

(1) This section applies with respect to a benefit that is an inducement or reward for the appointment of a person as a trustee of property or for joining or assisting in such an appointment.

(2) Subject to subsection (3), a person is guilty of an offence if the person—

(a) receives or solicits, or agrees to receive or solicit, from a trustee of property a benefit to which this section applies; or

(b) gives or offers, or agrees to give or offer, to a trustee of property a benefit to which this section applies.

(3) Subsection (2) does not apply to anything done with the informed consent of every person beneficially entitled to the property or in accordance with an order of a court.

(4) In this section, **"trustee of property"** includes—

(a) an executor or administrator appointed to deal with the property;

(b) a person who, under a power of attorney or a power of appointment, has authority over the property; and

(c) a person or a member of a committee managing or administering, or appointed or employed to manage or administer, the property on behalf of a person under an infirmity or incapacity of mind.

44. Bid rigging, etc.

(1) This section applies with respect to a benefit that is an inducement or reward for—

(a) refraining from submitting a tender, proposal, quotation or bid;

(b) withdrawing or changing a tender, proposal, quotation or bid; or

(c) submitting a tender, proposal, quotation or bid with a specified price or with any specified inclusions or exclusions.

(2) A person is guilty of an offence if the person—
  (a) receives or solicits or agrees to receive or solicit a benefit to which this section applies; or
  (b) gives or offers or agrees to give or offer a benefit to which this section applies.

45. Protection of public property and revenue, etc.

(1) A person is guilty of an offence if the person fraudulently or otherwise unlawfully—
  (a) acquires public property or a public service or benefit;
  (b) mortgages, charges or disposes of any public property;
  (c) damages public property, including causing a computer or any other electronic machinery to perform any function that directly or indirectly results in a loss or adversely affects any public revenue or service; or
  (d) fails to pay any taxes or any fees, levies or charges payable to any public body or effects or obtains any exemption, remission, reduction or abatement from payment of any such taxes, fees, levies or charges.

(2) An officer or person whose functions concern the administration, custody, management, receipt or use of any part of the public revenue or public property is guilty of an offence if the person—
  (a) fraudulently makes payment or excessive payment from public revenues for—
    (i) sub-standard or defective goods;
    (ii) goods not supplied or not supplied in full; or
    (iii) services not rendered or not adequately rendered,
  (b) wilfully or carelessly fails to comply with any law or applicable procedures and guidelines relating to the procurement, allocation, sale or disposal of property, tendering of contracts, management of funds or incurring of expenditures; or
  (c) engages in a project without prior planning.

(3) In this section, "**public property**" means real or personal property, including money, of a public body or under the control of, or consigned or due to, a public body.

46. Abuse of office

A person who uses his office to improperly confer a benefit on himself or anyone else is guilty of an offence.

47. Dealing with suspect property

(1) A person who deals with property that he believes or has reason to believe was acquired in the course of or as a result of corrupt conduct is guilty of an offence.

(2) For the purposes of this section, a person deals with property if the person—
  (a) holds, receives, conceals or uses the property or causes the property to be used; or
  (b) enters into a transaction in relation to the property or causes such a transaction to be entered into.

(3) In this section, "**corrupt conduct**" means—
  (a) conduct constituting corruption or economic crime; or

(b) conduct that took place before this Act came into operation and which—
   (i) at the time, constituted an offence; and
   (ii) if it had taken place after this Act came into operation, would have constituted corruption or economic crime.

47A. Attempts, conspiracies, etc.

(1) A person who attempts to commit an offence involving corruption or an economic crime is guilty of an offence.

(2) For the purposes of this section, a person attempts to commit an offence of corruption or an economic crime if the person, with the intention of committing the offence, does or omits to do something designed to its fulfilment but does not fulfil the intention to such an extent as to commit the offence.

(3) A person who conspires with another to commit an offence of corruption or economic crimes is guilty of an offence.

(4) A person who incites another to do any act or make any omission of such a nature that, if that act were done or the omission were made, an offence of corruption or an economic crime would thereby be committed, is guilty of an offence.

[Act No. 7 of 2007, Sch.]

48. Penalty for offence under this Part

(1) A person convicted of an offence under this Part shall be liable to—
   (a) a fine not exceeding one million shillings, or to imprisonment for a term not exceeding ten years, or to both; and
   (b) an additional mandatory fine if, as a result of the conduct that constituted the offence, the person received a quantifiable benefit or any other person suffered a quantifiable loss.

(2) The mandatory fine referred to in subsection (1)(b) shall be determined as follows—
   (a) the mandatory fine shall be equal to two times the amount of the benefit or loss described in subsection (1)(b);
   (b) if the conduct that constituted the offence resulted in both a benefit and loss described in subsection (1)(b), the mandatory fine shall be equal to two times the sum of the amount of the benefit and the amount of the loss.

49. Custom not a defence

In prosecution of an offence under this Part, it shall be no defence that the receiving, soliciting, giving or offering of any benefit is customary in any business, undertaking, office, profession or calling.

50. Impossibility, no intention, etc., not a defence

In a prosecution of an offence under this Part that involves a benefit that is an inducement or reward for doing an act or making an omission, it shall not be a defence—
   (a) that the act or omission was not within a person's power or that the person did not intend to do the act or make the omission; or

(b) that the act or omission did not occur.

PART VI
COMPENSATION AND RECOVERY OF IMPROPER BENEFITS

51. Liability for compensation

A person who does anything that constitutes corruption or economic crime is liable to anyone who suffers a loss as a result for an amount that would be full compensation for the loss suffered.

52. Liability for improper benefits

A person who receives a benefit the receipt of which would constitute an offence under section 39, 40 or 43 is liable, for the value of the benefit, to the following persons—
  (a) if the receipt constitutes an offence under section 39, to the agent's principal;
  (b) if the receipt constitutes an offence under section 40, to the person advised; or
  (c) if the receipt constitutes an offence under section 43, to the persons beneficially entitled to the property.

53. Liability—miscellaneous provisions

(1) A person liable for an amount under section 51 or 52 shall also be liable to pay interest, at the prescribed rate, on the amount payable.

(2) Nothing in section 51 or 52 affects any other liability a person may have.

(3) An amount for which a person is liable under section 51 or 52 to a public body may be recovered by the public body or by the Commission on its behalf.

(4) For greater certainty, nothing in the Government Proceedings Act (Cap. 40) prevents the Commission from instituting civil proceedings to recover amounts under subsection (3).

(5) A person is not entitled to any amount under section 51 or 52 in relation to a particular instance of corruption or economic crime if that person was a party to the corruption or economic crime or that person did a related act that also constituted corruption or economic crime.

54. Compensation orders on conviction

(1) A court that convicts a person of any corruption or economic crime shall, at the time of conviction or on subsequent application, order the person—
  (a) to pay any amount the person may be liable for under section 51 or 52; and
  (b) to give to the rightful owner any property acquired in the course of or as a result of the conduct that constituted the corruption or economic crime or an amount equivalent to the value of that property.

(2) If the rightful owner referred to in subsection (1)(b) cannot be determined or if there is no rightful owner, the court shall order that the property or equivalent amount be forfeited to the Government.

(3) In making an order under this section, a court may quantify any amount or may

determine how such amount is to be quantified.

(4) An order under this section may be enforced by the person in whose favour it is made as though it were an order made in a civil proceeding.

55. Forfeiture of unexplained assets

(1) In this section, **"corrupt conduct"** means—
- (a) conduct that constitutes corruption or economic crime; or
- (b) conduct that took place before this Act came into operation and which—
  - (i) at the time, constituted an offence; and
  - (ii) if it had taken place after this Act came into operation, would have constituted corruption or economic crime.

(2) The Commission may commence proceedings under this section against a person if—
- (a) after an investigation, the Commission is satisfied that the person has unexplained assets; and
- (b) the person has, in the course of the exercise by the Commission of its powers of investigation or otherwise, been afforded a reasonable opportunity to explain the disproportion between the assets concerned and his known legitimate sources of income and the Commission is not satisfied that an adequate explanation of that disproportion has been given.

(3) Proceedings under this section shall be commenced in the High Court by way of originating summons.

(4) In proceedings under this section—
- (a) the Commission shall adduce evidence that the person has unexplained assets; and
- (b) the person whose assets are in question shall be afforded the opportunity to cross-examine any witness called and to challenge any evidence adduced by the Commission and, subject to this section, shall have and may exercise the rights usually afforded to a defendant in civil proceedings.

(5) If after the Commission has adduced evidence that the person has unexplained assets the court is satisfied, on the balance of probabilities, and in light of the evidence so far adduced, that the person concerned does have unexplained assets, it may require the person, by such testimony and other evidence as the court deems sufficient, to satisfy the court that the assets were acquired otherwise than as the result of corrupt conduct.

(6) If, after such explanation, the court is not satisfied that all of the assets concerned were acquired otherwise than as the result of corrupt conduct, it may order the person to pay to the Government an amount equal to the value of the unexplained assets that the Court is not satisfied were acquired otherwise than as the result of corrupt conduct.

(7) For the purposes of proceedings under this section, the assets of the person whose assets are in question shall be deemed to include any assets of another person that the court finds—
- (a) are held in trust for the person whose assets are in question or otherwise on his

behalf; or

(b) were acquired from the person whose assets are in question as a gift or loan without adequate consideration.

(8) The record of proceedings under this section shall be admissible in evidence in any other proceedings, including any prosecution for corruption or economic crime.

(9) This section shall apply retroactively.

[Act No. 7 of 2007, Sch.]

56. Order preserving suspect property, etc.

(1) On an *ex parte* application by the Commission, the High Court may make an order prohibiting the transfer or disposal of or other dealing with property if it is satisfied that there are reasonable grounds to suspect that the property was acquired as a result of corrupt conduct.

(2) An order under this section may be made against a person who was involved in the corrupt conduct or against a person who subsequently acquired the property.

(3) An order under this section shall have effect for six months and may be extended by the court on the application of the Commission.

(4) A person served with an order under this section may, within fifteen days after being served, apply to the court to discharge or vary the order and the court may, after hearing the parties, discharge or vary the order or dismiss the application.

(5) The court may discharge or vary an order under subsection (4) only if the court is satisfied, on the balance of probabilities, that the property in respect of which the order is discharged or varied was not acquired as a result of corrupt conduct.

(6) A person who is served with an order under this section and who contravenes it is guilty of an offence and is liable on conviction to a fine not exceeding two million shillings or to imprisonment for a term not exceeding ten years, or to both.

(7) In this section, **"corrupt conduct"** means—

(a) conduct that constitutes corruption or economic crime; or

(b) conduct that took place before this Act came into operation and which—

(i) at the time, constituted an offence; and

(ii) if it had taken place after this Act came into operation, would have constituted corruption or economic crime.

[Act No. 47 of 2016, s. 24.]

56A. Appointment of receiver

(1) The Commission may, at any time with leave of the court, appoint a receiver for such property as is suspected by the Commission to have been acquired through corrupt conduct.

(2) The appointment of a receiver under subsection (1) above shall be in writing signed by the Director or Assistant Director.

(3) The receiver shall have powers of management, control and possession of the property for which he is appointed.

(4) The Commission or the receiver shall, at the time of the appointment or soon

thereafter, serve a notice on the person who has or who appears to have custody or control of the property, and, where the property is required under any written law to be registered, a similar notice shall be served on the respective registrar:

Provided that where the property is situated outside Kenya, the notice shall not be necessary but the Commission shall have the power to liaise with foreign governments, government departments and international agencies for the confiscation, management, control and repatriation of the property.

(5) A person served with a notice under the foregoing subsection shall not, except by authority of a court order, deal with the property in any manner inconsistent with the instructions of the receiver.

(6) A person who contravenes subsection (5) shall be guilty of an offence and liable to a fine not exceeding two million shillings or to imprisonment for a term not exceeding ten years, or to both for a first offence, and to imprisonment for a term not exceeding ten years without the option of a fine for a subsequent offence in respect of the same property.

(7) For avoidance of doubt, a receiver may be appointed under this section in respect of any kind of property whether tangible or intangible, movable or immovable, and including buildings, income, debts, bank deposits, business concerns, stocks and other properties.

(8) The receiver shall keep proper books of account and give quarterly reports to the Commission, and may pay the costs of receivership out of the property for which he has been appointed.

(9) A person aggrieved by the appointment of a receiver under this section may request the Commission in writing to set aside the appointment in return for an offer of deposit of some reasonable security, or he may apply to the High Court for setting aside or variation of the appointment on the ground that—

(a) he has offered to the Commission a reasonable security which has not been accepted by the Commission; or

(b) he has in his possession evidence to show that, on a balance of probabilities, he acquired the property otherwise than through crime or civil wrongs.

(10) An application to the High Court under subsection (9) shall be heard *inter partes*, and the Commission shall be entitled to cross-examine the applicant and to call evidence in rebuttal.

[Act No. 7 of 2007, Sch.]

56B. Out of court settlement

(1) In any matter where the Commission is mandated by this Act or any other law to institute civil proceedings or applications, it shall be lawful for the Commission to issue a notice or letter of demand to the person intended to be sued, and may, in such notice or letter, inform the person about the claim against him and further inform him that he could settle the claim within a specified time before the filing of court proceedings.

(2) The Commission may negotiate and enter a settlement with any person against whom the Commission intends to bring, or has actually brought, a civil claim or

application in court.

(3) The Commission may tender an undertaking in writing not to institute criminal proceedings against a person who—

 (a) has given a full and true disclosure of all material facts relating to past corrupt conduct and economic crime by himself or others; and

 (b) has voluntarily paid, deposited or refunded all property he acquired through corruption or economic crime; and

 (c) has paid for all loses occasioned by his corruption conduct to public property.

(4) A settlement or undertaking under this section shall be registered in court.

[Act No. 7 of 2007, Sch.]

56C. Recovery of funds and other assets

(1) Any funds recovered by the Commission shall be paid into the Consolidated Fund.

(2) Notwithstanding any provision in this Act or any other written law, any asset or property, whether movable or immovable, recovered either in the course of, or upon conclusion of investigations, or upon commencement of court action or proceedings, whether such proceedings are of a civil or criminal nature or upon conclusion of such proceedings, shall be surrendered to the Permanent Secretary to the Treasury.

[Act No. 10 of 2010, s. 78.]

PART VII
EVIDENCE

57. Unexplained assets, etc., as corroboration

(1) Unexplained assets may be taken by the court as corroboration that a person accused of corruption or economic crime received a benefit.

(2) For the purposes of this section, the assets of an accused person shall be deemed to include any assets of another person that the court finds—

 (a) are held in trust for the accused person or otherwise for or on his behalf; or

 (b) were acquired from the accused person without adequate consideration.

58. Presumption of corruption if act shown

If a person is accused of an offence under Part V an element of which is that an act was done corruptly and the accused person is proved to have done that act the person shall be presumed to have done that act corruptly unless the contrary is proved.

59. Certificates to show value of property, etc.

(1) In a prosecution for corruption or economic crime or a proceeding under this Act, a certificate of a valuation officer as to the value of a benefit or property is admissible and is proof of that value, unless the contrary is proved.

(2) A court shall presume, in the absence of evidence to the contrary, that a certificate purporting to be the certificate of a valuation officer is such a certificate.

(3) In this section, "**valuation officer**" means a person appointed, employed or

authorised by the Commission or the Government to value property and whose appointment, employment or authorisation is published by notice in the *Gazette*.

60. Rule, etc., relating to accomplices

For the purposes of any rule or practice requiring the evidence of an accomplice to be corroborated, a person shall not be considered an accomplice of a person accused of an offence under Part V only because—

    (a) the person received, solicited or agreed to receive or solicit a benefit from the accused person; or

    (b) the person gave, offered or agreed to give or offer a benefit to the accused person.

61. Certificates to show office and compensation

(1) In a prosecution for corruption or economic crime or a proceeding under this Act, a certificate of an officer of a body as to a person's position with the body or the person's compensation is admissible and is proof of that position or compensation in the absence of evidence to the contrary.

(2) A court shall presume, in the absence of evidence to the contrary, that a certificate purporting to be the certificate of an officer of a body is such a certificate.

PART VIIA
EXECUTION

61A. Execution against the Commission

Notwithstanding anything to the contrary in any law, where judgment or an order has been given against the Commission for payment of money by way of damages or otherwise—

    (a) no execution or attachment in the nature thereof shall be issued against the Commission or against the assets, debts or bank deposits of the Commission;

    (b) the Director shall, except if there is an appeal or application pending against the judgment or order, cause to be paid out of the funds of the Commission provided expressly for such purposes in the annual estimates, such amounts as may be payable under the decree to the person entitled thereto;

    (c) no property of the Commission shall be seized or taken by any person having, by law, power to attach or distrain property without the previous written permission of the Director.

[Act No. 7 of 2007, Sch.]

PART VIII
MISCELLANEOUS

62. Suspension, if charged with corruption or economic crime

(1) A public officer or state officer who is charged with corruption or economic crime

shall be suspended, at half pay, with effect from the date of the charge until the conclusion of the case:

Provided that the case shall be determined within twenty-four months.

(2) A suspended public officer who is on half pay shall continue to receive the full amount of any allowances.

(3) The public officer ceases to be suspended if the proceedings against him are discontinued or if he is acquitted.

(4) This section does not derogate from any power or requirement under any law under which the public officer may be suspended without pay or dismissed.

(5) The following shall apply with respect to a charge in proceedings instituted otherwise than by or under the direction of the Attorney-General—

(a) this section does not apply to the charge unless permission is given by the court or the Attorney-General to prosecute or the proceedings are taken over by the Attorney-General; and

(b) if permission is given or the proceedings are taken over, the date of the charge shall be deemed, for the purposes of this section, to be the date when the permission is given or the proceedings are taken over.

(6) This section does not apply with respect to an office if the Constitution limits or provides for the grounds upon which a holder of the office may be removed or the circumstances in which the office must be vacated.

(7) This section does not apply with respect to a charge laid before this Act came into operation.

[Act No. 18 of 2014, Sch.]

63. Suspension, etc., if convicted of corruption or economic crime

(1) A public officer who is convicted of corruption or economic crime shall be suspended without pay with effect from the date of the conviction pending the outcome of any appeals.

(2) The public officer ceases to be suspended if the conviction is overturned on appeal.

(3) The public officer shall be dismissed if—

(a) the time period for appealing against the conviction expires without the conviction being appealed; or

(b) the conviction is upheld on appeal.

(4) This section does not apply with respect to an office if the Constitution limits or provides for the grounds upon which a holder of the office may be removed or the circumstances in which the office must be vacated.

(5) This section does not apply with respect to a conviction that occurred before this Act came into operation.

64. Disqualification if convicted of corruption or economic crime

(1) A person who is convicted of corruption or economic crime shall be disqualified from being elected or appointed as a public officer for ten years after the conviction.

(2) This section does not apply with respect to an elected office if the Constitution sets out the qualifications for the office.

(3) This section does not apply with respect to a conviction that occurred before this Act came into operation.

(4) At least once a year the Commission shall cause the names of all persons disqualified under this section to be published in the *Gazette*.

65. Protection of informers

(1) No action or proceeding, including a disciplinary action, may be instituted or maintained against a person in respect of—

  (a) assistance given by the person to the Commission or an investigator; or

  (b) a disclosure of information made by the person to the Commission or an investigator.

(2) Subsection (1) does not apply with respect to a statement made by a person who did not believe it to be true.

(3) In a prosecution for corruption or economic crime or a proceeding under this Act, no witness shall be required to identify, or provide information that might lead to the identification of, a person who assisted or disclosed information to the Commission or an investigator.

(4) In a prosecution for corruption or economic crime or a proceeding under this Act, the Court shall ensure that information that identifies or might lead to the identification of a person who assisted or disclosed information to the Commission or an investigator is removed or concealed from any documents to be produced or inspected in connection with the proceeding.

(5) Subsections (3) and (4) shall not apply to the extent determined by the court to be necessary to ensure that justice is fully done.

66. Obstructing persons under this Act, etc.

(1) No person shall—

  (a) without justification or lawful excuse, obstruct or hinder, or assault or threaten, a person acting under this Act;

  (b) deceive or knowingly mislead the Commission or a person acting under this Act;

  (c) destroy, alter, conceal or remove documents, records or evidence that the person believes, or has grounds to believe, may be relevant to an investigation or proceeding under this Act; or

  (d) make false accusations to the Commission or a person acting under this Act.

(2) A person who contravenes subsection (1) is guilty of an offence and is liable on conviction to a fine not exceeding five hundred thousand shillings or to imprisonment for a term not exceeding five years, or to both.

67. Conduct outside Kenya—offences

Conduct by a citizen of Kenya that takes place outside Kenya constitutes an offence under this Act if the conduct would constitute an offence under this Act if it took place in Kenya.

68. Regulations

The Minister may make regulations generally for the better carrying out of the provision of this Act.

PART IX
REPEAL, TRANSITION AND AMENDMENTS

69. Interpretation

In this Part—

"**former Advisory Board**" means the Advisory Board under the repealed Act;

"**repealed Act**" means the Prevention of Corruption Act (Cap. 65) repealed by section 70.

70. Repeal of Cap. 65

The Prevention of Corruption Act (Cap. 65) is repealed.

71. Offences under repealed Act

(1) This section applies with respect to offences or suspected offences under the repealed Act committed before this Act came into operation.

(2) This Act, other than Part V, applies, with any necessary modifications, with respect to offences described in subsection (1) and, for that purpose, such offences shall be deemed to be corruption or economic crimes.

(3) For greater certainty, this section—

(a) does not apply with respect to any act or omission that, at the time it took place, was not an offence; and

(b) is not to be construed as authorising the imposition of a penalty that, under section 77(4) of the Constitution, could not be imposed.

72. Temporary Director, etc.

(1) The person who, immediately before the establishment of the Commission, was the head of the anti-corruption unit of the Kenya Police Force shall become the temporary Director of the Commission upon the establishment of the Commission.

(2) The temporary Director under subsection (1) shall cease to be the temporary Director upon the appointment of a Director under this Act.

(3) For greater certainty, the temporary Director under subsection (1) shall have and may exercise and perform all the powers and functions of the Director until the Director is appointed and may participate in any deliberations of the Advisory Board for the purposes of section 8(3).

73. Transfer from anti-corruption unit of the Kenya Police Force

(1) The conduct of all ongoing operations of the anti-corruption unit of the Kenya Police Force, including all ongoing investigations, shall, on the commencement of this Act, be transferred to the Commission.

(2) All assets of the anti-corruption unit of the Kenya Police Force shall, on the commencement of this Act, become assets of the Commission.

(3) Without limiting the generality of subsection (2), the assets that become assets of the Commission shall include all files and documents, including electronic documents, associated with ongoing or past operations of the anti-corruption unit of the Kenya Police Force, including ongoing or past investigations.

(4) The Kenya Police Force shall render such assistance to the Commission as the Commission requests to facilitate the transfer, under this section, of the operations and assets of the anti-corruption unit of the Kenya Police Force to the Commission.

(5) For greater certainty, this section does not result in the transfer of any staff of the anti-corruption unit of the Kenya Police Force to the Commission but the Commission may receive such staff as it considers advisable on secondment.

74. Amendment of section 42 of Cap. 22

Section 42 of the Limitations of Actions Act is amended by inserting the word "or" at the end of paragraph (h) and inserting the following new paragraph immediately after paragraph (h)—

> (i) a proceeding to recover an amount for which a person is liable under section 51 or 52 of the Anti-Corruption and Economic Crimes Act, 2003 or a proceeding under section 55 or 56 of that Act.

FIRST SCHEDULE

[Section 8, Act No. 7 of 2007, Sch.]

PROVISIONS RELATING TO THE STAFF OF THE COMMISSION

1. Qualifications for appointment as Director or Assistant Director

(1) To be appointed as the Director or as an Assistant Director, a person must satisfy the following qualifications—

(a) the person must be knowledgeable about or experienced in at least one of the following—
  (i) law;
  (ii) public administration;
  (iii) accounting and financial matters; or
  (iv) fraud investigation; and

(b) the person must be of outstanding honesty and integrity.

(2) The Advisory Board shall not recommend a person who is not qualified under this paragraph.

2. Vacancies, acting Assistant

(1) If the office of the Director or an Assistant Director becomes vacant, the Advisory Board shall, within three months, recommend a person to be appointed to fill the vacancy.

(2) During the illness or absence of an Assistant Director or a vacancy in the office of an Assistant Director, the Advisory Board may appoint a member of the staff of the Commission as an acting Assistant Director.

(3) The Advisory Board may at any time revoke an appointment under subparagraph

(2) and appoint another member of staff of the Commission as acting Assistant Director.

3. Term of office of Director or Assistant Director

(1) The term of office of the Director or an Assistant Director shall be five years:

Provided that an Assistant Director may be appointed for a term of four years to avoid having the Assistant Director's term expire on or around the time the Director's term expires.

(2) A person who has held office as Director or Assistant Director may be reappointed, but may not serve as the Director for more than two terms or as an Assistant Director for more than two terms.

(3) A director shall, unless his office becomes vacant by reason of his death, resignation, or ceasing to hold office under paragraph 5, continue in office until he is reappointed or replaced by a new director appointed under the Act.

[Act No. 7 of 2007, Sch.]

4. Resignation of Director or Assistant Director

(1) The Director or an Assistant Director may resign by a written resignation addressed to the President.

(2) A resignation is effective upon being received by the President or by a person authorized by the President to receive it.

5. Removal of Director or Assistant Director

(1) The appointment of the Director or an Assistant Director may be terminated only in accordance with this paragraph.

(2) The President, on the recommendation of the Advisory Board, may terminate a person's appointment as the Director or an Assistant Director if the person—

   (a) contravenes paragraph 6(1) of this Schedule;

   (b) is adjudged bankrupt; or

   (c) is convicted of an offence under the Penal Code or this Act or an offence involving dishonesty.

(3) The President may terminate the appointment of the Director or Assistant Director if a tribunal under this paragraph finds that the Director or Assistant Director—

   (a) is unable to perform the functions of his office by reason of a mental or physical infirmity; or

   (b) was involved in a corrupt transaction.

(4) The Advisory Board may request the Chief Justice to appoint a tribunal if the Advisory Board is of the view that the Director or an Assistant Director—

   (a) may be unable to perform the functions of his office by reason of a mental or physical infirmity; or

   (b) may have been involved in a corrupt transaction.

(5) The Advisory Board shall give a copy of the request under subparagraph (4) to the President at the same time as the request is made to the Chief Justice and the President may suspend the Director or Assistant Director pending the final resolution of the matter.

(6) Upon receiving a request under subparagraph (4), the Chief Justice shall forthwith

appoint a tribunal of three members, one of whom the Chief Justice shall designate as the chairman.

(7) Each member of the tribunal shall be a person qualified to be appointed as a judge of the High Court or the Court of Appeal.

(8) The tribunal shall conduct an inquiry in accordance with such procedures as it may determine.

(9) The procedures of the tribunal shall be consistent with the rules of natural justice.

(10) Within thirty days after concluding its inquiry, the tribunal shall—
- (a) publicly announce its finding and reasons; and
- (b) submit a report to the President.

6. Restrictions on activities of staff

(1) After being appointed, no staff of the Commission, including the Director or an Assistant Director, shall—
- (a) be employed in any other work or business;
- (b) hold any other public office; or
- (c) take any active part in the affairs of any political party or support any candidate for election to a public office.

(2) A person who holds a public office and is seconded to the Commission does not contravene subparagraph (1) only by virtue of continuing to hold that public office as long as the person performs no duties of that public office while seconded to the Commission.

7. Disciplinary code

(1) The Director shall issue a Code for the Commission providing for the discipline of its staff.

(2) The Code may provide for investigations and for the determination, including by a hearing, of matters that may be in dispute.

(3) The Code may provide for penalties up to and including dismissal and may include provisions for the recovery of costs arising from loss of or damage to property of the Commission.

8. Removal of other staff

In addition to any other ground on which, under this Act, a member of staff of the Commission (not being the Director or an Assistant Director), may be removed from office, the member may be so removed by the Director on the ground that the member has breached the Code issued under paragraph 7 of this Schedule or on the ground that the Director no longer has confidence in the member's integrity:

Provided that no member of staff shall be removed from office under this paragraph unless he has first been given a reasonable opportunity to show cause why he should not be so removed.

9. Protection from personal liability

(1) No action or proceeding for compensation or damages shall be brought against the Director, an Assistant Director, an investigator or any staff of the Commission in respect

of anything done or omitted in good faith under this Act.

(2) This paragraph shall not relieve the Commission of any liability.

SECOND SCHEDULE
[Section 22, Act No. 7 of 2007, Sch.]

PROVISIONS RELATING TO MEMBERS OF THE ADVISORY BOARD

1. Appointment of nominated members

(1) This paragraph provides for the appointment of a member of the Advisory Board nominated by a body under section 16(2)(a).

(2) The nominating body shall submit the names of two nominees to the Minister.

(3) The Minister shall submit the names of the nominees to the National Assembly for approval within seven sitting days after receiving them.

(4) The National Assembly shall, within fourteen days after it first meets after receiving the names of the nominees—

    (a) consider the nominees and either approve one of the nominees or reject both of them; and

    (b) notify the Minister as to its approval or rejection under subparagraph (a).

(5) If the National Assembly approves a nominee, the Minister shall, within fourteen days after receiving the notification of the National Assembly, forward the name of the nominee to the President and the President shall, within fourteen days after receiving the name, appoint the nominee as a member of the Advisory Board.

(6) If the National Assembly rejects both nominees submitted by the nominating body, the Minister shall, within fourteen days after receiving the notification of the National Assembly, request the nominating body to submit a new nominee to the Minister and subparagraphs (3), (4) and (5) and this subparagraph apply with necessary modifications with respect to that new nominee.

(7) In nominating and approving persons to be members of the Advisory Board, the nominating body and the National Assembly shall have regard to—

    (a) the honesty and integrity of the person and the person's knowledge and experience; and

    (b) the importance of representing Kenya's diversity on the Advisory Board.

(8) Within seven days after any vacancy arises in the membership of the Advisory Board, the Minister shall request the nominating body to submit nominees under subparagraph (2) and the nominating body shall do so within twenty-one days after being requested to do so.

(9) The following shall apply with respect to the initial appointment of the Advisory Board following the commencement of this Act—

    (a) each nominating body shall submit its initial nominees within twenty-one days after the commencement of this Act;

    (b) the Minister shall wait until sufficient nominees are approved to form a quorum before submitting the names of the approved nominees under subparagraph (5);

(c) within fifteen days after a sufficient number of the members of the Advisory Board are appointed to form a quorum, the Minister shall call a meeting of the Advisory Board for the purposes of nominating the initial Chairman and Vice-chairman.

2. Term of members

(1) The term of office of each nominated member of the Advisory Board shall be five years.

(2) A person may not serve more than two terms as a member of the Advisory Board.

(3) A member of the Advisory Board shall, unless his office becomes vacant by reason of his death, resignation or ceasing to hold office by virtue of paragraph 4, continue in office until he is reappointed or replaced by another member appointed under the Act.

[Act No. 7 of 2007, Sch.]

3. Resignation

(1) A nominated member of the Advisory Board may resign by a written resignation addressed to the President.

(2) A resignation is effective upon being received by the President or by a person authorized by the President to receive it.

4. Termination of appointment

The President, on the recommendation of the Advisory Board, may terminate a person's appointment as a member of the Advisory Board only if the person—

(a) is unable to perform the functions of his office by reason of a mental, or physical infirmity;

(b) is adjudged bankrupt;

(c) is convicted of an offence under the Penal Code (Cap. 63) or this Act or an offence involving dishonesty; or

(d) is absent from three consecutive meetings of the Advisory Board without reasonable excuse.

5. Disclosure of personal interest

(1) A member of the Advisory Board who has a direct or indirect personal interest in a matter being considered or to be considered by the Advisory Board shall, as soon as reasonably practicable after the relevant facts concerning the matter have come to his knowledge, disclose the nature of his interest to the Advisory Board.

(2) A disclosure of interest in a matter shall be recorded in the minutes of the meeting of the Advisory Board and the member shall not be present while that matter is being dealt with by the Advisory Board and shall not take part in any deliberations or vote relating to the matter.

6. Allowances

The Commission shall pay the members of the Advisory Board such allowances and expenses as are determined by the Minister in charge of finance in consultation with a committee of the National Assembly designated by the National Assembly for that purpose.

7. Protection from personal liability

(1) No action or proceeding for compensation or damages shall be brought against a member of the Advisory Board or any other person authorized by the Advisory Board, in respect of anything done or omitted in good faith under this Act.

(2) This paragraph shall not relieve the Advisory Board of any liability.

THIRD SCHEDULE
[Section 21.]
PROVISIONS AS TO THE CONDUCT OF BUSINESS AND AFFAIRS OF THE ADVISORY BOARD

1. Meetings

(1) The Advisory Board shall have at least four meetings in every financial year and not more than four months shall elapse between one meeting and the next meeting.

(2) Meetings shall be convened by the Chairman, or in his absence by the Vice-chairman.

(3) Unless three quarters of the members otherwise agree, at least fourteen days' notice of a meeting shall be given to every member.

(4) A meeting shall be presided over by the Chairman, or in his absence by the Vice-chairman or in both their absences, by a person elected by the Advisory Board at the meeting for that purpose.

2. Voting

A decision of the Advisory Board shall be by a majority of the members present and voting and, in the case of an equality of votes, the person presiding at the meeting shall have a second or casting vote.

3. Minutes

Minutes of all meetings shall be kept and entered in books kept for that purpose.